When Violence Begins at Home

Possible Predictors of Domestic Violence

The National Coalition Against Domestic Violence has produced a list of questions whose answers may provide clues to a man's potential for violence:

1. Did he grow up in a violent family?

2. Does he use force or violence to "solve" his problems? Does he have a quick temper? Does he overreact to little problems and frustrations? Is he cruel to animals? Does he punch walls or throw things when he's angry?

3. Does he abuse alcohol or other drugs?

4. Does he have strong traditional ideas about what a man should be and what a woman should be? Does he think a woman shouldn't work, should take care of her husband, and should follow all his wishes and orders?

5. Is he jealous of your other relationships (not only those with male friends but also those with female friends and with family members)? Does he keep tabs on you? Does he want to know where you are at all times? Does he want you with him all the time?

6. Does he have access to guns, knives, or other lethal instruments? Does he talk about using them against people? Does he threaten to use them to get even?

7. Does he expect you to follow his orders or advice? Does he become angry if you do not fulfill his wishes or if you cannot anticipate what he wants?

8. Do his mood and behavior go through extreme highs and lows? Is he extremely kind one time and extremely cruel the next?

9. Are you afraid of him when he gets angry? Is not making him angry important to you? Do you do what he wants you to do rather than what you want to do?

10. Does he treat you roughly? Does he physically force you to do what you do not want to do?

Without effective early intervention, abuse can escalate in severity and sometimes can lead to death. If someone is hurting you or someone you love, please call:

National Domestic Violence Hotline
(800) 799-SAFE (7233)
(800) 787-3224 (TTY)   *All calls are handled in strict confidence.*

TITLES IN THE HUNTER HOUSE *VIOLENCE-FREE LIVING* SERIES

OTHER RELATED TITLES

Praise for the first edition

"The author ... offers a resource guide to help women in painful relationships take control of their lives."

— *Journal of Social Work Education*

"[Wilson's] writing style is clear and direct, whether she is identifying abusive behaviors or outlining the history of violence against women from ancient Babylonian times through the Middle Ages to the present.

"The book is primarily by and about women who are beaten and verbally abused by men—and offers a tremendous amount of practical advice for that group."

— *KLIATT*

"Wilson's book ... is equally valuable for victims and for the professionals who help them.

"This book answers every conceivable question about domestic violence.... Books like *When Violence Begins at Home* will help us to survive the tunnel until we reach the more non-violent light.

— Michael Pastore, *The Octopus*

"*When Violence Begins at Home* is a definitive guide addressing the needs of multiple audiences, including battered women from various backgrounds, teenage victims of dating violence, educators, community leaders, and even the batterers themselves."

— *The Bookwatch*

ORDERING

Trade bookstores in the U.S. and Canada please contact:

Publishers Group West
1700 Fourth Street, Berkeley CA 94710
Phone: (800) 788-3123   Fax: (510) 528-3444

Hunter House books are available at bulk discounts for textbook course adoptions; to qualifying community, health-care, and government organizations; and for special promotions and fund-raising. For details please contact:

Special Sales Department
Hunter House Inc., PO Box 2914, Alameda CA 94501-0914
Phone: (510) 865-5282   Fax: (510) 865-4295
E-mail: ordering@hunterhouse.com

Individuals can order our books from most bookstores, by calling **(800) 266-5592**, or from our website at **www.hunterhouse.com**

PROJECT CREDITS

Cover Design: Jil Weil, Jinni Fontana
Book Production: Hunter House
Copy Editor: Kelley Blewster
Indexer: Nancy D. Peterson
Acquisitions Editor: Jeanne Brondino
Editor: Alexandra Mummery
Publishing Assistant: Herman Leung
Office Assistant: Joe Winebarger
Publicist: Jillian Steinberger
Customer Service Manager: Christina Sverdrup
Order Fulfillment: Washul Lakdhon
Administrator: Theresa Nelson
Computer Support: Peter Eichelberger
Publisher: Kiran S. Rana

When Violence Begins at Home

A Comprehensive Guide to Understanding and Ending Domestic Abuse

Second Edition

K. J. Wilson, Ed.D.

Hunter House PUBLISHERS

Hunter House Inc., Publishers
PO Box 2914
Alameda CA 94501-0914

LIBRARY OF CONGRESS CATALOGING-IN-PUBLICATION DATA

When violence begins at home : a comprehensive guide to understanding and ending domestic abuse / K.J. Wilson.— 2nd ed.
p. cm.
Summary: "Resource for victims of abuse and their caregivers, significantly updated with guidance on everything from indicators of an abusive relationship to domestic violence legislation, as well as information on date rape drugs, cyber-stalking, effectiveness of batterer intervention programs, and more"—Provided by publisher.
Includes bibliographical references and index.
ISBN-13: 978-0-89793-455-8 (pbk.)
ISBN-10: 0-89793-455-5 (pbk.)
1. Wife abuse—United States. 2. Wife abuse—United States—Prevention.
3. Family violence—United States.
HV6626.2W55 2005
362.82'92'0973—dc22   2005013711

Manufactured in Canada by Transcontinental Printing

9 8 7 6 5 4 3 2 1   Second Edition   06 07 08 09 10

Contents

Quick Contents

A list of sections that may be of immediate importance to some readers, arranged alphabetically.

Foreword

Every January, I receive requests from the media for statistics on the increase of domestic violence on Super Bowl Sunday. Many shelters for battered women have reported such an increase, but there are no hard data. I remember that one year a public service announcement concerning domestic violence was aired during the television broadcast of the football game. That announcement should be repeated every year.

Without a doubt, one can say that watching games of heated competition arouses strong emotions that can lead to violence. Witness the riots that have occurred at some soccer games and the fights in the stands at baseball and football games. In her work counseling batterers, Anne Ganley found that these men were unable to distinguish their emotions, that arousal was almost inevitably expressed as anger.

For the first time in the United States, a major athletic organization, the Seattle Mariners baseball team, has joined the Washington State Coalition Against Domestic Violence and KIRO-TV for a statewide, season-long educational campaign "Refuse to Abuse."

The National Advertising Council and the Family Violence Prevention Fund have collaborated on a national publicity campaign, "There is no excuse for domestic violence," which has had an impact on government and the corporate world.

There is hope.

Dr. Wilson undertook a monumental task when she decided to write *When Violence Begins at Home: A Comprehensive Guide to Understanding and Ending Domestic Abuse.* She traces the origins of violence against women from its roots in patriarchal society dating back thousands of years to the beginnings of the grassroots battered women's movement in the 1970s. Until then, the existence of domestic violence had been either denied or tacitly approved by law and custom.

Since then, the private practice of beating women into submission in the home has been publicized as a threat to the welfare of society as a whole. A network of shelters for battered women and their children has been established. Domestic violence has been defined as a crime and penal codes have been revised. Advocacy and support groups for victims/survivors have been formed. Public and private service agencies have developed programs to educate personnel and the community about the dynamics of domestic violence, its effects, and its treatments.

Twenty years seems like a long time. Advocates sometimes despair that despite all of these efforts to overcome violence in the home, it appears to be increasing. But domestic violence is not on the increase; it is the reporting of its incidence that has increased—a sign that our outreach has been successful. Women are breaking away from the abuse of their husbands and partners, and we need to protect them in the process and help them reconstruct their lives. Domestic violence is a social disease for which we as a society must take responsibility.

Twenty years is but a moment in time considering the thousands of years that made violence against women a worldwide tradition. We need to acknowledge the great strides that have been made to date. Grassroots organizing has been successful in bringing about change at local, state, national, and international levels. The Violence Against Women Act of 1994, passed by Congress and signed into law by President Bill Clinton, will have far-reaching effects in our struggle against domestic violence. As I write this foreword, the Second World Congress on Family Law and the Rights of Children and Youth is meeting in San Francisco. A key topic of the conference is domestic violence and its profound effect on all dimensions of a child's development. The latest effort at outreach has been made by the U.S. Postal Service, which has put the toll-free National Domestic Violence Hotline number (800-799-SAFE) on the covers of two hundred million thirty-two-cent stamp booklets.

There is hope.

In this book, Dr. Wilson has done a superb job in summarizing what we have learned and what we have accomplished over the last twenty years in responding to domestic violence. She speaks from her own experience as a survivor of violence and stalking, and describes the period in her own life when she went underground. She also speaks as an authority from her experience working with battered women's centers and her comprehensive knowledge of research on the subject. Her simple, straightforward style of writing is refreshing and easily understood. This book answers once and for all every question people have asked about the dynamics of abusive relationships.

Although my book *Battered Wives* has been credited as the catalyst for the battered women's shelter movement, I chose two arenas with which I was already involved as my personal commitment in creating change: the criminal justice system and politics. In San Francisco, we (attorneys, law students, advocates, and service providers—all women) formed the Coalition for Justice for Battered Women to take on the male bastion of law enforcement. Our objective was to establish that *domestic violence is a crime* and to make radical changes in police procedures in response to domestic violence calls. We had the backing of then Mayor Diane Feinstein who directed her police chief to work with us on a new general order, which includes provisions that Dr. Wilson describes in her chapter on the legal system.

Changes in police policy necessitated reevaluation of the prosecutor's handling of spouse abuse cases. Having the district attorney file charges of abuse as a crime against the state reduces the potential for recrimination by the defendant and increases the likelihood that the battered woman will cooperate with the prosecution. Expert witnesses can dispel misconceptions the jury may have about battered women. It took twenty years, but now we have a domestic violence unit within the San Francisco Police Department to investigate cases. We also have a specialized domestic violence unit in the district attorney's office providing vertical prosecution (one attorney handling the case throughout).

The role of the judiciary must not be minimized. Educating judges can be a problem because of their discretionary power and the assumption that they are above public reproach. Last year, the *San Francisco Examiner* revealed that San Francisco municipal court judges were using "civil compromise" in domestic violence misdemeanor cases. Defendants were being let off with an apology and a few hours of counseling. Those of us who had orchestrated changes in policies of the criminal justice system were shocked.

Supervisor Barbara Kaufman called for public hearings, and the judges were outraged that we dared to challenge their discretionary privilege. But the civil compromise clause is a legal option for cases involving neighborhood disputes, property damage, or petty theft. It was never meant to be used in the disposition of domestic violence caseloads. The California legislature backed our position and passed a bill to prohibit the misuse of civil compromise in domestic violence cases. As this is being written, activists are working with the legislature to cover child and elder abuse as well.

The California legislature also eliminated the option of diversion to a counseling program for defendants in domestic violence misdemeanor cases on the basis that it was too lenient. The law now requires that a defendant who is placed on probation for committing a crime against an intimate partner shall be subject to certain conditions: completion of a year of specialized counseling for batterers, a minimum period of thirty-six months on probation, and automatic issuance of a protective order.

Dr. Wilson states that the Texas Council on Family Violence considers traditional counseling, family therapy, and mediation inappropriate in a battering intervention. Mandating couple's counseling or mediation places the battered woman at a disadvantage and in further jeopardy.

We are not dealing with domestic disputes or communication problems. The batterer communicates quite clearly that he is the head of the household and will use force to maintain that power over family members. We are dealing with abject, unreasonable *violence*. Not having dinner ready on time can trigger a severe violent episode. Appropriate intervention must deal with the batterer's violent behavior. *You cannot mediate violence.* This bears repeating over and over again.

Unfortunately, the California legislature has not yet understood that message. Despite the 1990 recommendation of the National Council of Juvenile and Family Court Judges that no judge mandate mediation in cases in which family violence has occurred, California's judiciary persists in blocking attempts to exempt domestic violence cases from our mandated mediation of child custody and visitation "disputes." The best we have been able to get is the right of the battered woman to have a separate hearing without the presence of her battering spouse, to have a supporter accompany her during the hearing, and to presume that mediators and judges will be trained in the dynamics of domestic violence. If the latter were true, judges and mediators would understand the danger they are courting. Sheila Kuehl and Lisa Lerman warn that the battered spouse should have her attorney, or one recommended by an advocate, review any agreement reached in a mediation process before signing it. Agreements under this mandate have a greater potential for a breakdown.

It took years for battered women's advocates to add consideration of spousal abuse as a policy (along with child abuse) for determining custody. But the plea that the father have unsupervised visitation "is in the best interests of the child" still prevails, no matter how violent his nature. There are enough reported incidents where battered women *and* their children are killed during the process of separation or divorce. What else do we need to convince the legislature of the mediation folly?

San Francisco's Commission on the Status of Women created a subcommittee to look at a citywide response to domestic violence following the murder of Veena Charan by her husband in 1990. Except for one thing, she had done everything by the book over a period of fifteen months. She obtained a restraining order and was awarded temporary physical custody of her nine-year-old son. She sought a divorce and participated in mediation through Family Court Services as mandated by California law. She cooperated with the prosecution of her husband on felony wife beating. The one thing she didn't do was to avail herself of the safety of a shelter for battered women and their children.

Joseph Charan was sentenced to twelve months in jail. The sentence was suspended, however, in lieu of conditional probation: domestic violence counseling, a stay-away order, and thirty days in jail. A few days later, before reporting to probation, he murdered his wife in front of schoolchildren and teachers before killing himself.

The investigation showed that the judge was not informed of the many police contacts the defendant had prior to the current criminal charge. Joseph Charan had violated the restraining order both in San Mateo County where his wife worked and in San Francisco where she resided. He had also vandalized her home, scrawled graffiti, and rammed his car through the garage door. He made several attempts to kidnap their son at school.

Judges need to have a complete file on prior incident reports as they can be an indicator of homicide risk. The defendant should be taken into custody immediately after sentencing and processed by the probation department. The delay because of case overload can, and did, result in a death sentence for Veena Charan despite the stay-away order. All governmental departments that were involved in any way were cooperative in tracing Veena Charan through the system to determine what went wrong. All except the Family Court Services director, who claimed immunity because of client confidentiality. The presiding judge of Family Court and the city attorney backed her position. Members of the investigating committee were frustrated. They needed to know what impact mediation had on Veena Charan.

Since then, unsuccessful attempts have been made to amend the mediation clause in the law to exempt cases in which there is a history of violent episodes. A father's rights still prevail over the endangerment of wife and child. But each time a bill is introduced, more legislators become sensitive to the issue.

There is hope.

The latest ploy in the struggle to explore and prevent domestic homicides is the California state law that permits counties to create Domestic Violence Fatality Review Teams. The legislation is fashioned pretty much by guidelines for existing Child Fatality Review Teams, but it left out one very essential piece of the legislation—how to deal with confidentiality. Already San Francisco's Mental Health Department has declared that information from client files cannot be shared with the death review team without a waiver.

The problem of confidentiality can be resolved by requiring each committee member to sign a confidentiality agreement that information provided the review team will remain confidential and will not be used for any reason other than that for which it is intended. A violation of the agreement would constitute a misdemeanor. The law could state that this statute overrides contradictory codes of ethics from individual professions. The identity of the person is not the interest of the review team. Seeking clues based on the experience of the individuals to find the gaps in our response systems, recognizing signs of homicidal risk, and preventing fatalities is the mission of the death review teams.

Successful prosecution depends not only on the education of all branches of the legal system (both civil and criminal), but also on the battered woman herself. They all need to know that violence unchecked increases in frequency and severity, and sometimes leads to murder. With the cooperation of law enforcement officers, the Family Violence Prevention Fund in San Francisco has produced and made available manuals on procedures (including custody and visitation) for police, district attorneys, and judges.

Unless your local criminal justice system is enlightened about the lethality of domestic violence, is willing to adopt new and revised criminal justice policies, or you have enough political clout to get the state legislature to mandate these changes, then perhaps the protection order is the route to go. Either way it is necessary to watchdog the system and see that these orders are enforced. Personnel changes make education a never-ending process.

I remember the time in the early 1980s when politicians in San Francisco discussed issues instead of launching personal attacks on each other. No politician then dared to omit support of shelters for battered women as a key campaign issue. If laws in your state are obstructive rather than productive in dealing with domestic violence, it will be necessary to form political coalitions to publicize the problem and urge passage of remedial legislation at the state level. Funding for domestic violence programs was a key campaign issue in the last election for governor of California.

If we are to make substantive changes in the law, we have to be more involved in electoral politics. It isn't enough to form a Coalition Against Domestic Violence to lobby the state legislature: we need to change its makeup. We need to educate candidates for office and get commitments or planks in their campaign platforms to further efforts toward *prevention* of domestic violence. We need to elect more women who will challenge the status quo and push issues not always embraced by their male counterparts. Mayor Rita Mullins of Palatine, Illinois, was newly elected chair of the Women's Caucus of the U.S. Conference of Mayors in San Francisco this month. During her two-year term she intends to focus on combating domestic violence, increasing affordable child care, and creating a mentoring program for women who are, or who want to be, mayors. The gender gap in elections is growing.

There is hope.

In counseling battered women, there is a fine line between warning them and frightening them. Women should not be discouraged from leaving a dangerous situation. They should be educated regarding the inevitable escalation of the violence and offered help in putting together a safety plan. Although great strides have been made to provide recourse and safety to battered women, the systems we have developed are not uniform nor fail proof. But with persistence and continued advocacy, public awareness, and support, we shall overcome the obstacles we have encountered.

I was lucky to have had Eleanor Roosevelt as a role model. Her words have been an inspiration. "You gain strength, courage and confidence by every experience in which you really stop to look fear in the face.... You must do the thing you think you cannot do."

Dr. K. J. Wilson did. Her contribution is immeasurable. This book will be the bible of domestic violence advocates for years to come.

— Del Martin
San Francisco, June 1997

Preface

My name is Debby Tucker and I'm an advocate. I am honored to provide opening remarks for the Second Edition of *When Violence Begins at Home*. Karen Wilson has updated what was already an exceptionally useful overview of the knowledge we've gained in our movement to end violence against women, a movement that is now thirty years strong. Once again she has taken on the enormous task of sharing that accumulated knowledge in an effort to assist others who seek to design responsive programs or who simply wish to better understand the many and varied strategies we must employ if we are indeed to stop the violence.

This book provides a valuable supplement to the skills demanded by successful advocacy. Armed with the wealth of information contained in these pages—along with a willingness to take risks, a measure of creativity, receptivity to new information, a commitment to empathetic listening to the victims who are the true experts, and the maturity to admit when something isn't working as well as was hoped—one will only improve one's effectiveness as an advocate.

Karen and I both worked with SafePlace, in Austin, Texas, an organization that actively nurtures both the skills listed above and the philosophy behind the material you'll encounter in the chapters to come. That philosophy is rooted in two fundamental beliefs: that any woman can become the victim of domestic violence, and that we must stop trying to find out "what's wrong with her" and instead must hold the abuser responsible.

I'd like to describe some of my experiences as an advocate during each of the three decades of the movement and to touch on the issues that still challenge us today as we continue to expand the movement to end violence against women and gender-based violence against men. I was a volunteer and a staff member at the first rape-crisis center and first shelter in Texas. I cofounded the Texas Council on Family Violence, our state coalition, which in 1996 reestablished the National Domestic Violence Hotline (800-799-SAFE). I cofounded the National Network to End Domestic Violence, which wrote and worked to pass the federal Violence Against Women Act in 1994. I now direct the National Center on Domestic and Sexual Violence, based in Austin, Texas, where I consult, train, and advocate for change. I co-chaired the U. S. Department of Defense Task Force on Domestic Violence, and I remain active in congressional advocacy, especially on the issue of domestic and sexual violence in the military. By providing a sense of the movement's history I hope to help the reader place Karen's work in a context and to encourage a new resolve to remain true to the guiding principles that have served as our foundation.

The First Decade: 1975–1985

When local groups began developing services to assist domestic-violence victims in their communities, saving lives was often their top priority, and sometimes the only one. Before then, when battered women literally ran for their lives they had nowhere to turn. Advocates responded by opening shelters and providing services that assisted "well women in crisis." We didn't really know what we were doing, except for knowing that we didn't want to replicate the lack of responsiveness victims seemed to encounter when they approached professionals in other fields.

We weren't sure what feminism meant; we just knew that certain things were wrong. We didn't know that sexism was the root of the problem of family violence. For many of us, however, feminism ultimately helped us define what to do. At first, we didn't realize the ways in which we ourselves were being changed by what we learned. Most of us didn't have college degrees in social services, business, women's studies, or law, but we had a burning desire to create safety for individuals and to change the acceptance of violence against women implied by the apathy we saw in those around us.

What was most important in the beginning? It was addressing the fact that everywhere women turned for help they encountered rules and regulations. Women needed a place to go so their abusers couldn't find them and their children, yet actual refuge was unavailable in most (if not all) communities. For many of us, Del Martin's book *Battered Wives* was our bible. She noted that social services wouldn't provide financial support to a victim if she still resided with the offender, yet the victim often lacked the resources to move out without help. We saw this catch-22 played out in our communities. Criminal-justice agencies suggested that women divorce the abuser and cautioned law enforcement against becoming involved in civil or family matters.

Initially we thought we'd simply give women a place where they could rest and hide for a few days or a couple of weeks before they moved on, but soon we realized that most planned to go back to the abuser. Some actually needed help to find a new place to live because they had run for the last time, but we weren't very organized in our responses to that need. Back then, we thought providing a Greyhound bus ticket to a relative's or a friend's home was big support. We underestimated the persistence of batterers and had to learn from the women themselves how dangerous their situations truly were.

We began to push for other players in the system to pay attention, get involved, and respond more appropriately. We first turned to local police and prosecutors and urged them to respond in a way that actually provided protection for victims. We even dared to want a measure of accountability from the system and a challenge to the offender to change his behavior.

As our understanding of the multifaceted nature of the problem evolved, we began pushing other social-service agencies to provide women with what they actually needed rather than with merely what the agencies wanted to offer. We recognized that we were creating social *change* rather than just more social services. This philosophy came to be well understood across communities and states. Seemingly very isolated communities began to see that battering wasn't about the woman. "But for the Grace of God Go I" was the clearest way we communicated our conviction that what might separate a battered woman from a nonbattered one was the luck of the draw; we pointed out that any of us could have the misfortune to become involved with a person willing to use violence.

The well-entrenched belief that the woman was the cause of the problem influenced the responses of both the criminal-justice system and the helping agencies. Asking for assistance from these systems often brought with it a huge risk. Women who compromised their safety by reaching out for help sometimes found themselves the focus of the system—as parents, as persons with mental illness, or as the cause of the violence against them.

Witnessing this, advocates banded together within their states and began working with legislators to create laws and public policy that forced systems and professionals to change the way they responded to both victims and perpetrators. We told service providers in all branches of the system about their proper roles and about how they could best respond to battered women and their children. Taking these steps didn't necessarily endear us to others, and our approach didn't always have the desired effects. We learned that to advocate effectively for change in how battered women were treated, we had to build bridges; we had to listen and not just tell.

We began to garner the support of private citizens, organizations, businesses, churches, and other groups. Local operations grew from being run solely by volunteers or having just a couple of paid employees to employing staffs of several people. We had to learn how to manage our growth, and we were challenged by our lack of sophistication coupled with our commitment to doing things differently. Because of our desire to try organizational styles like the "feminist collective" or "nonhierarchical management," we often rejected information from others that might have helped us. Our attempts to break out of the norm were difficult since none of us knew much about the unconventional models we hoped to emulate, but they did create some positive results. We adopted an important openness in the management of our organizations based on the belief that people have a right to information that affects them. We tried new ways of working with women. We realized that shelter residents should have a say in how a shelter was run because it was their home. This was radical stuff, but it also created some fun moments.

I remember the rebellion of August 1978 in the Austin shelter, when women petitioned the staff to buy white bread and to quit making them eat only the honey-wheat variety. The health-food activists among our volunteers and staff reluctantly agreed to the white bread if they could offer voluntary workshops on nutrition and could help with the cooking. Empowered by the success of these efforts, the residents challenged the fact that only the staff and volunteer quarters had a TV set, when they liked to watch TV as well. A happy compromise was reached when the staff negotiated the womens's use of the TV for limited hours each evening in exchange for the removal of the Harlequin Romance book collection. More than just brokering a single agreement, we had spawned a management style. We had set a tone that would carry forward and be an important philosophic underpinning of how to run a shelter.

The Second Decade: 1985–1995

In 1984 the U.S. Surgeon General created a task force on family violence, held hearings on the topic, and released a report that addressed the epidemic proportions of the problem. In 1986 Congress enacted the Family Violence Prevention and Services Act and the Victims of Crime Act, both of which gave states leverage to create more services. The laws also gave voice to the millions of victims in this country by underscoring the fact that domestic violence was an issue of national importance.

President Carter established an office in the White House that offered technical assistance to fledgling programs attempting to provide safety to battered women and their children with only minimal resources and often open hostility from their communities. We were accused of "breaking up families" and recruiting women to be lesbians, some of the same kinds of attacks from the far right that still plague us today. But today we are much more sophisticated in responding to such attacks. We don't let them divide us the way we sometimes did twenty years ago.

Then Carter was defeated in his bid for reelection by Ronald Reagan. The first day President Reagan was in office he closed the White House office on domestic violence. I was in Washington, D.C., at the time and took home two large boxes of publications that would otherwise have been thrown away. Advocates realized that our efforts at the national level would no longer be well received, so we shifted our focus to building state coalitions and learning how to pass state legislation. We urged the criminal-justice system to respond more appropriately to domestic-violence calls and to arrest perpetrators. We pushed for warrentless arrest of batterers, training for law enforcement, and policies and procedures to be written with our input. Sponsored by our state coalitions, we enjoyed our first successes while wearing hose and heels: Dressed up for Capitol Lobby Days, we asked state legislators to invest funding in these programs and to match federal funds.

Those of us running local and state programs began to hear criticism that the programs served only a select few. We often responded with, "What do you mean? We do lots of public education and our doors are open!" We were busy helping survivors who were coming through our doors and didn't notice those who weren't coming in or calling. We gradually became conscious of our own lack of awareness and our failure to create broad support for women of all ethnicities, races, and social classes. Too many of us came from a frame of reference rooted in white, middle-class America; we noticed that our movement's leadership included few women of color. Slowly we embraced diversity in our leadership and in our thinking, but there was much more to be done to make the movement reflect our values.

In the early nineties we realized that the federal government might be more receptive to addressing family violence now that a different president was in office. The Domestic Violence Coalition on Public Policy was formed, leading to the establishment of the National Network to End Domestic Violence (NNEDV). Although every state had a coalition, only about half had a staff member working for the interests of all the agencies and battered women in that state. And few organizations had the resources to work together at the national level. Forming the NNEDV was a big step toward creating a presence in D.C. We began drafting what would become the Violence Against Women Act—just in case we got a chance to introduce it in Congress.

The Third Decade: 1995–2005

And we did! In 1994 two dramatic events influenced one another to significantly change the landscape: the criminal trial of O.J. Simpson and the enactment of the Violence Against Women Act (VAWA). Congress, with the encouragement of the Clinton administration, may never have been willing to take up and immediately pass our proposed legislation had it not been for the heightened awareness of the issue of family violence engendered by Simpson's trial as well as the encouragement of the Clinton administration.

VAWA provides increased support at the federal, state, and local levels for the effort to end domestic violence. One of the provisions of the act I am most proud of is the stipulation that criminal-justice agencies may not be awarded federal funding unless they have an advocate partner, a local domestic violence agency signing up to work closely with them to implement the project. This was our way of ensuring that police departments, prosecutors' offices, and other criminal-justice agencies would be influenced by ongoing relationships with advocates, who we hoped would share our movement's vision and guiding principles with those inside the system. We must remain vigilant if we want to change the system to make it more responsive to women, rather than simply helping women to negotiate the system.

Since VAWA was enacted, billions of dollars have been spent on training, technical assistance, and development of services to reach out to all victims of domestic violence. One of the largest organizations in the world, the U.S. Department of Defense (DoD), is undergoing a huge shift in its understanding of family violence and its approach to dealing with the problem. As Karen describes in the new chapter devoted to the military response, the Defense Task Force on Domestic Violence provided a blueprint for the DoD to modify how it addresses prevention and intervention, and slow progress is being made to implement the recommended changes. I have often told myself that if an organization as large as DoD can change, we can make a difference anywhere.

In the mid-1990s we also began to pay closer attention to complaints that we relied too heavily on the criminal-justice system. We began to ask which batterers were being sent to jail and which to "treatment." Which survivors were being pressured into attending parenting classes and which were losing their children to abusers and to child welfare? What was meant by the criticism that some survivors were uncomfortable with the services being provided? These questions have provoked profound self-examination among leaders in the movement. They have also influenced the writing of the federal Violence Against Women Act Reauthorization of 2005. This proposed legislation greatly broadens how the needs of victims are addressed both by building on what we've learned about influencing the criminal-justice system and by asking that housing, financial support, medical care, job training, and other needs be more thoroughly considered.

We have become more sophisticated in recognizing that many victims face challenges in addition to the violence, including chronic homelessness, poverty, addiction, and mental illness. We must expand our thinking and accept that there is much to learn from others, yet we must preserve the core of our movement's underlying philosophy and mission. We would only lose effectiveness if we allowed our focus to become diluted so that we became simply a social-service charity ministering to the unfortunate.

This book is a vital resource for people who want to end family violence. All of us must recognize that we have to keep learning. We must acknowledge that although we know much more now than we did thirty years ago, to end domestic violence in the next three decades we must work together to challenge its pervasiveness in our society. With every step we take to build safe, supportive families and a culture that condemns the use of violence, we move closer to ending violence against women.

— Deborah D. Tucker

Executive Director
National Center on Domestic and Sexual Violence

Acknowledgments

In the course of writing this book, I had the pleasure of talking with numerous women and men in Texas and across this nation. One thing became abundantly clear to me as a result of our discussions: These incredible people diligently work to end violence in the home because of their desire for justice and their respect for humanity. While their contributions are frequently unrecognized, they continue their quest with a compassion and a willingness to share that is nothing less than remarkable. This book is the product of their wisdom, passion, and guidance. To the many people who so willingly shared their gifts with me, I offer you my gratitude and appreciation.

I would like to extend a special thank you to Susan Brownmiller, Del Martin, and Deborah D. Tucker for their generous review of this book and their expert guidance.

I am continually touched by the support and encouragement I receive from the dedicated staff, board of directors, and volunteers at SafePlace (formerly the Austin Center for Battered Women). I find that the company of these fine individuals has enriched my life in more ways than I could ever express. Their relentless, loving efforts to end domestic violence continue to motivate and inspire me. I consider it an honor and a privilege to stand with the SafePlace family in our struggle.

I would like to extend a special thank you to the SafePlace staff and volunteers, both past and present, who so generously offered their insight and support on this project. My gratitude goes out to Wendie Abramson, Erin Clark, Kelly White, Pat Clark, Dana Grasso Gillispie, Lucy Muñoz, Barri Rosenbluth, Sara Slater, Coni Huntsman Stogner, Matt Starr, Kelly Sullivan Garcia, Rebecca Lightsey, Rand Metcalfe, Margaret Bassett, Tiffany McMillan, Betty Davis, Vivian Rogers, Julia Spann, Joan Carter, Mary Kay Sicola, Gin Keller, Murilyn Pinkosky, Holly, Martha Peine, Anne Spellacy, Theresa Pritchard, Margaret Young, Angela Atwood, Darlene Strayn, Dana Little, Wicket Davidson, Juanita Salinas, and Lisa Rivera Capper. Several SafePlace staff and volunteers, including Laura Hopingardner, Patsy Flores, Dina Ortiz, Sarah Hauck Seaton, Kim Cox, and Sara Sloan, helped to research materials for this project.

The past and present staff and volunteers at the Texas Council on Family Violence and the National Domestic Violence Hotline provided immeasurable support and assistance. I wish to extend a special thank you to Sheryl Cates, Ellen Fisher, Cyndy Perkins, D'An Anders, Susan Mathis, Diane Schultz, Tony Switzer, Anna Belle Burleson, Diane Perez, Sonia Benavides, Karen Buck, and Shaun Thompson.

This book would not have been possible without the expert guidance of the staff at Hunter House. I also wish to thank Kiran Rana and Dana Weissman, as well as Kathleen Niendorff, for their dedication to this important issue and their faith in my abilities. I am particularly grateful to Jeanne Brondino, acquisitions editor at Hunter House, for her ongoing thoughtfulness, support, and encouragement.

That I am alive and able to write this book is due, in part, to the support and assistance of my family and friends. My parents, Calvin and Carrie Wilson, gave me all the encouragement, support, and assistance I needed while respecting and honoring my need to find my own path. My brother, Billy Gage, and my nephew, Henry Goode, offered their assistance at a time when I was barely able to help myself. My dear uncle, Allen Hesser, gave me a safe haven and a loving heart at a time when I thought I'd never be safe again. My sister and my friend, Jan Conner, provided immeasurable love, support, and kindness. I extend my love and my gratitude to all of these dear people.

Barbara Stone, my teacher, my mentor, and my friend, always knew I could and helped me get there. Paulette Beatty, Nancy Sawtelle, Janeen Ashton, Abba Anderson, and Rhonda Snider gave of themselves in ways that helped me find my own strength. To all of you I offer my appreciation.

My gratitude goes out to Kalpana Sutaria, Mamata Misra, and all the members, past and present, of Saheli. Thank you for all that you have taught me and for giving me the opportunity to stand with you in our struggle for a more peaceful world.

To Michele Caruso, Sabrina Laurent, and all the staff at the Women's Resource and Services Office at Nicholls State University, I offer my admiration and my gratitude. I cannot begin to thank Gayle Jackson enough for the many journeys we have taken together. And to the members of the Domestic Violence Unit of Police Social Services at the Lafourche Parish Sheriff's Office, in Thibodaux, Louisiana, I extend my heartfelt thanks for teaching me that advocates come in many different forms.

A special thank-you goes out to the Voisin, Landry, and Bergeron families for opening your hearts and your homes to me and for always making me feel like family.

I find that sometimes the human language proves inadequate as an expression of the emotion that stirs my heart. I will try, however, to give thanks to those individuals who have blessed my life with their love and support. My deepest appreciation goes to my life partner and best friend, Barbara Voisin. Through her kindness, generosity, and humor she demonstrates to me every day what respectful and unconditional love is. I am especially grateful to Terri Leeth, who has traveled many miles with me. I am blessed with her company and her love. To Joel Maiorano, I wish to express my gratitude and deep affection for his faith, humor, and support. I have learned much from this kind man. Melinda Cantu fills my life with an abundance of love, laughter, and encouragement; she is the sister of my heart. Rose Hernandez's kind and gentle spirit provides comfort like no other. Stephanie Horgan is a loyal and loving force in my life. Miz Gail Rice moves me with her compassion and challenges me to action. Diane Rhodes never fails to tap my shoulder when I need it and lends me hers for my tears and my laughter. Julie Doll is a steadfast friend whose unselfish efforts to create social change remind me to never give up. Dear Andrea Edgerson inspires me with her courage, and Bernice Machala shows me the power of the human spirit. Jim Rigby, with his wicked sense of humor and deep commitment to social justice, leaves me in awe. I am a better person because of every one of you.

Dottie Davis's legacy continues to live on and inspires those of us fortunate enough to have shared time with her. I miss you, Dottie.

Lastly, to the many women who have so willingly shared their pain and their triumphs with me, I offer my grateful appreciation. You have taught me more than you will ever, ever know.

When Violence Begins at Home

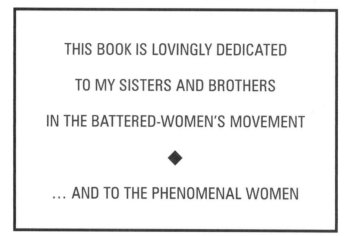

THIS BOOK IS LOVINGLY DEDICATED

TO MY SISTERS AND BROTHERS

IN THE BATTERED-WOMEN'S MOVEMENT

◆

... AND TO THE PHENOMENAL WOMEN

Introduction

I first became involved with the battered-women's movement in 1978, when I was working for a newly funded displaced-homemaker's program in a small rural community in Texas. Displaced-homemaker's programs, which evolved from the women's movement, were created to empower divorced, widowed, and separated women. Although the late seventies was a period of growth for battered-women's centers, many communities still lacked such resources, including the one I resided in. Consequently, many of those who turned to us for help were battered women. Almost thirty years later, I can still vividly recall the first "unofficial" hotline call I took from a battered woman. Because there were no women's shelters in our community and few or no services available to battered women, I remember my sense of helplessness and frustration. By 1979 I had begun researching the battered-women's movement in Texas. By 1980 I had developed a passion for this work.

I would like to say that my involvement in the battered-women's movement has been consistent for the last twenty-five years, but it has not. My growth and empowerment have taken a winding path, including my own involvement in abusive relationships and my turn at burnout. However, I keep returning to the movement. And as a result of my experiences and growth, each time I return I find that I am a better advocate. I have come to truly appreciate the importance of not only "talking the talk" but also "walking the walk." Along the way my commitment to ending domestic violence has deepened. I am fortunate to be able to fulfill my passion through the educational programs I offer to community groups, volunteers, advocates, and abused women. Together we share, we learn, we grow, and we struggle for change. And we are better people because of the process.

In the summer of 1994 I presented a workshop at the Sixth National Conference on Domestic Violence, sponsored by the National Coalition Against Domestic Violence. I returned home with a strong need to write about the women who dedicate their lives to this movement and whom I had come to know and love. Then, about a year later, Kathleen Niendorff, former board member of the Austin Center for Battered Women (CBW; now Safe-Place), met with Kelly White, then executive director of CBW, and Ellen Rubenstein Fisher, then associate director at the Texas Council on Family Violence, to discuss the possibility of writing a comprehensive summary of what we had learned about domestic violence in the preceding twenty years. All three women liked the idea. When asked who would be willing to tackle the formidable task, Kelly mentioned my name. The rest of the story is a blur of late nights, too much coffee, and little rest; the end product was the first edition of *When Violence Begins at Home.* I was guided by an unequivocal understanding that this book would both reflect my passion and be a part of my own learning, growth, and empowerment as a formerly battered woman.

When Violence Begins at Home approaches the topic of domestic abuse with the understanding that it does not occur in a vacuum. The effects of abuse on women and children touch every aspect of their lives and the lives of those around them. Domestic violence is a complex social problem that must be understood and seriously addressed by all community members if we truly expect to create a peaceful future for everyone.

Chapter 1, "The Dynamics of Abusive Relationships," defines domestic abuse and explores the myths and realities surrounding violent relationships. In Chapter 2, "The Effects of Family Violence on Children," I examine the behavioral and psychological consequences of growing up in an abusive family. Chapter 3, "Teen Dating Violence," describes the frightening phenomenon of violence in adolescent dating relationships. It also explains how programs implemented by SafePlace can serve as a model for addressing this problem.

Chapter 4, "The Intimate Relationship Between Substance Abuse and Domestic Violence," examines the complex connection between two ongoing plagues and identifies effective intervention strategies. In Chapter 5, "Battered Women and the Legal System," I explore the legal options and roadblocks many domestic-violence survivors encounter when appealing to the judicial system.

Many women exist in such fear of their batterers that they feel their only chance for survival is to live in hiding. Chapter 6, "Living Underground," describes how women can successfully plan for a life in hiding. Chapter 7, "The Oppression That Binds: Barriers to Living Violence Free," concerns the different challenges that confront women of color, lesbians, undocumented women, women with disabilities, older women, women in prison, and women residing in rural areas.

The impact of domestic violence extends far beyond the walls of the family home. Friends, family members, coworkers, employers, physicians, nurses, religious leaders, and congregation members all have an important role to play in the lives of women who suffer abuse. The community that seriously expects to eliminate this vicious problem must take an active stance against domestic violence *as a community*. The question "how do I help someone in an abusive relationship?" is answered in Chapter 8, "For Friends, Family, and Loved Ones: When Someone You Know Is Being Hurt." The chapter also provides a list of sensitive questions that concerned individuals can ask to determine if an abusive relationship exists. Chapter 9, "Domestic Violence and the Workplace," explores both the impact of domestic abuse on the workplace and the employer's role in helping to make the work environment safe for battered employees. In Chapter 10, "Battered Women's Health: The Response of the Medical Community," I discuss the responses and responsibilities of the medical community to abused women. Chapter 11, "Battered Women and Communities of Faith," outlines specific strategies the religious community can use to provide battered women with wise counsel and practical care. Chapter 12, "Domestic Violence and the Military," a new chapter for the second edition, explores the prevalence of domestic abuse in the military community, with a focus on the efforts of the Department of Defense Domestic Violence Task Force. Chapter 13, "Creating a Community Response to Domestic Violence," discusses strategies for developing a collaborative response to domestic abuse and highlights the community efforts made in Austin, Texas, to address the problem.

Intervention on behalf of abusive families can take different forms. Chapter 14, "Intervention Strategies for Battered Women and Their Children," discusses support groups and counseling options. Chapter 15, "Advocacy and Empowerment for Battered Women," another new chapter for this edition, explores the highly challenging—and rewarding—role of the domestic-violence advocate. Chapter 16, "Intervention and Prevention Programs for Batterers," examines the variety of treatment programs available for abusers. It also outlines important guidelines for choosing a program that addresses the safety needs of women and children.

Individuals who work toward ending domestic violence do so because they have a passion for peace. Too often, however, over time the nature of the work wears away advocates' energy and defeats their ability to share of themselves. In Chapter 17, "Loving Ourselves: Self-Care for Helpers," I explore what it means to experience burnout and how advocates can successfully avoid doing so.

Chapter 18, "The National Domestic Violence Hotline," describes the history of and services provided by the NDVH, which was revived in the mid-1990s as a result of hard-won federal funds and the careful stewardship of the

Texas Council on Family Violence. Finally, in Appendix I, "A History of Violence Against Women," I trace the history of domestic abuse from its origins in patriarchal society to the birth in the 1970s of the grassroots battered-women's movement.

Eighty-five percent of reported domestic violence is committed by men against women. This statistic is reflected throughout the book in my reference to the batterer as "he" and the survivor as "she." However, I do not wish to give the impression that battering among lesbians and gays does not exist or is less important than battering among nongays. Same-sex battering is as detrimental to the lives it touches as battering in any heterosexual relationship. As the Texas Council on Family Violence GLBT Caucus explains, the pain is the same. I apologize for any misunderstanding created by my use of this terminology, and I ask for your patience.

In the eight years since the publication of the first edition of *When Violence Begins at Home* I have received a wealth of positive feedback, much of it about the "user-friendly" nature of the book. In addition, survivors, advocates, state coalitions, teachers, students, social workers, counselors, therapists, law-enforcement officers, judges, lawyers, military personnel, employers, faith leaders, spiritual advisors, health-care professionals, and others have sought me out to share their stories and express their appreciation for the book. Numerous survivors have told me how the book "helped save my life." Without question, my dream that this resource would help at least one person has been greatly surpassed. I am humbled and honored that the labor of love I call my book has been of such service.

Much has happened in eight years. New research both reinforces and enhances our understanding of the complex problem of domestic violence. Creative and innovative programs continue to be developed to address the challenging needs of survivors and their children. The second edition of *When Violence Begins at Home* remains true to its original purpose in that it attempts to provide a comprehensive summary of what we have learned about domestic violence—but now it encompasses almost thirty years of work, study, and research. Building on the foundation of the original, this edition includes current research in such areas as the parenting behaviors of batterers, drug-facilitated sexual assault, stalking, cyber-stalking, child custody and visitation for batterers, pregnancy and domestic violence, and the effectiveness of batterer-intervention programs. Controversial issues such as women's use of force, child-welfare and "failure to protect" policies, welfare reform, and mandatory arrests are also introduced in this edition. The two new chapters result from many discussions I've had with readers over the last few years. Finally, many new resources have been included in the extensive directory located at the back of the book to reflect the ever-evolving wealth of books, websites, and agencies available to both survivors and helpers.

In 1998 the Austin Center for Battered Women (CBW) and the Austin Rape Crisis Center (ARCC) joined forces and became SafePlace. The group continues in its award-winning efforts to provide services to survivors of domestic and sexual violence and to their family members and friends. Innovative programs such as Disability Services ASAP continue to mark SafePlace as a leader in national efforts to end domestic and sexual violence. This edition examines these new programs and their impact on both the Austin community and the nation.

In 2000 I resigned my position as director of training for SafePlace to pursue a goal of providing educational programs at the national level. I am pleased to report that I have been able to accomplish that dream. I have been generously given the opportunity to facilitate trainings for a variety of groups, including state coalitions, local domestic-violence and sexual-assault programs, health-care facilities, the military, religious organizations, universities, and law-enforcement agencies. For two years I had the honor of serving as the senior trainer and consultant for the Louisiana Department of Justice Domestic Violence in the WorkPlace Initiative. I attribute my willingness to take the leap of faith into self-employment to the empowerment I gained as a result of writing this book and to the support and encouragement I received from the SafePlace staff, board, and volunteers. As I reminded those fine people upon my departure, my leaving signified just how well they did their job of helping women empower themselves. I continue to work with SafePlace, particularly the Disability Services ASAP Program, and am grateful to be able in some small way to help them make this world a better place for battered women and their children.

When I originally wrote this book, I had to wrestle with many old demons. I am proud to say that I have won. In the first edition, safety concerns led me to avoid using my full name and avoid including a picture of myself on the cover. I have made my peace with those concerns and now feel empowered to say, "My name is Karen Jeanine Wilson and I am the author of this book." I remain committed to helping others better understand domestic violence so that we may all do our part to end the problem. I will continue to address my safety concerns, but I will not be silenced. We have been forced into silence and shame for far too long. Never again, my sisters, never again.

...1

The Dynamics of
Abusive Relationships

Family violence is a simple phrase, but it encompasses a horrifying list of abusive behaviors, both physical and psychological, inflicted by one family member on another.... The list is endless. There is seemingly no end to the horrors some human beings can inflict on those whom this society calls their "loved ones."

— The American Medical News, *January 6, 1992*

Martha was twenty-seven when she met Phillip. The manager of a small business in a rural community, Martha was also attending night classes to complete a graduate degree. Phillip was self-employed and was well known in the community. He was handsome, charming, and witty. Unfortunately (as Martha saw it) he was also married. Three years passed and Phillip got a divorce. During that time Phillip had spent a lot of time around Martha's place of business. He would drop by to see the owner of the company and inevitably end up in Martha's office. When Martha learned of his divorce, she was secretly pleased. Here was her opportunity to go out with the man she was so drawn to. When Phillip asked her to lunch, she didn't hesitate.

They immediately began to see each other every day. Martha was so thrilled with all the attention that she didn't notice Phillip's irritation when she occasionally turned down lunch dates with him to meet her girlfriends. The first few months of their relationship were exciting and romantic. Phillip showered her with gifts and affection. Soon, however, Martha began to feel smothered by Phillip's constant demands on her time and attention. When Martha told Phillip she could no longer see him, he was furious and vowed to win her back. Then began a flood of flowers, gifts, telephone calls, and letters. Martha stood firm in her decision for a while but eventually began to miss Phillip. She finally agreed to see him again.

Shortly after their reunion Phillip moved in with Martha, and his attempts to control her escalated. He began telling her what he considered appropriate dress. He encouraged her to gain weight because he liked women with "meat on their bones," and then he made fun of her because her clothes were becoming tight. His constant phone calls continued, but now he required her to outline her whereabouts on a minute-by-minute basis. If she told him she would be home at five o'clock, the phone would be ringing as she walked in the door. If she was late, even by a few minutes, he would interrogate her. He began accusing her of having affairs.

Two years later Martha was ready to end the relationship. Phillip, however, wanted to marry her, and her refusals sent him into rages. Initially he threw or hit things, but eventually he began to push her when he was angry. Martha begged Phillip to leave. He moved in and out of her house so many times that she lost count. Each time he left he would harass her at home and at work so persistently that she would give in and let him return. She grew more and more afraid of him.

As Martha continued to refuse Phillip's proposals, he became increasingly abusive. Holidays were the worst. The last Christmas Eve they spent together, Martha found herself trapped under a seven-foot Christmas tree. While he held the tree on top of her, Martha felt the lights burning her arms. She silently prayed that she would never have to spend another holiday in fear.

Martha considered herself an intelligent, responsible woman. She held a professional position, attended graduate school, and was respected in her field. Privately, however, she was embarrassed and humiliated. Phillip had been born and raised in the area and was well liked there. He had friends in the police department and the county attorney's office, so Martha didn't feel safe approaching them about her situation. She thought about contacting the local battered-women's shelter, but Phillip's cousin worked there and Martha was afraid she would tell him. Her shame and fear prevented her from seeking help.

During the fourth and final year of their relationship, Phillip's abusive behavior reached its height. One evening, after another refused proposal of marriage, Phillip drove his truck into the back of Martha's car, pushing it into the closed garage door. It was three in the morning and the crash could be heard throughout the neighborhood; still, no one called the police. Phillip told Martha she would never be able to leave him. He threatened to kill both her and himself if she tried. He taunted her and said if she tried to get a restraining order against him, he would ignore it. Nothing would keep him from her.

Being abused and humiliated had become a way of life for Martha, but the final straw was the last time Phillip attacked her. Dragging her across the kitchen floor, he repeatedly kicked her in the stomach, back, legs, and arms with his steel-toed boots. Picking her up and throwing her into the kitchen table, Phillip held her down while he stomped on her hands.

When his rage had passed, Martha was left crumpled on the floor, bruised and bloodied. Phillip quietly approached her, crying, and said that if she had just done what he had wanted this wouldn't have happened. "You made me do this," was Phillip's explanation for his behavior. "If you don't marry me, I'll have to kill you. If I can't have you, no one else can either!"

Martha was now sure that if she didn't do something Phillip would kill her. Afraid to go to the local authorities, she decided to literally run away. She secretly planned her escape. She found the courage to tell her friends, family, and coworkers about her abusive relationship. Thankfully, all were supportive and offered help. Finally, after months of planning, Martha packed a bag, got into her car, and drove away. She left her home, her friends, her job, and her possessions. She had her life, however, and she was safe. She stayed on the run for the next few months, living out of a suitcase. Looking for a job was difficult, but she eventually found employment in another part of the country. Today Martha celebrates her new life and her peace. She knows what it is like to live in fear and has vowed never to live that way again.

What Is Abuse?

The strongest risk factor for being a victim of domestic violence is being a woman. According to the U.S. Department of Justice, there were 691,710 reported acts of nonfatal violence committed by current or former spouses, boyfriends, or girlfriends in 2001. In 85 percent of these assaults, the crimes were committed by men against women.[2] A Commonwealth Fund survey reports that nearly one-third (31 percent) of American women report being physically or sexually abused by an intimate partner at some point in their lives.[3]

Most people do not clearly understand the word *abuse*. Visions of broken bones and black eyes are the generally held impressions. Certainly these severe physical indicators are signs of abuse; however, abuse can be much less noticeable and much more insidious. It is not uncommon for women who have participated in workshops on domestic violence to approach me and confide that they have just realized that their ex-partners were abusive. They knew something was terribly wrong—they just didn't have a name for it.

To be effective advocates for battered women, we must have a working understanding of exactly what constitutes abuse. For our purposes abuse can be considered any repeated attempts to control, manipulate, or demean another individual using physical, emotional, or sexual tactics. The terms *abuse, battering, family violence, partner violence, intimate violence,* and *domestic violence* will be used interchangeably in this book.

Let's take a closer look at each of the three categories of abuse listed above: physical abuse, emotional abuse, and sexual abuse.

Physical Abuse

Physical abuse is any use of size, strength, or presence to hurt or control someone else. Although some of the behaviors listed below are clearly more dangerous than others, all show a lack of respect and an attempt to control the other's behavior. It is not necessary to use physical violence often to keep a partner in a constant state of fear. A batterer may actually use violence infrequently, as a last resort.

Abuse Involving Physical Contact Between People

Pushing

Pulling

Slapping

Biting

Choking

Shoving

Grabbing

Pinching

Spanking

Kicking

Spitting

Hair pulling

Arm twisting

Forced kneeling

Burning

Shooting

Stabbing

Restraining

Backhanding

Pushing into/pulling out of a car

Banging partner's head on wall or floor

Abuse of children

Abuse of animals

Hitting partner while she's pregnant

Standing or sitting on partner

Pinning partner against wall

Forcibly carrying partner

Punching with a fist

Attacking with an object or a weapon

Murder

Abuse Involving the Use of an Object

Throwing things

Breaking personal items

Driving recklessly

Trying to hit partner with car

Slamming doors

Tearing clothes

Breaking objects

Punching walls or doors

Sweeping things off tables or from drawers

Kicking furniture, car, or walls

Threatening with an object

Threatening with a weapon

Abuse Involving the Use of Size or Presence

Chasing

Unplugging phone

Stalking

Standing behind car to prevent driving away

Taking car keys

Sabotaging car

Taking credit cards, money, or checkbook

Trapping

Clenching fists as a threat

Standing in doorway to prevent exit

Locking partner out of house

Abandoning partner in dangerous places

Refusing to help partner when she is sick, injured, or pregnant

Emotional Abuse

Emotional abuse is any use of words, voice, action, or lack of action meant to control, hurt, or demean another person. This type of abuse is usually harder to define than physical abuse. At some time in their relationship almost all couples shout or scream things they later regret. Emotionally abusive relationships, however, are defined as involving repeated hurtful exchanges with a disregard for the partner's feelings.

While some emotionally abusive relationships do not involve physical abuse, all physically abusive relationships contain some emotional abuse. Emotional abuse is much more than name-calling. One of the dangers of this type of abuse is that it is frequently subtle and insidious. Many battered women describe emotional abuse as just as damaging as physical abuse, if not more so. According to one battered woman, "If you get beaten you at least have the bruises to prove it. With emotional abuse all you know is how much it hurts inside. That's where the scars are. How can you show that to someone? It comes down to your word against his."

Types of Verbal Abuse

Threatening to kill

Threatening to use violence

Making threats to children

Accusing partner of unfaithfulness

Calling names like whore, bitch, and slut

Leaving nasty messages on answering machine

Making insinuations

Making statements like:

"You're dumb."

"You're stupid."

"You're ugly."

"You can't do anything right."

"No one else would have you."

"Whose baby is it?"

Yelling

Using insults

Being sarcastic

Name-calling

Withholding approval, appreciation, or affection as a punishment

Sneering

Growling

Criticizing

Ignoring

Humiliating

Laughing at partner

Insulting family or friends

Threatening family or friends

Emotionally Abusive Actions

Being irresponsible with money

Controlling access to money

Displaying intense jealousy

Isolating partner from friends and family

Keeping partner up all night

Checking up on partner

Taking others' possessions

Making faces

Manipulating with lies

Threatening to divorce

Having affairs

Constantly questioning partner about activities

Not working

Keeping partner from working

Threatening to take custody of children

Denying access to phone

Threatening suicide

Threatening to harm self

Sexual Abuse

Sexual abuse is any sexual behavior meant to control, manipulate, humiliate, or demean another person. This is a confusing area for many people. For too long women have been taught that sexually submitting to the husband is a wife's duty. Historically, women have had little say about when, where, how, and with whom they engaged in sex.

Sexual violence is common in abusive relationships. Sex in these relationships is often used as a means to exert power over the female partner and to further shame and humiliate her. Frequently women are raped after a beating. Sexual deviancy, too, often occurs in these relationships. One battered woman reported being tied and bound with barbed wire while her husband and his friends repeatedly raped her.

Types of Sexual Abuse

Unwanted touching

Sexual name-calling

Unfaithfulness

False accusations about infidelity

Withholding sex as a punishment

Forced sex with partner

Forced sex with someone other than partner

Forced sex with animals

Hurtful sex

Insisting partner dress in a more sexual way than she wants to

Forcing partner to strip

Forcing partner to watch others have sex

Rape with an object

Unwanted sadistic sexual acts

Dispelling the Myths

Domestic violence, like other forms of violence against women, has long been shrouded in myths and fallacies. Many of these myths focus on the misconception that the woman has somehow caused her battering. They also serve to protect and isolate others who believe that "domestic violence could never happen to me." In addition, these myths sometimes offer comfort to rescuers who have been thwarted in their efforts to help battered women.

One of the problems for couples in abusive relationships is that they, like the general population, believe and promote these fallacies. Dispelling the myths helps couples understand the realities of their relationship and helps abused women begin to understand how they have been blamed for their own abuse. We must shatter these myths if we hope to understand abusive relationships and to help battered women empower themselves.

MYTH 1

Women are just as violent as men.

Fact

There are female batterers. There are women who batter their female partners and there are those who batter their male partners. However, data reported by the U.S. Department of Justice illustrate that women are five to eight times more likely than men to be hurt by an intimate partner.[4] Sociologist Richard Gelles notes that women are the recipients of more acts of intimate violence and suffer more serious injury than their male counterparts.[5] While domestic violence may be about the abuse of power in a relationship, it is also very clearly about gender violence.

Those claiming that women are just as violent as men frequently cite a 1985 National Family Violence Survey in which they say that the data revealed that there are as many (or more) battered men as there are battered women.[6] In fact, however, there are fundamental flaws with the instrument that was used in the study, the "Conflict Tactics Scale" (CTS), which was originally developed to capture the dynamics of interpersonal conflict in marital relationships.[7] One of the problems with the original instrument is that the questions did not distinguish between intent and effect. In other words, the CTS equated a woman pushing a man in self-defense, for example, with a man pushing a woman down the stairs. The second problem with the CTS involved the rank ordering of the violent acts. The manner in which the violent acts were ordered did not take into consideration the degree of injury sustained as a result of the violent act.[8]

Since 1985 the CTS continues to be evaluated and improved upon to better reflect survivors' experiences of domestic violence. Consistent, reliable data reported since then continue to prove that while some men do get battered, domestic violence is overwhelmingly a problem for women.

MYTH 2

Battered women are helpless, passive, and fragile; have little or no education, no job skills, and numerous children; and are usually women of color.

Fact

Our extensive work with battered women teaches us that, while the above may be true for some women, it is not applicable to all battered women. If anything is truly equal opportunity, it is battering. Domestic violence crosses all socioeconomic, ethnic, racial, educational, age, and religious lines.

MYTH 3

If a battered woman doesn't leave her partner, it must be because she enjoys the abuse.

Fact

Inherent in this myth is the notion that the battered woman is masochistic. Originating with Freud, the misconception is that the woman receives some sort of sexual gratification from the battering. A classic form of "victim blaming," this myth removes all responsibility for the abusive behavior from the batterer and unjustly places it upon the woman.

As a domestic-violence survivor, and having worked for many years with battered women, it has been my experience that battered women neither enjoy nor receive any type of sexual gratification from battering. This much we know: Broken bones, bruises, shame, fear, and humiliation are not sexy!

MYTH 4

Battered women are mentally unstable if they choose to stay in abusive relationships.

Fact

Another form of "victim blaming," this myth oversimplifies the reasons why women remain with their abusive partners. As we shall see later in this chapter, the dynamics of abusive relationships are complex and intense. And while some battered women have mental-health issues that influence their situations, this does not guarantee that they will stay with their partners.

Many battered women do exhibit behaviors that, to those of us outside the intimate relationship, may seem unusual or even bizarre. It is important to remember that as outsiders we are not living with the daily threat and fear of abuse or death. *These women are.* The constant threat of violence will begin to affect how a woman thinks, feels, and acts. What appear to be bizarre behaviors are often survival strategies women use to keep themselves safe and to control their environment to the best of their perceived abilities.

MYTH 5

Battered women have done something to cause the battering.

Fact

Another "victim-blaming" statement, this myth places responsibility for the batterer's behavior squarely on the woman's shoulders. Most battered women spend inordinate amounts of energy trying to placate and please their abusive partners. The reality of the situation is that no one else, including the woman, is responsible for the abusive partner's behavior. Though he is unwilling to accept it, the batterer alone bears that responsibility. The batterer *chooses* to abuse his partner, regardless of her behavior.

MYTH 6

Men who batter their partners are socially inept, socially inappropriate, or violent in all their relationships.

Fact

It is a common misconception that the batterer treats people outside the abusive relationship the same as he does his partner. This is typically not the case. Many batterers exhibit a Jekyll-and-Hyde personality. Batterers can be quite charming and delightful when they want to be. This is how so many women get pulled into relationships with them. Initially, the batterer may seem loving and attentive; eventually, however, his behavior becomes abusive.

This Jekyll-and-Hyde behavior also contributes to Myth 3. If a woman gathers the courage to reach out to a friend, family member, or coworker, and that person has seen only the charming side of the batterer, the listener may

find the woman's stories of abuse and terror difficult to understand. Consequently, people in whom a woman confides may not believe her or may think
there is something wrong with her.

Having said this, however, it is worth noting that sometimes a batterer's
behavior outside the abusive relationship is a good indicator of his potential
for violence with his partner. If he is violent with someone other than his partner, the chances of her getting seriously hurt rise tremendously.

MYTH 7

Alcohol and drug use cause battering behavior.

Fact

For many years it was believed that if an abusive partner curtailed his alcohol
or drug use, the battering would cease. These substances were blamed for the
batterer's behavior. We now know that being intoxicated or high is simply an
excuse for abusive behavior, not its cause.

It is true that many abusive relationships involve alcohol and chemical-
dependency issues. Battering and chemical dependency, however, are two
separate issues. Research indicates that even when a batterer quits drinking or
using drugs, the battering continues.[9] He will simply find something or someone else to blame for his behavior.

MYTH 8

Abusive relationships will never change for the better.

Fact

The key to changing an abusive relationship is the batterer's willingness to accept responsibility for his actions. If the batterer admits to the inappropriate-
ness of his actions, wants to change, and seeks counseling, then he has a
chance to recover. If the batterer will not accept this responsibility and refuses
to change, the woman's greatest chance for living nonviolently is to flee the relationship. If the woman is willing to set appropriate boundaries for herself,
believes in her value and worth as a human being, and develops and utilizes
the resources and support systems available to her to leave a violent relationship, she has taken a giant leap toward finding peace in her life.

A word of caution to anyone who thinks she may be in an abusive relationship: Abuse, whether emotional, physical, or sexual, does not just stop. In
fact, unless there is some type of intervention and change, abuse will actually
escalate over time, becoming more and more severe and perhaps even lethal.

MYTH 9

Battered women grew up in abusive families.

Fact

Many women who find themselves in abusive relationships did not grow up in violent households. Often these women come from gentle, loving families. What tends to be the standard, however, is that their families were traditional, with strongly held beliefs in prescribed sex roles. And while not all battered women saw their mothers battered or were themselves battered as children, we are beginning to learn that a high percentage of battered women are incest survivors.

Research indicates, however, that many men who batter lived in a childhood home where violence was present. In fact, witnessing or actually experiencing violence as a child has been identified as a risk factor for becoming a batterer.[10] The American Psychological Association Presidential Task Force on Violence and the Family explains, "Although children affected by violence do not necessarily grow up to repeat the type of abuse they experienced, studies document a strong connection between victimization in childhood and later involvement in some form of interpersonal violence.... In particular, children who experience multiple acts of violence, or violence of more than one variety, appear to be at greater risk of continuing the cycle of violence."[11] These men either saw their mothers being battered or were themselves abused. They also learned, through childhood and societal conditioning, that it is acceptable to use violence against women.

MYTH 10

A man who beats his partner must be mentally ill.

Fact

While some abusers do have mental-health disorders, they comprise only a small percentage of batterers A recent study evaluating the mental health of 840 men participating in four batterer treatment programs found that while 39 percent showed evidence of narcissistic or antisocial tendencies, only 25 percent showed evidence of a severe mental disorder.[12]

The American Psychological Association Presidential Task Force on Violence and the Family makes an important distinction among batterers with mental disorders. According to the APA, "Among them [batterers] are men whose mental disorders lead to their violence, as well as men who have a mental disorder in addition to their violent behavior.... Although these batterers should be held accountable for their violence and not excused because of their mental illness, they should also receive proper mental health treatment as well as interventions specifically intended to stop their violent behavior."[13]

The Truth about Abusive Relationships

In her book *Trauma and Recovery,* Judith Herman explains that the methods used to coerce hostages, political prisoners, survivors of concentration camps, and battered women are surprisingly similar. Batterers use a number of tactics beyond physical abuse to hold women in abusive relationships. According to Dr. Herman, methods of establishing control over another person are grounded in the "systematic, repetitive infliction of psychological trauma," a strategy intended to instill fear and a sense of helplessness and to lower a woman's sense of self.[14]

One of the primary motivators for abusive behaviors is to maintain power and control in the relationship. Ellen Pence, in her book *In Our Best Interest: A Process for Personal and Social Change,* outlines abusive behaviors used by batterers to maintain power and control:[15]

Economic Abuse

Trying to keep her from getting or keeping a job

Making her ask for money, giving her an allowance, or taking her money

Sexual Abuse

Making her do sexual things against her will

Physically attacking the sexual parts of her body

Treating her like a sex object

Using the Children

Making her feel guilty about the children

Using the children to deliver messages

Using visitation as a way to harass her

Threats

Making or carrying out threats to do something to hurt her

Threatening to take the children, commit suicide, or report her to child welfare

Using Male Privilege

Treating her like a servant

Making all the decisions

Acting like the "king of the castle"

Intimidation

Making her fearful by using looks, actions, gestures, or a loud voice, or by smashing things or destroying her property

Isolation

Controlling what she does, whom she sees and talks to, or where she goes

Emotional Abuse

Putting her down or making her feel bad about herself

Calling her names

Making her think she's crazy

Playing mind games

Based on the input of more than two hundred battered women, these abusive behaviors have been shown to work together to shame, humiliate, and instill fear in women so they become less and less able to act on their own behalf.[16]

See also the Equality Wheel and the Power and Control Wheel on the following pages. These were developed by the Domestic Abuse Intervention Project in Duluth, Minnesota, and have been adapted for other situations as well.

What Causes Domestic Violence?

The reason why a man would abuse his intimate partner has been the source of many debates in the last thirty years. Numerous theories abound, and no one theory is widely accepted by all practitioners, researchers, advocates, or academics.[17] The original work of the battered-women's movement, however, was based on a feminist theory that continues to drive much of the work today.

Feminist theory proposes that domestic violence is aligned with other forms of violence against women, such as rape, sexual assault, the trafficking of women, female genital mutilation, child marriages, and honor killings. The

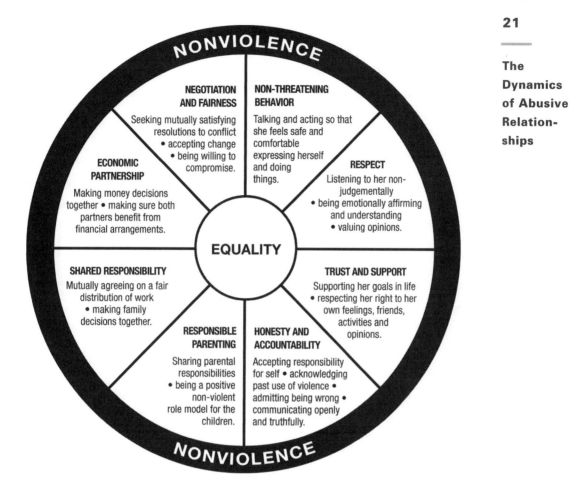

Equality Wheel

*Domestic Abuse Prevention Project, 202 East Superior St., Duluth MN 55802, (218)
722-2781, www.duluth-model.org. For a Spanish-language version see Appendix III.*

theory suggests that economic, social, and historical processes operate both directly and indirectly to support a male-dominated (patriarchal) social order
and the family structure itself. Patriarchy has led to the subordination of
women. Domestic violence, as well as other forms of violence against women,
are ways of maintaining this subordination.

According to sociologist Richard Gelles, "As with all forms of oppression,
patriarchal means of control are often subtle and deeply entrenched, with the
most violent forms not emerging until and unless patriarchal control is threatened—as when individual women leave or threaten to leave relationships or
groups of women assert their rights."[18]

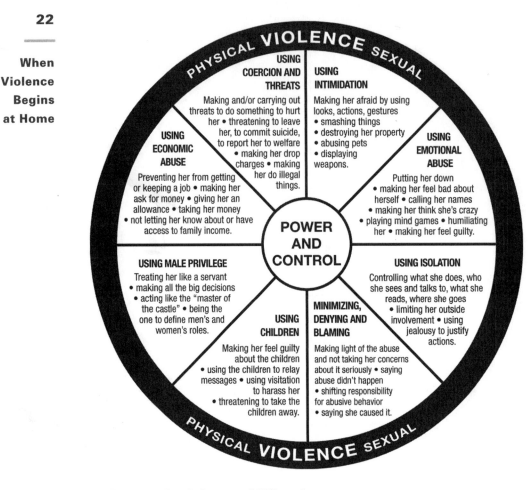

Power And Control Wheel

Domestic Abuse Prevention Project, 202 East Superior St., Duluth MN 55802, (218)
722-2781, www.duluth-model.org. For a Spanish-language version see Appendix III.

Building on the feminist theory, the exchange or "choice" theory provides one of the most succinct explanations for the cause of partner violence. Quite simply, men abuse women because they *can*. As a supplement to this explanation it should be noted that men *choose* to behave abusively toward their female partners because they can get away with it and because doing so gets them what they want.[19] One study tested the validity of the exchange theory and found that the men who believed themselves more isolated from the police, who were more powerful in their relationships with their partners, and who approved of men hitting their partners were less likely to consider being arrested as costly to them. Those men who perceived the costs of arrest as low were more likely to hurt their partners.[20]

The effects of abuse on battered women include psychological characteristics that greatly resemble those of hostages.[21] The implication here is that these characteristics are the *result* of being in a life-threatening relationship, not the *reason* for being in an abusive relationship.

Battering affects all types of women. However, there are some general characteristics that battered women develop in response to the abuse they suffer. Some of these are lowered self-esteem; accepting responsibility for the partner's actions; guilt; feelings of helplessness that affect how the women think, feel, and act; and denial, a survival strategy.

Lowered Self-Esteem

For many women, maintaining a positive sense of self is a daily effort. Women often begin to internalize the sexism that permeates our society and to discount their accomplishments, abilities, and self-worth. Adrienne Rich, author of *On Lies, Secrets, and Silence,* refers to this internalized sexism as self-trivialization.[22]

For women with abusive partners, the struggle with self-trivialization becomes even harder. One of the primary ways a batterer maintains power and control in the relationship is by demeaning and shaming his partner. She may begin to believe that she deserves no better because the batterer tells her exactly that. Even for women with a relatively strong sense of self, living with ongoing condemnation begins to take its toll. She will eventually begin to internalize her partner's criticisms and to believe them herself.

Acceptances of Blame for Her Abuse

As the woman's self-esteem erodes, she is also faced with a partner who constantly blames her for his abusive behavior. The batterer works hard to convince the woman that the abuse is her fault. I have known women who were beaten because dinner was late, dinner was early, children were crying, children were asleep, laundry was cleaned, laundry was cleaned but not folded correctly, and for a multitude of other excuses.

She increasingly accepts responsibility for her abusive partner's actions. Since she may already be experiencing self-trivialization, it becomes relatively easy for her to believe that she can alter her partner's behavior if she will only change—if she can only become a better wife, mother, cook, maid, lover, or mind reader.

In reality, a woman has no control over her abusive partner's behavior. No matter what she does or does not do, it is the batterer who *chooses* to hurt her. As she tries to appease and please him, all to no avail, her sense of failure and hopelessness continues to increase. Regrettably, her sense of failure further contributes to her diminished sense of self.

Guilt

A battered woman's feelings of failure contribute to and enhance her feelings of guilt. Battered women continually ask themselves, "Have I done everything I can do to make him change? Is there anything I could have done that I didn't?" Complicating the sense of failure is the fact that battered women are not allowed to express their feelings and frustrations, or, if they do, they are discounted. The inability to express themselves makes abused women angry. Anger, however, is just another feeling they are not allowed to express.

Battered women begin to internalize the feelings of anger, creating a volcano of emotions that will not simply lie dormant. Women turn the anger on themselves, and it is manifested as guilt. Feelings of guilt then further erode their self-esteem, producing a vicious cycle of low self-esteem, self-blame, anger, and guilt.

Feelings of Helplessness and Passivity

With continued abuse women may begin to exhibit characteristics such as submissiveness, passivity, docility, dependency, and an inability to act, make decisions, or even think. Adoption of these postures is an instinctive response to a life-threatening situation. Battered women are not really passive; instead, they have developed strategies for staying alive. Other survival strategies include denial, attentiveness to the batterer's wants, fondness for the batterer (accompanied by a fear of him), fear of interference by authorities, and adoption of the batterer's perspective.

Denial and Minimization of Abuse

The battered woman's feelings of anger and fear may become so overwhelming that she turns them off to be able to cope with her everyday life. She may begin to deny the seriousness of her situation or minimize the abuse she faces. As mentioned above, denial is a survival strategy. Denial on the part of an abused woman may include the following components:[23]

- ◆ Assumption that the batterer is a good man whose actions stem from problems that she can help him solve

- ◆ Denial that the abuse ever occurred

- ◆ Denial that the batterer is responsible for the abuse, which instead she attributes to external forces

- Belief that she is the instigator of the abuse and thus deserves the punishment
- Denial that she would be able to survive without the batterer's support (emotional or financial)
- Belief that marriage and/or following the beliefs of her religion, which may tell her to obey her husband, are more important than her personal welfare

We frequently talk to women who claim they are not battered because the abuse they suffered didn't require a trip to the hospital. In one case, I spoke with a woman whose husband had pointed a loaded gun to her head. She minimized the violence of this act by explaining that because he hadn't hit her she wasn't really an abused woman.

Understanding Women's Reactions to Abuse

The concept of "learned helplessness" first made its appearance in psychological literature in the 1960s. By the 1970s the notion was reconceptualized into the "battered woman syndrome." According to Dr. Mary Ann Dutton, with the George Washington University, the theory attempts to "explain a victim's inability to protect herself against the batterer's violence," an inability that "developed following repeated but failed efforts" to protect herself.[24]

Advocates have long criticized the effectiveness of applying this concept to domestic-violence survivors. In her article "Critique of the 'Battered Woman Syndrome' Model," Dutton explains that there are several concerns with the model as it is applied to battered women. First, she points out that there is no single profile of the effects of battering on all women. Yet the term *battered woman syndrome* "suggests that the psychological impact of battering is defined by a common set of symptoms."[25] Second, the term does not have a clearly defined set of criteria. Third, the term itself implies an image of pathology. According to Dutton, "A woman characterized as suffering from 'Battered Woman Syndrome' is typically viewed as flawed, damaged, disordered or abnormal in some way. Although it is true that many battered victims suffer negative effects of battering, syndrome language necessarily places the emphasis on pathology, not on the whole picture that also includes the battered woman's strengths and efforts, as well as others' responses to the situation."[26]

In their book *Battered Women as Survivors: An Alternative to Treating Learned Helplessness,* Edward Gondolf and Ellen Fisher sought to critique the effectiveness of the concept of "battered woman syndrome" by studying the help-seeking behaviors of six thousand battered women in fifty shelters in

Texas. According to the researchers, "The most outstanding of these findings is that the battered women are active helpseekers. The women's helpseeking appears to increase as the batterer becomes more apparently dangerous and incorrigible. The women, in sum, are not the passive victims that notions of learned helplessness would imply. They are in fact 'survivors,' in that they assertively and persistently attempt to do something about their abuse. They contact a variety of help sources where one would expect to find assistance. The help sources, however, do not appear to muster the decisive intervention necessary to stop the cycle of violence."[27]

The implications of Gondolf and Fisher's research are significant. If survivors are reaching out for help but not getting the assistance they need, perhaps efforts to "diagnose" battered women should be refocused and targeted to improving the responses of the systems that are in a position to help.

Who Is the Batterer?

We know that batterers come from all professions, educational backgrounds, religious affiliations, sexual orientations, and ethnic backgrounds. They match the full range of physical descriptions. However, batterers do have some characteristics in common, including a belief in the use of violence, the use of defense mechanisms to justify abusive behaviors, pathological jealousy, and a dual personality.

Belief in the Use of Violence

Men who batter do so because they can and it works. Abusive men have received the message that violence against women is acceptable behavior. This message may have come from a variety of sources, including the batterer's childhood family and our society. When societal institutions such as the judicial system fail to hold men accountable for their violence, they actually collude with the batterers to perpetuate the violence.

Defense Mechanisms

Typically, the batterer does not accept responsibility for his actions. Instead, he develops a number of defense mechanisms to explain why he batters, including the following:

- *Rationalization:* "I just wanted her to listen to me."
- *Denial—Minimizing:* "I only pushed her."
- *Denial—Claiming loss of control:* "A man can only take so much."
- *Blaming:* "If she hadn't provoked me...."

Batterers not only deny responsibility for their actions; they also often deny that any type of abusive behavior has taken place. It is not unusual to hear women say that after a severe beating they were told it never happened and they had imagined the whole thing. Women are encouraged by their batterers to question their own judgment and reality. "Don't you remember falling down the stairs?" a batterer may ask. Batterers will tell their partners they must be losing their minds. After a while, abused women begin to feel as though they are.

Jealousy

The abusive partner is jealous of any relationships the woman has, including those with other men, women, children, and even pets. Anything that takes time away from him is seen as a threat. One of the greatest fears a batterer has is that his partner will abandon him. This manifests itself in extreme jealousy and possessiveness. He believes that if he can completely control her, she won't leave. Batterers rely so heavily on their partners that they are willing to do anything to keep them from leaving—even maiming or killing them. It is not uncommon for batterers to become severely depressed, even suicidal, if they think their partner is going to leave.

To feel secure, the batterer must be overly involved with his partner. Constantly monitoring her time, not allowing her free time to be with others, and questioning her whereabouts are just a few of the ways in which a batterer will monitor his partner. Women have shared stories with me about batterers who would take them to work, pick them up for lunch, pick them up after work, and call throughout the day to make sure they were there. And although they may be constantly monitored, abused women are still accused of being unfaithful.

In one particularly brutal relationship, a batterer placed a tape recorder under their bed so he could monitor his wife while he was out of town. There was a television in their bedroom, and the recorder picked up a sitcom the woman watched. When the batterer returned from his trip and listened to the recording, he didn't hear the television show; he heard her with another man. Although she desperately tried to make him realize it was the television he was hearing, he refused to be convinced. She received several severe batterings because of her "infidelity."

Another reason for the batterer's constant manipulation of the woman's time and energy is his need to isolate her and make her dependent on him. If the woman's support system is reduced or destroyed, her dependency on him increases. The more she is tied to him, the greater her dependency and the less likely she is to leave him. Remember, her leaving is one of his greatest fears.

Dual Personality

Batterers typically present a different personality outside the home from the one they exhibit in the home, which complicates a woman's ability to describe her experiences to people outside the relationship. This behavior also helps to keep her tied to the relationship. The batterer does not always batter; many have periods when they can be very generous with their affection. The woman knows from experience that her partner is capable of being loving to her. If only she could get him to display his loving side all the time, she may reason, their relationship would be better. Thus, much of her time is spent trying to be the "perfect" wife and mother so he will continuously exhibit his loving side. Unfortunately this is a setup for her; the batterer will choose to batter her or not, regardless of her actions.

The Cycle of Abuse

According to Lenore Walker, author of *The Battered Woman,* violent relationships are not violent all of the time; rather, they often follow a three-phase cycle: tension-building, acute-battering, and honeymoon (which I prefer to call the "remorseful" phase). Unless the cycle is broken the violence will escalate in both frequency and severity. The following is a description of the cycle:[28]

Phase I: The Tension-Building Phase

- ◆ Less lethal forms of battering occur.
- ◆ The woman senses the tension and tries to placate the abusive partner to prevent the abuse.
- ◆ The woman minimizes minor incidents of abuse and blames herself for her partner's behavior.
- ◆ The woman denies that the tension will escalate to more severe battering even though it may have happened before.

Phase II: The Acute-Battering Phase

- ◆ The batter's rage escalates dramatically.
- ◆ Both the batterer and the woman accept the myth that he can't control his anger.
- ◆ Severe injuries occur as a result of the battering.
- ◆ The woman experiences shock and disbelief that the incident has occurred.

- ◆ The batterer expresses contrition over his behavior and makes promises to change.

- ◆ The batterer is charming and loving.

- ◆ The batterer offers gifts (flowers, jewelry, perfume, candy) to apologize for his behavior.

- ◆ The batterer begins to elicit feelings of guilt and sympathy from the woman.

- ◆ The batterer generates confirmation of his loving behavior from others.

- ◆ The woman's desire to believe he will change and the batterer's temporarily changed behavior reinforce her desire to stay in the relationship.

It is important to note that this cycle is not present in all violent relationships. And when it is present the three phases vary from couple to couple in terms of intensity and length of time in each phase. It is the third phase that tends to be the most insidious, as it is then that the woman is given false hope. The abused woman wants to believe that her partner can and will change. He gives her every indication, both verbally and through his actions, that he intends to change. It is during this phase that batterers often agree to counseling, only to claim they are "fixed" after attending a few sessions. Unfortunately, unless the batterer makes a conscious effort to change or the woman flees the relationship, the abuse will continue.

Possible Predictors of Domestic Violence

I am often asked how a woman can determine whether the man she is involved with is potentially abusive. The National Coalition Against Domestic Violence has produced the following list of questions, the answers to which may provide clues to a man's potential for violence:[29]

1. Did he grow up in a violent family?

2. Does he use force or violence to "solve" his problems? Does he have a quick temper? Does he overreact to little problems and frustrations? Is he cruel to animals? Does he punch walls or throw things when he's angry?

3. Does he abuse alcohol or other drugs?

4. Does he have strong traditional ideas about what a man should be and what a woman should be? Does he think a woman shouldn't work, should take care of her husband, and should follow all his wishes and orders?

5. Is he jealous of your other relationships (not only those with male friends but also those with female friends and with family members)? Does he keep tabs on you? Does he want to know where you are at all times? Does he want you with him all the time?

6. Does he have access to guns, knives, or other lethal instruments? Does he talk about using them against people? Does he threaten to use them to get even?

7. Does he expect you to follow his orders or advice? Does he become angry if you do not fulfill his wishes or if you cannot anticipate what he wants?

8. Do his mood and behavior go through extreme highs and lows? Is he extremely kind one time and extremely cruel the next?

9. Are you afraid of him when he gets angry? Is not making him angry important to you? Do you do what he wants you to do rather than what you want to do?

10. Does he treat you roughly? Does he physically force you to do what you do not want to do?

The Lethal Nature of Abusive Relationships

Without effective early intervention, abuse in relationships can escalate in severity and sometimes lead to death. In 2000 in the United States, 1,247 women were killed by their intimate partners.[30] When domestic violence results in murder, it is often a reflection of the community's failure to recognize the severity and potentially fatal consequences of the problem and to address its role in early intervention.

It also frequently occurs after the woman has been separated from her partner or has taken other action to end the relationship. Many people believe that leaving or separating from an abusive partner can solve domestic violence. The reality is, however, that trying to leave an abusive relationship can make life worse for a survivor and her children. According to the American Psychological Association Presidential Task Force on Violence and the Family, "the risk of serious or lethal violence may actually increase after separation. The greatest risk for serious injury or death from violence is at the point of separation or at the time when the decision to separate is made. Data from a U.S. Department of Justice National Crime Victimization Survey indicate that among women who were victims of violent assault by an intimate partner, women reported that the offender was an ex-spouse almost half as many times as they reported that the offender was a spouse."[31] Since our society continues to question why women stay in abusive relationships, it is crucial that we consider how dangerous and difficult it is for a battered woman to leave. Many women stay because of a reasonable fear that they will suffer severe injury or death if they attempt to end the relationship.

Unfortunately, when a batterer murders his partner, the tragedy is often portrayed as an unintentional "crime of passion" caused by the man's overwhelming love for the woman. Murder is, however, the ultimate expression of the batterer's need to control his partner's behavior.

Research indicates that when women kill it is much more likely to be in self-defense than when men kill.[32] Battered women who resort to homicide have usually tried, often repeatedly and unsuccessfully, to obtain protection from their batterers. Only a very small percentage of battered women kill their abusers to end the violence.

♦ ♦ ♦ *2*

The Effects of Family Violence on Children

Children who live in homes where there is family violence live in fear, confusion, and pain. A lot of our work is to help create a sense of safety for these children—safety to express themselves, safety to be themselves, and safety from abuse and fear. My hope is to give these things to them so that they may give them to their children and stop the cycle.

— Melinda Cantu, shelter director, SafePlace

If the family household is a nightmare for abused women, it is even more so for their children. For any child living in violence the basic need for a safe, secure home goes unmet. Children of battered women are victims, regardless of whether or not they are the direct recipients of violent acts. And children *are* the recipients of violent acts. Numerous studies in the last few years have clearly pointed to the connection between child maltreatment and domestic violence. Authors Jeffrey Edleson and Sandra Beeman report that in their review of over thirty studies, 30 to 60 percent of families experienced both child maltreatment and domestic violence.[1]

The violence that children are exposed to can take several forms. (For a list of abusive behaviors used against children please see the Child Abuse Wheel, on the facing page.) One form of abuse often seen in children from violent families is sexual abuse. Author R. Lundy Bancroft says several studies have il-

Child Abuse Wheel
Domestic Abuse Prevention Project, 202 East Superior St., Duluth MN 55802, (218) 722-2781, www.duluth-model.org.

lustrated the strong connection between domestic abuse and incest. According to Bancroft, "These studies, taken together, indicate that a batterer is about four to six times more likely than a non-batterer to sexually abuse his children... about half of incest perpetrators also batter the children's mother."[2] The best predictors of which batterers will sexually abuse their children include "the batterer's level of manipulativeness, entitlement or self-centeredness, his history of expecting and requiring that the child meet his needs, and past behaviors of his that introduce a sexual or romantic element to his relationship with the child."[3] Children whose mothers are battered may also be the victims of physical abuse by their parents. Almost one-half of the children of battered mothers are likely to be physically abused.[4] As violence against the mother grows in severity and frequency, children experience a 300 percent increase in physical violence by the male batterer.[5] In fact, the breaking point for many battered women is when the batterer begins abusing the children. That's when many women attempt to leave.[6]

Although battered mothers frequently try to shield their children from exposure to domestic violence, 80 to 90percent of children from abusive homes are able to give detailed descriptions of the violence.[7] As many as 3.3 million to 10 million children in the United States are at risk for exposure to domestic violence.[8] Children can be exposed to domestic violence in a variety of ways. They may hear their mother's screams or crying, the batterer's threats, glass breaking, or wood splintering. They may see the aftermath of abuse in the form of torn clothes, their mother's injuries, broken furniture, or wounded animals. Children who are exposed to domestic abuse suffer extreme emotional trauma and react with shock, fear, and guilt.

Children's lives are frequently disrupted by moves to escape domestic violence. They may lose considerable school time; flee their homes without taking books, money, or clothing; or live in the family car when shelters are unavailable. Many children of battered women who move to new school districts are unable to enroll in school if they lack birth certificates, immunization records, and other paperwork that was left behind when they and their mothers fled. Batterers, as part of their control of the family, frequently destroy such documents.

Parenting and Domestic Violence

The last decade has witnessed an increased interest in the effects of domestic violence on children. Within this context a growing body of research has explored the parenting styles of both the abusive and the battered parent. According to authors Edleson, Mbilinyi, and Shetty, "Exposure to domestic violence is often assumed to indicate being an eyewitness to violent events, but an expanded definition includes much more...." Their expanded definition includes the "child being used as a tool of the perpetrator."[9]

The Parenting Behaviors of Batterers

Bancroft and Silverman have recently published the first book focused exclusively on batterers' parenting behaviors. In *The Batterer as Parent,* the authors write that, compared with nonviolent fathers, batterers are more controlling and authoritarian, less consistent, and more likely to manipulate the children and undermine the mother's parenting.[10]

Battered mothers frequently report that their abusive partners intentionally involve children in violent acts. In a study of 114 battered mothers in four U.S. cities, researchers found that 73 percent of respondents reported that batterers used their children as "pawns" to indirectly get at the mother. Eighty-eight percent of the respondents reported that the abuser hurt them as punishment for their children's actions. About 20 percent of battered mothers reported that the batterer made the children watch him hit or sexually assault her, and 57 percent reported that the batterer blamed the mother for the abuser's excessive punishment of the children.[11]

It's clear that the parenting behavior of men who batter can have a negative impact on their children. One 1996 study found that children's relationships with their abusive fathers were often confusing, with children expressing affection for their fathers while simultaneously feeling resentment, disappointment, and pain over his abusive behavior.[12]

Bancroft explains that abusive men negatively impact their children or stepchildren in a variety of ways, including:[13]

1. Acting as role models who perpetuate violence

2. Undermining the battered mother's authority

3. Creating divisions within the family

4. Retaliating against the battered mother's attempts to protect the children

5. Using the children as weapons against the battered mother

Battering fathers are frequently able to perform parenting tasks well when they know they are being observed in custody evaluations or supervised visitations. According to Bancroft and Silverman, however, batterers may change their behavior once the outside observation has ended. The authors suggest that battering parents often pressure children to disclose confidential conversations the children had with evaluators or to relay a favorable message about the batterer to the evaluator and/or court.[14] Such behaviors have serious implications for custody evaluators, supervised visitation centers, mediators, and judicial officers.

The Parenting Behaviors of Battered Mothers

Not surprisingly, one clear finding from the research on battered mothers is that they appear to experience greater levels of stress than do their nonbattered counterparts. The increased stress does not, however, automatically equate to diminished parenting.[15] According to researchers, "Women who live in violent relationships are remarkably similar to comparison women in their beliefs about parenting, their self-reported parenting behaviors, and their observed interactions with their children. On such variables as providing structure, showing warmth, being emotionally available, and positively reinforcing their children, mothers from violent and nonviolent homes reportedly engaged in similar behavior."[16]

Various studies examining the use of corporal punishment by battered mothers indicate conflicting findings. When examined together, however, the studies do seem to indicate that abused mothers are more likely than other mothers to use some type of aggression against their children. It is important to note that these mothers were less likely to do so once they were safe.[17]

Regardless of whether abused women stay or leave the relationship, it appears that they often show concern for the safety of their children. Research indicates that such factors as child safety and economic support for the children's basic needs have heavily influenced battered women's decision-making process.[18]

Without question, the parenting behaviors of battered mothers do vary, with some mothers doing better than others. However, researchers and practitioners have frequently ignored the women's protective strategies. Instead, many have chosen to limit their focus to the more negative aspects of battered mothers' parenting behaviors. An article written by G.W. Holden and others points out that, "A search for pathologies of battered women and negative qualities of their parenting seems to be the wrong direction to pursue. Rather, the focus should be shifted to one that begins to recognize and document strengths and coping strategies of these women."[19]

The Struggle of Battered Mothers to Keep Their Children

Although a battered mother may be nonabusive, some states' child-abuse policies require children to be removed due to the abused mother's perceived inability to protect them from the batterer. Authors Evan Stark and Anne Flitcraft write, "Broad moral conceptions of women's responsibility for violence are implicit in state laws criminalizing 'the failure to protect.' … This is routinely interpreted to mean 'allowing' a child to become a covictim of or to witness violence against the mother."[20]

Child-protection and welfare workers commonly focus on "the best interest of the child" when making their determinations. This is typically reflected in identifying who can keep the child safe. Advocates argue, however, that focusing on "the best interest of the children" alone fails to consider contextual reality. The concept as it is narrowly defined fails to consider that it is in the best interest of children for intervening entities to also try to keep the abused mothers safe. Data suggest that when abused mothers are made safe, many children are also kept safe.[21] Concerned advocates also contend that applying "failure to protect" policies to battered mothers actually serves to revictimize and retraumatize them by taking their children from them. Instead, many advocates argue, child-protection and welfare agencies should take a stronger role in holding batterers accountable for their abusive behavior.

Recent legal challenges to the "failure to protect" policies call into question the effectiveness of such policies in promoting the safety and well-being of battered mothers and their children. In New York, severely battered women Sharwline Nicholson, Ekaete Udoh, and Sharlene Tillett went to court on behalf of themselves and their children. Their legal journey evolved into a class-action lawsuit that eventually traveled through the state and federal court systems of New York and impacted child-protection agencies across the U.S. The litigation, now in its fourth year, involves the rights of battered mothers whose children were removed from their custody by the City of New York's Administration for Children's Services (ACS). The mothers were not found to be unfit, to be neglectful, or to have perpetrated domestic violence. They were, however, being abused by their partners. After extensive hearings, federal judge Jack Weinstein, of the United States District Court for the Eastern District of New York, found that "the evidence reveals widespread and unnecessary cruelty by agencies of the City of New York toward mothers abused by their consorts, through forced unnecessary separation of the mothers from their children on the excuse that this sundering is necessary to protect the children."[22]

The decision in this case, known as *Nicholson v. Scoppetta,* forbids the ACS and various other defendants from removing children who have not been physically harmed, threatened, or neglected by abused mothers. While the city took the position that removal was consistent with protecting the children and that failing to prevent their witnessing violence was a form of neglect, Judge Weinstein found that the Constitutional rights of both the mothers and the children had been violated. Echoing what advocates have argued for years, he admonished that "Accusing battered mothers of neglect aggravates the problem because it blames the mother for failing to control a situation which is defined by the batterer's efforts to deprive her of control.... It's an ill-conceived way to think about this issue of neglect and it further victimizes women who are victims of domestic violence."[23]

The defendants appealed to the United States Court of Appeals for the 2nd Circuit, where the federal court permitted the injunction to stand. It did not, however, reach a conclusion. In late 2003 the circuit court identified several legal questions that were referred to the New York State Court of Appeals both for constitutional reasons and in deference to the state court's expertise in family law.[24] On October 26, 2004, the New York State Court of Appeals ruled unanimously that the child-welfare system cannot remove children from nonabusive parents simply because domestic violence is present in the home. According to Chief Judge Judith Kaye, "Exposing a child to domestic violence is not presumptively neglectful. Not every child exposed to domestic violence is at risk of impairment.... In many instances, removal of the child may do more harm than good."[25]

In an effort to address the safety needs of both children and battered women, many advocates are calling for increased cooperation between child-welfare and domestic-violence programs. Proponents argue that both groups share common concerns and problems. According to Susan Schechter and Jeffrey Edleson, "We share a common growing client population. Each field has a pressing need for increased public attention, resources, and for policy reform. As allies, rather than competitors, the fields have an enormous potential to mobilize constituencies for each other. Finally, as more and more communities call for coordinated interventions to stop family violence, agencies will be required to work together. A conceptual and practical linking of the needs of women and children would make these collaborations far more fruitful and change the way that we think about families."[26]

Characteristics of Children Living in Violent Homes

Children raised in violent homes learn many lessons. They learn how to keep family secrets. They learn how to get what they want through aggression and manipulation. They learn that people who love you hurt you. They learn that violence, albeit painful, is an acceptable part of life.

Children's responses to living with violence vary according to their age, gender, stage of development, and role in the family. Many other factors also play a part, such as the extent and frequency of the violence, repeated separations and moves, socioeconomic status, special needs of the child independent of the violence, length of time since last exposed to violence, and the child's connections to the nonabusive parent and other significant individuals and social supports. We do know, however, that the reactions of children exposed to family violence may include disruptions of normal developmental patterns that result in emotional, behavioral, physical, social, and cognitive problems.[27]

Regardless of their age, children living with domestic violence tend to have a strong sense of isolation and helplessness. Their initial method of solving problems is by hitting. They suffer from an extremely high level of anxiety and tend to have developmental delays. As the children mature, their degree of sympathy toward the mother diminishes and may be replaced by overt hostility.

In their book *Children of Battered Women,* Peter Jaffe, David Wolfe, and Susan Wilson list a series of characteristics that can be found in children who witness domestic violence. They include the following:[28]

1. A combination of limited tolerance for frustration, poor impulse control, and externalized or internalized anger

2. Sadness, depression, stress disorders, and psychosomatic complaints

3. Absences from school, predelinquent and delinquent behavior

4. Sexual acting out, running away, isolation, loneliness, and fear

5. A combination of poor impulse control and continual hopefulness that the situation will improve

6. Poor definition of self or a definition of self in the parenting role (role reversal)

7. Low self-esteem; sees self and siblings with few options or expectations to succeed

8. Increased social isolation, increased peer isolation, or complete identification with peers

9. Poor social skills

10. Feelings of powerlessness

11. Constant fear and terror for their life as well as for their parents

12. Confusion and insecurity

13. Increased deception, including lying, stealing, and cheating

14. Poor definition of personal boundaries and of others' personal boundaries

15. Little or no understanding of the dynamics of violence, and often an assumption that violence is the norm

16. Self-blame (depending on the age) for family violence, separations, divorce, and internal conflicts

17. Frequent participation in maiming or killing animals or battering siblings

18. Use of violence as a problem-solving technique in school, with peers, and with family

19. Poor sexual image, uncertainty about appropriate behavior, and immaturity in peer relationships

20. Heightened suicide risk and attempts; increased thoughts of suicide or of murdering parents

Infants

An infant who is raised in a violent family experiences a serious disruption in its basic need for attachment to the mother. Routines around sleeping and feeding may be anything but normal. The abused mother may be unable to handle the stressful demands of her infant. This distancing is recognized by the child and causes serious separation anxiety.

The early parent-child relationship sets the stage for the child's future relationships. If the early relationship is characterized by trust, consistency, and nurturing, the child's ability to develop positive relationships with others is greatly enhanced. If, however, the early parent-child relationship is marked by fear, inconsistency, and unmet physical and psychological needs, the child's future relationships are likely to be poorly formed. Such children also exhibit a higher frequency of behavioral and emotional problems.[29]

Infants and young toddlers may be injured in a battering incident by being caught between their parents. They may be accidentally hit, pushed, or dropped during a violent episode. The mother may hold the infant for its safety, but may quickly discover that the batterer has no regard for the baby's physical or emotional well-being.

Physical symptoms displayed by infants from violent homes often include a propensity for illness, irritability, and difficulty sleeping.

Toddlers and Preschool-Age Children

Even though small children may feel responsible for the violence that is occurring in their home, they still may be open to discussing it. They may suffer severe separation anxiety and be reluctant to leave their mother. They are often irritable, express somatic complaints, and are fearful of being alone. They may regress to earlier stages of functioning.

By elementary school, gender-related differences in children's reactions to family violence begin to emerge. Children look to their parents as role models. Boys who witness violence quickly learn that violence is an appropriate way of resolving conflict. Boys from violent homes are frequently described as being disruptive, acting aggressively toward objects and people, and throwing severe temper tantrums.[30] Girls may learn that victimization is inevitable and that no one can help change the vicious pattern that goes on in their home. They develop an assortment of somatic complaints and are more likely to display withdrawn, passive, clinging, and dependent behavior.[31] Children may practice what they have learned at home by fighting at school or in the neighborhood. These externalized behavior problems will undermine their adjustment to school and create consequences that can aggravate an already volatile home environment.

For elementary school–age children, exposure to abuse may also lead to significant emotional difficulties. They may live in shame, embarrassed by the family secret. Their experiences may undermine their self-esteem and confidence. And they may have few opportunities for activities outside the family because of the batterer's domination and control. They may experience guilt out of a belief that perhaps they could prevent the violence—if only they were better children, maybe their father wouldn't be so upset with their mother. They are often confused by the violence and have a divided sense of loyalty, both desiring to protect their mother and still respecting and fearing their father.

When children reach school age, teachers may recognize one or more of the following warning signs of physical abuse. While one or two of the signs are not necessarily an indication of abuse at home, a child displaying several of them should make a teacher suspicious.[32]

- Dirty clothing, body odor, or an unkempt appearance
- An unexplained injury
- Acting shy, withdrawn, or too eager to cooperate
- Arriving at school early and leaving late
- Not wanting to go home
- Wearing long-sleeved clothes in warm weather
- Talking about abuse
- Acting nervous, too active, or destructive

- ◆ Acting fearful of being touched by an adult
- ◆ Being absent from school with poor or no excuses
- ◆ Showing little hope of being comforted when in trouble
- ◆ Always searching for favors, food, or services
- ◆ Difficulty in getting along with other children

Teenagers

During adolescence children begin to develop intimate relationships outside their families, where they can practice the communication patterns they have learned. For some teenagers this means the beginning of violence within their own dating relationships. Adolescent girls may start accepting threats and violence from boyfriends.

Many teenagers have lived with violence in their families for years. In seeking independence and relief from family violence, some teenagers decide that running away may be an escape. Most interviews with runaway children and teenagers point to family violence as a major factor in the decision to leave home.[33] Some teenage boys handle their frustrations by exhibiting the behavior that has been most clearly modeled for them: by battering their mothers or siblings. Other teens begin to act out their anger and frustration in ways that result in delinquencies and the interventions of the juvenile justice system. Surveys of females in the juvenile justice system and in shelters indicate rates of sexual abuse and assault of over 70 percent.[34]

Other teenagers take on additional responsibilities to keep the peace and provide safety for their families. Older teens, especially girls and those with younger siblings, may assume parenting responsibilities. They may protect younger siblings during violent episodes and offer reassurance in the aftermath of the violence. They may feel they cannot leave home because they must protect their mothers and siblings. Obviously, such responsibilities are a heavy burden for any youngster.

Finally, teens who have been exposed to domestic violence are more likely to attempt suicide, abuse drugs and alcohol, engage in prostitution, and commit sexual-assault crimes.[35]

Behaviors of Children in Crisis

Children exposed to family violence may or may not be able to talk about their feelings and concerns. However, children's behaviors are good indicators of how well they are coping. New problem behaviors are not unusual for children in crisis. All children exhibit problem behaviors at some time; concern for the child is necessary if the level of the behavior is extreme.

Some behaviors to look for in a child in crisis include the following:

◆ Loss of appetite or any change in eating patterns

◆ Sleep disturbances such as nightmares or restlessness

◆ School problems such as refusing to attend, truancy, or a drop in performance

◆ Withdrawal

◆ Clinging to mother or siblings

◆ Shyness

◆ Fear of the dark

◆ Increased violent behavior such as kicking, hitting, or fighting

◆ Verbal abuse or talking back

◆ Regression such as bed-wetting, wanting a bottle, baby talk, and thumb sucking

◆ Inappropriate responses to discipline

◆ Temper tantrums

◆ Whining

◆ Oversensitivity

◆ Role reversal such as taking on a parenting role

◆ Testing and pushing limits as far as possible

◆ Stealing

◆ Lying

◆ Bowel irregularity or diarrhea

Posttraumatic Stress Disorder in Children

Children exposed to family violence exhibit symptoms similar to those suffering from posttraumatic stress disorder. PTSD is classified as a type of anxiety disorder by the American Psychiatric Association. The disorder may appear at any age following exposure to a psychologically traumatic event that is generally outside the range of typical human experience.

All of the following criteria must be met to qualify for a diagnosis of PTSD:[36]

1. Exposure to a stress or trauma that would create significant symptoms of distress in almost anyone

2. Reexperiencing the trauma as evidenced by at least one of the following: recurrent recollections of the event, recurrent dreams of the event, sudden acting or feeling as if the traumatic event were recurring because of an association with an environmental stimulus

3. Numbing of responsiveness to or reduced involvement with the external world, beginning some time after the trauma, as shown by at least one of the following: markedly diminished interest in one or more significant activities, feeling of detachment or estrangement from others

4. At least two of the following symptoms that were not present before the trauma: hyperalertness or exaggerated startle response, sleep disturbances, guilt about surviving when others have not or about behavior required for survival, memory impairment or trouble concentrating, avoidance of activities that arouse recollection of the traumatic event, intensification of symptoms by exposure to events that symbolize or resemble the traumatic event

As you can see from the information presented throughout this chapter, many of the reactions of children from violent families can be classified as responses to trauma. Children who live with violence may also display emotional symptoms that are quite removed from the initial trauma. Such symptoms may not be readily detectable as PTSD because they may be expressed in a manner that disguises their origins, such as running away, truancy, or dating violence.

Children's emotional development is closely connected to the safety and nurturing provided by the family environment. Children of violent families suffer a loss of faith that there is order and continuity in their lives. Normally, the family plays a crucial role in protecting children from traumatization and assisting in recovery when necessary. Children of violent families, however, are traumatized *by* the family environment.

Variances in Children's Reactions

Not all children who live with violence exhibit developmental difficulties. In a recent study of 228 children ages eight to fourteen years, 71 of them exhibited no problems. Of the remaining children, 41 showed mild distress symptoms, 47 exhibited problems with aggression and antisocial behavior, and 70 were classified as multiproblem.[37] Exactly how can these variances among children's reactions to family violence be explained?

Edleson points out that it is highly probable that children's experiences with family violence vary in a number of ways that must be considered when examining a child's reaction to the violence. Such differences include the following:[38]

1. The severity, frequency, and chronicity of violence in the family

2. The degree to which each child in the home is exposed to the violence

3. Other risks to which the child is exposed, including domestic violence with a new adult partner or the presence of a weapon in the home

4. The emotional and physical harm that exposure to domestic violence produces for each child

5. The risk of future harm

6. The unique coping skills of each child

7. Varying protective factors such as a caring parent, sibling, or other adult

There is also evidence that children's coping reactions can vary as a function of their developmental stage. Research with toddlers and preschoolers indicates that disruptions in their normal family functioning are associated with problem behaviors inside and outside the home.[39] While family disruption certainly has a negative influence on older children's social interactions, it has been suggested that older children are better able to cope with the stress because of their use of peers and schools as sources of information and support.[40]

...3

Teen Dating Violence

Eddie's got a fast car.
And he drives me to school.
My friends think he's cool.
And they wish they were me.
But they don't see when he hits me.
Or screams and calls me names.
Eddie's got a fast car.
Today he picked me up for school.
And we had another fight.
And he pushed my face into the dash.
And I'm confused and I'm scared.
Because tomorrow morning I'll wake up.
And I'll look out my window.
And he'll be sitting there.
And I'll have to get in.

Eddie's got a fast car.[1]

Battering finally received recognition as a serious social problem in the 1970s. Almost nothing was known, however, about teen dating violence. In her book *Dating Violence: Young Women in Danger,* therapist and battered-women's advocate Barrie Levy writes that when she talked about violence as something teenagers "might encounter when they grew up and had intimate relationships or got married, or about violence they may have witnessed between their parents, some of the young women revealed they currently or had already experienced violence from their adolescent boyfriends."[2]

Numerous studies in the 1980s confirmed what Levy suspected: Young women were in danger from their teenage boyfriends and in such high numbers as to elicit shock from the research community. A 2001 study published in *JAMA: Journal of the American Medical Association* reports that one in five high school students experiences physical violence in dating relationships.[3]

Levy defines abuse in teenage dating relationships as "a pattern of repeated actual or threatened acts that physically, sexually or verbally abuse a member of an unmarried heterosexual or homosexual couple in which one or both partners [are] between thirteen and twenty years old."[4] Dating violence is not unique to any particular class, community, or ethnic group or to heterosexuals. It appears to be prevalent in all populations.

Nor is dating violence a new phenomenon. As early as 1957, Eugene Kanin reported that during their last year of high school 62 percent of women surveyed had been victims of sexually aggressive acts perpetrated by young men they had dated. In 44 percent of the cases, the offender was either the woman's steady boyfriend or her fiancé. For 21 percent of the women, the sexually aggressive act was attempted or completed rape.[5]

Among high school and college students, abuse is more likely in a serious, rather than a casual, dating relationship.[6] The violence often begins when the couple perceives that they have entered into a monogamous relationship. This stage of the relationship appears to elicit expectations tied to sexual stereotypes, including the male's right to control his partner and the female's obligation to yield to his wishes. Teenagers involved in violent dating relationships also appear to express a greater acceptance of violence in marriages.[7]

Who Is the Teen Abuser?

Between 1997 and 1999 seven incidents of teen-perpetrated domestic violence received massive media attention in this country. One of the most publicized of these was the shooting in Jonesboro, Arkansas.[8] The media responded to the tragedies with questions about "youth violence" and "school violence." They failed, however, to acknowledge that in all the cases the perpetrators were male and the intended victims were female. In reality, the more appropriate question might have been about violence against women and girls. The failure to recognize and acknowledge that domestic violence perpetrated by teenage males is akin to domestic violence perpetrated by adult men may, in effect, hinder our ability to better understand this phenomenon.

It is important to note that no study has been able to prove that specific risk factors cause male teens to be violent against their dating partners. We do know, however, that there are several characteristics and life experiences that teen perpetrators share in common. While we cannot use these risk factors to determine definitively who will and will not abuse, they do give us a good idea of the commonalties among teens who choose to use violence against their partners. Some of them are listed here:[9]

1. Teen boys who abuse their dating partners are more likely to have experienced child abuse or neglect.

2. Witnessing domestic violence within the home appears to increase the risk for becoming abusive in adult intimate relationships.

3. Teen perpetrators are more likely to use alcohol or drugs than their nonviolent counterparts.

4. Adolescent males who abuse their dating partners are more likely to have sexist attitudes that support male domination over females.

5. Teen perpetrators are also more likely to associate with peers who support sexist attitudes.

Abusive Versus Healthy Dating Relationships

Many teenagers perceive jealousy, possessiveness, and abuse as "normal" in intimate relationships. For some teenagers abuse happens so often that it is an expected or accepted way to express love.[10] And many teenagers actually consider sexual coercion or hitting justifiable under certain circumstances.[11] In several studies, young men reported that their violence served to "intimidate," "frighten," or "force the other to give me something."[12] These claims are much bolder than those of violent adult men. Abusive husbands, for example, rarely admit that their aggression is manipulative; rather, they rely heavily on justifications based on being "out of control" because of such factors as alcohol, drugs, anger, or stress.[13]

There is some indication that young women think violence has a bad effect on their relationships, whether they are the ones being hit or the ones doing the hitting. Young men, by contrast, whether they are the abusers or the abused, believe that violence has either a positive effect or no impact at all on their relationships.[14] According to Patricia Occhiuzzo Giggans, executive director of the Los Angeles Commission on Assaults Against Women, "Dating and courtship among teenagers today have an injurious and, at times, potentially lethal dimension. It has become evident that one of the main reasons for this [development] is that our children do not have a clear sense of what constitutes a 'healthy relationship.' It is frightening to hear how many teens, from all economic, racial and cultural backgrounds, express how 'normal' physical, psychological and sexual control is within their own dating relationships and in those of their friends."[15] A nurturing love incorporates a wish that the loved one grow, flourish, and develop to his or her fullest potential. This attitude implies that each partner receives and encourages pleasure in other close friendships and independent activities. In an unhealthy love, one or both partners believe they cannot survive without the other. The desire to be together every minute develops into a need or demand for the partner to be continuously available.[16]

Teenagers often mistake jealousy as a sign of love. Many seem to be confused about the difference between jealousy and concern. Concern refers to caring for another person and focusing on her or his well-being and needs. It does not involve controlling behaviors. Jealousy, on the other hand, arises out of suspicions about rivalry and infidelity. It is based on a fear of losing something, which implies ownership—and people do not own one another. Jealousy can lead to inappropriate and abusive behaviors in an attempt to guard a possession. If a person is viewed as a possession, she or he is not being respected as a human being.[17] A healthy relationship is based on an ongoing process involving commitment, flexibility, respect, and honesty. When someone chooses to share his or her life with us, we are being offered a gift. We should value the gift and all the beauty and challenges that accompany it.

Patterns in Abusive Teen Relationships

Patterns of abuse in teen dating relationships are similar to those in adult battering relationships. They involve the same elements of control and jealousy, enforced by emotional and physical abuse. Teenagers and adult battered women describe the same range of violent experiences, from slaps and shoves to beatings and attacks with weapons.

Each year, an alarming number of young women are murdered by their boyfriends. Approximately 20 percent of female homicide victims are between ages fifteen and twenty-four. Typically, investigation into the victim's dating relationships reveals patterns of control and physical abuse.[18] The violence in teen dating relationships, however, is not always physical. Many young women are severely emotionally damaged by partners who repeatedly demean and control them. Teenage batterers use a variety of threats to enforce their demands. They may make direct threats against the girlfriend or her family, or may threaten to kill themselves. A batterer's suicide threats can be terrifying to a young woman, especially if he has made previous attempts. Batterers may threaten to expose embarrassing secrets, often regarding their partners' sexual behavior. A batterer may force his girlfriend to steal money from her parents or give him money she has earned. Some young women have been coerced by boyfriends to engage in illegal acts such as shoplifting, prostitution, and drug dealing. Threats to report the young woman's illegal activity add to the batterer's ability to control her.[19]

Teenage batterers, like their adult counterparts, refuse to accept responsibility for their actions and blame their partners for the abuse. Often the teenager's behavior is blamed on jealousy. Almost any action on the young woman's part—whether talking to another young man, not being home when the boyfriend calls, or going out with girlfriends—is labeled as provocative. Both high school and college students view jealousy as a major cause of dating violence. Uncontrollable anger has also been cited as a primary cause of dating violence.[20]

Teenagers report that conflicts about sex often lead to violence.[21] Date rape accounts for 67 percent of the sexual assaults reported by high school and college women. Young women between ages fourteen and seventeen represent an estimated 38 percent of those victimized by date rape.[22] Repeated sexual assault and sexual coercion in intimate relationships contribute to feelings of worthlessness, humiliation, and shame that gradually undermine a young woman's ability to escape. It is often difficult for young women to even identify sexual abuse in their relationships. This may be due to their inexperience and limited education about sexuality. It may also be a result of a societal tolerance for sexual assault when it is associated with romantic involvement. Young women with more traditional values have reported that they are more accepting of rape as well as less sure of what constitutes rape.[23] Young women may also feel that it is useless to try to stop a partner who is intent on rape. One study found that one of every six women interviewed believed that when a man became sexually aroused, it was impossible to stop him or for him to stop himself.[24]

Unique Aspects of Teen Dating Violence

Although young couples in violent relationships share some commonalties with their older counterparts, there are several youth-specific aspects to their relationships. Pressure to conform to peer-group norms contributes to an emphasis on having a dating partner. Peer pressure can be intense, and the fear of being different or of violating peer-group norms can create rigid conformity or enormous stress. Definitions of what is "normal" masculine or feminine behavior are often extreme and fit stereotyped patterns of dominance and passivity.[25] Frequently, teenage boys will begin to establish such patterns when their violent dating behaviors are reinforced by members of their peer group and by society as a whole.

Expectations of a girlfriend may include that she give up activities and other relationships in order to give priority to her boyfriend. Female socialization may also lead a young woman to assume responsibility for solving problems within the relationship.[26] Expectations of a boyfriend may include that he be sexually aggressive, make all the decisions in the relationship, and control his girlfriend's activities and behavior.

Teenagers have fewer resources and much less mobility than do most adults. If they are members of a minority group or are poor, their lack of power and of access to resources is compounded. Young women are often unable to avoid the abusers because they attend the same school. They are not free to move out of their neighborhoods or to change schools. This contributes to a young woman's feelings of fear and entrapment.

While young women are more likely than young men to talk to someone about their violent relationships, they often hesitate to talk to teachers, counselors, clergy members, or law-enforcement officers. Instead, young women tend to seek out friends and, to a lesser degree, family members for help. In one study of high school students in violent relationships, 25 percent told no one, only 26 percent told their parents, and 66 percent reported the abuse to friends.[27] Young women may feel that seeking help from adults would be pointless, especially when societal institutions have not addressed the problem or communicated a willingness or ability to respond. Teenagers' hesitancy to seek help from parents may be due to the fact that they are struggling for independence and want to solve problems themselves or with their peers. They may fear, justifiably or not, that if told of the abuse, their parents would curtail their independence and control future decisions about their relationships or other aspects of their lives. In addition, the isolation, shame, and fear a young woman experiences who is being abused may also prevent her from reaching out to those who could help.

Barri Rosenbluth, director of school-based services for SafePlace, explains that even when young women do reach out, some families do not take the problem seriously. Sometimes they will pressure the young couple to stay together, especially if the pair has a child. Other adults may assume that their daughters are overreacting, acting out, or "going through a phase." Some parents minimize the bonding that takes place between teenagers and expect them to easily break off a dating relationship. School personnel may become impatient with their misbehavior and, without recognizing the danger the young woman faces, insist that such behavior not be displayed at school.[28] Adults have access to legal and social services that may be unavailable to teenagers or that may be accessed only if parents or guardians are involved. This is a barrier for many youths who resist telling their parents or other adults about the abuse. Many battered-women's centers cannot shelter teenagers unless they are "emancipated." Emancipation is usually defined as maintaining a separate residence from the parents or having a child.

Teenagers may not take legal action in their own name, and few states permit minors to use civil and criminal laws that specifically relate to domestic violence. In other states, general laws such as civil harassment statutes can sometimes be applied. Few laws exist, however, that protect teenagers from abusive dating relationships. Temporary restraining orders may be unavailable to young women unless the application is made by the parents.

Special At-Risk Populations

Special circumstances exist for many young women that make them vulnerable to dating violence. Pregnant teenagers, young women of color, and gay and lesbian youth are especially at risk for relationship violence.

Pregnant Teens

Both adult and teenage women are at greater risk for violence when they are pregnant.[29] Studies of battered women report that between 25 and 60 percent of them were abused during pregnancy.[30] In an informal survey of more than two hundred pregnant teenagers in several large metropolitan areas, 26 percent reported they were in a relationship with a male partner who was physically abusive. Sixty-five percent of those abused had not talked with anyone about the abuse, and none had reported the abuse to law-enforcement agencies.[31] Abuse during pregnancy includes, but is not limited to, blows to the abdomen, injuries to the breasts and genitals, and sexual assault. Abused women suffer a higher number of miscarriages than do nonbattered women. Batterers may even prevent or sabotage their partners from obtaining appropriate medical care during pregnancy.

In addition to the injuries sustained by the women, negative health effects of battering during pregnancy are evident in low infant birthweight. The percentage of low-birthweight infants is approximately twice as high among battered women as among nonbattered women.[32]

Teens of Color

Evelyn White, author of *Chain Chain Change: For Black Women Dealing with Physical and Emotional Abuse,* maintains that young women of color are especially vulnerable to dating violence.[33] According to White, "Young black girls get conflicting messages about their identities. A girl's identity is not just based on who or what she believes she is, but also what society tells black girls they are. This is extremely painful because I believe that the first message black girls get is that they aren't good enough.... It is the rare black girl who can develop her own identity outside the external societal forces, both black and white, that tell her what she should be.... I think that this inability to find our own voice, our own being, keeps black girls vulnerable to the demands and expectations of others that are so prevalent in abusive relationships."[34] If a young woman feels that her options for success are limited by racism, she may depend on the dating relationship to define her future, and her feelings may keep her tied to her abusive partner. She may expect to be blamed or not taken seriously if she were to seek help. In addition, she may be unwilling to discuss her problems with anyone out of a protectiveness for her boyfriend that arises from understanding his struggles in a racist society.[35]

Young women from Asian and Pacific Island communities, in which dating and sexuality are possible sources of shame, are also vulnerable to dating violence. According to Mieko Yoshihama, Asha Parekh, and Doris Boyington, "The low status they hold in the traditional Asian/Pacific family hierarchy as children and as females, compounded with a culturally based emphasis on maintaining harmony even if it is at the cost of the individual's well-being, continues to discourage these teenagers from asserting their rights and needs. Because of their powerless position, their needs as victims may remain unaddressed."[36]

Like their Anglo peers, Asian/Pacific teenagers often remain silent regarding their violent relationships. Young women from Asian/Pacific communities who do seek help are often revictimized because of the insensitivity and discriminatory behavior of their families, their communities, and the professionals they turn to for help.[37] In most Asian/Pacific cultures, dating issues and sexuality are considered taboo and are not discussed. A young woman who has been dating or has been sexually active loses her respectability, according to the traditional values of her community. These teenagers face the burden of keeping both the violence and the dating relationship secret from their parents. The shame and guilt associated with dating intensifies the teenager's idea that she is responsible for the violence.[38] Not only is it difficult for these young women to turn to their families for support; many may believe that seeking professional help would only create problems by bringing more shame to their families. A value that is shared by most Asian/Pacific cultures is that of enduring and suffering without complaint. Both men and women value silence and acceptance as a way of handling difficulties with honor. There is pressure to keep silent to prevent family shame, which presents a dilemma for young women traumatized by the pains and concerns of the moment. They may minimize the violence in their lives and believe that they should not be reacting so intensely to it.

Other factors for young women from Asian/Pacific communities that can contribute to their entrapment in violent relationships include fear of exposure and lowered self-concept. In an effort to control his partner, an abusive young man may threaten to tell her family about their dating relationship. In addition, any acts of sexual violence further affect the young woman's feelings of self-worth.[39]

Gay and Lesbian Teens

Another group at risk for dating violence is teenage gays and lesbians, who often do not recognize the problem of relationship violence and may even deny its existence. Lesbian and gay teenagers may not define the relationship they have with a person of the same sex as a dating relationship. Therefore, the concept of "dating violence" may seem irrelevant to them. The confusion about norms and roles that characterizes nongay teenage relationships is even more pronounced in teenage gay and lesbian relationships. A lack of visible role models and relationships adds to the uncertainty. If a gay or lesbian teen lacks role models for what's healthy in a relationship, a partner's control and abuse may be accepted as normal. It requires a lot of courage to come out, or identify oneself as gay or lesbian, to friends and family. Fear of identifying as gay or lesbian, or fear of homophobic responses from parents, peers, and others, may keep teenagers from telling anyone about their relationship and seeking help if it turns violent.[40]

If teenage gays and lesbians are not out, the secrecy of their relationship adds to their low self-esteem and vulnerability to isolation and abuse. It may also cause them to feel unable to trust anyone outside the relationship, making it difficult to seek support if a partner is abusive. While nongay teens often have trouble reaching out to adults for support, teenage gay and lesbian couples may be as isolated from their peers as they are from adults. The secrecy of the relationship also allows the threat of exposure to be used as a weapon to intimidate and maintain control. Such unwanted exposure is known as "outing."[41]

Dating and Drug-Facilitated Sexual Assault

Researchers report that teens and young adults are four times more like to be the victims of sexual assault than women in all other age groups.[42] In the vast majority of these cases the victim knows the perpetrator. A recent study funded by the U.S. Department of Justice indicated that "about 9 in 10 offenders were known to the victim. Most often, a boyfriend, ex-boyfriend,

The past few years have witnessed a considerable increase in the number of reports of drug-facilitated sexual assaults of older teens and young adults. At least twenty different drugs have been used in such attacks. Although alcohol remains the most widely used date-rape drug, others such as gamma hydroxy-butyrate (GHB), Rohypnol, and Ketamine are increasingly being misused as "knock-out drops" to render victims helpless.[44]

Common Date-Rape Drugs

Perpetrators use the variety of drugs listed below because they act rapidly, some within twenty minutes. They have a variety of effects, including disinhibition, passivity, loss of will to resist, muscle relaxation, and permanent anterograde amnesia (a form of amnesia where new events are not transferred to long-term memory, so the sufferer is not able to remember anything that occurs after the onset of this type of amnesia for more than a few moments).[45]

GHB (street names include Liquid Ecstasy, Soap, Easy Lay, Vita-G, and Georgia home boy)

GHB, a central-nervous-system depressant, is a colorless, odorless liquid with a slightly salty taste that can be easily masked when dissolved in any type of drink. Intoxication requires as little as one teaspoon of the liquid. The drug, which causes a victim's muscles to relax, acts in as little as ten to fifteen minutes. It also affects the victim's memory so that she or he frequently doesn't recall events that occurred shortly after ingesting it.[46] It can cause coma and seizures, and when combined with other drugs such as alcohol it can cause nausea and breathing difficulties. It may also produce withdrawal effects, including insomnia, anxiety, tremors, and sweating.[47]

Rohypnol (street names include Rophies, Roofies, Roach, and Rope)

Rohypnol is the trade name for flunitrazepam. It is not approved for use in the United States and its importation is banned. Manufactured legally in Europe and both legally and illegally in Mexico, its intended purpose is as a sedative and tranquilizer. Illicit use of Rohypnol appeared in this country in the early 1990s. It was originally packaged in foil-backed, clear plastic "blister packs" in doses of 1 mg and 2 mg. It has now been reformulated so that it turns clear beverages blue and produces haziness in colored liquids. When dissolved in a drink, however, it remains odorless and tasteless.[48] Symptoms of ingestion include rapid loss of inhibition and loss of consciousness that may progress quickly to coma.

Ketamine (street names include Special K and Vitamin K)

Since 1970 ketamine has been approved for both human and animal use as an anesthetic. About 90 percent of the drug sold legally is intended for veterinary use. Certain doses of ketamine can cause dreamlike states and hallucinations. In high doses it can cause delirium, amnesia, impaired motor function, high blood pressure, depression, and potentially fatal respiratory problems.[49]

The Penalties for Using Date-Rape Drugs

Drugging someone without his or her knowledge or consent is a crime. It is important to note that having sex with someone who cannot give consent because of the mental or physical effects of alcohol or drugs can be considered rape.

In 1996 Congress passed the Drug-Induced Rape Prevention and Punishment Act as an amendment to the Controlled Substances Act. The amendment established federal penalties of up to twenty years' imprisonment and fines for anyone convicted of committing a crime of violence, *including rape,* by administering a controlled substance without the victim's knowledge or consent. State laws may also be used to prosecute these crimes.[50]

Protecting Yourself

The National Women's Health Information Center provides a number of recommendations to help women protect themselves against date-rape drugs:[51]

- ◆ Don't accept drinks from other people.
- ◆ Open drink containers yourself.
- ◆ Keep your drink with you at all times, even when you go to the bathroom.
- ◆ Don't share drinks.
- ◆ Don't drink from punch bowls or other large, common, open containers.
- ◆ Don't drink anything that tastes or smells strange. Sometimes GHB tastes salty.
- ◆ If you choose to drink alcohol, have a nondrinking friend with you to make sure nothing happens.
- ◆ If you think you have been drugged and raped:
  - – Go to the police station or hospital right away.

– Get a urine test as soon as possible. These drugs leave your system quickly. Rohypnol leaves your body seventy-two hours after you take it. GHB leaves the body in twelve hours.

– Don't urinate before getting help.

– Don't douche, bath, or change clothes before getting help. These things may give evidence of the rape.

You can also call a crisis center or a hotline number to talk with a counselor. Two very helpful hotlines are the National Domestic Violence Hotline, at (800) 799-SAFE (7233), and the Rape Abuse Incest National Network, at (800) 656-HOPE (4673).

The Effects of Teen Dating Abuse

While both young men and young women report having inflicted and received physical abuse, the experiences and consequences are not the same for the two sexes. And in heterosexual relationships females are more likely to be the victims of severe forms of physical and sexual violence.[52] Young women respond to the trauma of dating violence with anger, fear, and surprise. The major emotional response batterers exhibit is sorrow. Women outnumber men by almost a three-to-one margin in cases in which victims report severe emotional trauma.[53] Rape has a devastating impact on the mental health of survivors, with nearly one-third of all rape victims developing rape-related posttraumatic stress disorder sometime in their lifetimes.[54]

Some of the most common responses following rape or battering—which may or may not be symptomatic of rape-related PTSD—are anxiety, depression, disruption of social functioning, problems in sexual functioning, suicide attempts, sleep disturbances, hostility, somatic complaints, and obsessive-compulsive symptoms.[55] In addition, young women often experience confusion combined with feelings of helplessness and powerlessness.[56] Symptoms unique to teenage survivors are sudden personality changes, drops in school performance, withdrawal from school or social activities, flagrant promiscuous behavior, sudden phobic behavior, self-destructive or risk-taking behavior, drug or alcohol abuse, development of eating disorders such as bulimia or anorexia, and alienation from peers or family.[57]

Teenage rape survivors face four major issues. First, there is a sense of loss of personal integrity. This can be devastating to a young woman who is still in the process of defining who she is and separating from her parents. When this work is interrupted, there is often a regression to the safety of earlier stages of development. Second, teenagers have a need to believe they can control their environments. Rape or battering upsets a teenager's perception of her ability to control her world and affects her ability to trust in herself, others, and the world around her. A third issue is the damage done to a teenager's emerging sexual identity. A rape experience may have serious repercussions for future sexual encounters, which may be coupled with the feeling of violation. A fourth issue deals with the damage done to a young woman's self-esteem. She is likely to internalize blame for the rape or battering. False assumptions, such as "I am bad" or "I deserve to be raped or battered," reinforce an already shaky sense of self and can lead to severe self-esteem problems.[58]

If Someone Is Hurting You or Someone You Love

It can be very difficult for teenagers to determine whether a relationship is abusive. In addition, many barriers make it hard for parents to help teenagers who are in abusive situations. The questionnaires that follow can help teenagers and parents make assessments and get help.

Are You in an Abusive Relationship?

If you are dating someone and are unsure if your relationship is abusive, ask yourself the following questions:[59]

Are you dating someone who—

◆ is jealous and possessive toward you, won't let you have friends, checks up on you, or won't accept breaking up?

◆ tries to control you, is bossy, gives orders, makes all the decisions, or doesn't take your opinion seriously?

◆ is scary, threatens you, or uses or owns weapons?

◆ is violent, has a history of fighting, loses his or her temper quickly, or brags about mistreating others?

◆ pressures you for sex, is forceful or scary around sex, thinks women are sex objects, tries to manipulate you into having sex by saying things like "If you really loved me, you would...," or gets too serious about the relationship too fast?

◆ abuses drugs or alcohol and pressures you to use them?

◆ blames you when he or she mistreats you? Says you provoked them, pressed their buttons, made them do it, led them on?

◆ has a history of bad relationships and blames the other people for all the problems?

◆ believes that men should be in control and powerful and that women should be passive and submissive?

◆ makes your family or friends worry about your safety?

If you answered yes to several of these questions, chances are you're in an abusive relationship. Another good measurement is to simply ask yourself, "Do I feel like I'm being mistreated?" If you answer yes, then you are.

There are many kinds of abuse, from "joking" remarks about women to tickling, forced sex, slapping, pushing, and threatening with weapons. Emotional abuse can be particularly confusing, especially when it takes the form of "friendly" playing around. Teasing is a good example. If you feel embarrassed, hurt, humiliated, or inadequate as a result of your partner's comments, you are being emotionally abused.

If your dating partner has slapped, pushed, or threatened you, it's important to take it seriously. It means he or she is trying to control you, and there's a good chance it will get worse unless you do something about it.

Every teenager has certain rights and responsibilities in a dating relationship. These rights and responsibilities are a part of all nurturing, loving, and caring relationships. Some of them are listed below.[60]

Your Rights

◆ To refuse a date without feeling guilty

◆ To ask for a date and accept no as an answer

◆ To say no to physical closeness

◆ To end a relationship

◆ To have an equal relationship

◆ To have friends other than your dating partner

◆ To participate in activities that don't include your dating partner

◆ To have your own feelings and be able to express them

◆ To set limits—that is, to say yes or no or to change your mind if you choose

◆ To have your limits, values, feelings, and beliefs respected

◆ To say "I love you" without having sex

◆ To be heard

◆ To be yourself, even if it is different from everyone else or from what others want you to be

Your Responsibilities

◆ To determine your limits and values

◆ To respect the limits, values, feelings, and beliefs of others

◆ To communicate clearly and honestly

◆ To ask for help when you need it

◆ To be considerate

◆ To check your actions and decisions to determine whether they are good or bad for you

If your partner is hurting you and you're not sure what to do about it, an excellent first step is to reach out to people who can help you. Battered-women's centers throughout the country help teenagers just like you. No matter how alone you may feel, there are lots and lots of people out there who have gone through what you're going through. They understand how hard this may be for you and all the confusion you may feel.

The telephone number for the National Domestic Violence Hotline is (800) 799-SAFE (7233). Call the hotline and they will give you the telephone number of the center nearest you. When you make these calls, you won't have to give your name unless you want to. Making these calls requires a lot of courage. Remember that the people at the center will work with you to help you get safe and stay safe.

Is Your Teenager in an Abusive Relationship?

If you are a parent and think your child is in an abusive relationship, there are steps you can take to help her. Young adults are more willing to talk about their relationship if they feel safe and supported.

Asking your daughter the following questions in a warm, supportive manner may help her open up to you about her situation:[61]

◆ What happens when your partner doesn't get his or her way?

◆ Is your partner extremely jealous?

◆ Does your partner ever threaten you?

◆ Does your partner ever tell you what to wear, how to do your hair, or how to wear your makeup?

◆ Does your partner ever hold you down, push you, or hit you?

◆ Does your partner ever try to keep you from seeing other friends or from doing things you'd like to do?

Really try to listen to your daughter without judging, assuming, or giving advice, and try to believe what she tells you. Let her talk about her partner, and don't let your anger get the best of you when she tells you what a wonderful or loving person her partner is. Try to understand that she can both love and hate her dating partner.

If you are unable to listen without getting angry, blaming her, or trying to tell her what to do, chances are she will be unwilling to have further conversations with you about her relationship. Realize, too, that the possibility of her listening to your advice is slim. The bottom line is that the more she becomes isolated from you, the more dependent she will be on her abusive partner for emotional support. The more emotionally connected she is to her partner, the harder it will be for her to get help. Let her know you love and support her. Tell her you are concerned about her safety, but try not to be critical of her partner, no matter how terrible you think the person is. Make sure she knows that no one has the right to hurt her, no matter what she thinks she has done to deserve it. Offer to go with her to get help, or give her the number for the National Domestic Violence Hotline.

Try to arrange to spend both time alone with your daughter and time with her around her friends and loved ones. Opportunities to be with people who are loving and nonviolent will remind her that she can be loved without being abused.

There will be times when it's appropriate to put your energies into rescuing your child. Sometimes, however, such efforts can become counterproductive. For example, a parent's continued insistence that her daughter stop seeing her partner is likely to lead to no-win arguments and the daughter's refusal to discuss the situation. This helps neither person and shuts down the lines of communication. Try to resist the temptation to continue your rescue effort when it seems harmful to you or to her. As difficult as this may be, try to go about your usual activities and keep in touch with people you can rely on for support, including your local battered-women's center.

There may come a time when the stress of your daughter's relationship is more than you can handle. If so, you may need to limit your discussions with your daughter. If you find yourself too angry, critical, or depressed to be supportive, ask another trusted family member or friend to stand in for you. Explain to your child in the most loving way possible that you need a break. Be sure to make it very clear that you love her and want her to be safe, but that your feelings of helplessness, fear, or anger make it impossible for you to help at this point. Let her know you will resume discussions about her relationship as soon as possible, and be sure she has other support people she can rely on.

If your son is the violent person, do everything possible to get him into a family violence program or to a counselor. Be a positive role model for your child, and actively demonstrate equality and respect through your own relationships with others. Identify to your child the negative consequences of his behavior. Let his girlfriend know that you understand that he is in the wrong and that she should not stay with an abusive partner, even if he is your son.[62]

What Teenagers Do and Don't Need from Family and Friends

As a parent or other concerned adult, remember that young people do not easily reach out to adults. Adults must not hold back or wait for teens to ask for help; rather, we must actively help them define healthy and abusive relationships. Our youths need us to be supportive and honest, not minimizing, blaming, or punitive.

The lists below will help adults relate to and assist teenagers who are in abusive relationships:[63]

In relating to a teenager, don't—

◆ be critical of the teenager or her partner

◆ ask blaming questions such as "What did you do to make him hit you?" or "Why don't you just break up?"

◆ pressure her to make decisions

◆ forbid the couple to see each other (the abused partner is likely to secretly see her abuser anyway, and secrecy further entrenches her in the relationship)

◆ talk to both teenagers together (the abused partner will not feel free to say what she feels)

◆ assume that she wants to end the relationship or that you know what's best for her

In relating to a teenager, do—

◆ listen to and believe her

◆ take her relationship seriously

◆ offer to go with her to get help or to talk to a professional

◆ let her know that violence under any circumstances is unacceptable

◆ let her know she has the right to be loved without violence

- be a role model for healthy relationships

- help her obtain legal and other protection (such as getting a restraining order, filing charges, or changing phone numbers)

Intervention and Prevention Strategies

To reduce teen dating violence in any community, a comprehensive prevention and intervention response must be developed. Programs must be funded and implemented in schools, health clinics, battered-women's shelters, and the courts. They should be coordinated efforts that involve everyone who comes in contact with teenagers, including school personnel, counselors, health-care practitioners, police, parents, and other teenagers. Strategies must be employed at several levels. As Barrie Levy explains, "Like other kinds of violence against women, abuse in adolescent dating relationships must be dealt with at multiple levels because it is caused by a set of interacting societal/institutional, community, family and personal factors."[64]

Beginning at the institutional level, social institutions that both support and promote male domination should be called to account and changed. For example, the media and entertainment industries, which so often target our young people, must be held accountable for their objectification of women and their ever increasing tendency to glorify violence.

Attempts should be made to educate not only young couples in violent relationships but all youths. Educational programs should be directed toward elementary-school, middle-school, high-school, and college students. Information about dating violence should emphasize the importance of peers in supporting nonviolent relationships.

School personnel should also be educated about dating violence and trained in intervention strategies. Health and counseling personnel should be trained to question students about dating violence.

Campus resources, including intervention programs and support groups, should be made available to teenagers in abusive relationships. Every effort should be made to publicize these services so teenagers will use them. Since teenagers involved in violent dating relationships tend to seek out peers for assistance, efforts should be directed at informing the peer group about the availability of such programs.[65]

Education about dating violence is needed for all populations, regardless of race or class. However, vast differences exist between and within populations, and generic messages and programs can often be ineffective. Special populations, such as lesbian and gay youth, young men and women of color, and pregnant and parenting teenagers, should be reached with messages that are targeted specifically to them. Teenagers must also be educated and empowered to carry out their own prevention activities. In some schools, students have organized campus speakouts and public forums. Students should be trained as peer leaders and challenged to engage in activities designed to change social policies that perpetuate violence.

Some school systems have begun to implement these and many other strategies. School policies have been developed to reinforce the message that dating violence is unacceptable. Personnel have been educated about the issue and trained in intervention strategies, and intervention policies have been established for personnel who witness violence among young couples.

Intervention Programs for Teen Abusers

The last few years have witnessed a slow increase in the number of intervention programs for teen batterers. According to researchers Dean Peacock and Emily Rothman, "They have been developed by courts, survivor advocacy agencies, batterer intervention programs and community based agencies that serve youth."[66] The programs vary in terms of both structure and methodology. Most utilize a psychoeducation-group format, meeting weekly for one to two hours and running for twelve to fifty-two weeks. Group discussions typically include topics like healthy and unhealthy relationships, sex-role stereotyping, coping with anger or rejection, and the effects of alcohol or drug use.

Parents receive information regarding the program and in some communities are involved in it on an ongoing basis. Depending on the program, participants who reoffend may be expelled from the group or asked to restart it; those who are expelled may face severe penalties from the probation department or court.[67]

The Expect Respect Program

Large numbers of children and teens can be reached through schools; for this reason intervention and prevention programs targeting teen dating violence have begun to appear on school campuses. One of the early leaders in this effort was the SafePlace Expect Respect Program, a peer-support and education project dedicated to helping teens establish safe and healthy dating relationships and to addressing the needs of youth who are at risk due to family violence and bullying. Now recognized nationally as a model violence-prevention program, Expect Respect began in 1988 as the Teen Dating Violence Project when a high school teacher asked SafePlace (then the Austin Center for Battered Women) to help take action against teenage dating violence.

The Expect Respect Program has four components:

1. Counseling and support groups for students who have experienced abuse and those who have witnessed domestic violence

2. Classroom presentations on the topics of dating violence, sexual harassment/assault, and healthy relationships

3. The SafeTeens Leadership Program

4. The Bullying Prevention Program

Each of the components is examined more closely below.

Counseling and Support Groups

The program provides in-school crisis intervention and supportive counseling for youths of all ages who have experienced sexual or domestic violence. Program counselors utilize play-therapy techniques and peer support groups to help children communicate their feelings, increase their sense of personal safety, and build healthy coping skills.

In middle and high schools, the program also sponsors weekly groups for young people who have had personal experience with abuse in their dating or family relationships. Counselors utilize the twenty-four-session Expect Respect curriculum to help youths increase their knowledge of, skills for, and expectations for healthy relationships. Separate groups are held for young men and young women. The groups meet on campus during school hours and are limited to approximately twelve students each. Participants are referred to the program by principals, teachers, school nurses, or counselors. Many adult women who use SafePlace services have referred their daughters and/or sons to the groups. Other teenagers are self-referred or attend at the urging of friends. Those interested sign up voluntarily. Except when it involves child abuse or threats of homicide or suicide, information shared in the support groups remains confidential.

The program uses a combination of educational and group-counseling methods to examine abusive relationships—including their underlying dynamics—and healthy relationships. Groups follow a four-phase curriculum. In the first phase, members learn how to define their experiences and learn to name (acknowledge) the abuse. In the second phase, members discuss their personal experiences, with the goal of confronting their beliefs about the abuse and affirming their rights to respect and safety. In the third phase, facilitators present information on such topics as recognizing controlling behavior, effective communication, assertiveness training, and conflict resolution without violence. The fourth phase involves bringing closure to the group and evaluating its effectiveness using feedback from group members and school staff.[68]

Classroom Presentations

Classroom presentations are made in schools, church groups, and other youth settings to raise awareness of dating violence, sexual assault, sexual harassment, and healthy relationships. Expect Respect staff and trained community volunteers serve as presenters.

Safe Teens Leadership Program

Middle and high school students can help prevent bullying, sexual harassment, and relationship violence by raising awareness in their communities and schools. In Expect Respect's Safe Teens Leadership Program, student groups participate in six hours of training to increase members' knowledge and understanding of violence prevention and their leadership skills for dealing with the issue. Safe Teens groups develop and put into action projects for raising awareness and effecting positive changes at school.

The Bullying-Prevention Program

This component of the program assists schools in stopping and preventing bullying and sexual harassment using a schoolwide approach. Strategies include establishing a campus leadership team; developing school policies and practices for responding to incidents and disclosures; conducting a survey of students, faculty, and parents; classroom lessons; and training school staff and parents. The goal of the program is to involve all members of the school community in creating a safe and respectful school environment.

◆

Barri Rosenbluth, director of school-based services at SafePlace, developed *Expect Respect: A Support Group Curriculum for Safe and Healthy Relationships* to help other programs replicate the Expect Respect support groups.[69] Written specifically for school counselors and others working with youths, the manual can be used in a variety of settings. It features instructions for twenty-four hour-long group sessions on such topics as dating rights and responsibilities, jealousy, communicating assertively, fair fighting, and ending a relationship.

The Expect Respect Program, which has been active in virtually every school in Austin, continues to grow rapidly. During the 2004–2005 school year it sponsored nineteen support groups at fifteen middle and high schools in the Austin area. In addition, four groups were conducted in elementary schools for children who had experienced sexual or domestic violence. During the 2003–2004 school year over 2,000 middle and high school students participated in classroom presentations, and over 3,575 parents, school personnel, and other professionals received training. SafePlace has expanded its services to reach young adults in churches, juvenile detention centers, substance-abuse programs, and other nonprofit and governmental agencies.

In 2004 SafePlace hosted its fifth annual Bullying to Battering Conference, an event designed to help schools and community-based agencies build partnerships for safer schools. Fifty-seven educators and advocates from Texas and across the U.S. learned how to work with others in their communities through school policy initiatives, curriculum, counseling, staff training, and other methods to reduce and prevent bullying, sexual harassment, and dating violence in schools.

The Expect Respect Program helps teenagers better understand their rights and responsibilities so they may avert the suffering that comes from years of abuse in violent relationships. Mary, a fifteen-year-old participant, says it best: "I was scared to talk about it at first, but now I know I didn't do anything wrong—that it wasn't my fault at all. Now I'm going to help others who may have the same fears I had."

...*4*

The Intimate Relationship Between Substance Abuse and Domestic Violence

The social expectations about drinking and drinking behavior in our society teach people that if they want to avoid being held responsible for their violence, they can either drink before they are violent or at least say they were drunk.

— *Richard J. Gelles*[1]

Considerable evidence supports the contention that alcohol abuse and violence are related, both within the family and outside of it. Studies have consistently found alcohol to be involved in one-half to two-thirds of homicides, one-fourth to nearly one-half of serious assaults, and more than one-fourth of rapes.[2]

Substance Abuse and Violent Men

Depending on the study, reported alcohol abuse among batterers varies from 16 percent to 79 percent.[3] Abusive men with severe alcohol problems are just as likely to abuse their partners when drunk as when sober. They are more likely to inflict serious injuries on their partners than abusive men who do not have a history of substance abuse. In addition, substance abusers are more likely to sexually attack their partners and to be violent outside the home.[4]

Reported drug abuse among batterers ranges from 8 percent to 30 percent.[5] Many drugs have been implicated in acts of violence, including marijuana, cocaine, opiates, hallucinogens (such as LSD), and stimulants. Each has a different physiological effect on its user.[6] Evidence suggests that of these drugs amphetamines may be the only ones that possibly cause violent behavior. Amphetamines heighten excitability and muscle tension and may lead to impulsive acts. The behavior that follows amphetamine use is related to both the dosage and the personality of the user prior to taking the drug: High-dosage users who already have aggressive personalities are likely to become more aggressive when using amphetamines.[7]

Does Substance Abuse Cause Family Violence?

Although there is a documented connection between substance abuse and family violence, we should not make the assumption that substance abuse *causes* domestic abuse. According to Del Martin, author of *Battered Wives,* "Alcohol is one of several factors that often contribute to the circumstances in which marital violence occurs. It may be used as an excuse for violence and it may trigger arguments that lead to violence. But, contrary to conventional beliefs, it is not necessarily a direct cause of violence and therefore does not help to explain the causes of wife-beating."[8]

The relationship between alcohol abuse and domestic violence is both confusing and complex. According to Edward Gondolf, a psychiatric research fellow at the University of Pittsburgh and a sociology professor at Indiana University of Pennsylvania, there are currently three theories that attempt to describe the connection.[9] The first, the "disinhibition" theory, states that drinking breaks down people's inhibitions and leads to antisocial behavior. The evidence for this theory is that people often behave differently when they are drinking from how they behave when they are sober. The implication is that violence is caused by alcohol abuse. The second theory, the "disavowal" theory, emphasizes the role of social learning in the alcohol/violence relationship. Substance abuse accompanied by violence provides the opportunity for socially learned rationalizations, or excuses, for the violent behavior. In this theory substance abuse is used as an excuse for deliberate acts of violence. The third explanation, the "interaction" theory, suggests that the interaction of a variety of physiological, psychological, and social factors explains the relationship between alcohol abuse and violence. The combination of these influences determines the degree to which an individual will be violent when drinking.

Perhaps the best evidence against the disinhibition theory comes from cross-cultural studies of drinking behavior. Craig MacAndrew and Robert Edgerton reviewed evidence regarding how people from different cultures react to alcohol. They proposed that if the pharmacological properties of alcohol are the direct causes of behaviors engaged in when drinking, then there should be very little variation in such behaviors across cultures.[10] Contrary to what they expected, the researchers found that drinking behavior varies greatly from culture to culture. In some cultures individuals become passive; in others they become aggressive. Also noteworthy is their discovery that the difference in behavior appears to be related to what people in each society believe about alcohol. If the cultural belief is that alcohol is a disinhibitor, people who drink tend to become disinhibited. If the cultural belief is that alcohol is a depressant, drinkers become passive and depressed.

In our society there is a widespread belief that alcohol releases violent tendencies. According to MacAndrew and Edgerton, when people are drinking they are given a time-out from the normal rules of social behavior. The denial of family violence, not only within the family but also by society, and the belief that alcohol is a disinhibitor combine to provide a socially acceptable explanation for violence. In essence, being intoxicated gives the batterer something other than himself to blame for his behavior.

Alan Lang and his colleagues tested this cross-cultural research.[11] College-student subjects were randomly assigned to one of four groups. Two groups received tonic water, and two groups received tonic water and vodka. One of the groups receiving tonic water only and one receiving vodka and tonic were accurately told what they were drinking. The other two groups were misled: The tonic-water-only drinkers were told they were drinking vodka and tonic, and the vodka-and-tonic drinkers believed they were drinking tonic water that had been decarbonated. Aggression was measured by assessing the intensity and duration of shocks the subjects believed they were administering to Lang's associates. Fine motor skills were also measured, by having subjects place objects of various shapes into matching holes. The researchers found that drinking alcohol, regardless of whether or not the subjects knew they were drinking, affected fine motor skills. They also discovered that the most aggressive subjects were those who thought they were drinking, regardless of whether their glasses actually contained alcohol.

Morton Bard and Joseph Zacker report that in 1,388 cases of domestic assault, nearly half of the abusive men said they were drinking at the time of the assault. When blood-alcohol tests were administered, however, less than 20 percent of the men were legally intoxicated.[12]

Despite the evidence against the disinhibition theory, some researchers persist in asserting that alcohol and drugs cause violent behavior.[13] This perception is also common among the general public. It appears that in our society domestic violence is more comprehensible when inflicted by a person who is intoxicated. An abused woman can avoid seeing her partner as abusive, instead thinking of him as a heavy drinker or an alcoholic. For the abused woman the link between alcohol consumption and violence often offers a way for her to understand her partner's abusive behavior and gives her false hope that if he would only stop drinking the violence would cease.[14] Families that interpret their domestic problems in this way usually focus on the husband's drinking problem rather than on his abusive behavior. The belief that alcohol is the problem also appears to contribute to a failure to follow up on violence in evaluation interviews, a failure to adequately describe violence in case reports, and a failure to address violence in treatment programs.[15]

In reality, the facts paint a different picture from one that supports the notion that alcohol is the problem in violent homes. Battered women with substance-abusing partners who eventually seek treatment for their drug or alcohol addictions consistently report that during recovery the abuse not only continues but often escalates, creating greater levels of danger. In cases in which battered women report that the level of physical abuse decreases during recovery, the women often report a corresponding increase in other forms of abuse such as threats, manipulation, and isolation.[16]

Edward Gondolf suggests that both alcohol abuse and domestic violence may be caused by underlying needs for power and control associated with distorted perceptions of masculinity.[17] Heavy drinking among men has been shown in American culture to represent toughness, risk taking, virility, and sexual prowess. Women, however, drink for quite different reasons. Heavy drinking among women is more likely to be related to depression and to be used to sedate the emotional trauma associated with battering.[18] According to the American Psychological Association Presidential Task Force on Violence and the Family, one study found that the presence of abuse in a woman's past was the greatest predictor of alcohol or drug abuse.[19]

Ascribing causality to substance abuse and domestic violence simplifies a highly dynamic and complicated relationship. Sociologist Richard Gelles explains, "Except for the evidence that appears to link amphetamine use to family violence, the portrait of the alcohol and drug crazed partner or parent who impulsively and violently abuses a family member is a distortion. If substances are linked to violence at all, it is through a complicated set of individual, situational, and social factors."[20]

Battered Women and Substance Abuse

It is not always the batterer who is an alcoholic; some battered women have substance-abuse problems. In fact, domestic violence increases women's risk of addiction, depression, attempted suicide, and a range of other health and mental-health problems. Results of a study of 481 battered women seeking emergency-room services indicated that battered women have an eight-times-higher risk of attempting suicide than nonbattered women, a six-times-higher risk of drug abuse, and a fifteen-times-higher rate of alcohol abuse.[21] Approximately 7 to 14 percent of battered women have alcohol-abuse problems.[22]

Although women may in general drink less than men, they appear to be more susceptible to the physical consequences of drinking.[23] Women are more likely to develop liver disease with a lower level of alcohol consumption than men. Native American women between ages fifteen and thirty-four are thirty-six times more likely than white women to have cirrhosis of the liver. Although African American women tend to drink less than white women, they are more than six times as likely to develop liver disease. Women are twice as likely as men to develop and die from cirrhosis, pneumonia, or other alcohol-related diseases. In addition, female alcoholics die at rates fifty to one hundred times higher than do male alcoholics.[24] Low self-esteem, feelings of inadequacy, and depression consistently appear in women with substance-abuse problems. They often feel lonely, isolated from positive support networks, and less worthy of help than do men who abuse substances.[25]

Women's substance-abuse problems do not cause their physical abuse. Instead, some women may use alcohol to self-medicate against the emotional and physical pain associated with battering. Self-medication with legal or illegal drugs is both an expression of a desire to exert a measure of personal control and an attempt to numb the pain of the experience.[26] Judith Herman, author of *Trauma and Recovery*, explains that "Traumatized people who cannot spontaneously dissociate [create a self-induced hypnotic trance state] may attempt to produce similar numbing effects by using alcohol or narcotics."[27] Tragically, in attempting to ease her pain, a chemically addicted battered woman may actually increase her danger. Drugs and alcohol make her less aware of, and less responsive to, cues of forthcoming violence. Less able to escape, she is more likely to fight back, thus increasing the likelihood of serious injury. She may also be less aware of injuries she has suffered.[28]

For battered women, secondary problems such as substance abuse partially result from their feelings of entrapment in a relationship wrought with escalating violence, a sense that is reinforced both within and outside the relationship. Within the relationship, the batterer's coercive control, exercised over a wide range of the woman's activities, severely affects her sense of personal freedom and heightens her feelings of fear and frustration. Outside the relationship, ineffective, inappropriate, or blaming responses from those to whom the woman reaches out for help also contribute to her feelings of entrapment. Isolated within the relationship and blocked from without, the battered woman seeks to meet her needs to the best of her perceived abilities. Self-medication may seem her only alternative. When it no longer offers sufficient relief, she may attempt suicide.[29]

Many battered women report that their chemically dependent partners initiated them into drug use and then sabotaged their efforts to quit. Threatening to disclose his partner's substance abuse to local authorities or significant others is another tactic the batterer may use to control her.[30] According to one battered woman, "He would buy my drugs for me because he said he liked me better when I was stoned. When he got mad at me, though, he'd flush my dope down the toilet and threaten to tell my boss I was a junkie."

Women's substance-abuse problems are frequently viewed as less serious than men's, and their condition may be more frequently misdiagnosed. Many chemically dependent battered women are addicted to drugs that were prescribed to them by health-care providers from whom they sought help.[31] Tranquilizers such as benzodiazepines are the most commonly prescribed medications for posttraumatic stress disorder and a variety of other ills. They are effective for short-term use in the immediate aftermath of a traumatic event, but their long-term use carries some risk of addiction.[32] Battered women who regularly use tranquilizers or analgesics, who have chronic symptoms that are unresponsive to treatment, who register vague complaints, and who frequently visit clinics may be labeled as difficult, demanding, or noncompliant patients who do not deserve serious attention. Such labeling, and the resulting ineffective responses on the part of health-care providers, illustrates the importance of properly identifying domestic violence when treating female patients.

A Comparison of Alcoholism and Battering

Although substance abuse and domestic violence are related, they are separate issues with several crucial differences. Whereas substance abuse is primarily harmful to the user, domestic violence is primarily harmful to the person being abused. And although statistics indicate that equal numbers of men and women may be chemically dependent, men are overwhelmingly the perpetrators of violence and women overwhelmingly its recipients. Eighty-five percent of the victims of domestic violence are women.

Another difference lies in how various service agencies deal with children who are exposed to domestic violence versus substance abuse. Domestic-violence services have a longer history of responding to children than do chemical-dependency services. Children comprise about two-thirds of the residents in most battered-women's shelters. In contrast, most substance-abuse treatment programs for women are not equipped to serve mothers with children.

A disease model is typically applied to chemical dependency, and a sociopolitical one to domestic violence. Battering is not a disease but rather is a deliberate and intentional behavior. Many alcohol treatment programs operate from a "sobriety first" philosophy; battered-women's shelters operate from a "safety first" philosophy.

Whereas domestic violence is a criminal act, chemical dependency is criminal only in specific situations. There has been a stronger criminal-justice response to drunk driving and drug abuse than to the battering of women.[33]

Battering and alcoholism are alike in some respects. One important similarity is the tendency for both alcoholics and batterers to discount their behavior and to minimize the severity of their chemical abuse or violence. Both batterers and alcoholics blame others, make excuses rather than accept responsibility for their actions, and exhibit Jekyll-and-Hyde personality changes. Both frequently attempt to regain control, make empty promises, and create false hopes. Both violence and substance abuse occur more and more frequently as they progress. Inevitably, over time both cause increasing trauma and more problems in almost all areas of family and personal life.

Partners of both alcoholics and batterers often minimize the impact of the addiction or the violence on the family. The denial process of not feeling, not trusting, and not talking dominates the family. When coupled with violence, alcoholism doubles the need for denial and creates an even greater sense of hopelessness for family members.[34] As Claudia Black, author of *It Will Never Happen to Me,* puts it: "Remember, the goal of family members in attempting to live through these problems is the same—minimize the conflict, adjust, placate, act-out, drop-out—do anything, but be sure to survive."[35]

Substance Abuse Recovery Programs and Batterer Treatment Programs

Anyone working with families in which both domestic violence and substance abuse are present must recognize that full recovery for the family will not usually occur unless both issues are addressed. For the dually affected family, the reemergence or continuation of either violence or substance abuse can trigger the recurrence of the other. Studies have consistently shown alcohol abuse to

75

The Intimate
Relationship
Between
Substance
Abuse and
Domestic
Violence

be a major predictor of a person's dropping out of a batterers' treatment program. Studies have also shown that domestic violence contributes to alcohol relapse.[36]

Recognizing the complex relationship between domestic violence and substance abuse is a first step toward providing effective services for both the battered woman and the batterer. It is crucial that battered-women's advocates and substance-abuse counselors recognize the similarities and differences between the two problems. To enhance the possibility of effective collaboration, advocates in both fields should familiarize themselves with the philosophies, strategies, and assumptions of the other.[37]

Self-help programs such as Alcoholics Anonymous (AA) promote and support emotional and spiritual health and have helped countless alcoholics get and stay sober.[38] These programs, however, were not designed to address battering and are thus ineffective in helping batterers to change their abusive behavior. Treatment for substance abusers who batter must mandate involvement in a program designed specifically to address the attitudes and beliefs that support batterers' behavior.

In cases involving both substance abuse and domestic violence, the pattern seems to be to give first priority to providing treatment for the substance abuse. In AA, this is known as "sobriety first." In fact, substance-abuse programs often neglect relationship violence based on the erroneous assumption that the violence will subside with sobriety. Some municipal courts repeatedly refer domestic-violence cases to substance-abuse treatment programs rather than to batterer's treatment programs.[39]

In batterers' treatment programs, men who are chemically dependent are frequently referred to alcohol- or drug-rehabilitation programs, AA, or Narcotics Anonymous as a prerequisite to their participation. There is no assurance, however, that the two programs will reinforce each other. In fact, approaches and assumptions in conventional drug- and alcohol-recovery programs often contradict the counseling provided in most batterers' treatment programs. In AA the focus is primarily on one's self. Batterers' treatment programs, in contrast, emphasize the impact of the batterer's behavior on his family. The objective in such programs is for the batterer to become less self-centered. Furthermore, AA recovery programs often implicate the batterer's partner as codependent or coalcoholic and utilize family-treatment strategies that may put an abused partner in a dangerous position. By contrast, batterers' treatment programs view the partner as caught in an enforced state of compliance and dependency where abuse and threats force her into submission. AA emphasizes that alcohol abuse is a disease; batterers' treatment programs emphasize that violence is a choice. AA emphasizes the number of sober days and meetings attended; batterers' treatment programs are concerned with increasing the abused woman's feelings of safety as a result of her partner's treatment.

Besides the differences that exist between programs to treat substance abuse and those to treat batterers, there are also several important similarities between the two. Both AA and batterers' treatment programs confront denial and the minimization of destructive behaviors. Both address rationalizations used to justify behaviors, and both urge participants to take personal responsibility for their behavior. Both promote the importance of utilizing support to reduce social isolation. Finally, both assert that individuals can and should stop their destructive and dangerous behaviors, and both emphasize the personal change that is necessary on a daily basis over the long term to do so.[40]

Again, it is absolutely critical that batterers who abuse alcohol or other drugs address both problems directly and concurrently, not only to maximize their families' safety but also to lessen the possibility of relapse. True recovery requires much more than abstinence from a substance or a behavior. It includes adopting a lifestyle that enhances all aspects of emotional well-being, a goal that cannot be achieved as long as the battering continues. Recovery programs for family violence and substance abuse must begin with screening and assessment for both problems. According to Gondolf, "Decisively addressing alcohol abuse may be essential to increasing the effectiveness of wife assault programs, and confronting wife assault may improve the effectiveness of alcohol treatment programs."[41]

Service providers need to ask their clients direct questions to determine whether domestic violence has occurred. As with any sensitive issue that has been perpetuated by denial, questions should begin with the least threatening and lead to the more direct. The following list offers an example of how questioning might progress:[42]

◆ Do you and your partner argue often?

◆ If either of you drinks, is your personality different when you're drinking?

◆ Does your partner ever lose his or her temper, throw things, or threaten you?

◆ Do arguments ever end in pushing, shoving, or slapping?

◆ Has your partner ever used a fist or a weapon against you?

◆ Have you ever been concerned about the safety of your children?

For dually affected families, services should be offered in the following order: (1) address safety issues, (2) begin recovery for alcoholism and/or other drug abuse, (3) before the alcohol/drug program ends, begin a treatment program for the violence, and (4) provide ongoing support for both sobriety and the elimination of violent behavior.

Never assume that once someone is clean and sober the problems associated with domestic violence will automatically cease. Unless the abuse is addressed, the underlying issues of power and control are still in place. And from the perspective of the abuse survivor, if by chance the abuse stops when the drinking stops, the fear, guilt, and anger she has experienced will not automatically disappear and should be addressed.

The Abused Partners of Men in Recovery for Substance Abuse

Often, partners of batterers who enter substance-abuse recovery programs are directed into self-help programs such as Al-Anon and codependency groups.[43] As with other traditional treatment responses, however, these groups were not designed to meet the needs of battered women and often inadvertently set them up for further harm. The goals of codependency treatment typically include helping family members of addicts get self-focused, practice emotional detachment from the substance abuser, and stop their enabling or codependent behaviors. Group members are encouraged to define their personal boundaries, set limits on their partners' behaviors, and stop protecting their partners from the harmful consequences of the addiction. These strategies can be very helpful for women whose partners are not abusive. For battered women, however, they will likely result in an escalation of the abuse, including physical violence.

Battered-women's advocates and substance-abuse counselors often disagree about the labeling of battered women as codependent. Many domestic-violence workers feel the label blames the victim. In battering relationships the behaviors described as enabling or codependent are often forced, coerced, and maintained by abuse. Furthermore, they often serve as battered women's survival strategies. Battered women are often highly sensitive to their partners' moods as a way to determine levels of danger. They may focus on their partners' needs and cover up for them to avoid being beaten. Seen in this light, a battered woman's behaviors are not codependent but instead are survival strategies undertaken to maintain her safety and the safety of her children. When battered women are encouraged to stop these behaviors they are in essence being persuaded to stop doing what may be keeping them alive.[44] Some of the principles behind the concept of codependency reflect valid concerns that can be helpful when placed in the proper context. Equally impor-

77

The Intimate
Relationship
Between
Substance
Abuse and
Domestic
Violence

tant, however, is the realization that attempts to eliminate a battered woman's survival strategies, without offering her viable alternatives, can and will endanger her life.

Service providers should always remember the following key points when working with battered women whose partners are in recovery for substance abuse:[45]

1. Guarantees for the woman's safety in the relationship can never be based upon the promises of her abusive partner.

2. If she is still in the battering relationship, she may deny or minimize the danger she is in. Family or couple's counseling is not safe for the battered woman until the violence has been addressed.

3. Believe her and tell her the violence is not her fault. Do not join the batterer in his denial or minimization of the abuse.

4. Codependency concepts are not appropriate in trying to understand why women remain in violent relationships.

5. Dispel any belief that the violence will stop when she or the batterer becomes clean and sober.

6. Work with her to assess her safety and to develop a safety plan.

7. Share information with her about her options and resources, including battered-women's services, protective intervention, and legal choices.

Battered women need to understand the purposes and limitations of resources like Al-Anon and codependency groups. Equally important, they need to receive accurate and complete information about domestic-violence services and similar resources so they can make informed choices and set realistic expectations.

Battered Women in Recovery for Substance Abuse

Just as it is crucial for treatment programs that target chemically addicted batterers to address both the violence and the substance abuse, it is important for chemically addicted battered women to have access to treatment for substance abuse as part of a program that addresses all aspects of their well-being. Yet there are issues that hinder the effective delivery of alcohol- and drug-treatment services to all women who need them. While nearly one-third of the estimated ten million alcoholics in America are women, less than a quarter of the patients at publicly funded alcohol-treatment centers are women. At drug-

79

**The Intimate
Relationship
Between
Substance
Abuse and
Domestic
Violence**

treatment centers, about 30 percent of the patients are women.[46] All women, and battered women in particular, face several obstacles to their recovery from substance abuse, including shame, fear, denial, and service programs ill-equipped to meet their special needs.

Shame is perhaps one of the hardest obstacles for women to overcome. In 1991 Sheila Blume summarized the differences commonly found between male and female alcoholics and found that a key disparity is that women are more stigmatized for their substance use and abuse.[47] The stigmatization, along with an unwillingness on the part of many physicians, mental-health professionals, police, and courts to identify battered women as chemically dependent, is detrimental to early intervention and treatment. Shame may also contribute to women's own denial of their substance-abuse issues. One of the main reasons why Hispanic women alcoholics often do not acknowledge their problem is the strong sanctions within their culture against women's drinking.[48] Fear is another powerful factor that can keep chemically dependent battered women from dealing with their addictions. They may fear reprisal or abuse from their partners, losing or being unable to take care of their children, or punishment from local authorities.

Batterers often oppose their partners' attempts to seek help, including help for substance abuse. They may sabotage their partners' recovery by preventing them from attending meetings or appointments, or they may increase the violence or threats to reestablish control. Some battered women decide to leave substance-abuse treatment when their participation appears to compromise their safety.[49]

A major deterrent to women seeking help for substance abuse is the lack of child care at treatment facilities. Most alcohol and drug treatment centers do not provide child care, much less allow children to accompany their mothers who need inpatient treatment. According to Diane Rhodes, senior director of programs at SafePlace in Austin, Texas, "Taking their children with them is a first priority for many of our residents. They often feel there is no one they can trust with their children's safety. In these situations a woman will refuse treatment unless she is guaranteed that she can take her children with her."

Frequently, women lack either the money or the insurance to pay for treatment, a disadvantage that may keep them from seeking help or may force them to accept the services they can afford rather than those they need. One study of women entering treatment for alcoholism reported that African American women face greater financial difficulties, are more likely to abuse multiple drugs, and experience a greater sense of alienation than do white women.[50] The results suggest that black women and other women of color have more or different barriers to overcome in entering treatment than do white women. In addition, African American, Hispanic, and Native American women have fewer alcoholism services available to them than are available to men of the same ethnicities. When a woman of color is also a lesbian, services specifically designed for her needs are almost nonexistent. Of 540 rehabilitation centers in Texas, only 17 are exclusively for females and only one is specifically for Hispanic females.[51]

Drug-addicted pregnant women have the additional problem of finding a treatment program that will accept them. There is a tremendous fear among service providers concerning liability issues associated with treating addicted women who are pregnant. In New York City, of seventy-eight drug-treatment programs surveyed, 54 percent refused to admit pregnant addicts, and 87 percent refused to take pregnant, crack-addicted women on Medicaid.[52]

Research shows that women receive the most benefit from drug-treatment programs that provide comprehensive services for meeting their basic needs, including access to food, clothing, and shelter; transportation, job counseling and training, legal assistance, and educational opportunities; parenting training; family or individual therapy; medical care and child care; social services and social support; assertiveness training and family planning services.[53] Traditional male-oriented drug-treatment programs may not be appropriate for women because they often do not provide these services. Granting more women access to substance-abuse treatment is not feasible until such programs offer sensitive, effective, nonracist, and antihomophobic treatment. Failure to design programs and policies that meet women's needs results in programs that are either underutilized or ineffective.

Approximately 30 percent of AA membership is female.[54] A substantial number of women drop out of AA due to frustration with the patriarchal model of the twelve-step programs. As an alternative, women's groups have formed that have adapted the twelve steps to better meet women's spiritual needs and nurture their well-being.[55] These groups provide a sensitive and effective alternative to the more traditional, male-oriented recovery programs.

Creating an Empowered Response to Substance Abuse

At the same time that chemically dependent battered women are confronting substance-abuse programs ill-designed to meet their needs, they may also be dealing with domestic-violence programs that are poorly prepared to serve them effectively. Many battered-women's shelters have strict rules forbidding the use of alcohol and other drugs in the shelter, restrictions that are necessary to provide a healthful environment for the other residents, who usually include both women and children. However, offering chemically dependent battered women shelter without addressing their substance abuse is setting them up to fail. And refusing shelter to chemically addicted women sends a message that may reinforce their depression, frustration, and desperation. Some battered women stop abusing substances once they find safety; others stop if they become pregnant. Neither will likely be the case, however, for the truly addicted battered women. Expecting the chemically *addicted* battered woman to respond the same as the chemically *abusing* battered woman is unrealistic.

At SafePlace an increasing number of residents have substance-abuse problems. According to one staff member at the shelter who is also a twenty-year veteran in the movement, "We do seem to be working with more chemically addicted women. We're also seeing a big difference in the drug of choice. Crack is definitely more popular, and this is a particularly serious addiction to address." One of the reasons why SafePlace is serving more women with substance-abuse problems may be because of a change in attitude among staff and volunteers over the last decade or so. Advocates now are more informed about substance abuse and are less likely to blame and judge chemically addicted women. A nonjudgmental environment allows residents to be more open about their addictions and the problems they create.

SafePlace's admission policy was changed in the 1990s to reflect less victim blaming attitudes about substance abuse. All women seeking shelter continue to be screened for substance abuse during their initial assessment, but no woman is ever turned away because of a drug problem. Chemically addicted women are admitted to the shelter with the understanding that their substance use will be addressed with their counselor or advocate. Women are asked if they are interested in addressing and changing their drug-using behavior. If they express a desire to go into treatment, they are provided with the appropriate resources. SafePlace works closely with the Austin Family House, an inpatient treatment center and halfway house for women and their children, including offering on-site support groups for chemically addicted survivors of domestic abuse.

These changes have greatly improved SafePlace's ability to help abused women. Residents at the shelter now are routinely given opportunities to address both their safety and their recovery needs. According to one SafePlace advocate, "We've really gotten away from that 'bad girl' attitude that shames and blames the woman. Now we focus on the behavior, which is more consistent with the movement's empowering philosophy."

81

The Intimate
Relationship
Between
Substance
Abuse and
Domestic
Violence

...5

Battered Women and the Legal System

Systemic solutions to domestic violence must be adopted. Policies that on their surface should be useful—that is, greater police arrests or enforced use of protective orders—have repeatedly floundered on the shoals of indifference by other critical actors.[1]

— *Eve and Carl Buzawa, authors of* Domestic Violence: The Criminal Justice Response

Many of the justice system's attitudes and responses toward domestic violence have historically prevented battered women from getting the help they need. The justice system's response to incidents of domestic abuse has often been inadequate and has left survivors confused and discouraged. On the one hand, a court's lenient response may encourage a batterer to believe that violence against a family member is acceptable; on the other, imposing a jail sentence may punish not only the abuser but also his family by depriving it of financial support.

Domestic-violence laws—and their enforcement—vary greatly from state to state and city to city. It is often difficult for battered women to know what to expect when they turn to the justice system for help. Some women may get the assistance they need, but others may be further victimized. Furthermore, the system simply fails to protect some women, including undocumented immigrants, women involved in crime, and lesbians.

Understanding the Justice System

The legal response to domestic violence consists of a complex network of processes, people, and laws, any of which a battered woman may become involved with. To gain access to the help they need, battered women are often implicitly expected to understand the legal system. But it often stumps even the experts; thus it's understandable that it may seem intimidating and frightening to a layperson.

The justice system encompasses law-enforcement officers, prosecutors, and the courts. To better understand the system it is helpful to grasp the distinction between the *criminal* process and the *civil* process. The differences between the two can have a profound effect on battered women.

The criminal-justice system deals only with crimes, which are acts in violation of penal law (the branch of law dealing with crimes and their punishments). A crime is considered an injury to the state and is prosecuted as such. The rationale for treating a crime as an injury to the state, rather than as an injury to the individual or group that was directly affected by the crime, is to protect all citizens from a criminal who may strike again and thus must be deterred or punished. A crime can be prosecuted regardless of whether the victim takes action. That's even true in the case of domestic violence: The criminal-justice system can decide to prosecute a batterer even if the battered woman doesn't take any action. In fact, women are not always able to make the prosecution process work, such as when the woman has been murdered.

The civil system deals with all the legal processes and matters that don't involve crimes, including breach of contract, divorce, custody, property rights, recovery of money for injury, and a variety of other issues. Civil cases are typically initiated when one party sues another party; the legal remedy is usually an order by a judge. If the judge finds that the case presented by the party bringing the suit has merit, she or he can order the party being sued to do certain things or to pay money to the party bringing suit. It is important to remember that in the civil process no one can be sent to jail as part of the remedy, except through contempt proceedings (when a judge takes action against a party for failing to follow the court's orders). Contempt proceedings, which may involve a jail sentence or a fine, more closely resemble criminal proceedings than they do civil ones.[2]

Mandatory Arrest Policies

In situations of domestic violence, mandatory, or pro-arrest, policies require that a police officer arrest a suspect if there is probable cause to believe that an assault has occurred. Mandatory arrest policies do not require or take into consideration the consent or objections of the survivor. According to Eve and Carl Buzawa, authors of *Domestic Violence: The Criminal Justice Response,* the adoption of mandatory arrest policies has been based on the belief that they are necessary to change police officers' behavior. Theoretically, mandatory arrest policies seek to eliminate an officer's discretion in making arrests. As the Buzawas explain, "Proponents of mandatory legislation and administrative policies also recognize that most officers do not have adequate knowledge [for] handling domestic violence cases or actively disapprove of police intervention. Implementing rigid pro-arrest policies, therefore, tries to force change in behavior without necessarily changing officer attitudes. Attitudinal change, although apparently considered less important, would then occur at some later point, if at all, by training officers [in] the rationale of the policy and by conversion due to their immersion into the procedure."[3]

Mandatory arrest policies first became popular among police departments after Lawrence Sherman and Richard Beck published a 1984 study examining the relationship between arrest and domestic-violence recidivism. After analyzing 314 cases in Minneapolis, the researchers concluded that arrest was the most effective means of deterring batterers' violent behavior.[4] By 1986, a survey of U.S. police departments found that as many as one-third had changed to mandatory arrest policies because of the Sherman and Beck study.[5] The American Bar Association endorsed such policies, and the federal Violence Against Women Act (VAWA), passed in 1994, encouraged police departments to adopt them.[6] Most states currently have codified mandatory arrest policies.[7]

The debate over the effectiveness—and appropriateness—of such policies generates a great deal of disagreement and division among domestic-violence experts.[8] Although their long-term implications have yet to be definitively determined, opposing camps offer arguments in support of their respective positions. According to Barbara Hart, legal director of the Pennsylvania Coalition Against Domestic Violence, "The leading research in the field demonstrates that where police arrest perpetrators of domestic violence rather than separating the couple or mediating between the victim and offender, the arrested perpetrators are significantly less likely to recidivate within six months than those [toward] whom the police take conciliatory action. Arrest more effectively deters perpetrators than any other law-enforcement action, even if a case does not result in conviction. Further, victims of domestic violence who call the police appear to be less likely to be assaulted again by their partners than those who [do] not."[9]

Mary Koss, with the University of Arizona, counters this argument. She writes:

> Evaluations of mandatory arrest in Minneapolis, Minnesota; Metro-Dade, Florida; Colorado Springs, Colorado; Milwaukee, Wisconsin; Charlotte, North Carolina; and Omaha, Nebraska, indicated that although arrest seemed to initially deter violence in employed men (but not unemployed men), in the long run battering increased.... [W]omen's satisfaction with police response is highest if officers comply with their preference, whether it is to arrest or not to arrest the offender. Uniform policies of mandatory arrest rob women of choice and are oversimplified, given the varied domestic situations women face and the strategies they choose to deal with abuse. The original research team that implemented and evaluated mandatory arrest laws in the six aforementioned metropolitan areas has concluded that they should be repealed."[10]

In her highly controversial work, *Insult to Injury: Rethinking Our Responses to Intimate Abuse,* Linda Mills highlights the "racial divide" inherent in both the justice system and mandatory arrest policies. Men of color are more likely to be arrested and prosecuted for domestic-violence crimes at disproportionately higher rates than Caucasian men.[11] According to Mills, "Without considering who actually gets arrested, it appears that a mandatory arrest policy does in fact prevent more acts of violence than it is likely to cause. However, when one considers who is most likely to get arrested by criminal justice personnel, a very different picture emerges."[12]

A 2001 study found different levels of support for mandatory arrest policies among Caucasian and African American women. Seventy-nine percent of Caucasian women supported the adoption of mandatory arrest policies, but only 53 percent of African American women did.[13] As Mills explains, "[I]t is critical to remember that many women of color are reluctant to seek intervention from the police[,] fearing that their contact with law enforcement will serve to exacerbate the diverse assaults on their public and private lives."[14]

Women Arrested for the Use of Nonlethal Violence

Two disturbing trends in the last few years are the increases in dual arrests (when battered women who use force against their abusive partners are arrested along with the partners) and in arrests of women for domestic violence. Family-violence data from Connecticut illustrate this point: In 1987 women comprised 11 percent of the total arrests for domestic violence; by 1997 that figure had risen to 18 percent.[15] Data from Boulder, Colorado, indicate that in

1997 women comprised 12 percent of those arrested for domestic violence. In the first six months of 1999 that number had doubled to nearly 25 percent.[16] Some believe that the increase in female arrests represents a backlash against the adoption of mandatory arrest policies. David Hirschel and Eve Buzawa, both with the University of Massachusetts at Lowell, explain, "As *a consequence of the nationwide* move to preferred and mandatory arrest policies in intimate partner violence cases, arrest rates for intimate partner violence have increased dramatically. It was anticipated that the rates of males arrested for domestic violence would increase. What was less expected was a concurrent, and proportionally greater, increase in female arrests.... Whereas in some cases the female partner is the sole person arrested, other cases involve the arrest of both her and her partner, resulting in a *dual arrest*."[17]

When Women Use Force

The increase in the number of women arrested for domestic assault has raised concerns among domestic-violence experts. Many advocates are calling for a better understanding of women's use of nonlethal violence so the justice system can best respond to both survivors and perpetrators. As briefly discussed in Chapter 1, some women do batter their male or female partners. Some of the women arrested under mandatory arrest policies may certainly fall into this category. What is equally possible, however, is that some female survivors who use force against their abusive partners are being erroneously identified as abusive.

A 2004 study conducted in Portland, Oregon, evaluated the characteristics, criminal histories, and past domestic-violence histories of 5,578 men and 1,126 women arrested for domestic assault against a heterosexual intimate partner. Several gender differences emerged. The women were more likely to be arrested along with their partner than were the men (34 percent versus 7 percent.) A higher proportion of the arrested males were violating existing protection orders when they committed the offense being reviewed, and more of the men had used substances immediately before the assault. Victims of arrested males, as opposed to victims of arrested females, were more likely to report that there had been recent escalations in the frequency and severity of the abuse. Finally, the female victims of the arrested males were significantly more likely than the male victims of arrested females *to feel threatened by their partners and to report wanting to end the relationship.*[18] Researchers concluded:

> To the extent that women continue to be arrested for domestic assault, either individually or through dual arrests, prosecutors and judges should carefully consider whether continued prosecution is warranted. Many of the women in this study did not have a background that is

consistent with premeditated or instrumentally aggressive behavior. As such, it seems likely that some of these women may have been arrested for engaging in defensive tactics following an attack by their intimate partner. Moreover, at least as compared to the men, these women as a group appear to be at low risk to engage in continued aggression or criminality.[19]

Erin House, legal advocacy coordinator for the Domestic Violence Project/SAFE House, in Ann Arbor, Michigan, identifies five common reasons why battered women use force against an abusive partner. They are:[20]

◆ self-defense, including trying to escape

◆ to try to stop or dissuade the batterer from continuing to assault

◆ as a "preemptive strike" (trying to "induce" an assault in an effort to minimize the harm, embarrassment, and disruption to their lives that the assault would cause)

◆ avoiding the use of force has not kept the woman safe

◆ retaliation for a history of abuse

Dr. Shamita Das Dasgupta, with Manavi, Inc., an advocacy program for Asian survivors of domestic violence, points out that researchers have identified both self-defense and other possible reasons for women's use of force against their partners, including wanting to gain emotional attention, expressing anger, and reacting to frustration and stress. According to Dasgupta, these reasons alone do not fully explain women's use of force. "To compartmentalize women's motivations for engaging in violent behavior towards intimate partners as either self-defense... or retaliation and other intentions... is to disregard the complexities of women's lives. A broad theoretical perspective that considers the interactions of social, historical, institutional, [and] individual variables in women's violence would provide a better understanding of it."[21] A deeper comprehension can only be attained through further study and research.

Battered women's use of force may prevent an immediate assault, but it will not stop the violence. In fact, it may increase the chances that she will be seriously injured. In addition, using force may lead to a survivor's arrest and incarceration. Some advocates argue that the use of force is never acceptable. As a proponent of nonviolence I can certainly understand that sentiment. As a survivor who fought back, however, I also know the conditions under which I felt the need to use force. It is important to remember that *understanding* why survivors use force is not the same as *condoning* it. We as advocates are better able to respond to survivors' needs if we understand the motivations driving their actions. As Erin House explains, "Advocates may be concerned that law enforcement will be upset that they are 'advocating for a criminal.' These situations are undeniably difficult, and each case requires significant analysis. However, advocacy agencies must not back down from complicated situations and they must not deny services to a battered woman who has used force because they do not want to deal with responses from law enforcement and the court system. If the advocate assesses that the woman who used force is a battered woman in a domestic violence relationship, they should advocate for her."[22]

At the same time, we advocates must examine our own attitudes regarding women's use of violence. On the one hand, battered women's use of force against an abusive partner may be considered a contradiction to their expected gender roles. Women are not "supposed" to be aggressive or to use force, even in defending themselves from harm. Unfortunately, survivors who use force may be seen as "bad" or "dangerous" and denied services they seriously need. On the other hand, some people may question survivors who never physically resist their attackers, implying that they are "passive." Dasgupta points out that society has conceptualized battered women as "...passive and helpless. Yet, even the most subservient and fearful battered woman [employs] shrewd survival strategies on a daily basis to keep her children and herself alive."[23]

Determining the Primary Aggressor

Dual arrests often occur because the arresting officer is unable to determine the primary aggressor. In particular, survivors of same-sex partner violence are especially vulnerable to being arrested along with their abusive partners. Unable to make a determination based on gender, arresting officers may be more likely to erroneously conclude that there is "mutual battering."[24]

In some situations police officers base their decision about whom to arrest on "visible signs of injury." However, this can be an ineffective and problematic approach when trying to determine the primary aggressor. According to House, "When battered women use force to resist attack, to free themselves, or to retreat from an attack they are often likely to leave visible injuries.... We must remember that batterers... are making conscious decisions about what kinds of injuries to inflict.... Batterers report tailoring their assaults so as not to leave visible injuries.... Additionally, battered women who are dark skinned are less likely to show immediate redness or bruising and the batterer knows that."[25]

As our understanding of same-sex partner violence increases, we are beginning to recognize that gender is not the most effective criterion for determining the primary aggressor; nor is counting how many times who hit whom. Effective determination of the primary aggressor is dependent upon examining the *context, intent,* and *effect* of the actions of both parties. In addition, since domestic violence is defined by a repeated pattern of abusive behaviors, one incident of physical force does not necessarily indicate that the individual is abusive. Looking beyond the current incident—specifically at prior domestic-violence incidents, criminal histories, and the potential for future violent behavior—may help to ensure that the arresting officer is making a fair and accurate determination.[26] In addition, House recommends that the following be considered when trying to determine the primary aggressor:[27]

- ◆ Batterers often try to manipulate their partners into pushing or hitting them first to give the batterer "justification" for "defending" himself/herself.

- ◆ Get a description of the entire incident, from start to finish. If the person is consistently vague, avoids answering your questions, or changes the subject, you may be talking to a batterer.

- ◆ If the person you are speaking with makes repeated efforts to turn the conversation toward you and away from himself/herself, this may be a sign that he/she is the batterer.

- ◆ A survivor will usually admit to using force.

- ◆ A batterer will either deny using force or will couple the admission with some form of justification or rationalization.

- ◆ A survivor will not always admit to being afraid of her/his partner. If she/he does admit to being afraid, then ask for specifics about what the survivor is afraid the partner will do. A survivor should be able to give specifics and details.

- ◆ During questioning, a survivor may describe ways in which she/he tries to control her/his behavior, such as "I try to stay out of his way," or, "I try not to make her mad." A batterer may respond to the question "What have you done to stop the violence?" by describing the ways he/she controls the partner: "I try to keep her in the bedroom until she is calmed down," or, "I make sure she doesn't leave the house because I'm afraid of what she might do to herself."

- ◆ A survivor will often try to defend the battering partner by emphasizing the batterer's good qualities.

- ◆ A batterer, while claiming to be the victim, will emphasize his/her partner's "faults."

◆ A batterer is an expert at manipulation and at "selling" him-/herself to others.

Protection for Battered Women under the Legal System

In most states women have a choice of three legal strategies to protect themselves against domestic violence:[28]

1. Divorce or legal separation from the abusive husband

2. A civil protection order that requires the batterer to stop abusing, threatening, or harassing the woman

3. Criminal prosecution of the batterer

In some situations women may be able to obtain both criminal enforcement and civil protection orders.

The rest of this section examines civil protection orders in detail.

Civil Protection Orders

A civil protection order, now available in all fifty states and the District of Columbia, is an order issued by a civil court judge in response to a written petition from a battered woman. Other names for protection orders include:[29]

◆ stay-away order

◆ order of no contact

◆ injunction for protection

◆ harassment order

◆ restraining order

◆ stalking protection order

◆ orders not to abuse, harass, contact, etc., that are part of bail, probation, or parole conditions

◆ emergency, temporary, or ex parte order

The order usually commands the abusive partner (a spouse, former spouse, or lover) to stop abusing, harassing, or threatening the woman and to stay away from her. It can also contain other provisions, such as rules governing child custody and visitation (which may be supervised or unsupervised); eviction of the abuser from the family home (even if it is held in his name); prohibition of the batterer from contacting the woman at her residence, school, or place of employment; a requirement that the batterer get counseling or participate in a substance-abuse or batterers' treatment program; restrictions against firearm possession; and other forms of relief that the court deems appropriate.[30] If the protection order is violated, courts may hold the violator in contempt, impose fines, or incarcerate the violator, depending on state laws.[31]

The remedies provided by protection orders are separate from divorce and separation procedures. Even if the woman plans to file for divorce, she may still need a civil protection order because her only recourse if the batterer violates the divorce decree would be to return to court. By contrast, a violation of the civil protection order would provide for his immediate arrest.

Civil protection orders are also distinct from criminal-justice remedies. Other than in New York State, petitioning for a protection order does not prohibit a woman from bringing criminal charges against the offender at the same time. Some judges recommend that domestic-violence survivors consider pursuing their cases both civilly and criminally, at least in those involving aggravated assault and battery.[32] In a case involving criminal prosecution, a protection order may help prevent the batterer from retaliating, intimidating, or exerting undue influence on the woman. In a family-based crime, the defendant often has both a strong sense of having been wronged and easier means to retaliate against the woman. In addition, long-standing emotional ties and socialization factors can influence a woman to withdraw as a prosecution witness and interfere with the criminal-justice goals of punishing the offender and deterring future crimes. By prohibiting contact and evicting the batterer from the home, civil protection orders can often address the unique circumstances of criminal assault between intimate partners and thus increase the likelihood that the criminal prosecution will proceed. Many women, however, do not want the batterers charged criminally or jailed; they simply want the violence to stop. Others are fearful of entering into an adversarial criminal procedure against their abusers. For these women, civil protection orders may offer the only form of legal protection.[33]

Obtaining a Protection Order

In some states, a woman may ask the court for an order without the aid of a lawyer. This is called appearing *pro se* (meaning "for yourself"). In other states, an attorney must be present, whether it's a private attorney, a pro bono (no fee) lawyer from Legal Aid or from a law-school clinic, or a government attorney.

Sometimes a woman can get an immediate, short-term, emergency protection order (an ex parte order) on the basis of her own testimony and without the abuser being present. Before an emergency order can be extended to cover a longer period, it is served on the abusive partner and followed by a full court hearing at which the batterer has an opportunity to appear. In some cases it may take months to find and serve the batterer, hold a court hearing, and issue a longer-term protection order. Longer-term protection orders can be in effect for periods ranging from six months to two or more years.[34]

Limitations of Protection Orders

Although they offer many potential benefits, protection orders have historically had several limitations. First of all, it may be difficult for a woman to obtain an order. All states have mechanisms for issuing emergency protection orders, and many have low filing fees, especially if the case involves a spouse or former spouse. In some situations, however, it may take several weeks for a woman to obtain a protection order, and the process sometimes involves prohibitively high lawyer fees and court costs. Furthermore, domestic violence frequently occurs during evenings or on weekends, when most courts are not in session. Not all states provide for issuing emergency protection orders after hours.[35]

The utility of protection orders can depend on whether they provide the requested relief in specific-enough detail. Unfortunately, few guidelines exist for judges to use in interpreting the statutes and determining which types of relief are authorized and appropriate for individual cases.

One of the greatest limitations in the effectiveness of civil protection orders is that they have not always been consistently enforced. Few courts have developed guidelines or procedures for arresting and punishing violators, resulting in a great deal of confusion over those issues.[36] One study examined 355 temporary and permanent protection orders issued in Denver and Boulder, Colorado. A year after they had obtained temporary orders, 60 percent of the women reported that their partners had violated the order at least once. Women who had obtained permanent orders were as likely as those with temporary ones to report violations. The women in the sample made a total of 290 separate calls to police to report order violations; however, only 59 arrests were made in those incidents. While women were very satisfied with the police response to the abusive incident that had led them to seek a court order, their ratings of the police response to order violations fell drastically. For various reasons—including a fear of retaliation, a belief that doing so would not help, and a lack of awareness that doing so was an option—very few women returned to court to seek a violation hearing.[37]

Similarly, research surveying the experiences of seventy-five battered women in Denton County, Texas, who had protective orders found that while respondents to the survey generally felt very positive about the process of applying for and receiving the order, nearly half were dissatisfied with the enforcement process. Comments indicated that some law-enforcement officers were reluctant to make arrests, seemed unfamiliar with the orders, or dismissed the women's fear and pleas for help.[38]

(Police officers' uncertainty about making arrests in cases involving violations of protective orders may stem from a long-standing, general legal prohibition against making a warrantless arrest for any misdemeanor unless it occurs in an officer's presence. In recent years laws have been passed in numerous states allowing warrantless arrests for misdemeanor domestic violence.)

According to the National Institute of Justice, 60 percent of protective orders are violated within one year.[39] Criminal sanctions are still the most common mechanism used to enforce protective orders. The violator may be charged with a felony, a misdemeanor, or contempt of court. In most states felony treatment is reserved for repeat violations or for violation of orders issued in cases involving aggravated offenses. In some states, a combination of these options may apply, depending on the original offense for which the order was given or the number of times the order was violated.[40] In any event, enforcement of protection orders continues to be procedurally complex for both police and courts.[41] Criminal sanctions for violating protective orders are crucial, but they can only be imposed if law enforcement and judges are aware of their existence. According to the Office for Victims of Crime, "A major enforcement issue arises when no system is in place for verifying both the existence of a valid protective order and its terms and conditions."[42]

Other limitations in the effectiveness of protective orders include inadequate funds for training and supervising clerks who assist battered women seeking an order; difficulty in serving protection orders, thereby placing women in danger during the days or (sometimes) weeks until service has been made; and ineffective or nonexistent monitoring to determine whether batterers are complying with the terms of the order.[43]

Positive Effects of Protection Orders

Despite their limitations, obtaining protection orders seems to have a positive impact on battered women's sense of personal control and self-confidence. The women surveyed in Denton County, Texas, generally indicated that the orders worked well to help them protect their children, gain a sense of control, reduce their fear, and begin the process of divorce. The majority of them felt empowered by the protection-order experience, describing positive changes in self-perception that were not necessarily tied to the practical effects of the orders, including acting on their own behalf, reducing their feelings of helplessness, using the legal system, and sending a strong message to the batterer that abuse would not be tolerated.[44]

Regardless of the capacity of protective orders to help women feel empowered, those that aren't enforced offer little protection and may actually increase women's danger by creating a false sense of security. Batterers routinely violate orders, especially if they believe there is no real risk of being arrested. For enforcement to work, courts need to monitor compliance, women must report violations, and law-enforcement officials, prosecutors, and judges should respond sternly to reported violations. Domestic violence requires a coordinated response from each part of the justice system, which in turn must act in collaboration with social-service and advocacy groups. Civil protection orders, as part of the solution, cannot be fully utilized or enforced by any one of the groups without cooperation from the others. For example, law-enforcement officers may be reluctant to file reports or make arrests if they do not believe that prosecutors will follow through or that judges will impose appropriate sanctions.[45] To encourage respect for the court's authority and to increase compliance with protection orders, courts should develop, publicize, and monitor a clear, formal policy regarding their violation, one that specifies procedures for both law-enforcement officers and judges.[46]

In 1992, Massachusetts became the first state with a computerized database of all domestic-violence protective orders issued within the state. The Massachusetts Registry of Civil Restraining Orders was designed to provide both law-enforcement agencies and the courts with prompt and accurate information to assist them in responding appropriately to each domestic-violence situation. Encouraged by the success of the Massachusetts registry, several states have established local or statewide registries and have improved their procedures for verifying protective orders.[47]

Attitudes about domestic violence must also be challenged. Several judges interviewed for a study conducted by the National Institute of Justice acknowledged that they first had to change their views of domestic abuse in order to respond to it effectively. Whereas they had originally thought of domestic violence as a relationship problem, they later came to see it as a complex issue involving persistent intimidation and physical injury. In effect, they now view domestic abuse as a violent crime that is as serious as any other form of assault and battery. In addition to altering their views about the nature and seriousness of domestic violence, the judges reported a change in their perception of the court's proper approach to handling requests for civil protection orders. They no longer view the hearings as an extension of divorce court, which calls for a negotiated settlement of a private problem; rather, they now regard such proceedings as the application of an immediate civil remedy to criminal behavior.[48]

The federal Violence Against Women Act actually strengthens protection orders and if actively enforced may help to alleviate battered women's struggles. Under the act's "full faith and credit" provision, a valid protection order—which includes those issued in all fifty states, Indian tribal lands, the District of Columbia, the U.S. Virgin Islands, Puerto Rico, American Samoa, the Northern Mariana Islands, and Guam—must be enforced everywhere throughout the U.S.[49] In additional to the full faith and credit law, federal domestic-violence laws exist whose violation may result in criminal prosecution and punishment. They make it illegal to cross state lines or tribal lands with the intent to commit domestic violence or engage in conduct that violates a protection order. They also make it illegal to commit interstate stalking or to possess a firearm or ammunition while subject to protection orders that qualify under federal law.[50] Walter Tenney, domestic-violence specialist with Police Social Services at the Lafourche Parish Sheriff's Office, in Thibodaux, Louisiana, encourages all law-enforcement officers to familiarize themselves with the federal laws. According to Tenney, "Many people don't realize there are federal laws out there that help domestic-violence victims. I'm always thinking about federal laws. In fact, I actively look for violations in the federal code. If I see something in a case report that is a federal offense, I follow up on it. Perpetrators need to be held accountable, and federal laws are in place to do that."

The National Stalker and Domestic Violence Reduction Act authorizes the inclusion of civil protection orders in all national Crime Information Center databases. However, only nineteen states have begun to enter their protection orders since the FBI began accepting them in the national registry in 1997. In the fall of 1998, the national registry contained only 97,136 entries, less than 5 percent of the two million orders thought to qualify. According to the Office of Victims of Crime, "Until a complete national registry is available, states' ability to give full faith and credit to each other's protective orders is compromised. Thus, to date, the goal of establishing a separate, comprehensive national protective order registry remains unrealized."[51]

Dealing with Stalking

Stalking is a criminal activity encompassing a series of actions that, if removed from the context of domestic violence, could constitute legal behavior. For example, sending someone flowers and waiting for her outside her place of work are activities that on their own are not criminal. Coupled with an intent to instill fear or injury, however, such actions may constitute a pattern of behavior that is illegal.[52] Each state has its own definition of stalking, and it is important for battered women to learn their state's definition. For a listing of state statutes regarding stalking, visit the website of the National Center for Victims of Crime, at www.ncvc.org, and click on "Stalking Resource Center." Or call your state coalition on domestic violence, which should be able to explain the state's stalking laws. Phone numbers for all state domestic-violence coalitions are listed in the Resources section at the back of this book.

Although every stalking case is different, a stalker's behavior typically grows more threatening and violent over time. The stalker's activity generally escalates from what initially may be bothersome and annoying but legal behavior to obsessive, dangerous, violent, and potentially fatal acts. This section examines stalking laws and offers suggestions for what women can do if they're being stalked.

Antistalking Legislation

The primary objective of antistalking legislation is to intervene in a suspected stalking case before the behavior results in physical harm. The two most immediate and typical forms of intervention are arrest and protection orders.[53] Stalking first became the object of widespread public concern in 1989 when Rebecca Shaeffer, a popular young actress, was shot to death by an obsessed fan who had stalked her for two years. Although it was the death of a celebrity that first attracted media attention, stalking victims are women from all walks of life, most of whom are trying to end a relationship with a man. Some battered-women's advocates believe that up to 80 percent of stalking cases occur in a domestic-violence context.

The initial publicity about Shaeffer's death resulted in a rush to pass anti-stalking legislation. California passed the first in 1990, and by 1992 twenty-seven states had enacted similar laws. Today, all fifty states and the District of Columbia have antistalking laws. States designate as stalking a variety of acts ranging from nonconsensual communication to harassment. To be convicted of stalking in most states, the stalker must display a criminal intent to cause fear in the woman. The conduct of the stalker must be "willful," "purposeful," "intentional," or "knowing." Many states do not require proof that the defendant intended to *cause* fear, just proof that he intended to commit the act that *resulted in* fear. If the woman is reasonably frightened by the stalker's conduct, the "intent" element of the crime has been met. Many states have both misdemeanor and felony classifications for stalking. Misdemeanor stalking offenses generally carry a jail sentence of up to one year, felony offenses three to five years. Most also include provisions to lengthen the sentence in certain cases, such as if the stalker brandished a weapon or violated a protective order. Some states allow incarceration for as long as ten years for repeat offenses.[54]

Drafting effective antistalking legislation that withstands constitutional challenges is a difficult task. In some cases, the distinction between lawful activity and stalking activity is hazy. Defendants seeking to challenge antistalking laws usually argue that the laws are so broad that they infringe upon constitutionally protected speech or activity. By January 1996, the U.S. Justice Department had identified fifty-three constitutional challenges to stalking statutes in nineteen states. For the most part, courts uphold the laws.[55] This was not the case in Texas, however, when in September 1996 the Texas Court of Criminal Appeals threw out the state's three-year-old antistalking law, declaring it unconstitutionally vague because it did not protect First Amendment rights.[56] Texas now has a more specific antistalking law. Many states have amended their initial antistalking laws, in part due to concerns about constitutional challenges and other issues that arose in implementing the laws. Many of the original statutes, for instance, did not specifically prohibit threats or assaults on non–family members, such as the woman's new intimate partner. In general, the revised laws include specific requirements regarding "intent" and "credible threat," broaden definitions, refine wording, stiffen penalties, and emphasize the suspect's pattern of activity.[57]

The effectiveness of stalking laws varies from state to state depending on the language of the law and the attitudes of those enforcing it. A detective's time and effort mean little if the city or county prosecutor won't take the case. A district attorney can't obtain a conviction if the law leaves gaping loopholes. For example, some states have overly specific stalking laws that allow stalkers to avoid certain items on the laundry list of prohibited actions while continuing to terrorize women. A shortcoming of nearly every stalking code is that penalties are not stiff enough. The National Institute of Justice has encouraged legislators to make aggravated first-time stalking a felony offense rather than a misdemeanor.[58] Most states have ignored the institute's recommendations. Even when a state's stalking laws are well written, the attitudes of local law enforcement can prevent a case from ever reaching trial.

Making the Judicial System Accountable

For the most part, the burden of proof falls on the battered woman to show that she has been victimized through the act of stalking. The National Coalition Against Domestic Violence has outlined the following suggestions to help make law-enforcement agencies and the judicial system accountable to battered women.[59]

1. The woman should keep detailed records of her reporting of the incident(s), including a copy of the police report, statements expresssing concern about the police or judicial system's treatment of her, what

services were offered to her, the results of any court proceedings related to the incident, and details of the proceedings.

2. If the woman is not satisfied with the enforcement of the law or feels that the incident is not receiving the attention to which it is entitled, she should write a letter to the chief of police, the state's attorney, the chief judge, the attorney general, and a crime-victims advocacy group. The letter should clearly identify the following: whether the woman's life is in immediate danger, the nature of the problem, and facts about how and why the incidents fit the pattern of stalking as defined by the state's stalking law. The letter should also include detailed information from police or court reports and descriptions of what action was not taken or enforced by law enforcement or the judicial system. It should clearly state a request for appropriate action from the persons to whom the letter is addressed.

3. Fax or hand deliver the letters immediately. Copies of the letters should also be sent to all addressees by certified mail with return receipt.

4. Copies of the letters, in addition to copies of the dated return receipts, should be given to a trusted individual.

5. Seek a lawyer's advice for possible legal action.

Keeping a Stalking-Incident Log

The Stalking Resource Center, part of the National Center for Victims of Crime, advises victims of stalking to maintain a log of stalking-related incidents and behavior. According to the center, "Recording this information will help to document the behavior for restraining order applications, divorce and child custody cases, or criminal prosecution. It can also help preserve your memory of individual incidents about which you might later testify."[60] The log should be used to document all stalking behavior, including harassing phone calls, letters, e-mail messages, acts of vandalism, and threats communicated through third parties. It should include the following information for every incident:

Date

Time

Description of incident

Location of incident

Witness name(s)

Witness address(es) and phone #(s)

When were police called (date and time)

Police report #

Officer name

Officer badge #

When reporting any incident to law enforcement, always write down the officer's name and badge number for your own records. Even if the officer does not make an arrest, you can ask him or her to create a written report. Request a copy of the report, and attach it to the log along with a photograph of the stalker and photocopies of restraining orders and other relevant documents. Keep the log in a safe place and tell only those whom you trust where it is. Because the information could be introduced as evidence in a court proceeding or inadvertently shared with the stalker, do not include any information that you do not want him to see.

Documenting stalking behavior can be difficult and draining. However, advocates at your local domestic-violence program can provide support, information, and assistance with safety planning.

If You Are Considering Taking Legal Action

When battered women try to utilize the justice system to protect themselves, they are often thrown into a strange and frightening world. When they lack access to sensitive and well-informed legal advocates, lawyers, clerks, police officers, or judges, they often give up in frustration and disgust. The following is offered as a guide for battered women who are considering taking legal action against their abusive partners.

First, I strongly encourage you to contact your local domestic-violence program to discuss your situation with a legal advocate. If your community does not have such a program, advocates at the National Domestic Violence Hotline can help you (see Resources for contact information for the NDVH).

Protection Orders

After you have obtained protection orders, carry them with you *at all times*. Leave a certified copy at the local police precincts where you live and work, where the batterer lives, and where your children go to school or day care. Make sure that wherever you are likely to encounter the batterer, the police in that area have been notified that an order is in effect.

When Children Are Involved

If at all possible, do not leave your children at home with the batterer, even if they are not in danger, because doing so may weaken your custody case later. Immediately upon leaving your abusive partner, seek temporary custody of your children as part of the legal proceedings in your civil protection order. Ask your lawyer to arrange to have the court order provide that you will not have to be alone with the abuser when he picks up the children for a visit. Arrange to exchange the children at a relative's home, a church, a public place, or another safe location. If possible, involve a third party in making arrangements and transferring the children for visits and, if necessary, in supervising visits.[61]

If your children are being abused, call your local shelter immediately to discuss the procedures for getting help from the child protection office.

Recommendations for Child Visitation and Custody Arrangements

In 1999 the National Council of Juvenile and Family Court Judges (NCJFCJ) issued the following recommendations to judges for effective interventions in domestic-violence and child-abuse cases. While these are only recommendations and there is no guarantee that the judge you appear before will follow them, they may serve as a helpful resource as you make decisions about what is best for you and your children.

In cases of domestic violence where children are involved—[62]

1. Interventions should be designed to create safety, enhance well-being, and provide stability for children and families.

2. Children should remain in the care of their nonoffending parent (or parents) whenever possible. Making adult survivors safe and stopping the abuser's violence are two important ways to do this.

3. Community leaders should design interventions and responses that are appropriate to the wide range of families experiencing domestic violence and child maltreatment.

4. Judges should have and use powers that specifically enable them to ensure the safety of child and adult survivors.

5. Where there is domestic violence in a child-protection case, judges should make orders that keep the child and nonabusive parent safe, keep them together whenever possible, hold the perpetrator accountable, identify the service needs of all family members, and create clear,

detailed visitation guidelines that focus upon safe exchanges and safe environments for visits.

6. The juvenile court should prioritize removing the abuser before removing a child from a battered mother, and should work with child-welfare and social-service agencies to ensure that separate service plans for the abuser and the survivor are developed.

Rehabilitative Maintenance

Also known as temporary alimony, rehabilitative maintenance involves the payment of financial support for a specified length of time after separation. You can request rehabilitative maintenance in your protection order and can use the payments to help finance education, job training, or counseling.[63]

Building Your Case

Whichever legal route you choose, the more evidence you have that shows you were subjected to abuse, the stronger your case. Police logs, medical records, photographs, and the testimony of those who heard a fight or saw your physical condition afterward can provide good courtroom evidence. Some battered women have kept journals describing the abuse, including dates and times, and have later found them to be very helpful. To establish the evidence, call the police as soon as possible during or after an incident, and ask your neighbors to call, too. Seek medical treatment and tell the doctor the full story. Ask your doctor to take photographs of your physical condition, or take them yourself. Torn or bloody clothing and anything used or threatened as a weapon should be kept with the photographs in a secure place until they are turned over to a lawyer or prosecutor.[64]

Legal Procedures to Be Wary of

Two measures to be suspicious of are forced mediation for domestic-violence complaints and mutual protection orders. When domestic violence is present, the power structure of a relationship is not in equilibrium, which can seriously impede the mediation process. Unfortunately, mediation is often suggested as a way to avoid "wasting" court time and resources. The National Council of Juvenile and Family Court Judges has recommended that no judge mandate mediation in cases in which family violence has occurred.[65]

Mutual protection orders, which have been discouraged by law in several states, include language stipulating that both persons refrain from harassing and assaulting the other. Typically issued by a judge with the consent of the parties, they may sound harmless until you are abused and call the police for help. The police may refuse to help, and they may even arrest you because they cannot tell who the likely aggressor is, given that both parties have been ordered not to harass the other. The mutual protection order keeps the police, the courts, and the batterer from acknowledging that a criminal act has occurred. Avoid any such restraints on your legal options.[66]

Legal Recourses for Lesbians and Gays

Although most domestic-violence programs are designed for nongay women, and police may be reluctant to intervene in a lesbian or gay relationship, there is hope. In numerous states, domestic-abuse laws cover unrelated adults of the same sex. In all states, criminal law prohibits physical assault and threats. Lesbians and gays interested in utilizing these laws can seek arrest and prosecution of abusive partners.[67]

Legal Recourses for Older Women

In addition to the domestic-violence statutes that are available to all battered women, older women can often get help in the form of information or direct assistance from the state or local office on aging or the state adult-protective service.

The most important goals of the justice system should be to assure both the short-term and long-term safety of battered women. Accordingly, it should support efforts to reduce their isolation, enhance their safety, and promote their self-esteem. Simultaneously, the justice system must understand why battered women find it so hard to realistically assess their situations and to regain control of their lives. Responsibility for the violence must be assigned firmly to the batterer, and the survivor's struggles must not be dismissed as masochistic enjoyment of the abuse.

...6

Living Underground

Getting started can be very hard for people who have trouble with beginnings. After all, where do beginnings begin?

— Dorothy Bryant

In the early morning hours of July 28, 1991, I arose after having spent an exhausting evening being harassed and threatened by my abusive boyfriend. I packed a small suitcase and waited for my mother, father, brother, and nephew, who were soon to arrive. Upon seeing me, my brother confided to my mother that he had seen a lot of scared people in his life, but never anyone as scared as I. He was right. I was about to begin running for my life and I was terrified.

Before me lay a journey that was to prove both difficult and demanding. But it was also the beginning of my new life. Several years later, while working at the Austin Center for Battered Women (now named SafePlace), I began receiving calls from women interested in learning how they could live underground. They had heard through the grapevine that I had done so and had survived. I found myself sharing my story with numerous women trying to survive in the same way I had.

Over the years I have had the pleasure of meeting a few other women who have lived underground as a means of escaping an abusve relationship. Our stories are surprisingly similar. We all made and carried out our plans without the benefit of talking with anyone else who had accomplished the feat. We gathered bits of information from various sources, including battered-women's centers, lawyers, and loved ones, and used what we learned, coupled with common sense, to protect ourselves. That we are alive today is testimony to the effectiveness of our efforts.

The suggestions in this chapter are based on my personal experiences and those of other women, as well as on information currently available to the public. Historically, battered-women's advocates and others have often maintained that guidance about how to live underground should not be published because it could help a batterer find his partner. However, we have reached a point where such logic no longer serves battered women. Books and other resources are available that outline step by step how to learn someone's address, telephone number, and social security number.[2] By contrast, little assistance is available to help a battered woman thwart her partner's efforts to find her. This chapter is intended to fill that void.

Making the Decision to Live Underground

First, it is important to understand exactly what living underground means. It does not involve an organized network of shelters, organizations, or agencies that have the resources to hide or support survivors trying to escape violent relationships. Nor is it similar to a witness protection program. When a survivor of domestic violence makes the decision to live underground it means she is taking the steps to hide and protect *herself.* Those of us who chose to live underground did so because we were terribly afraid that our batterers were going to either kill us or harm our children. Our decision represented the final effort to save ourselves and our families after many other strategies had failed. According to Holly, a survivor of an eighteen-year abusive marriage who escaped it and lived underground, "I wanted to begin living rather than surviving."

I strongly urge you to seriously consider your decision to go underground. There are no "official" strategies for living in hiding. Each situation is unique, and in reality it is truly difficult to just disappear. Living underground requires an incredible amount of planning and secrecy and can be very dangerous. You must be committed not only to ending your abusive relationship but also to severing ties with almost everything and everyone familiar to you. You will probably need to leave the community and perhaps even the state in which you reside. You are the best judge as to whether, how, and where you should go underground. But please also remember that with careful, thoughtful planning, it is possible to escape and to create the life you want. If you are in immediate danger I strongly encourage you to contact your local domestic-violence program prior to making any decisions about your life.

All of us who have lived underground had trustworthy people and monetary resources to help us escape. You will need to evaluate your own situation. In addition, if you currently have criminal charges pending against you, are on probation for a prior conviction, are the legal guardian for someone who needs you, or need specialized medical care, then living underground may not be the best choice for you. It could mean you would be breaking the law or hurting yourself or someone else. Still, if any of the above scenarios exist for you, or if you do not have trustworthy friends or relatives or adequate financial resources, do not despair. Contact your local battered-women's shelter and ask for help. The people at the shelter are a valuable resource. They will help you address your safety needs and explore your options.

The women I've talked to who successfully lived underground did so without children. Taking children underground is much harder than going by yourself, and there are serious legal ramifications if you do so. All states have criminal laws against parental kidnapping, also referred to as "custodial interference." The laws vary as to whether parental kidnapping is a felony or a misdemeanor. In some states it becomes a felony only if the child is transported across state lines. The legal situation for unwed parents, joint-custodial parents, and sole-custodial parents varies from state to state. In some states there is no criminal violation if the abduction occurs prior to the issuance of a custody order.[3]

In addition to criminal penalties, there may be other custody problems if you move a child from her or his "home state." Typically, you can obtain a custody order in the state where the child has lived for the last six months. If you move with your child to another state, the state you left has jurisdiction over your child for at least six months. This means the child's other parent may file for custody in the "home state" and you must go back to participate in that suit or risk having your custody rights taken away. If you can prove that an emergency exists and you must protect your child, you may be able to get a temporary custody order in the new state. Temporary custody orders are generally only good for ninety days, and the "home state" still has jurisdiction.

You should be aware that almost all states have missing-children's clearinghouses to assist in the location, recovery, and return of missing and parentally abducted children. In addition, almost every school in the country (public, private, and parochial) sends the name, birth date, and grade level of every student attending the school to the National Center for Missing and Exploited Children three or four times a year.[4]

The information presented here is not intended to serve as a substitute for sound legal advice. If you are considering living underground with children, I encourage you to talk to both a lawyer and a legal advocate at your local battered-women's center.

Changing Your Name or Social Security Number

One of the first questions I am asked when people discover that I have lived underground is whether I changed my name. Neither I nor any of the women who contributed to this chapter changed our names or social security numbers. If you are considering a change of name or social security number, the following information may be beneficial, though it does not substitute for sound legal advice. I urge you to discuss these options with a trustworthy lawyer.

Changing Your Name

State statutes for name changes usually require publication of the change in order to notify creditors and others who have a right to know. To prevent your batterer from discovering your name change, a motion can be made to the court for you to directly notify all your creditors and other interested parties (such as a probation office, the Immigration and Naturalization Service, or the military). This alleviates the need to publicly announce your name change. Another alternative is to request that you be allowed to publish a notice that simply says you are changing your name, without indicating your new name, and requests that anyone with questions contact your lawyer or the court. You must also ask the court to keep the records confidential or to sequester the file along with any papers containing the confidential information. This includes not listing anything on the docket sheet that would reveal your current address and new name. You will need to explain the danger you face and make clear that you can keep this information from your batterer only if it is completely inaccessible to everyone.

If you are divorced or were never married to your batterer but have children with him, the same procedure for changing your name is followed, but the process will be more difficult. If you change your children's names, the father must be notified so he has an opportunity to argue against it if he so desires. Ask the court not to list the children's new names on the batterer's copy of the papers.[5]

Changing Your Social Security Number

The Social Security Administration (SSA) has long had a process for an individual whose life (or whose child's life) is threatened by another person to obtain a new social security number (SSN). In the past, unfortunately, the procedure was not widely known about and was difficult to follow. In particular, the SSA required the individual to prove that the abuser had either misused the individual's SSN or could be expected to misuse it to locate the individual. This changed in 1998. The SSA now assumes that the misuse of someone's SSN is possible in all abuse or harassment cases.[6]

To obtain a new social security number, apply in person at any Social Security office. You will need to take the following information with you:[7]

1. Evidence of your age, identity, and U.S. citizenship or lawful alien status

2. If you have changed your name, evidence of your former and new names

3. If you are requesting SSNs for your children, evidence showing that you have custody

4. Evidence documenting the stalking, harassment, or abuse

The SSA will assist you in obtaining any additional corroborating evidence, if needed. The administration considers the best evidence of the stalking, harassment, or abuse to be evidence from third parties such as police, medical facilities, doctors, or courts (for example, protective orders or court findings). Other potential evidence could include letters from shelters, family members, friends, counselors, employers, or others with knowledge of the situation.[8]

The potential impact of changing your SSN includes a variety of challenges that you should be aware of prior to making the decision. The National Coalition Against Domestic Violence outlines several of them:[9]

◆ The inability to get a passport or other federal documentation due to the lack of a birth certificate under the new identity

◆ The loss of previous work history, resulting in the survivor having to accept positions for which she is overqualified or has no experience

◆ Difficulties or delays in receiving federal or state benefits such as welfare, disability, or social security insurance

◆ Difficulty trying to prove past abuse if past medical records and court papers are under a different name

The Social Security Administration does not destroy the original SSN when a new SSN is assigned. The original and new SSNs are cross-referenced in the administration's records to make sure the individual gets credit for all earnings The SSA maintains the confidentiality of all its records and will not disclose information about an individual's SSN without the individual's consent, unless it is required by law to do so. In addition, the administration has extra security measures in place for situations in which a new SSN has been assigned based on harassment, abuse, or life endangerment. To prevent third parties from inappropriately accessing the new SSN, the SSA requires that anyone requesting information about a record properly identify himself or herself as the subject of the record. An individual requesting information in person must present documentary evidence. An individual requesting information over the phone must provide six pieces of identifying information, which the SSA can verify from its records.

Governmental entities that, by law, can have access to your new SSN include law enforcement; government agencies administering entitlement, health, and welfare programs (such as Medicaid, Medicare, and veterans benefits); the Internal Revenue Service; the Immigration and Naturalization Service; the Selective Service; the Department of Health and Human Services; state motor-vehicle agencies; and congressional representatives.[10]

Protecting Your New SSN

Credit bureaus and other third parties have the ability to cross-reference SSNs in their databases. The Social Security Administration has no control over what such entities do with an individual's SSN. Use a great deal of caution when giving out your new number. According to the National Coalition Against Domestic Violence, "Employers and financial institutions will likely need the SSN for wage and tax reporting purposes. Other private businesses may need the SSN to do a credit check.... Sometimes, however, they simply want the SSN for general record keeping. It is not necessary to give a business the SSN just because they ask for it. However, a business may not provide the service or benefit if a[n] SSN is not provided."[11]

Consider the following when you are asked for your SSN:[12]

◆ Give your SSN only when it is absolutely necessary. If possible, use other types of identification.

◆ It is perfectly acceptable to ask questions regarding the request. For example:

– Why do you need my SSN?

– How will you use my SSN?

– Can it be kept confidential?

– What will happen if I don't give you my SSN?

– Will my SSN be shared with others?

Be aware that, by itself, changing your social security number will not fully protect you. If you otherwise fail to cover your tracks, there are a variety of ways in which the batterer can find you. That is the topic of the next section. Do not be discouraged, however; later in the chapter we will discuss ways to conceal your location.

How You Can Be Found

Anything that connects you to your past may give the batterer a way to find you, including your continued use of old credit cards, having your mail forwarded by the postal service, having school or medical records forwarded, telephone contact with persons from your past, or having money transferred from an old bank account to a new one. This section examines some of these scenarios.

Information such as your address and social security number can often be obtained through a written request for your driver's-license record, which lists traffic violations and accident reports. Your batterer can request copies of tickets you have received, which may reveal your current address and telephone number. However, states vary as to what information they will release to the public. Some states have a policy of informing an individual if his or her driver's-license record was pulled. You may want to check with your state's office of drivers' records about its policies. You can also be traced through motor-vehicle registrations. Again, states' motor-vehicle-records departments have varying policies regarding the information they make available to the public. Contact your state's department of transportation to learn its policy.

When completing a form to conduct any kind of business with a governmental agency, only fill in the minimum required information. Ask the agency if it allows personal information to remain confidential in certain situations. If possible, use a post office box, and do not provide your middle initial, home phone number, or social security number.[13]

If your batterer has your social security number, he can discover the address you have used for dealings with certain businesses and credit card companies. He can also trace you through a variety of public records, including voter-registration records.[14] Voter-registration information, which often lists the voter's latest home address and social security number, is available upon request and can be accessed with either your name or your social security number. Never reveal an unlisted telephone number when you register to vote. An unlisted telephone number that is part of your voter-registration information is considered available to anyone as part of a public record.

Numerous public records can be accessed at the county and parish levels. The following is a brief list of records that may disclose your location and that can be obtained with just your name:

◆ Amended judgment

◆ Assumption agreement

◆ Assignment of mortgage

◆ Breach of lease

◆ Change of name

◆ Divorce

◆ Guardianship

◆ Involuntary bankruptcy

◆ Judgment

◆ Lien

◆ Power of attorney

◆ Revocation of power of attorney

◆ Separation

◆ Trust agreement

◆ Voluntary bankruptcy

The address listed on records such as these should not be where you actually live. Instead, use a post office box, preferably one in a city where you do not reside (more about how to deal with mailing addresses appears later in the chapter).

Likewise, pet, hunting, and fishing licenses are considered public record. Copies of them can be obtained by using only your name and will probably list your telephone number and address. Remember, if you put an unlisted number on a license, it becomes public information because you chose to put it on a public record.

If you request that a U.S. post office forward your mail, your batterer can obtain your forwarding address for a small fee. His request may be made by mail or in person. According to the Privacy Rights Clearinghouse, "Residential addresses of post office box holders are generally confidential. However, the U.S. Postal Service will release a residential address to any government agency, or to persons serving court papers. The Post Office only requires verification from an attorney that a case is pending. This information can be easily counterfeited. Private companies, such as Mail Boxes Etc., are often more strict and will require that the person making the request have an original copy of a subpoena."[15]

Cyberspace Information

When I went into hiding, in 1991, the issue of Internet safety was not even a consideration. Today, advanced technology has made the Internet a valuable resource that you can use in planning and executing your escape. On the flip side, however, your batterer can use the same technology to locate you. He can do so through a variety of online resources, including the following:[16]

- ◆ Search engines such as www.yahoo.com and www.google.com
- ◆ Online phone directories and reverse phone directories such as www.switchboard.com and www.reversephonedirectory.com
- ◆ Court, parish, and government records
- ◆ Tax-appraisal records
- ◆ Voter-registration records
- ◆ Membership lists of civic organizations
- ◆ Membership lists of parent-teacher associations
- ◆ Information brokers such as www.knowx.com, www.docusearch.com, www.usafind2000.com, and www.peoplefind.com

Planning Your Escape

It takes extensive planning and careful attention to detail to prepare to escape an abusive relationship and live underground. The women who contributed to this chapter planned for lengths of time ranging from four months to three years. This section outlines the preparations you will need to make, including arranging for a contact person, finding a lawyer, and dealing with issues related to your finances, mail, moving, telephone, and house.

Under no circumstances should you tell your batterer you are leaving. If your relationship is so dangerous that you would consider living in hiding, revealing your plans will only jeopardize your safety. Your batterer must believe that life is proceeding as usual. Any suspicious questions or behavior on your part can lead to a fatal confrontation. According to one survivor, "You will never do anything more important than this escape. You can't afford to make a mistake."

Arranging for a Contact Person

If you decide that living underground is what you need to do, the next step is to line up a contact person. Carefully evaluate your existing relationships with family members and friends to determine whether there is someone you can trust who would be willing to help you. You must be able to trust this person with your life, and she or he must be willing to help you through the long haul. Depending on the danger you face, you may need to live underground for a long time, and your contact should be the only one who knows your whereabouts while you are underground. Choose no more than two people to serve as your contacts.

Talking to a Lawyer

If it is safe to do so, ask a close friend or relative for the name of a good lawyer. If you are not comfortable doing this, call your local battered-women's shelter and ask if they can refer you to one. Another option is to call several lawyers listed in the telephone book until you find one you feel you can trust. One survivor recommends interviewing three attorneys. "They usually offer a free thirty-minute introductory session," she says. "Get an hour and a half of free legal advice as soon as possible." A lawyer can provide information regarding stalking laws, civil protection orders, changes of name and social security number, divorce, wills, and other legal issues. If you are married, consider filing for divorce immediately. Before you depart, have the request for divorce written. Ask your lawyer to have it delivered a few days after you leave. A strong message must be sent that this move and the divorce are ending the relationship.

Your Finances

As soon as you decide to go into hiding, begin saving money. Living underground is expensive. Eating out, even fast food, can cost up to twenty dollars per person per day. You may need to borrow money from family or friends for your expenses. Several of us had to do this.

Do not leave a paper trail. Plan to take as much money in cash or traveler's checks as possible. Under no circumstances should you write checks or withdraw money from an old account or a joint account while you are underground. If you have a joint account, wait to withdraw money until immediately before your departure. If the account is in your name alone, you may want to close your savings account the day before you leave and wait until later to close your checking account. If your employer owes you money, have them send the checks to your contact person's post office box.

When planning your move, do not make long-distance calls from your house to your new area or to family or friends, and do not allow anyone else to, either. Likewise, do not use a long-distance calling card tied to your home phone number. You may also want to avoid using your cell phone for local or long-distance calls. In each of these cases, the calls are listed on your monthly phone bill. Your batterer can use the numbers listed on the bill to discover your location or to harass your friends or family members. Although my batterer and I were not married, he was able to obtain a copy of my last telephone bill. Fortunately, none of the people I had called knew where I was. Regrettably, however, he used the telephone numbers to harass some of them.

For long-distance calls, pay cash for a temporary calling card that you can buy at a convenience store or other retail outlet and that leaves no paper trail. For local calls use a land line only. If your contact person needs to reach you, ask her to call you either at work or at specific times when your abuser is not around.

Your Mail

There are two ways you can have your mail forwarded. Both options require that all your mail be routed through your contact person. Make arrangements with this person to open a post office box for your mail. Ideally, the mailbox should be in a location other than the city where your contact resides, and it *must* be in a location different from where you are hiding. Your contact will need to collect your mail and forward it to you. Once the box is established, call your creditors and have them forward your bills to it.

The other option is to have the post office forward your mail to your contact's post office box. Remember, however, that if you go through the postal service, your batterer can get a copy of your forwarding address. If you do this, be absolutely certain that your contact person is using a post office box for your mail. Under no circumstances should your contact person use a home address for your forwarded mail.

Your House

When I made the decision to live underground, I resigned myself to abandoning my house and defaulting on my loan. After discussing the situation with my lawyer and contact person, however, I instead arranged to give my contact power of attorney to take care of the property for me. Power of attorney allows your contact to conduct business transactions on your behalf. It is an excellent way to avoid detection and yet not lose property you own. I gave my contact power of attorney to conduct business related only to the house I owned, including allowing her to rent it out for me. The bottom line is that I did not default on my loan and ruin my credit.

If your contact does not want the responsibility of renting out your house, power of attorney will allow him or her to turn the property over to a real estate agent who can rent it out. If you find yourself in a similar situation, talk to your contact person and your lawyer about using this strategy to protect property you own.

The Move

When planning your move, check and double-check the dates and times when your batterer will be out of the house for at least eight hours. Days when he has a business trip or special meeting scheduled are safer than most. One survivor reports, "Even though I knew my ex-husband was meeting and entertaining out-of-town clients, he still came home four hours early. The movers and I missed him by forty-five minutes." Knowing that my batterer had a very unpredictable schedule, I made arrangements for family members to move my possessions into storage so I could leave immediately upon their arrival. This may have saved my life. My batterer showed up less than an hour after I left.

If you hire a moving company, do not give them your telephone number. Be very direct in telling them that this is a confidential move. Under no circumstances should the moving company call your house. Advise them that you will contact them to confirm the move.

If you use moving boxes, hide them in a safe place or store them at a trusted neighbor's. Breakables can be wrapped in clothing, towels, and sheets. Take as much out of your house as you can. It will be much easier to return something later than to get something you forgot. If in doubt, take it. Be sure to take anything that has sentimental value to you as this may be your last chance to save it.

Other Considerations

If you write down any of your plans, keep them where your batterer cannot find them, such as at work or with your contact person. Your contact person can help you check and double-check your plan.

In arranging for a place to live while in hiding, all of us initially stayed in locations distant from our contact person. Some women had found jobs before their moves; others had not. I lived with trusted relatives in various locations for three months before I found a job and was able to move my possessions to a semipermanent location. Whether you immediately move to a new location or live on the run, as I did, your contact person should be the only person who knows your whereabouts all the time.

Living in Hiding

Plan on living underground for at least a year. One formerly battered woman reported living underground for two and a half years. Once you have begun your new life, it is absolutely crucial that you continue to protect yourself and guard your location. This section discusses how you can keep yourself safe while you begin to rebuild your life.

Your Mail

During the entire time you live underground, continue to use your contact person's post office box for all credit card and other bills that may show up on a credit report. Throughout this time your contact will need to forward your mail to you. For local bills, such as gas and electricity bills, open a post office box in your community. Under no circumstances should you receive any mail at your home address.

If you write to friends or relatives, place the addressed letter in another envelope and mail it to your contact person to mail it for you. If you mail it from your location, it will be postmarked with the name of your city or one close to you.

Your Finances

If you open a new savings account, the bank will require your social security number for income tax purposes. Don't forget that your batterer can find your location if he has access to your social security number. Consider opening a joint savings account with your contact person at a financial institution near the city in which your contact person resides. Give the bank your social security number; however, the address on the account should be your contact's post office box. If you need money, your contact can make the withdrawal and forward it to you.

When opening a new checking account, consider opening a joint account with your contact person and using her or his social security number. That way your batterer will be unable to trace your social security number to the account.

Avoid using your middle initial on your checks or other documents. Middle initials are typically used to differentiate among people with common names. At this stage you want to blend in, not stand out.[17] The only personal information that should appear on the checks is your name (less the middle initial) and mailing address. Your mailing address should be the post office box that you have opened in your new community. If a cashier asks for a home phone number then give out your work or other number.

Contact the three credit bureaus, Experian, Equifax, and Trans Union, and alert them to your situation. Ask them to "flag" your record to avoid fraudulent access.[18]

Your Telephone

When setting up an account with your local telephone company, ask for an unlisted and unpublished phone number. Explain your situation and discuss how you can make certain that your name and number are never disclosed in any manner to anyone. Stress the danger you face and your safety needs. Avoid making calls to family or friends from your underground location, which would allow people with caller ID on their telephones to discover your location. If you must call someone from your underground location, ask the telephone company if you can order Caller ID Blocking (also referred to as Complete Blocking or Per Line Blocking), which will ensure that your phone number is not disclosed when you make calls from your home phone. One of the safest ways to contact anyone from your past is in writing in the manner previously discussed.

You may also want to avoid calling 800, 888, and 900 numbers from your home phone. Calls made to those numbers are recorded by a service called Automatic Number Identification and will also appear on the called party's bill at the end of the month. If you do call 800 numbers, consider using a pay phone.[19]

Last, consider having your name removed from all so-called reverse directories. Published by phone companies and direct marketers, these lists allow anyone who has just one piece of information, such as a phone number, to discover where you live. Contact your local telephone company for instructions on having your name removed from any such directories.[20]

If you choose to use a cellular phone, consider purchasing a disposable phone. These phones are preprogramed with a specific number of minutes and do not require you to establish an account with a local cell phone company.

Safety in Cyberspace

One of the best ways to determine how much personal information about you is on the World Wide Web is to conduct a search for yourself. On a regular basis, check several websites and search engines, including the free sites listed in the section above titled "Cyberspace Information." You may want to consider paying a few information brokers to search for you in order to see what is available to others.

Find websites for the courts of any county or parish that you've lived in; also check the websites of any federal courts that you have used in the past. In the communities where you currently or previously resided, conduct an online search for land records, tax-assessor records, marriage licenses, and voter-registration records. Look for information on the websites of any organizations that you are affiliated with, including work, school, volunteer organizations, professional associations, and sports teams. If you locate information about yourself on any of these sites, request that this information be removed immediately due to safety reasons.[21]

If you find information about yourself on the Internet that is correct and potentially dangerous, you have a couple of options. Some websites have a form or e-mail address you can use to request removal of your information; however, if the web page has been saved ("cached") or archived by another website or search engine then the information may be online forever. The faster the information is removed the better, but it is unlikely that published information can ever be completely deleted from the web. If it is a public record you may need to fill out an official petition, request, or letter. If the information about you is extremely dangerous you may want to consider speaking with a lawyer regarding your legal options.[22] Depending on the accuracy and sensitivity of the information, it actually may be better to leave some of it in a database. If you attempt to remove your information from certain sites, you may be, in essence, confirming that it is correct, thus increasing the likelihood that it will be sold to more information brokers.[23]

To prevent further information about you from making its way to the World Wide Web, consider the following:[24]

- If you use e-mail make sure it does not contain identifying information such as your name or address.

- If you post an opinion on a website or ask a technical support question, consider giving your name and the *wrong* city. If there is enough information about you on the web you may be able to hide that which is accurate amongst that which is inaccurate.

- Do not enter any personal information into an online directory.

Personal Safety

Your personal safety is actually at a higher risk when you are living in hiding. Few people will know where you are, so if something happens to you you may be unable to access help as easily. One way to address your safety needs is to have a solid personal-safety plan in place. Appendix II contains a sample safety plan for your use. If you need help developing a personal safety plan your local domestic-violence shelter can provide valuable assistance.

While living underground it is best to act as though your batterer knows where you are. Keep all doors and windows securely locked. Carefully look outside before leaving your house. Drive by your house or look at your front door before entering. Change the times when you come and go. Don't be predictable.

Consider renting a security apartment, which is a unit in a building with a front entrance and access from a hallway rather than from outside. Don't put your name on the tenant's list at the front of the apartment building.

Show a picture of your batterer to as many neighbors as possible. Explain your situation and let them know he is dangerous. Ask them to call the police if they see him anywhere near your house.

Plan an escape route out of your house or apartment in the event that he breaks in. If you live in a two-story structure, buy a "fire ladder" at a hardware store and keep it under your bed.

Ask your local police department if they will send someone out to assess your home security and to point out what needs attention. Many police departments provide this service for members of their community. Also ask to speak to someone in the assault unit, and explain your situation to that person. Ask how the assault unit handles domestic-violence calls. Get the person's name and make sure you give them yours. Give the department copies of any protection orders you have in force against your batterer, even if it was issued by a court in another state. This groundwork may help if your batterer is able to find you.

Other Considerations

As you begin opening new accounts and establishing residence in your new community, be prepared to explain your situation to neighbors, your employer, and others who need to know. Although it was embarrassing to reveal my situation to strangers, I found most people receptive and concerned for my safety.

Make sure your new employer understands why you are living underground, and ask that no information be given to anyone about you, regardless of the circumstances. Show your batterer's picture to your employer, and ask that the police be called if he appears at your place of employment.

Never forget how easy it is for someone to get your address, telephone number, and social security number. Use your post office box as little as possible. Always try to route your mail through your contact's post office box. Never give out your home address or telephone number.

It may help to try to think like your batterer to anticipate what he may do to find you. This will allow you to stay at least one step ahead of him.

After a year, consider finding a permanent place to live. Even if your batterer has not contacted you at your underground address, assume he has discovered your location. One more move will get you even farther from your batterer and will be well worth the work. And this time you will be moving toward something rather than running away from someone.

The Joys and Challenges of Living Underground

Women I've talked to who went underground initially experienced strong feelings of loneliness and isolation. Being unable to entertain friends or family, giving up friendships, the fear of being located by the batterer, living alone in a new city—all of these circumstances proved very challenging to each of us. I was particularly angered by the fact that I was having to live my life as if I had done something wrong. I also became very tired of explaining my abusive relationship to strangers.

For each of us, however, something miraculous began to happen after a few months. We became aware of a newfound serenity in our lives. According to one survivor, "At one point I actually realized that my batterer really wasn't going to call me on the phone or show up on my doorstep." Each of us used that time to begin healing from the years of abuse we had suffered. As we began to reclaim our lives, we experienced what I refer to as a rebirth. Not many people have this opportunity. Today, our lives are very different from those we once knew. Best of all, we now live with peace in our hearts and in our lives.

...7

The Oppression That Binds: Barriers to Living Violence Free

The oppression of women knows no ethnic nor racial boundaries, true, but that does not mean it is identical within those differences.

— *Audre Lorde*[1]

Over the past thirty years, the battered-women's movement in the United States has made enormous strides in establishing shelters and other domestic-violence programs. In addition, a large number of social-service agencies now address the problem of domestic violence. To effectively advocate for all battered women, however, domestic-violence programs and other agencies must provide services that are tailored to women's varying cultural and group identities and that operate from an understanding of women's diverse backgrounds. Insensitivity to such differences alienates battered women and fails to meet some of their specific needs.

All women face barriers when trying to escape battering relationships. The barriers can be grouped into four basic categories:[2]

1. **Personal barriers** such as shame, fear, lack of personal resources, and lack of emotional support

2. **Relationship barriers** such as being denied access to money, transportation, or jobs, as well as the physical abuse itself

3. **Institutional barriers** such as immigration policies, cultural insensitivity, a lack of services, discrimination, sexism, and other forms of oppression

4. **Cultural barriers** such as language differences, beliefs about marriage and the family, gender roles, and religious beliefs

Combined, these barriers create formidable obstacles that women must address and overcome in order to live their lives violence free.

Two factors contribute to the continuation of violent relationships. The first is the degree to which women are isolated from key support systems. Our society continues not only to marginalize but also to make invisible women of color, older women, lesbians, women with disabilities, and other communities of women. When societal oppression is coupled with women's isolation from friends and family, their risk of being abused greatly increases. Second, society's ongoing reluctance to provide access for women to such resources as education, skills, and jobs can foster women's dependency on their partners. Together, social isolation and dependency help keep women stuck in violent relationships that may eventually cost them their lives.

This chapter briefly summarizes the major barriers women of color and other communities of women must address when confronting abusive relationships. In each case notice how the combination of personal, relationship, institutional, and cultural barriers increases women's isolation and dependency.

Women of Color

Women of color make widely divergent choices in coping, functioning, and empowering themselves. The term "women of color" itself encompasses many heteregeneous populations that are highly diverse with regard to ethnic and racial background, religious beliefs, cultural values, economic status, family structure, occupation, and lifestyle. In addition, differences exist even among women from the same ethnic and racial groups.[3] Social scientists have come up with terms to distinguish the various ways in which women of color relate to their outer worlds. An *acculturated* woman of color is one who has chosen to assimilate into white society and has rejected the general attitudes, behaviors, customs, and rituals of her culture of origin. A *bicultural* woman of color has pride in her racial and cultural identity and yet is comfortable operating in the white world. A *culturally immersed* woman of color has openly rejected white values, embracing the identity and traditions of her cultural group. Finally, a woman of color with a *traditional* interpersonal style usually has limited contact outside her community of color, may be older or newly immigrated, and speaks only the language of her traditional culture. Depending on a woman's place on the acculturation continuum, the challenges to helping her address her abuse vary.

While there is great diversity among women of color, one common barrier they all face is the racism that exists in our society. Racism, at both the individual and institutional levels, affects the quality of services and support battered women of color receive. In fact, the level of racism present in a particular community will help determine whether any services are made available to battered women of color. The next several sections examine the issues faced by specific racial and ethnic groups of women survivors of domestic violence.

African American Women

In addition to sexist and racist attitudes and practices, battered African American women face a number of other barriers they must address to be able to live violence free.

Internalized Societal Images

The image of African American women as long-suffering victims can create misunderstanding about the abuse in their lives. According to Evelyn White, author of *Chain Chain Change: For Black Women Dealing with Physical and Emotional Abuse,* "The images and expectations of black women are actually both super and sub-human.... This conflict has created many myths and stereotypes that cause confusion about our own identity and make us targets for abuse." Negative and conflicting images may make black women wonder who they really are and what their partners and society expect from them.[4]

The Family

Many African Americans have mothers, fathers, sisters, and brothers who are not blood relatives yet are considered as much a part of the family as biological kin. Socialization in the black family is an important part of the identity of the abused woman. She may have intense loyalty to her extended family and strong views about the importance of privacy and respect within the family unit. Although the support network of the extended family enriches the black community, it can also be a problem for women who approach loved ones about the violence in their lives: Family and friends may have divided loyalties and may feel they are being pressured to take sides.[5]

Religious Beliefs

123

The
Oppression
That Binds:
Barriers to
Living
Violence
Free

African American women, who typically comprise about 70 percent of black congregations, often have strong religious beliefs dating back to early childhood. Religious beliefs or fear of rejection from the church may keep women in abusive relationships.[6]

Conflicting Loyalties

According to White, because African American women and men live in the same racist society, the women cannot help but be sympathetic to what the men suffer. "We know that the black family has been damaged by slavery, lynchings and systematized social, economic and educational discrimination. Though we have surely been divided as black men and women, our mutual suffering has prevented us from completely turning our backs on each other."[7] Many black women in violent relationships fear that if they report an abusive partner, he will be treated more harshly by law-enforcement officials because he is a man of color, a double bind that may prevent the women from reaching for help.[8]

Shelter Services

Some African American women may be reluctant to leave a familiar network of neighbors, family, and friends to live in a shelter with a group of people they don't know. In addition, many shelters are predominantly staffed by persons that black women have learned to mistrust. And if the shelter is located in a white neighborhood, black women may feel more vulnerable, visible, and exposed.

Regrettably, shelters are not immune to the racism that exists in society, and some can be run in ways that are insensitive to the needs or perspectives of black women.[9] According to Pat Clark, a former advocate with SafePlace, in Austin, Texas, "One of the hardest things for black women to deal with is to leave their homes and live in a shelter that is almost completely staffed by white women. It's definitely a trust issue. Our community believes that you don't put your trust in the white system. To do so implies you're turning against your own race."

Latinas

Latina and *Hispanic* are general terms used to refer to Spanish-speaking women from Mexico, Puerto Rico, the Dominican Republic, Cuba, Guatemala, Nicaragua, El Salvador, the rest of Central America, and all the countries of South America. The terms also encompass individuals who were born in the United States and call themselves Mexican Americans, Chicanas, Cuban Americans, or Nuyoricans (people of Puerto Rican descent who were born in New York). All have different histories and cultural backgrounds.[10]

Latinas are an extremely heterogeneous group not only with respect to country of origin, but also with respect to race, education, income, age, religion, marital status, number of years in the United States, language, acculturation, and cultural values. All these factors play a part in understanding the dilemmas of Latinas in abusive relationships.

Cultural Expectations

The Latino culture is a patriarchy with a long-established social system. Women are often relegated to the roles of wife and mother. It is not socially acceptable to be divorced, to marry several times, or to remain single and have children out of wedlock. For these reasons it may take some time for battered women to consider leaving their partners. According to Myrna M. Zambrano, author of *Mejor Sola Que Mal Acompañada: For the Latina in an Abusive Relationship,* "Latinas have little representation in political and economic arenas. We are not only denied equality by American society, but by our own Raza, by our own men. It is time that we demand and take the place we deserve, a seat beside them, with full voice and vote. Until we are recognized as true partners, we will not command the respect that is necessary to make rape and physical abuse a thing of the past."[11]

The Family

Latinas usually look toward the family as the center of culture. Being a woman in Latino culture implies responsibility to a husband or other significant males such as fathers and brothers. Family relationships are dictated by a definite authority structure based on age, gender, and role. In addition, the authority of the family itself is respected. Individual needs often defer to family unity and strength. For battered women this often means tolerating abuse for the sake of family pride and preservation. Problems are usually kept in the home. Counseling may be received from a priest or other respected authority, but help from other outside agencies is rarely sought.[12]

Lucy Muñoz, a former advocate with SafePlace, explains that the people most important to battered Latinas—that is, their families—are also those least likely to support them if they leave the violent relationship. According to Muñoz, "When we marry we are supposed to stay married—no matter what happens. If we try to leave abusive marriages our families do not support us. In fact, they will often try to make us return."

Guarded Trust

125

The
Oppression
That Binds:
Barriers to
Living
Violence
Free

Latinas are not accustomed to revealing their feelings to outsiders and may find it difficult to express themselves to strangers. If battered Latinas do seek help outside of their family, they may be reluctant to discuss the abuse. Details about their personal lives are reserved for those whom they trust.

Financial Barriers

Latinas are more concentrated in low-paying, semiskilled occupations than is the overall workforce. The money battered women need to be able to move or to obtain a lawyer is not always available. For Latinas who drop out of school, poor education and lack of skills make it difficult to get better-paying jobs. Additionally, because of racial discrimination, opportunities for job advancement are not always comparable to those afforded white women.[13]

Religious Beliefs

Latinas often accept their situations with resignation, believing their family life is the way God wants them to live. They may feel that the power to change dosen't lie in their hands or may prefer to accept a bad situation rather than attempt to correct it, because doing so may be seen as arrogance before God.

In addition, a lack of information about birth control and limited access to it, combined with other aspects of Catholic doctrine, often result in Latinas having larger families, which can make it difficult to move or to find affordable child care.

Language Barriers

Being abused is embarrassing to discuss, and talking about it is even more difficult when language and cultural barriers exist. Even if women speak English they may be uncomfortable using it to express their feelings.

Asian Women

The term "Asian" is typically used in the United States to identify people from China, Japan, Korea, and other east Asian Countries. "Asian" can also be used to describe people from Vietnam, Laos, Cambodia, Tibet, and the Philippines, and the term is sometimes used in a broader context to refer to people from the entire Asian continent.

Many battered Asian women have a difficult legacy to bear. The abusive treatment they receive grows out of deeply rooted cultural and social values from both their country of origin and the United States. Although traditional Asian cultures can be a source of strength, they also contribute to a tolerance of domestic violence. The unequal status of women and the right of men to beat them has been asserted for centuries in many parts of Asia.[14]

The Family

Mutual obligation and self-reliance within the extended family structure are valued in many traditional Asian cultures. If there is a conflict between an individual's needs and the family's goals, the family's goals are given priority. Maintaining family harmony often comes at the expense of women, particularly wives and daughters-in-law. Interdependence of family members and the importance of mutual help and support are deeply ingrained values. Reporting the batterer's abuse to outsiders can make an Asian woman feel disloyal. Her socialization may cause her to believe that she has brought shame to her family, either because she thinks she is in some way responsible for the abuse or because she reported it.

Support Systems

Asian families who resettle in the United States frequently leave behind aunts, uncles, grandparents, and cousins. This extended family, which makes up the traditional Asian support system, acts as a mechanism for controlling domestic violence. With the loss of the extended family, the support and control it provides are also lost.

Children

Some Asian women fear that moving away from an abusive husband will mean losing or, at the least, stigmatizing their children. Their community often reinforces the belief that women must not leave their family and community.[15]

Family Privacy

Another barrier for some Asian women who need help is a traditional attitude toward "private" issues. Most battered women feel ashamed about their abuse, but the feelings may be even more pronounced for some Asian women. It is considered inappropriate to discuss family matters outside the family since to do so is thought to bring shame to the family.

Self-Control

Emotional control is considered a mature trait in many Asian cultures. Open displays of pain or anger are thought to be immature and unworthy of civilized adults, particularly women. For this reason, some women seldom express their true feelings and emotions, except among very close relatives or friends.

Self-Blame

127

The
Oppression
That Binds:
Barriers to
Living
Violence
Free

Assuming responsibility for problems is considered virtuous and is particularly valued in women. While a tendency toward self-blame is also common among many American women, the Asian woman's self-blame should be considered in the context of her cultural socialization rather than as a manifestation of low self-esteem.

Resignation

Perseverance and the acceptance of suffering are highly valued virtues among traditional Asian cultures. What appear to be passivity and apathy in a battered Asian woman are often culturally based responses to adversity.

Respect for Authority

Many women from traditional Asian cultures are socialized not to question the commands or decisions of persons in authority and not to express their own wishes or opinions. The Western values of direct self-expression and self-determination are unfamiliar concepts. A battered Asian woman's respect for authority may prevent her from asking for help or from questioning racist treatment by a service provider.

Lack of Information

Some battered Asian women don't seek help about their violent relationships because they don't know that domestic violence is wrong. Many do not even realize that battering is a crime and punishable by law or that they have legal rights and can press charges.[16]

South Asian Women

South Asia includes the geographical area of the entire Indian subcontinent: India, Pakistan, Sri Lanka, Nepal, Bhutan, and Bangladesh. Although there are strong similarities among the social and cultural structures of the various South Asian nations, the region is not monolithic.[17] India itself has at least sixteen official languages and hundreds of dialects nestled within each language. Although Hinduism is the most popular religion in India, a variety of other major religions are observed there as well, including Christianity, Islam, Jainism, Buddhism, Sikhism, Sufism, Zoroastrianism, and Judaism.[18]

   Power relations between men and women are intertwined with other structures of social hierarchy such as class and caste. In addition, the relationship between two women of the same household is affected by their relations to the men in the household and by the men's relationships to each other. Familial relations are also characterized by a hierarchy based on age.[19]

The Family

Group and family identity are emphasized in most South Asian cultures, and family ties are further complicated by the presence of extended family. Since group identity is given priority, battered women may hesitate to make decisions to end abusive relationships before they consider the feelings of other family members. Women may consider not only their parents' wishes but also those of their grandparents and other significant relatives.

Arranged marriage is still a norm in these cultures. The relationship between a man and a woman may initially begin with a relationship between their families. Separation, divorce, and remarriage may not be considered options for fear of shaming and dishonoring the family. In addition, there may be pressure from the family on the woman to reconcile and continue living with the batterer.[20]

Family Privacy

Within traditional South Asian families, strict rules about privacy, intended to maintain family honor, dictate that family matters are not shared with outside individuals. Neighbors and friends, however, may gain the status of relatives by establishing a close emotional kinship with a family.[21]

Isolation

According to Kalpana Sutaria, cofounder of Saheli, a grassroots advocacy program for Asian battered women in Austin, Texas, a fear of being isolated from the family is one of the greatest barriers for South Asian women to overcome. She says, "Even more than a lack of resources, Asian Indian women's fear of loneliness and isolation keeps them tied to abusive relationships. I continue to hear, over and over again, 'Who are going to be my friends? Am I going to be all alone?' " The absence of a protective support system of family, friends, and neighbors increases South Asian women's social isolation and their dependency on the abusive relationship. In addition, many are forbidden by their abusive husbands to contact friends and family or to develop friendships. They may be denied access to postage, money, telephones, and transportation.[22]

Shelter Services

For South Asian women who already feel emotionally and culturally isolated, the unfamiliar nature of shelters may heighten their sense of alienation. Additional complications may arise from their unwillingness to trust shelter staff, police, and other support personnel. Services considered standard for other groups of women may be both unfamiliar and uncomfortable for South Asian women. The food provided at the shelter may create problems, especially if the women are vegetarian. Most South Asian women are uncomfortable about undressing in front of anyone. The informal habits women often display in exclusively female surroundings can make some South Asian women feel very ill at ease.[23]

129

The
Oppression
That Binds:
Barriers to
Living
Violence
Free

Native American Women

As with other communities of women of color, there is tremendous diversity within the Native American culture, which encompasses many different languages, traditions, and spiritual beliefs. The United States recognizes 365 Native American tribes with two hundred distinct languages. Further complicating the issue of heterogeneity is the ongoing migration between reservations and urban areas.[24] A battered Native American woman may have a different perspective on her situation based on whether she grew up in an urban setting or on a reservation.

The Historical Context of Domestic Violence among Native Americans

Varying rates and patterns of abuse exist among different tribes. It is important to note, however, that domestic violence is a relatively new phenomenon in the Native American culture. Abuse of both Native American women and children by Native American men can be traced to the introduction of alcohol, Christianity, and the European hierarchical family structure. Women from the Sacred Shawl Women's Society, on the Pine Ridge reservation, in South Dakota, report that while domestic violence existed in prereservation society, it was both rare and severely reprobated.[25] Many traditional Native American histories indicate that when domestic violence did occur, the community responded. The batterer would be banished or ostracized, or retaliation was left to the male relatives of the victim.[26] One possible reason why abuse rarely happened in prereservation society can be traced to tribal legends that asserted the sacredness and importance of women in the spiritual, economic, and political realms.[27] Traditional methods of addressing domestic violence were eliminated or limited with the advent of a Western European criminal-justice process.

Societal Oppression

Several factors have accompanied the increase in domestic violence in Native American communities, including the removal of Native Americans from their ancestral lands, suppression of religious and cultural practices, forced removal of children into foster homes and boarding schools, the disruption of traditional living patterns compounded by the poverty of reservation life, and a 90 percent reduction in the Native American population from the advent of European contact to the establishment of reservations. These dramatic changes in tribes' social, spiritual, and economic structure have drastically undermined their traditional ways of life.[28]

The Family

The Native American family is an extended one that includes aunts, uncles, grandparents, cousins, and adopted relatives. The nuclear family of mother, father, and children is considered a household within the family.[29] Native American families are very close. If domestic violence occurs, the family is expected to take care of the problem. If a Native American woman goes outside the family for help, she may be ostracized by her family and the batterer's family.

The Reservation

Some Native American women have resided on the same reservation for their entire lives. If a battered woman leaves her reservation to go to a shelter, she is forced to leave both familiar surroundings and her support system. Furthermore, many women residing on reservations live in such poverty that they do not have access to telephones, transportation, or child care. In many cases remote areas of the reservations actually lack either telephone lines or a transportation system. Some battered Native American women do not speak English. All of these factors severely impact women's ability to seek help.[30]

Confidentiality

Confidentiality is a major issue in small communities. Sanctions within tribal or clan groups or other subgroups are often more severe for an informant than for an abuser. Although the community may view the behavior of the batterer as undesirable, the decision to contact the outside legal system or to reveal details of intimate family life is often seen as disloyal. In addition, group dynamics and relationships may cause battered women themselves to regard outside intervention as unwelcome.[31]

Spirituality

131

The
Oppression
That Binds:
Barriers to
Living
Violence
Free

Native American spirituality can be a source of profound support, comfort, and healing for many battered women. According to Karen Artichoker, coauthor of *Domestic Violence Is Not Lakota/Dakota Tradition,* it can also serve to keep them in abusive relationships. A belief in the interconnectedness of all things is frequently used by batterers and other family members to encourage women to remain in violent relationships.

Trust

Many Native American women have a high level of mistrust for white agencies and service providers. This attitude, while it is understandable given the historically oppressive way in which white society has treated Native Americans, may keep a battered woman from reaching out for help. In many cases, when battered Native American women do reach out, they are confronted with helpers who are insensitive to their unique lifeways and culture.

The remainder of the chapter looks at the unique barriers faced by other groups of battered women.

Immigrant Women

Women and children comprise approximately two-thirds of all legal immigrants in the United States. Battered immigrant women often suffer from several forms of discrimination because of their gender, race, and immigration status.[32] A 2002 study of women murdered in New York City reports that 51 percent of those who were foreign born were killed by their domestic partners, versus only 45 percent of those who were born in the U.S.[33] Domestic violence is thought to be more prevalent among immigrant women than among U.S. citizens.[34] Some researchers believe that higher domestic-violence rates among immigrant women result from two main factors: the fact that they may have come from cultures that accept domestic violence and the fact that they have less access to legal and social services than U.S. citizens. In addition, immigrant perpetrators (and survivors) may believe that the penalties (and protections) of the U.S. legal system do not apply to them.[35]

Laws Affecting Battered Immigrant Women

Despite the expanding awareness of the devastating consequences of domestic violence, battered immigrant women remain marginalized and out of reach of helpful services. U.S. immigration laws and policies have never reflected the needs of women. In the past, women who entered this country were forced to due so under the doctrine of coverture, which states that the husband is the head of the household and that the wife's nationality and residence follows his. This put immigrant women at risk from domestic violence. In addition, since the mid 1980s a climate of racism and intolerance against immigrants has intensified, resulting in their being portrayed as threats to the economic, cultural, and political life in the United States and blamed for increased unemployment and crime. As a result, Congress codified a number of measures that severely restricted immigration into the country, including the 1986 Immigration Marriage Fraud Act (IMFA).[36] The IMFA created additional obstacles for immigrant women seeking lawful permanent residence in the United States on the basis of their marriage to either a U.S. citizen or a lawful permanent resident.

The Violence Against Women Act (VAWA) of 1994 gave battered immigrant women the option of petitioning on behalf of themselves and their undocumented children to become legal permanent residents without having to rely on abusive spouses, and the Violence Against Women Act of 2000 built on these provisions.[37] In particular, VAWA 2000 removed the U.S. residency requirement and the "extreme hardship" requirement for immigrant women to receive VAWA protections; it allows battered immigrant women to obtain lawful permanent residence without leaving the country; it restored access to VAWA protections for immigrants regardless of how they entered the country; and it created a new type of visa, the U-visa, that allows some victims of serious crimes to attain lawful permanent residence. Immigrant women who are survivors of domestic violence, sexual assault, stalking, or trafficking are eligible for the U-visa.[38]

Although the harsh impact of the IMFA has been somewhat softened by amendments to the act in 1990 and 1991, and despite the Violence Against Women Act, battered undocumented women remain largely unable to access the help, services, and legal resources available to them.[39]

Accessing Legal Services

Immigrant women may be unfamiliar with how to access the legal system for any type of assistance. They may not realize that domestic violence is against the law, that they have legal options, or that there are agencies and community resources available to support them.

Even if battered immigrant women do manage to get legal help, family-law practitioners who are competent to deal with domestic-violence issues are often untrained in immigration law. Likewise, immigration lawyers who are able to assist with visa matters and applications for lawful permanent residence may lack knowledge of the domestic-violence issues their clients face. As a result, amendments to immigration statutes that specifically apply to battered women may remain unutilized because of the lack of integration and communication between family-law attorneys and immigration attorneys.

133

The
Oppression
That Binds:
Barriers to
Living
Violence
Free

Obtaining Permanent Residence

Battered immigrant women are often faced with the threat of deportation not only from the Immigration and Naturalization Service (INS) but also from their spouses. This is a particularly effective way for batterers to maintain power and control over their wives. If women try to escape abusive relationships, they may risk their ability to obtain lawful permanent residence, which may rely solely on their husbands' cooperation with the INS. They may face deportation to their country of origin. For women who have fled persecution in their home country, deportation could mean torture, jail, or death. For others it could mean a return to a life of extreme poverty, disease, and little or no opportunity.

Some battered immigrant women seek asylum in the U.S. to escape domestic violence in their home countries. Rodi Adali Alvarado experienced years of abuse in Guatemala at the hands of her husband. Her repeated requests for help were ignored by the Guatemalan police and courts. In 1995 she came to the United States specifically to escape the violence. She was granted asylum in 1996. Since then, however, immigration courts have made conflicting rulings that have left her case unresolved. Former Attorney General Janet Reno acted on Alvarado's behalf; later, Attorney General John Ashcroft took the case under advisement. After delaying his decision for a number of years, he announced in January 2005 that he would leave office without deciding the case. A Department of Homeland Security spokesperson told the Associated Press that it would not deport Alvarado. However, only a favorable decision on asylum will give her the legal status she requires in order to bring her children to the United States. In the interim, Alvarado—and numerous other women in similar situations—are left in limbo.[40]

Perhaps one of the worst threats is that women may have to leave their U.S.-born children. Once deported, women can be excluded from the United States for five years. Deportation is something most battered immigrant women are not willing to risk. If they are unaware that they may have other legal avenues through which to obtain lawful permanent residence, most will be reluctant to leave a violent relationship.[41]

Community Resources

In a 1992 study conducted by the Texas Department of Human Services and the Texas Council on Family Violence, shelters in Texas reported that the community resources most accessible to battered immigrant women were counseling, immigration information, and education. The community resources most difficult for immigrant survivors to utilize were employment and housing.[42] Most family-violence shelters do not provide battered immigrant women with services different from those available to women who are United States citizens. Shelters may want to help but often have limited bilingual staff and a limited understanding of the unique needs of immigrant women and how to help them.

Language Barriers

Often, immigrant survivors of domestic abuse lack sufficient English-language skills to enable them to seek help or use resources. Women who cannot speak English cannot communicate with their neighbors, the police, lawyers, doctors, or advocates. They may even become alienated from their children or working husbands who gain fluency in English, or may become more dependent on family members to interpret the culture for them.[43]

Cultural and Social Barriers

Cultural and social isolation prevents many battered immigrant women from readily seeking help. We must consider the experiences of immigrant women in light of both their current social interactions in the United States and those in their countries of origin. Cultural norms concerning a woman's place, family, marriage, sex roles, and divorce may contribute to an environment in which an immigrant woman feels isolated and powerless to escape the violence.

Financial Barriers

Immigrant women are often economically dependent on their partners to a greater extent than most women who are citizens or lawful permanent residents. Economic dependence is intensified due to the impact of immigration laws concerning employer sanctions and hiring practices as well as those that may make immigrant women ineligible for most forms of public assistance and income entitlement programs.[44]

Health Services

Many immigrant survivors do not know how to gain access to health services. Even when they are able to access such services, language barriers can make it difficult to discuss their health problems. Women may be reluctant to discuss certain aspects of their anatomy with male medical personnel, and they may not want their children to interpret for them.[45]

135

The
Oppression
That Binds:
Barriers to
Living
Violence
Free

Lesbians and Gays

Although the battered-women's movement has been advocating for survivors of domestic violence and their children for many years, little has been done to address the problem in the lesbian and gay community—a sad irony considering that lesbians helped to start many of the domestic-violence programs in the country. Violence in lesbian relationships occurs at about the same frequency as violence in nongay relationships.[46] Battered lesbians and gays suffer the same types of physical, emotional, and sexual abuse as their nongay counterparts. Gin, a survivor of same-sex partner violence, describes a particularly frightening incident she endured: "She caught me off guard when she burst through the door and punched me in the stomach. She proceeded to punch me several more times, then she grabbed me by the neck and pushed me against the wall yelling, 'If you ever leave me I'll kill you and then kill myself.'"

Homophobia

Although battering among lesbians and gays bears definite similarities to nongay battering, lesbians and gays must confront some distinct barriers. Suzanne Pharr, writing in *Naming the Violence: Speaking Out about Lesbian Battering*, explains, "There is an important difference between the battered lesbian and the battered non-lesbian: the battered non-lesbian experiences violence within the context of a misogynist world; the lesbian experiences violence within the context of a world that is not only woman-hating, but is also homophobic. And that is a great difference."[47] Pharr defines homophobia as the irrational fear and hatred of people who love and sexually desire those of the same sex.[48] In most of the United States it is perfectly acceptable to be overtly homophobic. Unfortunately, battered lesbians and gays who reach out for help must overcome not only the fear of abuse from their partners but also the possibility of added victimization by homophobic service providers, law-enforcement agencies, prosecutors, and judges.

Myths and Stereotypes

While myths and stereotypes about nongay battered women flourish, they are even more numerous for battered lesbians and gays. In attempting to ascertain the causes of and contributing factors to same-sex abuse, many inaccurate stereotypes have evolved. One widespread misconception is that abusive women are stronger and characteristically more "butch" than battered women, who are stereotyped as more passive or "femme." Another harmful myth surrounding same-sex battering is that of "mutual battering." This is an example of victim blaming and is simply another way to minimize and dismiss same-sex abuse. While some battered lesbians and gays have been violent toward their abusive partners, such violence usually occurs in self-defense or possibly as a manifestation of rage at past abuse.[49]

Societal myths grow from misconceptions about lesbian and gay couples and from a simplistic understanding of the factors that contribute to men's domination over women. In addition, such myths frequently give batterers additional ammunition with which to further intimidate and control their partners. As long as our society continues to perpetuate these stereotypes, effective advocacy for battered lesbians and gays will be hindered.

The Lesbian and Gay Community

The lesbian and gay community's response to battering has been impacted by homophobia. Denial, minimization, and rationalization about abuse has been the community's way to protect itself from a society that is looking for reasons to condemn lesbians and gays as sick and perverted. In addition, the lesbian community may minimize lesbian violence because it doesn't want to destroy the myth of a "lesbian utopia."[50] According to Claire Renzetti, author of *Violent Betrayal: Partner Abuse in Lesbian Relationships,* "[a]cknowledging that lesbian battering is a serious problem may indeed be unpleasant, even painful, for the lesbian community. But until such acknowledgment is made, until victims' needs are effectively and sensitively met, and until batterers are challenged and held accountable for their behavior, all lesbians are unsafe and the struggle for the creation of a peaceful, egalitarian community of women is violently betrayed."[51]

Outing

One tactic of intimidation and control commonly used by abusive lesbians and gays is the threat of "outing" their partners. Outing is the unwelcome disclosure of a person's sexual orientation. Batterers may threaten to out their partners to family, friends, employers, and church communities if they attempt to leave the relationship. On the flip side, some survivors may not reach out for help for fear of outing a closeted abusive partner. Depending on the circumstances, outing can mean loss of a job, support systems, and even child custody.

Isolation

137

The
Oppression
That Binds:
Barriers to
Living
Violence
Free

Lesbians and gays frequently obtain their emotional support from other lesbians and gays. Many lesbians and gays share close friends with their partners, causing battered lesbians and gays to feel conflicted about whom they can talk to. They may fear shaming their partners before mutual friends or fear that their friends will take the abusive partner's side. On the other hand, survivors of same-sex battering may be isolated from the lesbian and gay community because of geographic location, fear of coming out, or lack of knowledge about how to find other lesbians and gays. They may see their abusive partners as their only support system.[52] The lesbian and gay community is frequently small, even in larger cities. In some cases the community is so small that anonymity and confidentiality cannot be assured.

It may be difficult for battered lesbians and gays who are closeted to turn to relatives for support. In addition, many lesbians and gays lost the support of relatives and nongay friends when they came out.

Safety

Battered lesbians face safety issues quite different from those of their nongay sisters. Batterers may try to enter shelters and support groups, claiming they are the ones being abused. If shelters fail to screen female visitors as effectively as they do male visitors, a female batterer's access to her partner is made much easier. Furthermore, although shelter locations are often secrets well guarded from men, they may be known to lesbian batterers if the batterers are a part of the local women's movement.[53]

The Legal System

In most states, domestic-violence statutes do not explicitly apply to lesbian and gay couples, and in states where they do apply, the police and the courts do not consistently or fairly enforce them in cases involving same-sex couples.[54] Police officers frequently minimize the violence that battered lesbians and gays experience and do less to intervene, resulting in more mutual arrests and in arrests being wrongly categorized under charges of disorderly conduct. The police frequently fail to inform battered lesbians and gays about local domestic-violence programs that may be of assistance. The result of these homophobic actions is that battered lesbians and gays and their abusive partners receive the message that violent behavior is not a serious crime.

Children

The homophobic fear of lesbians raising children may increase scrutiny by child-protective services of lesbian couples who have children. In addition, a battered lesbian may face custody battles if she prosecutes her abusive female partner and the children's father has been unaware of the fact that she is a lesbian.

Shelter Services

Shelter programs were developed to respond to the needs of women who are being battered by men, a reality that influences everything from philosophy and policy to actual services offered. In the past, shelters have feared that addressing same-sex abuse would jeopardize their programs' credibility or cause them to lose hard-won funding. This attitude is a manifestation of homophobia called *lesbian baiting:* attempting to control women by accusing them of being lesbians when they engage in behavior considered inappropriate. It prevents many domestic-violence programs from effectively meeting the needs of a population of women at risk for abuse.

If battered lesbians and gays do reach out to local domestic-violence programs, there is no guarantee that advocates will be understanding or sensitive to their needs. Like other forms of oppression, homophobia can and does occur among shelter staff. In addition, battered lesbians may enter a shelter where the residents are homophobic. For men in same-sex abusive relationships, there may be no shelter services available at all.

Older Women

Domestic violence among older people is a reality that is unlikely to simply disappear as the population continues to age. Today there are more people age sixty-five and older than in any other period in history. In 1900, 4 percent of the U.S. population was sixty-five or older and 40 percent was under eighteen. By the year 2020, 22 percent of the population will be sixty-five or older and 21 percent will be under eighteen.[55] As more baby boomers reach old age, the need for services for battered older women is likely to increase.

In the context of family violence, elder abuse is more frequently compared to child abuse than to spouse abuse, an attitude arising from the misconception that elder abuse is solely a problem related to caregiving. However, the parallel is fundamentally flawed. First, older women are not children, and to equate them to children is both paternalistic and condescending and ultimately demeans and devalues them. Moreover, treating older women like children ignores not only the differences between adults and children but also the range of abusive situations to which older women may be exposed.[56] Second, elder abuse does not always occur by a caretaker against a dependent victim. In a survey of older adults living in the Boston area, results indicated that 65 percent of the abuse cases were perpetrated by a spouse, while only 23 percent involved an adult-child caregiver abusing a parent.[57]

Even when the older woman is dependent upon others, the conditions of dependency are very different from those of children. Parents have a clear legal responsibility for children, unlike almost all caregivers of older adults. Unless proven otherwise, older women are considered to be competent individuals who are therefore responsible for decisions regarding their lives.[58]

Who Is the Battered Older Woman?

In a study conducted by the Community Care Organization of Milwaukee and the Wisconsin Coalition Against Domestic Violence, twenty-one battered older women, most of them in relatively good health, participated in in-depth interviews about the violence they had experienced. Most of the women who were abused by their partners had been abused for the entire length of the relationship. These women were extremely isolated and difficult to locate. The majority of them did not want to discuss the abuse with anyone, and few contacted agencies for help.[59]

Ageism

Older adults are especially vulnerable to abuse because of the social status they occupy. Systematic stereotyping and discrimination against older adults contribute to their isolation and devaluation. When battered older women reach out for help, service providers sometimes respond in an ageist manner. Ageism is a system of destructive, false beliefs about older adults. In addition, service providers may neglect to consider the special needs of battered older women.

Internalized Social Expectations

Battered older women were raised at a time when they were expected to stay at home and care for their children. Divorce was not considered acceptable because it was usually regarded as a woman failing in her primary role. Older women who have internalized rigid gender roles may be less willing to talk about their abuse or to seek help from community agencies.[60]

Self-Identification

Many older women do not identify themselves as abused. Some may see their relationships as normal. In addition, they may believe that battered women are exclusively young women with children, especially when media exposure of domestic violence is given predominantly to young women or to women with children. These images may leave society, including older women, with the impression that domestic violence doesn't occur in later life.[61]

139

The
Oppression
That Binds:
Barriers to
Living
Violence
Free

The Family

Adult children are often not supportive of a change in their parents' relationship. If the abuse has been hidden from the children for years, they often refuse to believe it when they are finally told. In some cases the children have seen the mother suffering the abuse, have become accustomed to it, and resent her sudden rebellion.[62]

Financial Barriers

Fear of financial insecurity often keeps older women in abusive relationships. Many battered older women are financially dependent on their abusive partners, creating a reality of their having to choose between continued violence or assured poverty. Fourteen percent of women age sixty-five and older are poor.[63] Some abused older women have no formal education or economic resources. They may find few employers willing to hire them, either because of age discrimination or because they have held only low-paying or part-time jobs or have not worked outside the home.

Employed older women may not earn enough to support themselves. Others may have no access to resources acquired during the relationship. Some women may be ineligible for social security because of their years of working at home. Women who are on their abusers' health insurance policies and have uninsurable preexisting conditions may fear losing their insurance.[64]

Aging in Place

The gerontological term *aging in place* refers to older adults' ability to remain at home as they age, as opposed to being forced to enter an institution to receive needed care because of a lack of personal or public resources. For battered older women, however, aging in place may mean continued abuse and isolation.[65] Many older women fear being placed in a nursing home if they leave their homes. Others are reluctant to give up a lifelong residence in exchange for a month or two in a shelter with no assurance of a permanent residence.

Furthermore, shelters are frequently geared toward the needs of younger women. Women who have not lived with small children for many years may find the stress of dealing with youngsters too great. They may be in poor health and have special needs that go beyond what the shelter program is able to meet.[66]

Isolation

Battered older women may have lost contact with family and friends. Support persons may have died and new friendships may have never developed. Retired abusers may go everywhere with their partners or may monitor telephone calls and mail. Battered women who do not drive or who are forbidden to drive may be dependent on their abusive spouses for transportation, mobility, and socialization.[67]

141

The
Oppression
That Binds:
Barriers to
Living
Violence
Free

Health

Natural cognitive and physiological changes occur as we age. Changes in vision, hearing, touch, pain tolerance, and mobility may limit the ability to live independently. In addition, years of abuse can create physical problems that can cause battered older women to feel, or to actually be, dependent upon their abusers. Some women feel obligated to take care of their abusers, who themselves may have serious health problems.[68]

Women in Rural Areas

For our purposes, the term *rural women* refers to women outside major U.S. urban centers. It should be noted that distinct regional differences affect the experience of rural living. In some parts of the Northeast, for example, rural communities are located closer to urban areas than are many in the Southwest. The isolation of rural living can seriously affect the challenges that battered women face.

Availability of Services

Appropriate services for rural battered women and their abusive partners are sadly lacking. Rural programs have access to fewer local funding sources, and larger funding agencies are often more inclined to allocate money to urban areas, where reports of larger numbers of people served make a program appear more cost-effective. In addition, many grants to such programs are funded for only one or two years.[69]

If women seek assistance from social-service programs, they are frequently confronted with staff who have little or no training in domestic violence and who fail to consider the social context of the woman's situation.[70] In many cases, it is necessary to refer battered women to services offered in urban areas. When a rural battered woman relocates to a shelter in an urban area, she often experiences an additional crisis because she is confronted with a strange environment and may be isolated from her local support network.

Conservative Attitudes

The attitudes and beliefs of rural communities often reflect a traditional, conservative bias. Women may be financially dependent upon their abusive partners. The rural church frequently provides ideological support to old traditions by preaching the virtues of the dependent status of women.

Denial is often high in rural communities. The false notion that domestic violence happens only in urban areas or to certain kinds of women is often present. Belief in the need to maintain family privacy at all costs and a lack of understanding regarding domestic violence may also hinder rural women's ability to flee abusive relationships. Some rural areas put such emphasis on maintaining the family that separated or divorced women are excluded from positive social outlets and even ostracized.[71]

Transportation

A lack of adequate public transportation contributes to the isolation of rural battered women. Private transportation may also be limited. An abusive partner may restrict access to car keys or may damage the automobile to prevent his partner from driving. Neighbors may live so far away that they cannot be easily reached. Some women may never have learned to drive and thus may be dependent upon family members or friends to provide transportation. Unfortunately, these relationships are often severed by the batterer or by the woman herself in an attempt to prevent further abuse.

Lack of Privacy

Many rural battered women lack the privacy of anonymity because they live in a small community where "everybody knows everybody." This situation can intimidate a battered woman, who may decide against taking public action because she does not want the facts of her home life revealed to the residents of her community. By contrast, some rural women may have too much anonymity. They may be so isolated, either geographically or by their abusive partners, that they remain unknown to other members of the community. If community members are unaware of what is happening to victims of abuse, they have no basis for offering help.[72]

Employment

Rural areas generally lack adequate job opportunities for women. In addition, conservative rural attitudes often make it difficult for women to seek and hold employment, particularly in nontraditional, higher-paying jobs. This leaves many battered women underemployed, if not unemployed and financially dependent.[73]

Child Care

For battered women trying to work outside the home, the shortage of child care in rural areas is a major problem. A lack of affordable and accessible child care not only curtails battered women's involvement in the paid labor force; it may also limit training opportunities.[74] Ultimately, this creates an additional burden for mothers attempting to work outside the home and support themselves independent of an abusive relationship.

Housing

The housing choices available to rural battered women who want to move out of their abusive homes may be limited or inadequate. One-third of U.S. residents live in rural areas, but two-thirds of all substandard housing is located there.[75]

Communication

Many rural homes do not have telephones or access to direct dialing. It may be a long-distance call to reach the nearest town with a shelter or other services. Many battered women cannot afford long-distance calls, and most probably do not want a record of such calls on the telephone bill for their batterers to see. Party lines, which still exist in some rural areas, present their own problems. Women may fear that someone is listening when they call for help, and they may be unwilling to ask the person to get off the line so they can make a private call.

Police

Rural police may have neither the time nor the resources to provide battered women with transportation or to stay with them to insure their safety. In addition, police response may be inconsistent because officers, who can come from any of several area law-enforcement agencies that may or may not receive the same training, may be unfamiliar with new legal developments pertaining to family violence. Some rural communities have no local law-enforcement body at all. Many have only one police officer, who may or may not be trained and certified. In some areas, the sheriff is located many miles away, in the county seat.[76]

Women with Disabilities

Comprehensive statistics about the abuse of people with disabilities are not widely available; however, professionals working with these individuals report that they suffer domestic abuse at the same rate, or perhaps more frequently, than the general population.[77] Although women with disabilities experience high rates of domestic violence, it is important to note that many men with disabilities also experience abuse.

The term *disability* can include a vast spectrum of conditions. I use it here to mean any of the following: physical disability (e.g., spinal cord injury, amputation), chronic disease (e.g., multiple sclerosis, rheumatoid arthritis), sensory disorder (e.g., hearing impairment, blindness), cognitive or learning impairment (e.g., mental retardation), acquired disability (e.g., traumatic brain injury, cancer, stroke), a congenital condition (e.g., cerebral palsy, muscular dystrophy), a condition labeled as a mental or psychiatric disorder (e.g., bipolar disorder, schizophrenia, major depression), age-related disability (e.g., Alzheimer's disease), and "hidden" illness (e.g., heart disease, diabetes, fibromyalgia).

In 1996, researchers at the Center for Research on Women with Disabilities (CROWD) conducted a national survey in which women with physical disabilities reported approximately the same incidence of sexual, emotional, and physical violence as the respondents without disabilities. It is noteworthy, however, that respondents with physical disabilities reported that they had experienced abuse for longer periods of time than respondents without disabilities (3.9 versus 2.5 years).[78] Respondents with disabilities also reported that their perpetrators sometimes withheld needed orthotic equipment (such as wheelchairs or braces), medications, transportation, or essential assistance with personal tasks such as dressing or getting out of bed.[79]

In a 2004 survey of domestic-violence and rape-crisis centers in the United States, 67 percent of respondents reported that their center had served people labeled mentally ill over the past year. Despite the high incidence of violence against people with disabilities, few respondents reported that their agency served people with cognitive disabilities (7 percent), with physical disabilities (6 percent), or who were blind, deaf, or had hearing loss (1 percent).[80]

There is some evidence that survivors with disabilities may be at risk for repeated victimization. Sixty-one percent of the sexual-assault survivors with disabilities who participated in counseling at SafePlace, in Austin, Texas, between 1996 and 2002 reported multiple perpetrators of violence. Approximately 90 percent of the perpetrators were *not* strangers to their victims.[81]

Battered women with disabilities face a number of barriers that may hinder them from getting the assistance they need. Researchers Margaret Nosek and Carol Howland note that "[f]or each disability type, different dynamics of abuse come into play. For women with physical disabilities, limitations in physically escaping violent situations are in sharp contrast to [limitations for] women with hearing impairments, who may be able to escape but face communication barriers in most settings designed to help battered women."[82]

Survivors with disabilities are often patronized and treated as children. They may be met with condescension and disbelief when they report abuse.

Limited access to appropriate information about domestic violence, loss of a caregiver, isolation, limited access to services, and a lack of appropriate services are just a few of the barriers that keep women with disabilities trapped in relationships that endanger their lives.

Denial of the Problem

Few people want to admit that the problem of domestic violence against people with disabilities exists. How could someone beat a woman who has a disability? The horrific nature of the abuse keeps many from effectively addressing the problem. It is precisely this denial that allows the abuse to continue unchecked. As a result, many police departments, social-service agencies, and women's shelters are ill prepared to deal with the violence that affects women with disabilities.

Physical Barriers

Although the passage of the Americans with Disabilities Act has sought to address the issue of buildings that are inaccessible to people with disabilities, many still exist. Some courtrooms, police stations, shelters, and other structures continue to have physical barriers that make it almost impossible for women with disabilities to utilize them. Barriers may include a building entrance with steps, agency policies that prohibit animals (including service animals), lack of accessible parking spaces, and lack of materials available in alternative formats (such as large print, audio, Braille, or simplified language). Other physical barriers include a lack of interpreters and of TTYs (special telephone systems that allow communication between users who hear and those who are deaf, hard of hearing, or have a hearing loss). The omission of these necessary services often prevents women with disabilities from obtaining and receiving help.

Physical barriers may be relatively easy to address, but it is also relevant to direct attention to attitudes that prevent access or are discriminatory.

Lack of Information

The level of awareness about domestic violence is not nearly as high among women with disabilities as it is among the rest of the population. Although information on abuse is becoming increasingly available to women with disabilities, there is a severe lack of educational materials on the subject that address the special needs and problems of this community.[83] For survivors who are deaf, hard of hearing, or have a hearing loss, for example, much of the literature about domestic violence uses syntax too complex to be well understood. Vocabulary can also be a problem: Words may have one meaning in English and another in sign. Even slight differences can create confusion, which further compounds the problem of discussing the sensitive subject of domestic abuse. Finally, many English words do not have exact equivalents in sign.[84]

Isolation

When women are isolated, whether due to a disability or otherwise, they are more likely to blame themselves for the abuse. With regard to sexual violence, because many people are reluctant to talk about sexuality in general and especially to individuals with disabilities, women with disabilities who have been sexually abused may go through life never fully understanding what has happened to them. Without appropriate information on domestic violence, battered women with disabilities are more likely than other women to assume that their experience is unique, and they are less likely to know where to go for help or even that help is available to them. If a woman does decide to seek help, she will be unable to access the help she needs unless the services are barrier free.

Community Factors

The community of people with disabilities is often close, strong, and insulated, particularly among persons who are deaf. The community's small-town atmosphere may limit a woman's chances of maintaining confidentiality if she reports her problem. Confidentiality is an important need for most battered women, especially when they first seek help. In addition, the sense of being insulated from the rest of society may create a greater dependence in the battered woman upon her partner, family, and community. A woman with a disability may be more afraid of threatening her support system than a woman who does not have a disability and who therefore has more alternatives for establishing a new support system. In addition, society's insensitivity to the problems of people with disabilities has fostered in many of them a mistrust of service providers and a fear of intervention into their personal lives.[85]

Loss of Caregiver

Getting help is often complicated by the fact that in many cases the batterer is providing personal assistance to the woman. When the person who is doing the abusing is also the caregiver, it may become incredibly difficult to reach out for help. If the batterer is removed from the home, the woman may be faced with having no personal care at all, a situation that could be life threatening. Faced with the choice of enduring abuse or having no one to feed, clothe, and care for them, many women will choose to continue living with their batterers.[86]

Transportation Barriers

147

The
Oppression
That Binds:
Barriers to
Living
Violence
Free

For battered women with disabilities, lack of transportation can become a major barrier to fleeing an abusive relationship. Many smaller communities offer no special transit services, and although larger urban areas may offer them, they are often inadequate. Most shelters do not have vehicles equipped to transport women using wheelchairs.

One survivor with a disability explains that in order to use the special transit service in her community, she had to call hours in advance of leaving her home. She says, "When I was trying to leave my abusive boyfriend, I couldn't use the service. Waiting at the curb for hours would have made me an easy target for him. [But to get a ride] I had to wait at the curb.... The van would not stop unless they saw me."

Lack of Appropriate Services

Nosek and Howland report, "In both the disability rights movement and the battered women's movement, it is generally acknowledged that programs to assist abused women are often architecturally inaccessible, lack interpreter services for deaf women, and are not able to accommodate women who need assistance with daily self-care or medications."[87] In a 2003 survey of 546 domestic- and sexual-assault programs in the United States, only approximately 9 percent of them reported that they included money in their annual budgets for accessibility or accommodations.[88]

A nationwide study conducted by CROWD of 598 programs that provide abuse-related services reported that on average the programs provided two services targeted specifically to women with disabilities. Eighty-nine percent of the programs provided fewer than five individualized services for women with disabilities. The most commonly provided services for women with disabilities were accessible shelter or referral to an accessible safe house or hotel (83 percent) and group counseling (73 percent). Nearly half (47 percent) provided an interpreter for women who were deaf. Only about one-third offered safety-plan information modified for use by women with disabilities or disability-awareness training for staff (35 percent). The services least likely to be offered were attendants who could provide personal care, which were available in only 6 percent of the programs.[89]

Some shelters' policies and procedures have the effect of keeping women with disabilities out. For example, Wendie Abramson, director of Disability Services ASAP at SafePlace, points out that women with mental illnesses are frequently "screened out" for shelter services by procedures requiring admissions counselors to deliberately question women about the medications they take. According to Abramson, "This is blatant discrimination and a possible violation of the ADA." As another example, for health and safety reasons many domestic-violence programs do not allow animals in the shelters. While this may be a sound policy in most cases, it will automatically screen out a woman who uses a service animal. In addition, survivors with disabilities may need to bring a personal-care attendant (who is not the abuser) or have modifications made in their daily chore assignments. Abramson recommends that shelters examine their existing policies and revise them with inclusion in mind.

Disability Services ASAP (A Safety Awareness Program)

Disability Services ASAP, at SafePlace, in Austin, Texas, began in 1996 as a small education and counseling program and has grown to include local, state, and national education programs about sexual, domestic,and caregiver violence against people with any type of disability. The Disability Services program includes six major components:

1. Abuse-prevention education and safety-awareness training for people with disabilities

2. Abuse-prevention training for service providers and for families of people with disabilities

3. Training for other professionals, including those involved in law enforcement, domestic-violence and sexual-assault programs, and disability-service agencies; plus consultation on how to reach out to people with disabilities and on techniques for providing accessible services

4. Counseling (in the Austin area) for people with disabilities who are victims of rape, sexual abuse, domestic violence, or caregiver abuse

5. A library that features over 450 items available for checkout in person or by mail to anyone within the United States

6. A comprehensive training curriculum, *Stop the Violence, Break the Silence,* that is available for a fee to those interested in addressing violence against persons with disabilities in their local communities

Since the program's inception, the number of survivors with disabilities who reach out for services has increased, and so have the requests for training and technical assistance from professionals located all over the country who want to know how they can be more responsive and effective in helping survivors with disabilities. Abramson says, "I think one of our greatest successes is that we're addressing the issue at so many levels. We're now working with various systems to improve their responses to abuse survivors."

Women in Prison

149

The
Oppression
That Binds:
Barriers to
Living
Violence
Free

The last few years have witnessed an increasing awareness of the needs of battered women in prison. According to Suzanne Donovan, former project specialist with the Texas Council on Family Violence, "Battered women in prison are no different than battered women seeking assistance through shelters or other domestic violence programs. In the last few years, advocates in the battered women's movement have come a long way in understanding the connections between women seeking shelter, those who are killed by their abusers, and those who kill their abusers, but much work remains to be done. Battered women in prison need support from their sisters outside."[90]

It's not easy to reach out to battered women in prison. Many people hold preconceptions about women who fight back against their abusers. Logistical problems often exist as well. Women's prisons are frequently located in remote areas, and some women in prison do not readily identify themselves as battered. Visiting a woman in prison can be intimidating, especially the first time. As Ellen Fisher, former executive director of the National Domestic Violence Hotline, says, "The first day I went to the prison, I stayed up the night before. I was afraid I wouldn't have anything to say, or to offer. After just thirty minutes of talking to her, I knew she was the same as me."[91]

Battered women in prison face barriers distinct from those encountered by women on the outside. It is crucial that they know that advocates and others outside are concerned about their well-being. We should provide support for any battered woman, regardless of whether she is charged with, convicted of, or acquitted of a crime. As advocates for all battered women, we have a responsibility to provide the best service possible based on the needs of each individual woman, regardless of the circumstances in which she finds herself.

Battered Women Defendants

Although battered women defendants have needs specific to their involvement with the criminal-justice system, many of their needs lie outside the courtroom. In cases where women have murdered their abusive partners, they may need to make peace with the deceased, to deal with their partner's family, or to address their emotional pain and that of their children. Despite the fact that she'll be undergoing trial and possible imprisonment, a defendant who is free on bail needs to go on with her everyday activities as best she can. Like other women, she may require housing, public assistance, and other support services.[92]

Battered Women Who Kill

Although women commit fewer than 15 percent of all homicides, they have historically received harsher sentences than men for the same crimes. In addition, homicides committed by women are seven times more likely to be in self-defense than those committed by men.[93] Prior to the 1990s, it was not unusual for women to receive sentences of forty-five years to life for killing their abusive partners. In stark contrast, abusive men who killed their partners served an average of two- to six-year terms.[94] Fortunately, some progress has been made. While some women still receive twenty- to twenty-five-year sentences for killing their abusive partners, in the last decade or so more have received shorter sentences.[95]

Women charged with homicide have the least extensive prior criminal records of any female offenders.[96] And, once released, women convicted of killing their abusive partners have an incredibly low recidivism rate.

The Prison Environment

According to one formerly battered woman in prison, "Prison has been another form of a nightmare. It is degrading, dehumanizing, and definitely a battleground, where only the strong or determined survive. You are no longer a person, you are a number. You have no rights, no privacy.... It is a garden of negativeness and only self-motivation can help you reach toward a better existence."[97]

Sixty-five to 95 percent of female prison inmates are victims of prior abuse, and approximately 50 percent are battered women. Many women incarcerated for felonies were acting in self-defense, were coerced into illegal acts by their abusive partners, or are taking the punishment for crimes committed by their abusers.[98] Despite the high percentage of abused women in prison, there are shortages of support groups for battered women and of classes to educate and inform the general prison population about abuse.[99] According to one female inmate, "I am in a facility that vaguely addresses abuse of any kind. There are two programs that are occasionally offered. Both of these programs are very good; however, they are not offered enough to the inmates. There are 110 women in this facility, and classes are limited to ten inmates."

Incarcerated battered women frequently need help with appealing their sentences and applying for and processing clemencies when their appeals have been exhausted. If advocates do not make themselves available to these women, who can they turn to for help? Correctional and parole personnel frequently have little or no understanding of the dynamics of domestic violence. Without appropriate training, similar to that offered by domestic-violence

programs to sensitize police, correctional and parole personnel can easily replicate the abusive behavior of a batterer.[100]

151

The
Oppression
That Binds:
Barriers to
Living
Violence
Free

After Incarceration

When women leave prison, they frequently have little or no support and are
unaware of services available in the communities to which they are paroled.
Liaisons are needed between the women awaiting parole and organizations
that provide services in a specific community.

Approximately 70 percent of incarcerated women are mothers. Many of
them lose their parental rights if their terms are longer than twelve to eighteen
months.[101] Battered women released from prison need help in reuniting with
their children. Numerous issues need to be addressed after such long separations.

Furthermore, as one former inmate explains, women coming home after
years in prison are generally treated as though they have more to prove than
men in the same position. "We have to work harder to prove ourselves worthy
of a good job, trust, respect and love. It's easier for men who are ex-convicts
because it is more acceptable for men to have committed a crime or to protect
themselves than it is for women."[102]

◆ ◆ ◆

Women from each of the communities examined in this chapter face unique
barriers when trying to escape violence at home, barriers that are multiplied
for women who belong to more than one group or culture. A battered lesbian
residing in a rural area may not only have to deal with an openly homophobic
community; she may also be confronted with a lack of services, communication barriers, and isolation. Individual barriers have a considerable impact on
women's abilities to escape battering relationships. In combination they form
an oppressive wall that helps to maintain abusive relationships and to keep
women trapped in situations that are both dangerous and life-threatening.

...*8*

For Friends, Family, and Loved Ones: When Someone You Know Is Being Hurt

Helping a battered woman is a process that may take a long time. We have to realize that she needs to move according to her own timetable and not ours.

— Erin Clark, manager of hotline services, SafePlace

In 2003 approximately 15 percent of the calls received at the SafePlace hotline were from friends, family members, and employers asking how to help someone they knew. Studies show that battered women often seek help from their informal support networks, including relatives, friends, and neighbors. In fact, it appears that the greater the violence, the more likely women are to seek help.[1] The manner in which we respond to those who turn to us for help can have a powerful impact on their lives—one that's either positive or negative, depending on the nature of our response. According to Judith Herman, author of *Trauma and Recovery,* "A supportive response from other people may mitigate the impact of the event, while a hostile or negative response may compound the damage and aggravate the traumatic syndrome. In the aftermath of traumatic life events, survivors are highly vulnerable. Their sense of self has been shattered. That sense can be rebuilt only as it was built initially, in connection with others."[2]

This chapter explores ways in which you can help an abused woman who has reached out to you. First, however, it shows how you can prepare yourself to be the best helper possible. (A related topic is advocating for battered women, which requires more advanced helping skills. Advocacy for battered women is addressed in Chapter 15.)

The Role of the Helper

In their concern for her well-being, many helpers advise a battered woman to "just leave." When she fails to heed their advice, helpers often turn away in frustration and anger. Don't make the assumption that the abused woman has not thought of "just leaving." It is quite possible that she has considered that option but also sees major obstacles associated with her departure.

One likely obstacle is a fear of retaliation from the batterer. A battered woman has just cause to fear for her safety. According to the Presidential Task Force on Violence and the Family, "The greatest risk for serious injury or death from violence is at the point of separation or at the time when the decision to separate is made."[3] In addition, battered women who leave are also at risk for harassment at work by the abuser, homelessness, and an overall decrease in their standard of living.[4] Contrary to what many may think, leaving in and of itself does not make a battered woman's life better. In fact, it may make it more difficult.

Try to imagine yourself in her situation. Imagine fleeing your home with nothing but the clothes on your back, the money in your pocket, and your children. If you are lucky you will have a safe place to stay for the night and perhaps the next several weeks. Your children will be scared and confused. Not only are you removing them from their home, but they will probably need to change schools. If your partner is particularly violent, you may need to refrain from contacting family or friends who might reveal your location. If you are employed and your employer is insensitive to your safety needs, you may have to quit your job. If you are not employed, you may be worried about supporting yourself and your children.

Escaping a violent relationship is a complicated, arduous, and dangerous process. Don't expect immediate results from your efforts to help a battered woman. You will need to be patient with her and prepared for her to vacillate between leaving and staying as she reviews her options and their possible outcomes. Also remember that, regardless of the decisions she ultimately makes, your support will have a subtle impact, even if you are unaware of it.

The ability to demonstrate unconditional acceptance is crucial when helping a battered woman to help herself. Try to suspend judgment when confronting behaviors and attitudes different from yours, and be flexible enough to accept her without imposing your values and ideals.

Helpers Versus Rescuers

In trying to be supportive, significant others can actually become overprotective to the point where they reinforce feelings of helplessness the abused woman is trying to overcome. There's a difference between helping someone and rescuing her. So-called rescuers tend to do things for the abused woman rather than helping and supporting her in her efforts to do for herself. Doing too much for someone implies that she is incapable of acting on her own behalf. The more the rescuer accepts the idea that the abused woman is helpless, the more the abused woman is forced into that role. Rarely does rescuing someone improve a situation. On the contrary, the more helpless and dependent an abused woman feels, the less able she will be to act on her own behalf.[5]

Some key differences between helpers and rescuers are listed below.

A helper—

- ◆ believes that a battered woman is in crisis, but with appropriate support, information, and resources can make her own decisions and determine her own fate

- ◆ listens for requests for help

- ◆ gives what the woman says she needs

- ◆ checks in with the woman periodically

- ◆ establishes and maintains appropriate boundaries

- ◆ does most of the listening

- ◆ supports the woman as she makes her own decisions and does her own work

A rescuer—

- ◆ believes a battered woman is helpless and needs someone to save her

- ◆ gives help even when it is not asked for

- ◆ fails to find out whether the help is welcomed

- ◆ gives advice instead of information

- ◆ gives what he or she thinks the woman needs

- ◆ does most of the talking and working

The goal in assisting a battered woman should be to help her empower herself to make the best decisions possible. Susan Schechter, author of *Women and Male Violence,* explains that "empowerment means gaining control over the decisions affecting one's life and finding access to the resources needed to live decently."[6] While you can certainly help a woman in crisis, it is ultimately up to her to change her own life and to create her own future.

Preparing to Be a Helper

Battered women have diverse backgrounds, personalities, and needs. There is no single solution applicable to all battered women. Try to be sensitive to individual differences and avoid treating women categorically.[7]

Before you can offer help to an abused woman, you need some understanding of the resources available in her community. Is there a shelter in her town? Do they offer support groups? What is the policy of her local police department toward domestic violence? How does she go about getting a restraining or protective order? Is there a batterers' treatment program in her community?[8] The National Domestic Violence Hotline, at (800) 799-SAFE (7233), can help put you in touch with battered-women's shelters and other agencies that can answer these questions.

Be aware that helping a battered woman often generates powerful feelings of anger, pity, fear, frustration, and sadness. To be helpful, you will need to be in touch with your feelings without being self-critical and without projecting them onto the abused woman. A positive self-image and a healthy sense of humor can help put emotions into perspective.[9] In addition, seeking support, information, and ideas from your local battered-women's shelter will help you address your frustrations and concerns as you help your friend.

Be very careful about directly intervening if you witness a woman being assaulted. Batterers can be incredibly dangerous, and jeopardizing yourself will not be of benefit to you or to the woman you are trying to help. The most effective action you can take when you see or hear someone being abused is to call the police as quickly as possible.

How to Help a Battered Woman

If an abused woman has reached out to you for help, you will need to listen to her, talk with her, provide her with support and information, and offer to help in whatever way you can. In your role as a helper, let her take the lead. Let her tell you what she needs rather than assuming you know what's best for her. One of the most important things you can do is to maintain some level of ongoing contact with her. Physical and psychological isolation are powerful control tactics used by batterers. An open line of communication between you and the battered woman can be a lifeline.

Let her know you are a nonthreatening, concerned ally who is able to see the reality of her situation and still respect her as a person. By all means, convey respect to her in every way possible. Do not admonish, patronize, or negatively judge her. Make and repeat clear statements about her value and rights as a person, such as, "You don't deserve to be treated that way," and, "No one, not even your husband, has the right to mistreat you." Express disapproval of her partner's abusive behavior, but do not be critical of him. For example, instead of saying, "John must be some kind of monster to hurt you like he did," a more appropriate response would be, "I'm really concerned about the way John treats you. No one has the right to mistreat you." If you focus on the batterer rather than on his behavior, the woman may become defensive and try to make excuses for him.[10]

Convey your concern for the woman's safety if things continue unchecked, but refrain from giving advice, even though you may be tempted to because of your desire to make sure she is safe. Giving advice falls under the function of rescuing, and you will be more valuable to her if you maintain the helper's role.[11] According to Erin Clark, manager of hotline services for Safe-Place, "If you try to rescue her by giving her advice, you're actually setting her up to feel like she's disappointed you if she doesn't do what you've told her. These feelings may prevent her from reaching out to you again in the future." Instead of saying, "You need to get out of that relationship before someone gets killed," a more appropriate remark would be, "I'm really concerned about your safety and wonder what's going to happen to you if this hitting doesn't stop." Stay away from "you" statements such as "you should," "you need to," and "you have to." Instead, use "I" statements such as "I'm concerned," "I'm worried," and "I'm afraid."

Let the woman know that she does not have to endure her situation alone and that she deserves support. Offer her the telephone numbers of local resources such as a battered women's shelter, but don't force information on her if she doesn't want it. If she refuses your offer, let her know that you respect her wishes and that you will hold on to the information in case she becomes interested in it at any point in the future.

Your friend may need you to brainstorm with her to solve problems. She may be so enmeshed in her crisis that she cannot see her options, such as staying at a shelter or another safe location; joining a support group; changing jobs; obtaining counseling, education, or training; filing for separation or divorce; and getting legal counsel.[12] Help her discover and develop her own resources, including money, friends, relatives, and employment. Encourage her to turn for support to people she can trust in addition to you. Suggest that she assess each relationship she has as a potential source of protection, emotional support, or practical help—or as a potential source of danger.[13] If she has children, ask how she thinks they are being affected. Support her concern about their emotional and physical welfare without blaming her. Point out that children are always deeply affected by domestic violence and deserve protection from it.[14]

The ideas listed below may be useful as you begin the helping process.[15]

Be Aware of Who She Is

Allow her to tell her story.

Let her know you believe her and want to hear about her experiences.

Let her know you care about her and are concerned about her safety.

Help her identify her feelings.

Support her right to be angry. Don't deny any of her feelings.

Be sensitive to the differences between women. Realize that no woman is a stereotype and that each has had diverse life experiences.

Respect the cultural values and beliefs that affect her behavior. Know that her beliefs may be a source of security for her and that their importance to her should not be minimized.

Know that she does not need rescuing.

Help her assess her resources and support systems.

Be Aware of Who You Are

Be aware of your own attitudes toward, experiences with, and reactions to violence.

Be honest about your limits of time and energy.

Be wary of any need you have to be an expert.

Don't give advice. A battered woman has had numerous people tell her what to do. She needs someone to listen to her and support her as she plans her own course of action.

Be conscious of your cultural biases, beliefs, and prejudices.

Do not express disappointment if the woman decides not to leave her violent partner. Be honest and explain your fear and concern, but let her know that you still care about and will support her.

You may be one of the first people in your friend's life to show her respect and support at a time when she most needs it. In return you will receive both the opportunity to see strength and courage in action and the knowledge that you have helped a woman to help herself.

Listening with Love

One of the greatest gifts you can give an abused woman is to listen to her with love. Listening with love differs from other types of interaction. It requires more effort and concentration than is needed for simple chatting. It is very different from focusing on what you are going to say or how you are going to react to what the speaker has said. Listening with love is an act of will requiring choice and effort. First, you must make a conscious decision to *listen*. This means not only hearing what she says, but also listening to her words and emotions with your entire being. This type of listening requires that you be completely present, clearing your mind of everything else and focusing on the person in front of you. Listening with love is a gift because it goes against our natural tendency to talk and to establish our own position. Let the woman tell her story without interruptions, and don't fear any silences that may occur. The woman will eventually break the silences. Use body language to indicate that you are listening. Lean toward her as she speaks, and nod your head to indicate your understanding.

Listening with love occurs at two levels: words and feelings. The conversation will usually begin on the level of words, or content. Supporting the woman as she expresses her feelings, however, is the most important aspect of listening with love. Remember, this may be the first time she has had the opportunity to verbally express the range of emotions she has experienced.[16]

As the conversation progresses, try using a technique known as *reflecting*. As the woman shares her story, digest and filter her words and the feelings behind them, and then reflect back to her your interpretation of what she is saying. For example, if she says, "John seems to be getting more and more violent with me," your response might be, "That must be really frightening for you." She will then either confirm or deny what you have reflected. One word of caution: Reflecting does not mean repeating word for word what the woman has said. It means reflecting back to her your *interpretation* of her feelings and words. Reflecting responses might begin with such phrases as, "It sounds like," "It seems that," "In your situation," and, "As you see it." Don't worry about reflecting back the "wrong" thing. If you do, the woman will correct you. In the previous example the speaker could have responded, "No, I'm more confused

159

For Friends,
Family, and
Loved Ones:
When Some-
one You
Know Is
Being Hurt

than frightened." Whether or not you reflect accurately, the woman will know you are present for her. She will know you are listening to her with love, and there is much comfort to be gained from that fact.[17]

If you want to be an effective listener, there are some pitfalls to avoid. First, don't give advice. Our natural tendency is to tell people how they should solve their problems. Giving advice, however, focuses the conversation on you and will not help the woman make the best decisions she can for herself. You also need to suspend your judgments and assumptions. Be as objective as possible, giving honest feedback that separates fact from your subjective opinions and emotions. Objectivity does not mean that you must be emotionally neutral. It is possible to communicate feelings of empathy and acceptance without passing judgment.[18] Listen without blaming, and believe what the woman tells you. Do not discount her fears that her partner may try to kill her if she leaves or if she stays. Also, beware of the temptation to think she is exaggerating. Telling you her story is probably very embarrassing for her, and she is not likely to exaggerate. By offering a safe, accepting place for her to talk, you will help her begin to break the silence. Don't get ahead of her as she speaks. If you find yourself formulating your response before she has finished her thoughts, back up; you are not truly listening to her. You have begun to focus on yourself, not her.

Battered women often express love for their abusive partners. They may hate his abusive behavior and know he can be dangerous, yet still have feelings for him. Confused feelings are a normal response for someone in this situation. Remember, many batterers are not abusive all the time. Rather than trying to convince her that she really doesn't love her partner, acknowledge and validate her mixed feelings. According to Erin Clark, "We find this really opens a door and allows us to make a connection with her." Validating rather than denying her feelings gives an abused woman a profound sense of relief and can help create a strong bond between you.

Be honest with the abused woman and with yourself. Do not pretend to have all the answers or deny that you are affected by your experiences with her. It is equally important, however, to be a warm, patient, and approachable listener who is sensitive to her feelings and needs.

This type of listening may at first seem strange and awkward. With time and practice, however, you will begin to feel the process become a part of who you are. It is a privilege to share this gift of love with people we care about, and it is comforting to know that we are connecting with each other at a deeper and more meaningful level.

160

**When
Violence
Begins
at Home**

Creating a Safety Plan

The abused woman you are helping may not be ready to leave her abusive partner. Rather than trying to convince her otherwise, such comments as the following will convey your concern and encourage her to think more deeply about her situation:[19]

◆ "I'm afraid for your safety."

◆ "I'm afraid for the safety of your children."

◆ "I'm worried it will only get worse."

◆ "I'm here for you when you are ready to leave."

◆ "You don't deserve to be abused."

The battered woman who decides to stay with her abusive partner may need a safety plan to help protect herself and her children from further violence. Ask her if she has thought about this and if she feels it would be helpful. If she expresses interest, ask whether she would like your help in creating such a plan.

First, she should be aware of warning signs or cues of forthcoming violence. She will probably be able to describe signs that are specific to her partner; however, some general warning signs are listed below.[20]

Physical Warning Signs

◆ Red face

◆ Clenched fists

◆ Clenched teeth

◆ Squinting eyes

◆ Glaring

◆ Heavy breathing

◆ Sweating

◆ Shaking or trembling of the arms, legs, or entire body

Behavioral Warning Signs

◆ Pacing

◆ Shouting

◆ Raising fist or leg as if to hit or kick

◆ Becoming argumentative

161

For Friends,
Family, and
Loved Ones:
When Some-
one You
Know Is
Being Hurt

- ◆ Hitting objects
- ◆ Staring the woman down
- ◆ Physically cornering the woman

Verbal Warning Signs

- ◆ Yelling
- ◆ Name-calling
- ◆ Making ethnic slurs
- ◆ Using nicknames she dislikes
- ◆ Making derogatory comments about her

Once she has identified the cues she needs to watch for, she can develop a step-by-step plan of action to help her protect herself and her children the next time she senses her partner escalating toward violence. A sample safety plan is provided in Appendix II.

When the abused woman sees her partner exhibiting any of the cues of forthcoming violence, it is advisable for her to leave the situation as quickly as possible. It is of no use to try to have a discussion with a batterer who is escalating toward violence. Having made a safety plan better enables the woman to take care of herself and her children when she feels she needs to escape a volatile situation.

Reaching Out to Someone You Think Is Abused

Do you suspect that someone you know is in an abusive relationship? Compare your observations about their relationship with the warning signs listed below:[21]

1. The couple avoids being around others, preferring to stay at home or to go out alone.

2. One person appears to make the decisions for both people.

3. The couple avoids discussing the relationship or focuses on only the good qualities and avoids discussing problems.

4. One person exhibits quick and inappropriate anger.

5. One person seems to be blamed for causing all the problems in the relationship.

6. You openly observe abuse such as yelling or name-calling; marks or bruises may be visible.

7. One partner exhibits violence toward objects or animals.

8. One person exhibits obsessive jealousy toward the other or accuses the other of infidelity.

9. The couple openly engages in intense and sometimes violent arguments.

10. One partner tries to isolate the other from significant others and may even sabotage friendships to prevent the other from receiving support.

11. The suspected batterer is secretive about his past.

12. One partner's needs seem to be more important than the other's.

In *Next Time She'll Be Dead,* Ann Jones warns women to "stay away from a man who disrespects any women, who wants or needs you intensely and exclusively, and who has a knack for getting his own way almost all the time. Any of the above should put you on guard. And if, when you back off, he turns on the solid gold charm, keep backing."[22]

If after reviewing these warning signs you still suspect that the woman is in danger, there are several steps you can take to reach out to her. Respectfully approach her and express your concern. It may be hard to break the taboo around privacy, especially if you don't know her well. You can initiate a conversation by saying something like, "I don't mean to pry, but I've noticed you seem really depressed lately. I just want you to know that if you ever want to talk, I'm available." If the woman appears open to a conversation, you may want to gently ask her some nonthreatening questions to help her begin to talk about her relationship. Some questions you could ask include the following:[23]

◆ Is your partner extremely possessive or jealous?

◆ Does your partner try to control your behavior by telling you where you can go or who you can associate with?

◆ Does your partner threaten or criticize you?

◆ Does your partner blame you for everything that goes wrong in the relationship?

◆ Does your partner treat you differently from the way he treats other people?

◆ Are you afraid when your partner gets angry?

If, in the course of your conversation with her, the woman continues to show signs of welcoming your help, continue in the ways discussed in this chapter. Don't be surprised, however, if she rebuffs you or denies her situation. If this happens, do not press her. Simply let her know you are available if she would like to talk.

Communication cannot be forced. Any relationship you develop with a woman whom you suspect is battered should occur naturally, and it can if you display a positive, friendly, and receptive attitude. You can be helpful to her simply by being available as a friend if and when she chooses to reach out for help.

$\bullet\bullet\bullet 9$

Domestic Violence and the Workplace

Domestic violence is not something we can simply ignore. It is not just a family problem. It is a crime that is damaging to individuals and their families, as well as to productivity in the workplace. We in corporate America cannot afford to stand on the sidelines if we hope to protect the well-being of our employees and the health of our compan[ies].

— *Jerome A. Chazen, chairman emeritus, Liz Claiborne, Inc.*[1]

Many battered women are working women. Domestic violence is a serious problem that does not disappear when women leave their homes and enter the workplace. Ninety-six percent of employed battered women experience problems at work due to the abuse they suffer.[2] The effects of domestic violence show in lost productivity, increased health-care costs, absenteeism, turnover, workplace violence, and lawsuits. One 1997 study reported that 37 percent of the women who experienced domestic violence felt that the abuse had an impact on their work lives in the form of lateness, missed work, their ability to keep a job, or missed promotions.[3] The Centers for Disease Control and Prevention estimates that the annual cost of lost productivity due to domestic violence equals $727.8 million, with more than 7.9 million paid workdays lost each year.[4] In a study of fifty battered women by the Victims Service Agency of New York, half of the respondents missed an average of three days of work per month because of abuse at home, 64 percent reported being late to work because of their abusers, and 75 percent used company time to telephone friends, counselors, physicians, and lawyers because they could not do so at home.[5] One 2000 study of female domestic-violence survivors found that 44 percent were left without transportation when their abusers either disabled the car or hid the car keys.[6] Domestic violence frequently affects women's health. Many battered women suffer from stress-related illnesses, depression, eating disorders, and substance-abuse problems.[7] In turn, these health problems affect job performance.

Workplace violence is a real concern for battered women and their employers. Homicide is the second leading cause of female workplace deaths.[8] In 1992, approximately 20 percent of women killed in the workplace were murdered by a current or former male partner.[9]

Economic self-sufficiency is crucial for battered women. Maintaining a job, earning money, and receiving health-care benefits are extremely important issues to women trying to escape abusive relationships. In addition, many abused women find some level of support and achieve a positive sense of self through their work. It may be one of the few areas in their lives where they feel competent and are treated respectfully.

Batterers often jeopardize their partners' employment. A batterer may disrupt a woman at work by either constantly calling her or showing up at inappropriate times and demanding to see her. Seventy-four percent of employed battered women are harassed by their abusive partners at work, either in person or over the telephone.[10] A batterer may keep his partner up until early morning hours so that she either oversleeps or misses work altogether. He may contact his partner's employer or coworkers and falsely accuse her of stealing from the company, abusing drugs or alcohol, or suffering from a mental illness, at the same time often expressing concern for her well-being and that of the company. A batterer's abusive behaviors at his partner's workplace affect not only the woman but also her coworkers. Although women are not responsible for the abusive behavior of their batterers, approximately 20 percent of employed battered women lose their jobs as a result.[11]

Welfare-to-Work Programs and Domestic Violence

An important source of income for some battered women has been welfare assistance. In the 1990s welfare benefits were impacted by changes in legislation aimed at getting welfare recipients off assistance and into the workforce. The Personal Responsibility and Work Opportunity Reconciliation Act of 1996 spurred the welfare-reform movement by eliminating the federal program Aid to Families with Dependent Children (AFCD) and creating Temporary Assistance for Needy Families (TANF), block grants through which states can provide cash assistance to needy families on a time-limited basis. The legislation also made far-reaching changes to child care, the Food Stamp Program, Supplemental Security Income (SSI) for children, benefits for legal immigrants, and the Child Support Enforcement program.[12]

According to the National Conference of State Legislatures, the purpose of TANF is to "provide assistance to needy families with children so they can be cared for in their own homes, and to reduce dependency by promoting job preparation, work, and marriage. States may also use funds on efforts to prevent out-of-wedlock pregnancies and encourage the formation and maintenance of two-parent families."[13] Adults receiving TANF are required to participate in work activities after receiving assistance for twenty-four months (subject to "good cause" exemptions by the state). In order to meet the minimum TANF work requirements, recipients had to work at least twenty hours per week in 1997–98, increasing to thirty or more hours in 2000 and beyond.[14] States are required to reduce assistance to a family for any period in which an adult member of the family refuses to engage in work as required under the TANF grant. A state may waive the penalty subject to good cause and other exceptions the state may establish. States may also completely terminate other assistance, including Medicaid, for an individual whose cash benefits are stopped for failure to work.[15]

Welfare Reform and Barriers for Battered Women

Women moving from welfare to work face a number of barriers, including a lack of affordable housing, quality child care, and adequate job training, education, or experience. Battered women moving from welfare to work may also face barriers caused by their abusive partners. Almost all of the studies investigating the connection between welfare and domestic violence have found that over half of the women receiving TANF had experienced physical abuse by an intimate partner at some point during their adult lives.[16] Between 9 and 23 percent of women receiving TANF report that they experienced abuse from a male partner *in the past year*.[17] According to Dr. Eleanor Lyon, with the University of Connecticut School of Social Work, "Although the specific behaviors and time frames differ across studies, the studies have consistently shown that rates of physical and sexual violence for women receiving TANF are significantly higher than for other low-income women from the same neighborhoods."[18]

Studies show that women who are currently experiencing domestic violence are interested in working and are as likely to be employed as those who are not. However, because of the batterer's abusive behaviors, battered women on TANF may have more difficulty sustaining their employment. The evidence of batterers' interference with women's efforts to obtain education, training, or employment, and to sustain these efforts over time, is alarmingly high. According to the 1998 U.S. General Accounting Office Report to Congressional Committees, batterers "often feel threatened by women's efforts to improve themselves and become financially independent."[19]

Batterers engage in a number of abusive behaviors to prevent their partners from finding or keeping employment, including "promising child care that they then fail to deliver; destroying or hiding items the women need for the [employment] activities; and inflicting visible signs of abuse, such as bruises, black eyes, and cigarette burns, so the women will be too embarrassed to go to training, work or a job interview."[20] A 2000 study found that 32 percent of the women enrolled in a job-readiness program in western Pennsylvania were told by their abusive partners that they would never be able to succeed at work or school. Twelve percent of the women were told by their partners that working mothers were bad mothers.[21] A Wisconsin study found that 30 percent of the women who reported current or past abuse also reported they had been fired or had lost a job because of domestic violence, and 35 percent said their education and training efforts had been hindered by their abusive partners.[22]

The Family Violence Option and TANF

As of August 2000, thirty-nine states had adopted the Family Violence Option, a provision of the federal welfare legislation that allows a state to temporarily exempt survivors of domestic violence from work requirements while they continue to receive services and take the other necessary steps toward self-sufficiency. It also allows battered women to apply for a waiver from cooperation with child-support-enforcement efforts.[23]

It is important to note that domestic-violence survivors are typically very cautious regarding whom they tell about the abuse. Many may feel that talking about the abuse will actually place them in *greater danger*. One study found that 70 percent of abused women did not disclose the violence to a TANF worker. Reasons included because they did not think it was the worker's business (32 percent); they were embarrassed (24 percent); they didn't think the worker had time to help them (10 percent); the worker seemed insensitive to them (6 percent); and they were afraid of losing their benefits (4.5 percent).[24] One comprehensive study of domestic-violence disclosure rates found that rates were higher when workers asked direct questions about abuse rather than providing information about the Family

Violence Option and then waiting for women to bring up the topic themselves. It is noteworthy that survivors reported it was better to be asked directly
about the violence.[25]

While some survivors may be willing to disclose the violence, there is no
guarantee the disclosure will be met with effective or appropriate responses.
One domestic-violence program in Chicago found that screening procedures,
poor interagency communication, TANF worker roles, and workers' attitudes
about domestic violence seriously hampered TANF workers' referral rates to
appropriate domestic-violence agencies.[26] According to Dr. Lyon:

> It should be clear that *passage* of the FVO [Family Violence Option]
> has not been enough to assure women's safety; instead, the way it is
> implemented is central.... Assisting battered women will require sen-
> sitivity to differences in women's strengths and needs, which can be
> achieved by providing safe and confidential opportunities for commu-
> nication, and attention to what individual women say they need to
> achieve both safety and self-sufficiency. Women should be given the
> opportunity for voluntary and confidential disclosure of domestic vio-
> lence, and be assessed for other issues that have been identified as
> barriers to employment. Women also need to be informed of all the
> implications of disclosure, and must have the opportunity to explore
> the consequences of disclosure for their ongoing safety. In order for
> TANF staff to engage in such initial screening safely and effectively, it is
> important that they receive specific training about the dynamics of do-
> mestic violence, and [about] women's highly variable reactions and
> sources of risk.[27]

Corporate Responses to Domestic Violence

Despite the prevalence of domestic violence, the corporate community has
not considered it a high-priority concern until relatively recently. Although
women comprise almost half of the workforce in the United States, only a few
corporations have taken leadership roles in the issue. This is beginning to
change, however, as an increasing number of corporate leaders recognize the
serious impact domestic violence has on both their employees' lives and their
companies.

In a 2002 survey conducted on behalf of Liz Claiborne, Inc., senior corporate executives in companies across the United States were interviewed
about their perceptions of domestic violence and the workplace. Fully 91 percent of the respondents believed that domestic violence affects both the private and the working lives of their employees, and more than 56 percent were
aware of employees who had been affected by domestic violence.[28] A 1994

study, also conducted on behalf of Liz Claiborne, Inc., found that 66 percent of those surveyed believed that a company's financial performance would benefit from addressing the issue among its employees, while only 30 percent said domestic violence was not serious enough to merit a companywide response. However, in both the 1994 and 2002 studies only 12 percent of the respondents said they believed that corporations should play a major role in addressing the problem of domestic violence. Instead, they said responsibility for dealing with the issue should fall to the family, social-service organizations, and the court system.[29]

Esta Soler, executive director of the Family Violence Prevention Fund and also of the National Workplace Resource Center on Domestic Violence, responded to the earlier survey: "Business leaders still feel that the responsibility for addressing domestic violence should fall to the family, despite the fact that the family's failure to deal with this problem has caused it to rise to crisis proportions. Abuse in the home is not just a private family matter. It is time for our society and corporate leaders to take responsibility for this problem."[30]

In 1995, the Corporate Alliance to End Partner Violence (CAEPV) formed to become a leading force in the struggle to end domestic violence. Founded by business leaders and focused on the workplace, it is the only national organization of its kind. It states that its mission is to "aid in the prevention of partner violence by leveraging the strength and resources of the corporate community. We believe that business plays an essential role in raising awareness of the issue and that our sustained efforts will help reduce and ultimately eliminate partner violence." CAEPV has brought together dozens of progressive companies who exchange information, collaborate on projects, and use their influence to promote change.[31]

Several corporations have made noble efforts to address domestic violence in the workplace. The rest of this section describes a few corporate programs, a program sponsored by a labor union, and a program in Texas designed to engage the corporate community there in addressing the matter.

Polaroid Corporation

Polaroid has developed both in-house services for its employees and initiatives at the local and national levels. The company's employee-assistance program (EAP), which provides employees with counseling and support on various issues, trains its staff to counsel victims of family violence and to refer batterers to community resources. Lunchtime seminars have been held throughout the company featuring guest speakers from local police departments and battered-women's shelters. Polaroid tries to accommodate employees affected by family violence who need time off in order to seek safety and protection, make court appearances, or arrange new housing. The company offers flexible work hours, short-term paid leaves of absence, and extended leaves without pay with the guarantee of the same position upon return.

In addition to its internal programs, Polaroid also donates money to community domestic-violence programs and, through its Domestic Violence Injury Documentation seminar, trains law-enforcement professionals in the photographic documentation of domestic-violence crimes. The seminar covers such topics as lighting and composition techniques for photographing victim's injuries and crime scenes. Seminar attendees also receive training in how to testify in court with evidential photography.[32]

Verizon Wireless

Among Verizon's priorities are raising awareness about domestic violence and ensuring the safety of survivors while they're at work. Employees can request a leave of absence, increased security at work, or a change in shift or work location. The EAP is available to employees twenty-four hours a day. The company's security response features a workplace violence-prevention policy that includes a focus on domestic violence. As president and CEO Denny Strigl explains, "When you think about it, corporations spend millions of dollars placing and training employees. It only makes sense to protect that investment by getting your employees the help they need to be safe from harm."[33]

Verizon Wireless is well known for its phone-recycling program, Hope-Line. Since 2001 the company has donated more than $8 million to domestic-violence shelters and prevention programs.[34]

Blue Shield of California

Blue Shield's Domestic Violence Initiative includes a variety of components. In partnership with local programs and shelters, it has provided domestic-violence prevention sessions for various businesses across California. It has produced kits for helping employers make workplaces safer for survivors of domestic abuse and a video on domestic violence and the workplace. It has reached out to the medical community on the topic of domestic abuse and is prominent in supporting local shelters.

The Limited, Inc.

Each associate of the company is provided with domestic-violence resource information in the employee handbook that is distributed annually. The company has conducted training sessions for all of its human-resource managers and executives. It has also sponsored forums on domestic violence and the workplace for human-resource executives of other companies in the greater Columbus and Albuquerque areas.

Marshalls, Inc.

Marshalls created the Marshalls Domestic Peace Prize, a fund to which employees may donate during the annual giving campaign. The fund gives periodic awards of ten thousand dollars to innovative programs working to prevent domestic violence.

American Federation of State, County, and Municipal Employees (AFSCME)

The labor union AFSCME has conducted nationwide trainings on domestic violence for all of its members. District Council 37, in New York City, offers comprehensive services to its members who experience domestic violence, including legal and social-service benefits.[35]

Liz Claiborne's Women's Work Program

Perhaps no U.S. corporation has done more to establish itself as a leader in domestic-violence intervention and prevention than Liz Claiborne, Inc. The company is continually seeking new ways to have a positive impact on the problem and has developed some innovative programs and policies.

Liz Claiborne's Women's Work program was created in 1991 with the mission of reaching out to women and their families to create positive social change in the issues affecting them. The program seeks both to educate the general public about domestic violence and to raise corporate America's awareness of the need to address the problem.[36] For more than a decade the company has implemented a wide variety of public-education campaigns using art, music, film, sports, and various products, and it came up with the tag line "Love is not abuse" to represent its long-term commitment to the issue.

Each October, which is National Domestic Violence Awareness Month, Liz Claiborne donates 10 percent of its sales from Charity Shopping Days as well as profits from sales of T-shirts and other commemorative items to local family-violence organizations. National Domestic Violence Awareness Month, sponsored by the National Coalition Against Domestic Violence, involves efforts at the national, state, and local levels to heighten awareness and understanding of the problem. Billboard and radio public-service campaigns have been developed in San Francisco, Boston, and Miami to help mobilize community groups and retailers.[37]

In 2003 Liz Claiborne joined forces with *Marie Claire* magazine and Polaroid to launch the No More Tour, a national bus tour and film festival that visited Washington, D.C., Atlanta, Austin, and Los Angeles during National Domestic Violence Awareness Month. In each city, activities included campus events with live musical performances, screenings of winning films from the

Stop the Violence student short-film contest, and book discussions.[38] The campaign has sought to raise awareness of family violence among the public at large and among the following groups specifically:

◆ *College students:* A survey was conducted in 1995 to determine their knowledge and perceptions of domestic violence and its impact on their lives.

◆ *Legal and medical establishments:* Programs have been designed to encourage awareness and intervention in these communities.

◆ *"Influentials":* Information on the issue of violence has been distributed to politicians, celebrities, and business and community leaders.

◆ *Corporate sector:* Surveys of Fortune 1000 CEOs were conducted in 1994 and 2002 to determine their understanding of family violence, and materials for display in employee areas were distributed.

Liz Claiborne also turned its attention inward, toward its own employees, by developing a written policy on domestic violence. (To see a copy of the policy, visit either of the following websites: www.loveisnotabuse.com/pdf/domestic_policy.pdf *or* http://endabuse.org/workplace/print.php?DocID =33014.) The company provides a nationwide employee-assistance program for its employees, their spouses, and anyone else with whom employees share a household. To get help, employees can either walk into the health-services department or, to maintain confidentiality, call a toll-free hotline and receive counseling and referrals. All division heads within the company are prepared to assist by referring an employee to health services or to the hotline and allowing time off from work to seek help. Seminars on family stress have been instituted as part of the Women's Work program and are open to all employees. The company has also instituted security measures for employees who feel threatened by a violent partner. At an employee's request the company will try to provide a parking space near the facilities and an escort to and from the employee's vehicle. The workplace is secured by guards or receptionists equipped with panic buttons.[39]

Company leaders have come to understand that their internal workplace efforts are just as important as their public-education campaigns. The company formed a Domestic Violence Response Team (DVRT), made up of representatives from the legal, security, and human-resources departments. The team's purpose is to increase employees' reporting of workplace concerns related to domestic abuse. When management becomes aware that abuse is affecting an employee at work, the DVRT meets to evaluate, plan, and take action to implement the best course of action. Focusing on security and performance needs, the team takes a comprehensive approach to each employee's situation. Appropriate training of personnel in each of the three departments involved in the DVRT has been a key component of the company's organized response.[40]

Drawing on the lessons learned from its internal and external campaigns, Liz Claiborne, Inc., has begun to reach out to others in the corporate sector to encourage them to take action against domestic violence in both the workplace and the community. According to Jane Randel, vice president of corporate communications, "In reaching out to other businesses, we've learned their motivation for getting on board is usually not about the 'bottom line'; it's more about the humanity of the issue, about caring for employees."[41]

Texas Council on Family Violence (TCFV)

The Texas Council on Family Violence is making great strides in reaching out to the corporate community in its state. In 1996 the agency produced an eighteen-minute training video for businesses titled *A Home Away from Home: The Impact of Domestic Violence on the Workplace.* In addition, TCFV staff have developed a training manual to help employers (1) effectively intervene when an employee is experiencing domestic violence, (2) design an organizational action plan to address domestic violence as it affects the workplace, and (3) educate corporate leaders about the financial, medical, and emotional impact of domestic violence on the workplace. The agency has also sponsored workshops for business professionals that feature presentations made by experts in workplace violence.

In 2003 TCFV formed the Texas Business Alliance to End Domestic Violence (TBA-EDV) with the goal of providing avenues and resources for Texas businesses to address domestic violence. TBA-EDV both addresses safety issues related to domestic abuse in the workplace and builds statewide support of domestic-violence programs. Many leading Texas businesses are members of the alliance, including Verizon Wireless, Univision, Clear Channel Worldwide, Motorola, Inc., Time Warner Cable, Mary Kay, Inc., Austin Community College, H-E-B, *Texas Monthly,* Seton Healthcare Network, Humana, and the Women's Chamber of Commerce of Texas.[42]

A Proactive Response to Domestic Violence in the Workplace

Although many corporate leaders still believe that the task of addressing domestic violence should fall primarily to social-service agencies and other such entities, corporations have a responsibility to support employees whose lives are affected by violence. The Occupational Safety and Health Administration (OSHA) has no specific regulations for preventing workplace violence, but the OSHA General Duty Clause does require employers to provide a safe and healthful working environment for all workers.[43]

Most corporate leaders agree that it is important to protect employees from domestic violence at work. Eighty-six percent of the respondents in the 1994 Liz Claiborne survey felt that companies have a responsibility for the general well-being of their employees. In fact, 58 percent of them sponsor domestic-violence awareness or survivor-support programs for employees, and nearly 75 percent offer domestic-violence counseling or assistance programs. Specific components of the programs included referrals (87 percent), counseling (72 percent), and company-paid benefits to cover physical or psychological care (70 percent).[44] The most effective workplace responses to domestic violence are proactive and build on a company's commitment to safety and support. Companies that invest in such efforts are able to protect lives and save millions of dollars in medical costs, lost productivity, damaged property, and avoided lawsuits.

Although domestic violence is a complex issue, workplace responses to it need not be. Employers may be able to effectively address the matter simply by modifying existing programs and policies that deal with human-resource concerns, workplace safety, and employee training.[45] The Family Violence Prevention Fund, in its publication *The Workplace Responds to Domestic Violence: A Resource Guide for Employers, Unions and Advocates,* makes specific recommendations, grouped into the following four categories: creating a fair workplace, creating a safe workplace, creating an informed and productive workplace, and creating a socially responsible workplace.[46] The rest of this section examines each of these topics.

Creating a Fair Workplace: Company Policies of Intolerance to Domestic Violence

The first step in creating a proactive response to domestic violence involves forming an interdepartmental management team comprising representatives from the human-resource, benefits, legal, medical, and security divisions (including the EAP). Employees who have experienced domestic violence should also be invited to participate. The team's mission is to review existing policies and programs to determine their sensitivity to employees experiencing domestic violence and, with the cooperation of the CEO, to design procedures that clearly convey the company's commitment to establishing a workplace that is intolerant of domestic violence.[47] Findings and recommendations for change should be reported to senior management. Guidelines concerning domestic violence should be communicated to all employees and should complement existing personnel and grievance procedures.[48]

Creating a Fair Workplace: Human-Resource Policies

All human-resource policies should recognize and be sensitive to the special needs of employees experiencing domestic violence, especially those relating to employee absences and supervisory procedures.[49] Women who are trying to escape abusive partners need time to plan, make necessary arrangements, and act. Policies should permit employees to take time off for court appearances and meetings with agencies and individuals that are offering help. If there is a high risk of death or physical assault, an employee may need to leave the area to escape the batterer for a length of time that depends on the situation. A policy that permits an employee to take an unpaid leave of absence under special circumstances can be lifesaving.

There may also be occasions when an employee is at such serious risk that she may need to relocate to escape her abusive partner. If a company has a policy of transferring employees to other job sites, employees at risk of life-threatening assault should be considered for relocation. This type of relocation requires special safety precautions, which include not disclosing the new location to coworkers at the original worksite except on a need-to-know basis, and removing the employee's name and other identifying information from all company directories and organizational charts.

Battered employees may require sick leave for special medical treatment—such as physical therapy or reconstructive surgery—of the physical trauma they have suffered. In addition, others in the home besides the battered partner are often affected by the abuse. An employee may need medical leave to care for a family member or other member of the household who has been hurt by the batterer.

Many performance problems, including those caused by domestic violence, can be addressed through existing personnel policies and programs. However, the complex nature of domestic violence may continue to cause performance problems until the violence is stopped and the employee receives the help she needs. Although performance guidelines should be consistently applied to all employees, a special effort should be made to consider all aspects of the battered employee's situation. Supervisors should attempt to make every accommodation possible within the framework of the guidelines. Company policy, which usually describes the process supervisors must use to address performance problems, should include referral to an employee-assistance program or other source of help.

Creating a Safe Workplace

In a survey conducted by the National Safe Workplace Institute of 248 corporate security and safety directors, 94 percent of the respondents said that domestic violence was a high-security problem at their companies. More than 90 percent had seen at least three cases of men stalking women. Sixty-four percent reported that their companies did not have explicit procedures for encouraging battered employees to report threats of domestic violence, and 61 percent reported that their companies did not have established procedures for protecting employees experiencing domestic violence.[50]

If a company has any form of security, it can prove valuable to employees who are being harassed by their abusive partners. Among the safety and security measures that should be examined are the safety of parking areas, the presence of full-time or after-hours security guards, monitoring and warning systems, limited-access key cards, and visitor policies.[51] Batterers can be extremely resourceful in gaining access to buildings and work sites; often they simply talk their way in. Security guards should be trained to handle the special safety needs of battered women. In addition, supervisors should be trained in company policies on violence and harassment and instructed to contact the appropriate persons when they know or suspect that an employee is being abused by her partner. In cases of domestic violence, confidentiality policies should extend beyond protecting personal information to include information about an employee's job title, work schedule, dates of service, and work site locations.

Additional safety measures that can help to protect battered employees are the following:[52]

- Relocating the employee's workstation
- Changing the employee's work schedule
- Showing a photograph of the batterer to receptionists and security personnel
- Installing security cameras near entrances to the employee's work area
- Escorting the employee to and from her car
- Placing silent alarms at the employee's workstations

If harassment is persistent, company security can call in local law enforcement, who can further involve the telephone company and others as needed. Some employers have obtained restraining orders on behalf of their abused employees, a step that may actually help to reduce the possibility of a batterer's retaliating against his partner who requests the order in her own name.[53] Companies can arrange for a meeting between security personnel and local law-enforcement agencies to facilitate the sharing of appropriate information and the development of collaborative working relationships. Emphasis should be placed on developing procedures for interacting with law-enforcement officials.

Creating an Informed and Productive Workplace: Employee-Assistance Programs

If a company provides an employee-assistance program, the program's staff, in collaboration with local shelters, should receive training in how to provide information and referrals to employees who are experiencing domestic violence. EAP staff can assist employees in several areas, including crisis intervention, problem solving, dealing with work issues, and accessing other company services.[54] Staff should have information about local battered-women's shelters and other helpful service agencies. In addition, they should be able to help employees create safety plans (see Appendix II for an example of a safety plan).

Creating an Informed and Productive Workplace: Employee Training

Whereas 57 percent of corporate leaders who responded to the 1994 Liz Claiborne survey believed that companies *should* have programs to provide their employees with information on domestic violence, only 42 percent of respondents said their companies actually *did* have such programs.[55] Many large corporations offer programs to promote employee wellness. Domestic-violence awareness and prevention programs can easily be incorporated into these efforts.

Workshops on domestic violence can be held as part of the employee-training program. For example, a domestic-violence survivor can be invited to speak about her experiences and the impact they had on her life and specifically on her work. Staff from local battered-women's shelters can be invited to discuss the topic. A training program for all supervisors can be established to provide guidance on how to respond when an employee experiences domestic violence. Specialized training can be arranged for company nurses, EAP staff, and others who may work with abuse survivors.

Additional employee training can be conducted in the following ways:

◆ Sponsor a companywide educational campaign that includes an acknowledgment from the CEO, in the form of a letter or memo to the staff, of the need for heightened awareness of domestic violence.

◆ Distribute educational materials about domestic violence to all employees.

◆ Display posters and brochures that examine the issue and send the message that there is no excuse for domestic violence.

◆ Make safety information available in private places, such as restrooms or paycheck envelopes.

◆ Include articles on domestic violence in the company newsletter.

Creating a Socially Responsible Workplace: Support of Local Domestic-Violence Programs

Effectively addressing domestic violence requires a collaborative effort from all parts of society, including the business sector. To support community domestic-violence programs, companies can consider adopting a local shelter and holding a drive in the workplace to collect monetary donations and such needed items as toys, clothing, diapers, personal-hygiene items, baby formula, food, furniture, office equipment and supplies, and perhaps company products. Employees can also volunteer their time.

Companies can work with and support local domestic-violence programs by having company representatives serve on boards, donating a percentage of their profits during National Domestic Violence Awareness Month (October), cosponsoring conferences and workshops on domestic violence, and sponsoring mentoring programs for shelter residents.

Responding to Battered Employees

To effectively respond to employees experiencing domestic violence, organizations must first take the abuse seriously and treat the employee respectfully. Battered women are often isolated and feel their situation is unique. A battered employee may be embarrassed to discuss her situation with anyone. Many battered women are afraid that no one will believe them. If a woman has previously raised the issue with someone and has been blamed or judged, or the abuse has been minimized, she may withdraw. Other women may deny or minimize the abuse to make their home situations more tolerable.

Supervisors can be of help by watching for the following warning signs of abuse among their employees.

Warning Signs of Domestic Abuse

◆ Physical indicators such as bruises, which the employee may attempt to hide with makeup or clothing

◆ Claims of being "accident-prone," which can be a way to cover up abuse

- Pregnancy, since abuse often escalates during pregnancy

- Signs of depression, including crying at work

- A mention of having stress at home

- Harassing telephone calls at work

- Frequent absences from work, especially taking vacation days sporadically and one to three days at a time

- Frequent doctor appointments

- Frequent references to a partner's anger or temper or an apparent fear of the partner

- Decreased productivity

- Inattentiveness

- Lack of access to such resources as money or a car

- Isolation from friends, family, and even coworkers

Reaching Out to Battered Employees

People are often reluctant to approach a woman whom they suspect is being abused. They may feel that to ask questions is to intrude into the woman's personal life. The key is to ask questions and offer comments that let her know you are concerned and that it is okay for her to bring up important personal issues. A good way to start is to say, "You're such a good employee, but you seem to be depressed lately. I want you to know I'm here if you want to talk." Or, "Can I help in any way?"

It is often very difficult for a battered woman to tell a supervisor or coworker that she is in crisis and is afraid of her partner. If she appears willing to talk, try asking clear, direct questions in a sensitive and caring manner. For example:

- Has your partner ever threatened to hurt you?

- Are you afraid of your partner when he gets mad?

- Does your partner try to control how you dress, whom you associate with, or what you do?

- Has your partner ever hit you or your children?

According to Jim Hardeman, former corporate EAP manager for Polaroid and founder of the Massachusetts-based consulting firm Workplace Violence Interventions and Strategies, direct questions about family violence should be asked when there is either evidence of abuse or a strong suspicion that the woman is being abused. Employee-assistance program and human-resources staff should, however, ask indirect questions of all female employees seeking counseling services, regardless of whether there is evidence of abuse. Hardeman offers the following as examples of indirect questions that should be asked:[56]

- I talk to many women who are having problems. Many of them are being hurt by a loved one. Are you in this situation?

- Many women I talk to are in relationships where their partners are abusing them in some way. Are you in a situation like this?

Certain questions should not be asked, as they tend to shut down the conversation. For example:

- Don't ask why she stays with her partner. Her inability to leave is a part of the crisis she is experiencing.

- Don't ask if she is a "battered woman." Many battered women deny or minimize the abuse they suffer and will not readily identify with the term.

- Don't ask what she has done to provoke the violence or why she thinks her partner is abusive to her. Both questions suggest that she is being blamed for the abuse.

If a battered employee discloses her situation and is comfortable discussing it with you, the following tips may be helpful:

- Encourage her to talk about her abusive situation and her feelings about it.

- Validate all of her feelings, including those of anger, shame, fear, guilt, confusion, and hopelessness.

- Let her know you believe her. Also let her know that the abuse she is suffering is not only illegal but also unacceptable to you and the company.

- Let her know you do not blame her for what is happening to her and that it is not her fault.

- Let her know that she is not alone and that she has your support and the support of the company.

- Gently remind her that domestic violence usually gets worse without outside intervention. Let her know there are domestic-violence programs that can help.

- Ask her how you can help.

◆ If she needs help with referrals, a place to stay, someone to talk to, information about battering, or information on creating a safety plan, refer her to appropriate internal divisions such as the company's employee-assistance program, a local battered-women's shelter, or the state's coalition against domestic violence. You can find out about your state's coalition by calling the National Domestic Violence Hotline, (800) 799-SAFE (7233).

Continue to check in with her as she struggles with her situation, but be aware that she may not be ready to take action. Resist the temptation to make decisions for her. Instead, allow her to make her own decisions, and be supportive whether she leaves or stays in the relationship. It may be helpful to review Chapter 8 of this book. Offering assistance and then stepping back is often the most difficult aspect of helping someone. It is, however, one of the most beneficial and empowering actions you can take.

...*10*

Battered Women's Health: The Response of the Medical Community

When physicians and nurses do nothing, even when the victim/ patient knows they know, they magnify the victim's anxiety, hopelessness, fear, and shame—her sense that she alone is responsible for her safety, that she alone is perhaps, after all, to blame.

> — *Ann Jones, author of* Next Time She'll Be Dead: Battering and How to Stop It[1]

Many battered women may never call the police, go to court, or flee to a shelter. A great number of battered women, however, do visit doctors and hospitals for treatment of injuries and stress-related illnesses. According to a 1998 report released by the National Institute of Justice and the Centers for Disease Control and Prevention, women make 693,933 visits to the health-care system each year as a result of injuries from physical assaults, the majority of which are for treatment of injuries inflicted by intimate partners.[2] A 1997 Department of Justice study reports that 37 percent of women admitted to an emergency room for violence-related injuries were abused by an intimate partner.[3]

183

Battered
Women's
Health: The
Response of
the Medical
Community

Edward Gondolf and Ellen Fisher, in a study of women in Texas shelters, found that 42 percent of them sought hospital care for their injuries.[4] Evan Stark and Anne Flitcraft reviewed the medical records of 3,676 randomly selected women with injury complaints at a major metropolitan hospital. Those identified as battered averaged one injury-related visit per year to the emergency room. Compare this with nonbattered women, who may make one injury-related visit to an emergency service in a lifetime.[5]

Medical costs associated with domestic violence are staggering. Direct medical and mental-health-care services for survivors total nearly $4.1 billion each year.[6] Studies indicate that domestic-violence survivors have 50 percent higher medical costs than individuals who do not experience partner violence.[7] Although numerous battered women seek emergency service, an even greater number are found in nontrauma caseloads. Twenty to 25 percent of obstetrical patients have a history of battering. Estimates of the proportion of patients in primary-care clinics who are battered women range from 28 to 38 percent.[8]

Health Risks for Battered Women

In her study of battered women who killed their abusive partners, Angela Browne found that their injuries ranged from bruises, cuts, black eyes, concussions, broken bones, and miscarriages caused by beatings to such permanent injuries as damage to joints, partial loss of hearing or vision, and scars from burns, bites, or knife wounds.[9] Lenore Walker, in *The Battered Woman,* groups the injuries of battered women treated in hospital emergency rooms into several categories. The first category is serious bleeding injuries, including wounds requiring stitches, especially around the face and head. The second category is internal injuries that cause bleeding and malfunctioning of organs. The women Walker interviewed reported damage to their spleens and kidneys and punctured lungs. The third category is damage to bones, including cracked vertebrae, skulls, and pelvises as well as broken jaws, arms, and legs. The fourth category is burns, including cigarette burns, burns from hot appliances such as stoves and irons, and burns from acids and scalding liquids.[10] One battered woman seeking shelter from the Austin Center for Battered Women (now SafePlace) described how her husband poured drinking alcohol over her and then methodically threw matches at her until she caught on fire.

According to Browne, the force with which an act is carried out, repetitions of the act, and the clustering of various violent acts determine the severity of the injuries. The clustering of violent acts during an assault frequently produces a distinctive pattern of injuries characterized by multiple injury sites.

Typically, the injuries are to the face and central areas of the body rather than to the extremities. Battered women are thirteen times more likely than other accident victims to sustain injuries to the breasts, chest, and abdomen.[11] Frequency of injury is also an indicator of domestic violence. A woman who goes to the emergency room with injuries three times has an 80 percent chance of being a battered woman, whether or not the injuries require sutures. High frequency of injuries and the presence of multiple injury sites increase the likelihood that a woman is being battered.[12]

Richard Gelles and Murray Straus asked battered women to compare their present health with their health prior to being beaten by their partners. Women who had experienced violence, especially severe violence, reported that their health, the amount of stress they were under, the chances of their feeling bad or depressed, and their drinking and alcohol problems were much worse than before the violence began. Gelles and Straus asked the more than three thousand women who participated in their survey to give a general evaluation of their health. The greater the violence experienced, the more likely it was that women reported their health as fair or poor. Battered women also reported that they stayed in bed due to illness an average of one day each month, which is twice as often as women from nonviolent homes.[13]

The stress of an abusive relationship increases women's risk of depression, suicide, and substance abuse.[14] One 1999 study found that women experiencing domestic violence were about twice as likely to be coping with some form of depression. Battered women have a rate of attempted suicide approximately five to eight times that of nonbattered women.[15] Battered women often have symptoms of posttraumatic stress disorder similar to those experienced by soldiers, hostages, and prisoners of war. Headaches, abdominal pains, and atypical chest pains are not uncommon. Physical problems associated with depression, such as backaches, gastrointestinal problems, fatigue, restlessness, loss of appetite, and sleep problems, are also common.[16] Complications of previous injuries—for example, recurrent sinus infections among women who have suffered fractured facial bones—are another source of medical illness among battered women. Many physicians have also noted that chronic illnesses such as asthma, diabetes, arthritis, hypertension, and heart disease may be exacerbated in women who are being abused.[17]

Abused women frequently experience significant changes in their eating habits. For many women the changes, though relatively short in duration, are concurrent with the violence. Battered women may be unable to eat because of nausea or may be able to eat but unable to keep the food down. For some battered women, regulating caloric intake may be the one area in which they feel they can exert influence in a world that otherwise appears beyond their

185

Battered
Women's
Health: The
Response of
the Medical
Community

control. *Choice* and *self-control* are terms that women repeatedly use to describe being thin.[18] Battered women's struggles with eating disorders are not simply to achieve thinness, but to gain control over their lives.

The sexual specificity of battering is evident by the frequency of abusive assaults during pregnancy. According to the findings of the U.S. Centers for Disease Control and Prevention and the American College of Obstetricians and Gynecologists (ACOG), domestic violence during pregnancy may be more common than preeclampsia, gestational diabetes, and neural-tube defects such as spina bifida.[19] Between 25 and 60 percent of abused women are assaulted during pregnancy. Stark and Flitcraft found that battered women are three times more likely than nonbattered women to be pregnant when injured by undetermined causes. As a result, they experience a greater number of miscarriages.[20] Other effects of battering during pregnancy include separation of the placenta from the uterus; antepartum hemorrhage; fetal fractures; low infant birthweight; and rupture of the mother's uterus, liver, or spleen.[21] The unfortunate reality is that the most common cause of death among pregnant women is homicide, frequently committed by an intimate partner.[22]

Sexual coercion and assault are common in abusive relationships. Women who have been repeatedly raped frequently experience vaginal discharge, itching, chronic yeast infections, burning sensations when urinating, and general genital discomfort. Vaginal and anal bleeding are not uncommon and often require internal and external suturing. Victims of sexual assault are also at risk of acquiring sexually transmitted diseases, including chlamydia, gonorrhea, syphilis, herpes, trichomoniasis, and HIV, the virus that causes AIDS.[23] Many battered women have been infected with STDs by batterers who force them into unprotected sex. Some batterers deliberately infect their partners to prevent them from having sex with other men. A direct link has been identified between battering and the spread of HIV and AIDS in women.[24]

The batterer's control frequently extends to the medical setting. He may limit the woman's access to routine or emergency medical care, remain with her constantly during her stay, or insist that she be released prematurely. He may also prevent her from taking her medication as prescribed, hide or destroy her birth control, or prevent her from keeping medical appointments.[25]

Public Policy and the Well-Being of Battered Pregnant Women

A number of recent, and highly publicized, criminal cases have brought to the public's attention the danger that many pregnant women face. Mark Hacking is accused of killing his pregnant wife, Lori, in Salt Lake City. Scott

186

⎯⎯⎯⎯⎯

**When
Violence
Begins
at Home**

Peterson was recently found guilty of killing his pregnant wife, Laci, in Modesto, California.[26] Not all cases of domestic abuse resulting in murder are reported in the national news, but certain ones have drawn widespread media attention. According to Dr. Diana Cheng, director of women's health at the Maryland Department of Health and Medical Hygiene, "People are interested in Laci Peterson and Lori Hacking because they seemed so normal and happy in their relationships."[27] In particular, the public outrage over the death of Laci Peterson and her unborn son, Conner, fueled the passage of the federal Unborn Victims of Violence Act, which many feel ultimately undermines *Roe v. Wade,* the 1973 Supreme Court decision that legalized abortion.

Although clinical study after clinical study has repeatedly called upon the health-care community to aggressively screen pregnant women for domestic violence to better address their safety needs and the needs of their unborn children, the medical community continues to fail to do so in a comprehensive and targeted way.[28] On the part of policy makers, instead of improving the criminal-justice and health-care responses to pregnant battered women, the passage of the Unborn Victims of Violence Act has been criticized by many advocates as nothing more than a political agenda disguised as an attempt to ensure the safety of pregnant women and their unborn children. The act was actually introduced while President Bill Clinton was in office. It passed in the House of Representatives but died on the Senate floor because Clinton promised a veto. After Peterson's murder it was reintroduced under the administration of President George W. Bush, passed in both houses of Congress, and signed into law in 2004. It makes a separate and punishable crime of knowingly or unknowingly harming or killing a zygote, embryo, or fetus while attacking a pregnant woman during the commission of a federal crime. It also gives personhood and rights to a zygote, embryo, or fetus at any stage of development, the provision that causes it to be widely viewed as an anti–abortion rights law.[29]

Speaking in July 2003 about the proposed legislation before the Subcommittee on the Constitution Committee on the House Judiciary, Juley Fulcher, public-policy director with the National Coalition Against Domestic Violence, gave voice to the concerns of thousands of women's advocates across the country. She said, "My role here today is to advocate for increased safety for battered women, which in turn will lead to healthier pregnancies and births. Unfortunately, the Unborn Victims of Violence Act (H.R. 1997) does *not* provide the protection that battered women need to obtain safety.... [O]ur response to the problem should be one that truly protects the pregnant woman by early intervention and prevention and not a reaction to a specific set of circumstances after the fact, however horrible and sad."[30] Many advocates believe that the act will actually work against battered women. According to Fulcher:

> This bill would, for the first time, federally recognize that the unborn embryo or fetus could be the victim of a crime. It would not be a large intellectual leap to expand the notion of the unborn fetus as a victim in other realms. In fact, some states have already made that leap and in those states women have been prosecuted and convicted for acts that infringe on state recognized legal rights of a fetus. While the Unborn Victims of Violence Act specifically exempts the mother from prosecution for her own actions with respect to the fetus, it is easy to imagine subsequent legislation that would hold her responsible for injury to the fetus, even for the violence perpetrated on her by her batterer under a "failure to protect" theory. Moreover, a battered woman can be intimidated or pressured by her batterer not to reveal the cause of her miscarriage and, if she is financially or emotionally reliant on her batterer, she may be less likely to seek appropriate medical assistance if doing so could result in the prosecution of her batterer for an offense as serious as murder. The long-term public health implications of such a policy would be devastating for victims of domestic violence and all women.[31]

The concerns of advocates such as Fulcher went unheard.

It is highly unfortunate that this law, which has also been referred to as "Laci and Conner's Law," although intended by some to oversee the safety of battered women and their unborn children, may ultimately serve to erode the rights of all women and further harm battered pregnant women.[32] It is important to note that Senator Dianne Feinstein (D-CA) introduced an alternative measure that would have imposed the same penalties as those prescribed in the Unborn Victims of Violence Act, but without recognizing the fetus as a person and without making harming it a separate crime. Feinstein's bill was rejected by a vote of fifty to forty-nine. According to Eleanor Smeal, president of the Feminist Majority, "The very fact that the majority in the Senate refused to vote for the exact same bill with one small change—not granting separate personhood to the fetus—shows that this legislation had nothing to do with protecting pregnant women, and everything to do with restricting women's rights. This is all part of the attempt by the right-wing to stop women's advancements, and to have legislation in place for when they capture the majority on the Supreme Court. This bill, along with others passed in states and federally, are traps waiting to be used to make abortion and birth control illegal."[33]

The Medical Community's Ineffective Responses to Battered Women

The Family Violence Prevention Fund, in collaboration with the San Francisco Injury Center for Prevention and Research, conducted a survey of all California hospital emergency departments to explore their capacity to respond to the overwhelming number of battered women seeking medical care. The study clearly demonstrated that battered women are not being identified by emergency-department staff and that most ER personnel are not being trained in identification and referral procedures.[34] In a study by Stark and Flitcraft of 481 women seeking emergency medical services, one in four women could be identified as battered, approximately nine times the number identified by emergency-service staff.[35] A study conducted by Carol Warshaw found that emergency-service staff reported explicit information about abuse in only 21 percent of cases involving identified battered women. Despite the existence of hospital guidelines for referring battered women to social-service agencies or shelters, no such information was given to women in more than 90 percent of the cases.[36]

Even in cases in which battering is not officially recognized, physicians seem to make diagnoses that select battered women from the general population of injured patients and treat them differently. Battered women are more likely to leave the emergency room with prescriptions for pain medications or tranquilizers: Only one in ten nonbattered accident victims receives such prescriptions, compared with one in four battered women. In addition, despite the serious injuries battered women suffer, physicians are less likely to clinically follow up on them than they are nonbattered women. When they do receive referrals to social-service agencies, battered women are typically sent to detox programs, drug-dependency units, mental-health clinics, hospitals, or counseling agencies, most of which approach alcoholism or depression as the primary problem and domestic violence as secondary.

Furthermore, abused women are referred to psychiatric staff five times more frequently than nonbattered accident victims. Battered women who complain of frequent headaches, stomach disorders, painful intercourse, and muscle pains but whose X rays and lab tests are normal are often labeled "neurotic," "hysteric," "hypochondriac," or "a well-known patient with multiple vague complaints." One in fifty nonbattered women leaves with such a label, compared with one in four battered women.[37] According to Stark and Flitcraft, "This highlights the tension between patient demand for help and medicine's frustration in the absence of overt physiological disorder. The use of such phrases to characterize patients makes it extremely difficult for them to get sympathetic, quality treatment."[38]

Battered women often make repeated trips to the emergency room, and the treatment they receive there over time tends to follow a certain pattern. At first, the visits are recorded simply as "repeated trauma." Their injuries are defined as the only need for medical care, and questions are focused primarily on obtaining diagnostic information. Patients are often interrupted or redirected when they mention social problems that do not conform to diagnostic reasoning.[39] Gradually, the accumulation of injuries is supplemented by physicians' notes about "vague medical complaints." Eventually, problems such as alcoholism, drug abuse, attempted suicide, depression, fear of child abuse, and a variety of alleged mental illnesses are recognized. At this point the actual source of women's repeated injuries may be noted, but the abuse is dismissed as a consequence of their problem with drugs or an emotional disorder. In shifting the focus from the women's conditions to the women themselves, labels such as "alcoholic," "addict," and "neurotic" are used to explain their continued suffering in a way that leaves the medical paradigm intact.[40] It appears that it is more convenient to blame the woman than to question the treatment approach.

The Medical Power and Control Wheel, shown on page 190, outlines how physicians' interactions with battered women often mirror the abusive partners' behavior. Neglect, inappropriate medication, isolation, blaming the violence on secondary problems such as alcohol, labeling, and punitive referrals (such as to psychiatric facilities) only serve to undermine battered women. The batterer's strategies of coercion, isolation, and control converge with these discriminatory and ineffective medical responses to make it extremely difficult for women to escape from abusive relationships.

Changing the Medical Paradigm

Effectively changing the medical paradigm, or the way of thinking that emphasizes treating the illness or disease rather than focusing on the patient's overall well-being, requires adjustments at many levels. Initially, health-care providers must recognize and educate themselves about the impact of domestic violence on the lives of millions of women. Second, effective strategies to identify and intervene in cases of domestic violence must be developed and utilized. Third, increased cooperation with other societal institutions and community-based organizations must be encouraged and supported. Finally, and perhaps most difficult, attitudes and values surrounding the role of health-care provision for women must be redefined to encourage the empowerment of female patients. The rest of the chapter explores each of these issues.

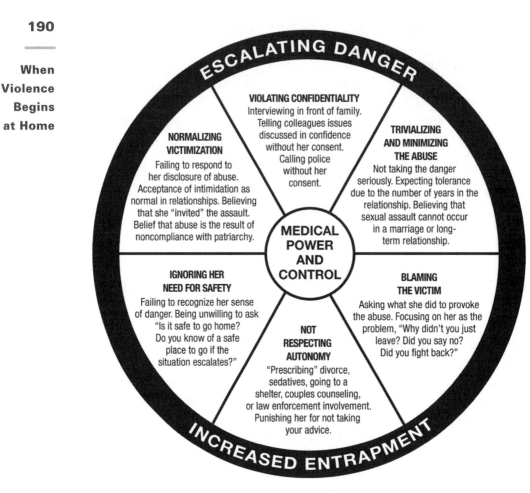

Medical Power and Control Wheel
*Developed by Pathways of Courage, Inc., Women's and Children's Horizons, 1511-
56th St., Kenosha WI 53140, (262) 656-3500, modeled after the "Power and
Control and Equality Wheels" developed by the Domestic Abuse Intervention Project,
202 East Superior St., Duluth MN, (218) 722-2781, www.duluth-model.org.*

Recognition and Education

Despite the medical community's history of inattention to domestic violence,
efforts to educate health-care providers have dramatically increased in the last
couple of decades. Today, medical responses to domestic violence extend from
the Office of the U.S. Surgeon General to such entities as the Centers for Disease Control and Prevention, the Family Violence Prevention Fund (a federally funded center for information on health and domestic violence), state
health departments, professional medical organizations, and public-health organizations. Almost every major association of health-care professionals has

produced comprehensive guidelines, standards of practice, and informational materials to assist medical practitioners in improving their recognition and treatment of battered women.[41]

In 1985 Surgeon General C. Everett Koop suggested that hospitals and trauma centers might prevent further violence by intervening. That same year the Nursing Network on Violence Against Women International was formed, with the goal of helping nurses to provide assistance and support to women in the process of achieving personal empowerment.[42] In 1991 the American Medical Association (AMA) announced the start of a campaign to address family violence as a major health problem, developing diagnostic and treatment guidelines for child abuse and neglect, child sexual abuse, domestic violence, and elder abuse and neglect. The AMA also played a key role in the formation of the National Coalition of Physicians Against Family Violence, which claims membership from more than seventy-five major medical organizations. The American Women's Medical Association, the American Academy of Family Physicians, the American Nurses' Association, the American College of Obstetricians and Gynecologists, and the American College of Emergency Physicians have also worked to create a medical response to family violence.[43]

Increasingly, state and local medical associations are taking a leadership role in addressing family violence. Medical associations in Texas, California, Florida, Iowa, Minnesota, North Carolina, Oklahoma, Oregon, and other states have initiated domestic-violence training and educational activities.[44] In 1992 the Texas Medical Association's (TMA's) Council on Public Health identified family violence as a priority. The council stressed the need for more emphasis on prevention and the importance of the physician's role in addressing the issue. Accordingly, in collaboration with the Texas Council on Family Violence, TMA developed a package of information, *Start the Healing Now: What You Can Do about Family Violence,* that was distributed to primary-care physicians throughout the state.[45]

Initiatives have emphasized the importance of educating medical students about domestic violence. Still, although many medical students now receive basic information on the issue, most medical, nursing, and social-work schools fail to provide students with in-depth instruction in the topic.[46] A 1998 study led by Dr. Elaine Alpert, of the Boston University School of Medicine, examined the content of 126 U.S. medical schools' curricula on family violence (including domestic violence, child abuse, and elder abuse), as well as deans' and students' perceptions of their schools' curricular offerings on the topic. In terms of percentage, a majority of deans reported that their schools' curricula addressed family violence. In terms of numbers, more deans reported that their schools' curricula addressed family violence than did in a similar study conducted in 1987. Unfortunately, however, neither total instructional time nor the amount of curriculum devoted to the issue during clinical training had increased since 1987. In addition, discrepancies existed between students' and deans' awareness of curricula covering these topics. The authors concluded that while the number of schools that reported offering family-violence curriculum had increased, there did not appear to be increased attention paid to the topic, based on time devoted to teaching.[47]

Identification and Intervention

Since 1992 the Joint Commission on Accreditation of Healthcare Organizations (JCAHO) has required that all accredited hospitals implement policies and procedures in their emergency departments and ambulatory-care facilities for identifying, treating, and referring victims of abuse. The standards require educational programs for hospital staff in domestic violence, elder abuse, child abuse, and sexual assault.[48] According to the Family Violence Prevention Fund (FVPF), "Screening for domestic violence provides a critical opportunity for disclosure of domestic violence and provides a woman and her health care provider the chance to develop a plan to protect her safety and improve her health."[49] In *Preventing Domestic Violence: Clinical Guidelines on Routine Screening,* the FVPF recommends the following:

1. That routine screening for domestic violence be carried out for all female patients over age fourteen in the following settings: primary care, obstetrics/gynecology/family planning, emergency department, inpatient, pediatrics, and mental health (routine screening means the provider inquires about domestic violence whether or not symptoms or signs are present and whether or not the provider suspects abuse has occurred)

2. That, within these settings, all practitioners and health organizations implement culturally competent programs to ensure routine screening of all female patients

3. That screening be carried out in private and through the use of straightforward, nonjudgmental questions asked in a culturally competent manner, preferably verbally, and in ways that increase the safety of abused patients and respect their autonomy

4. That the outcomes of the screening be documented confidentially

The physician's role in the intervention process includes not only screening and identification but also validation, appropriate medical treatment, mental-health assessment, clear documentation, safety assessment, appropriate referrals, and follow-up.[50]

The AMA has developed the following lists of indicators that health-care providers can look for as keys to diagnosing domestic violence.[51] In addition, some experts suggest that a patient's chart be flagged when a woman's partner calls to cancel the woman's appointment.

Physical Indicators of Abuse

◆ Type of or extent of injury that is inconsistent with the patient's explanation

◆ Injuries to the head, neck, breasts, chest, or abdomen

◆ Injuries that are consistent with a defensive posture, such as forearm bruises or fractures

◆ Injuries occurring during pregnancy

◆ Repeated or chronic injuries

◆ Multiple injuries or injuries in various stages of healing

◆ Frequent visits for complaints of pain without tissue injury or evidence of disease

◆ Symptoms of migraines, backaches, fatigue, sleep or appetite disturbances, chest pains, hyperventilation, gastrointestinal disorders, or gynecological problems

◆ Substantial delay between the time of injury and presentation for treatment

◆ Asking to see the physician at inappropriate times, such as before or after office hours, for seemingly minor injuries

◆ Evidence of assault to the genital area, indicating rape

Abuse of children and partners frequently occurs simultaneously; therefore, if abuse of one is identified, other family members should be carefully screened.

Behavioral Indicators of Abuse

◆ Thoughts about or attempts at suicide

◆ Depression

◆ Alcohol or drug use

◆ Appearing frightened, nervous, withdrawn, ashamed, evasive, or embarrassed

◆ Patient's being accompanied by her partner, who insists on staying close and answering all questions directed to the patient

◆ Reluctance to speak or disagree in front of the partner

◆ Intense, irrational jealousy or possessiveness on the part of the partner, either visibly or as reported by the patient

◆ Denial or minimization of the violence by either the patient or the partner

◆ Patient's exaggerated sense of personal responsibility for her relationship, including self-blame for her partner's violence

◆ Apparent noncompliance with a medical regimen prescribed for a chronic condition

Despite the initiatives set forth by JCAHO, many hospitals continue to lack standards of practice for managing domestic-violence cases. Basic hospital policy should include asking questions about battering in every unit and as a routine part of every physician's visit. Ineffective responses on the part of medical professionals contribute to women's entrapment in violent relationships, but supportive responses enhance women's opportunities to empower themselves and live free of violence. (The Advocacy Wheel, developed by the Domestic Violence Project, in Kenosha, Wisconsin, and reproduced on page 263, outlines the keys to empowerment-based advocacy for battered women and is a useful guide for anyone interested in helping them.) Effective assessment begins with a patient-centered interview conducted in private, away from family and friends. The need for the patient to trust the physician is especially important. The patient's safety may be jeopardized if the physician discloses a diagnosis of abuse to the woman's partner.[52] Interviews should address any history of trauma sustained by the patient as an adult, an overview of the dynamics in the relationship, a review of health and mental-health problems that may be associated with abuse, and consideration of risk to the children in the family.

To survive in battering relationships, women often deny, minimize, or forget incidents of control and violence. Conducting short interviews frequently and using significant events in a woman's life as markers for violent episodes can help physicians obtain more detailed information.[53] Physicians should routinely ask all women direct, specific questions about abuse. Although women may not bring up the subject of abuse themselves, many will discuss it when asked simple, nonjudgmental questions in a confidential setting. For example:[54]

195

Battered
Women's
Health: The
Response of
the Medical
Community

◆ Because abuse and violence are so common in women's lives, I've begun to routinely ask about it. Are you in a relationship in which you feel you are treated badly?

◆ What happens when you and your partner fight or disagree?

◆ Has your partner ever destroyed things that you cared about?

◆ Has your partner ever forced you to have sex when you didn't want to?

◆ Has your partner ever physically hurt or threatened you?

◆ Has your partner ever threatened or abused your children?

The physician's recognition and validation of the woman's situation is important. Silence, disregard, or disinterest convey acceptance of domestic violence. In contrast, recognition, acknowledgment, and concern confirm the seriousness of the problem and the need to address it. Physicians may choose to identify someone on their office staff who will be responsible for asking every patient about domestic violence. This person should be educated about appropriate questions to ask and knowledgeable about community resources.

Once the diagnosis of battering is established, physicians must convey to their patients concern, respect, and a willingness to offer ongoing support. Let the patient know that she doesn't deserve to be beaten and that she is not alone. Assert that domestic violence is illegal, assure her that it is not her fault and that many others are in the same situation, and ask whether she is interested in community resources. If the patient thinks it is safe for her to have written materials, offer her such information, including telephone numbers for local shelters, crisis services, and legal options. Physicians and therapists should *not* suggest that an abused woman enter couples' counseling with her batterer. Family therapy is inappropriate if domestic violence is occurring; it may actually increase the risk of serious harm.[55]

The possibility of life-threatening violence must always be considered, particularly if violence has resulted in hospitalization. The risk is significantly increased in any of the following circumstances: the woman believes her life is in danger; violence has resulted in previous hospital visits; the batterer has used a gun or knife, stalked her, or threatened to kill her or himself; or the couple is in the process of divorce, separation, or conflict over children.[56]

Routine safety assessment is particularly important for women who have left a violent relationship. In a sample of battered women seeking emergency service, two-thirds were either divorced or separated.[57] Ask a battered woman in this situation if she is safe and encourage her to take steps to protect herself and her children. Do not assure a battered woman of her safety after she has been discharged. The person most qualified to determine whether she will be safe upon leaving the hospital is the woman herself. Only she knows how dangerous her home situation is and when the time is right to leave.

It may be useful to help the patient determine her degree of entrapment by discussing ways in which the batterer might try to control her that could prevent her from defending herself, escaping, or using helping resources when she is threatened or hurt again. Offer to help her develop a safety plan in case violence reoccurs. Safety planning with battered women can address such concerns as going to a shelter or other emergency housing, accessing legal services, getting treatment for substance abuse, finding a women's support group, changing jobs, continuing education, applying for Temporary Assistance for Needy Families or other emergency assistance, getting counseling for children, and dealing with child or adult protective services. A sample safety plan can be found in Appendix II.

Since medical records assist in documenting the abuse, it is particularly important that they be accurate and legible. Include photographs or use a body map to detail the extent of the injuries. Even if the patient chooses not to proceed with legal action immediately, she might in the future and the records will be helpful.[58] In the mid-1990s, when some health-insurance companies began denying coverage to battered women, some advocates maintained that physicians should not write a diagnosis of domestic violence in the medical record as it might be used to deny the patient insurance coverage. Substantial pressure on the insurance industry forced them to change their policies of direct denial and instead to charge higher premiums. Although there is still concern that documenting the existence of domestic violence could adversely affect a woman's ability to obtain affordable insurance, the benefits of documenting it outweigh that possibility.[59]

The success of each stage of the intervention process depends on consistent communication between the patient and the health-care provider, including follow-ups with the patient. It is crucial that the physician support the patient in whatever decision she makes. At the same time, the physician should express concern for her safety and that of her children. Expressing disappointment in a battered woman's decision reinforces her feelings of low self-esteem and lack of control and may also make her less likely to return for help. Even if the woman does not immediately leave her abusive partner, the fact that a health-care provider is concerned about her suffering validates her feelings and reinforces her capacity to seek help when she feels ready to do so.

**Battered
Women's
Health: The
Response of
the Medical
Community**

In March 2004 the third U.S. Preventive Service Task Force (USPSTF) released its updated recommendations on routine screening for family and intimate-partner violence. The task force, an independent panel of private-sector
health-care experts appointed by the federal government, is mandated with
making recommendations on the effectiveness of clinical prevention services.
It based its suggestions on a report prepared by the University of Oregon's
Evidence-Based Practice Center and on judgements about the effectiveness of
screening for and interventions in domestic violence. Ignoring the repeated
recommendations for screening from organizations such as the American
Medical Association, the Family Violence Prevention Fund, and the National
Coalition Against Domestic Violence, the USPSTF concluded that there is insufficient evidence to recommend for or against routine screening for domestic violence in the primary-care setting.[60]

Writing in the journal *Family Violence Prevention and Health Practice*, Dr.
Linda Chamberlain explains the serious consequences of the panel's recommendation:

> The Task Force's conclusion that there is insufficient evidence to rec-
> ommend for or against screening for IPV [intimate-partner violence]
> may discourage the development of assessment and intervention ser-
> vices in the primary care setting for years to come. Professional medi-
> cal societies use the Task Force's recommendations as the basis for
> clinical practice guidelines. Private sector health care organizations
> and government agencies serving Medicare beneficiaries, military per-
> sonnel, and veterans use the recommendations to determine whether
> a service should be offered or reimbursed. Published versions of the
> Task Force's recommendations are used in textbooks to teach medical
> and nursing students about clinical preventive care.[61]

In the fall of 2003, well before the release of the task force's recommendations, the Family Violence Prevention Fund was asked to review and com-
ment on a draft of the recommendations. The FVPF's comprehensive report
outlined numerous problems with the draft and concluded by advising:

> The USPSTF draft statement is too limited in approach and in assess-
> ment of what literature was relevant. We feel strongly that a valid
> analysis must include the growing body of evidence published since
> 1996 recommendations that support the need for assessment and
> brief counseling for family violence as part of a behavioral health as-
> sessment. Women continue to accept routine inquiry, evidence exists
> to indicate that assessments can improve identification and some

health outcomes[,] and the public health benefits resulting from such assessments are significant.... **[W]e urge you to take the additional time necessary to consider a fuller body of research related to assessment for intimate partner violence before proceeding with a final recommendation.**[62]

The published USPSTF recommendations have generated heated reactions from both health-care professionals and battered-women's advocates. In a letter to the *Annals of Internal Medicine*, Dr. John Nelson, president of the American Medical Association, wrote:

> [W]e, along with our colleagues from the medical and domestic violence communities, strongly support assessment for abuse and urge every health care provider to continue or adopt this health-promoting practice.... The American Medical Association and the American Academy of Pediatrics stand by their policy of routine inquiry about abuse. Emerging research and experience confirm that when doctors and other health care providers talk to patients about domestic violence and offer referrals and help to victims, battered patients are more likely to protect themselves and their children.... Let us never minimize the positive role we can play to help victims. No provider should stop inquiring about family violence as a result of this USPSTF recommendation. We believe that a "wait and see" approach is ill-advised and will leave thousands of women without information that could help prevent further violence and save lives.[63]

Collaboration and Innovation

For battered women, the hospital can serve as a vital link to other crisis services. Health-care providers can smooth the way for frightened women by offering encouragement and support for them to seek more specialized help from shelters and battered-women's centers. The transition from hospital to battered-women's center is made even easier when there is a collaboration between the two. Every emergency facility should have a paid battered-woman's advocate either on staff or on call from a battered-women's center. Regrettably, few hospitals offer programs of this nature.

Programs such as Advocacy for Women and Kids in Emergencies (AWAKE), in Boston, WomanKind, in Minneapolis, and Project SAFE, in New Haven, Connecticut, are leading models for collaborative intervention programs between health-care systems and community-based battered-women's programs. Integrating the services of battered-women's programs, state domestic-violence coalitions, medical associations, medical schools, and hospitals, these groups have designed and implemented innovative programs that have successfully assisted battered women and their children and have helped educate the medical community about domestic violence.[64]

In a hallmark effort, the Family Violence Prevention Fund's National Health Initiative on Domestic Violence initiated and operates the National Health Resource Center on Domestic Violence (HRC). The center acts as the nation's clearinghouse for information on the health-care response to domestic violence and provides free technical assistance and materials to thousands of health-care providers each year. It is one of only five specialized resource centers that are funded by the U.S. Department of Health and Human Services.[65] Another recent, innovative project is the joint venture between the HRC and the Indian Health Service Administration for Children and Families (IHS), Sacred Circle, the National Resource Center to End Violence Against Native Women, and Mending the Sacred Hoop: STOP Violence Against Women Technical Assistance Project. The project works to strengthen comprehensive domestic-violence prevention strategies in fifteen American Indian/Alaska Native health-care facilities throughout the U.S. The project, which began in October 2004, is targeted for completion in March 2006.[66]

Empowerment of Female Patients

Events in the past few years exemplify both advancements and setbacks for successful domestic-violence intervention in the health-care community. They reflect a complex mix of society's denial of the prevalence and severity of abuse against women and children and a heightened understanding of the problem. An effective response to domestic violence extends well beyond instituting protocols or asking a few questions. It requires that as individuals we identify and question the power imbalances in our own lives and in the lives of those around us. Doing so allows us to begin to question the institutional and societal traditions that perpetuate violence against women.

Many battered women have been poorly served by a health-care system that too often focuses on medicine as a science and forgets that, above all, it is an art of healing. Good health goes beyond a rigid medical definition and is best expressed by the concept of well-being. The well-being of battered women depends heavily on their empowerment as users of the health-care system. How can women receive better health care if they are alienated by the established medical paradigm? Empowerment does not deny the individual woman her dignity or refute or discount her pain and fear.

As Jeanne Achterberg, author of *Woman as Healer,* says, "The growth and change in health care will obviously depend upon the breadth of our energies and the richness of our creative process."[67] Empowerment means eliminating

199

Battered
Women's
Health: The
Response of
the Medical
Community

the myths, prejudices, and preconceived notions about women and women's bodies. Empowerment means providing women with a safe, confidential environment where they can discuss, make decisions about, and be the ones to control their health and their lives. The empowerment of battered women involves the sharing of information so that everyone will be an equal partner in the patient-doctor relationship.

...11

Battered Women and Communities of Faith

As pastors of the Catholic Church in the United States, we state as clearly and strongly as we can that violence against women, inside or outside the home, is never justified.

> — *United States Conference of Catholic Bishops, November 12, 2002* [1]

[I]f we are serious about ending abuse and creating a model of how a faith community responds, we must be committed to giving the issue greater visibility, accepting that abuse is present in Jewish homes, fully funding the programs that serve abused women and their children, educating the entire Jewish community, and serving our youth and young adults with programs that teach them at the front end of their adult lives about healthy relationships.

> — *Millie Sernovitz, international president, and Loribeth Weinstein, executive director, Jewish Women International* [2]

Domestic violence occurs in all types of families, including the nonreligious, the marginally religious, and the devoutly religious. It occurs in families of all religious traditions. In a study of six hundred Methodist women, one out of six reported abuse by their husbands, and for one-fourth of those women the abuse involved physical battering.[3] According to a 1993 study conducted by the North American Council for Muslim Women, domestic violence (including a range of abusive actions from hitting to incest) against Muslim women and their children occurred in 10 percent of the Muslim population.[4]

Many women are pressured by the traditions, attitudes, and values of their religious or cultural groups to remain in abusive marriages. Some Christian women are often instructed to be submissive to their husbands, and many Jewish women have been taught that divorce just doesn't happen in their community. Muslim women are taught to devote themselves to their husbands and families. According to Mamata Misra, acting program director for Saheli, a grassroots advocacy program for Asian women, in Austin, Texas, "Religion plays such a critical role for Muslim women—not only in a spiritual way, but in a legal way as well." For all of these women, leaving their marriages feels like a betrayal of their religious beliefs and of the traditions and hopes of their communities.

For hundreds of years domestic violence has been the unmentionable sin. Historically, communities of faith, not unlike society as a whole, have ignored the problem. Battered women who have strong religious convictions need help not only with ending the abuse they suffer, but also with addressing the religious issues they face. Religious faith is a primary reference point in the lives of some women. When faced with a personal crisis, they will probably turn first to their priest, pastor, rabbi, or imam. Their religious leader is a trusted and known resource, and women may assume that he or she will know what to do. For other women, a religious leader may be the only resource in a small town or rural area. Unfortunately, many communities of faith have responded poorly or not at all to the issue of domestic violence.

In an effort to assess the validity of the claim that pastors hold a patriarchal attitude that predisposes them to respond ineffectively to battered women, James and Phyllis Alsdurf distributed a questionnaire to more than five thousand Protestant pastors throughout the United States. According to the Alsdurfs, "The opinion that pastors do hold such views was partially confirmed in our study. However, the comments from pastors revealed them to be a group concerned about women but torn by the theological perspectives they hold which conflict with this concern."[5]

Battered women of faith also find themselves torn. Any devout woman, no matter what her particular faith, may find herself in conflict between the teachings of her religion and her own safety. Of the nearly one hundred battered Protestant women in another study conducted by the Alsdurfs, approximately 75 percent stayed with their abusive husbands long after most women would have considered it safe. Rather than leave, they prayed for their husbands to change or for the ability to endure the abuse. Those who left generally did so after years of questioning whether or not there was adequate biblical justification for divorcing an abusive partner. Most of the women in the study reported that they received little sympathy or support within the church after revealing their abusive situation to others.[6] In addition, many of the women perceived their pastors as naive about the issue or afraid to get involved, especially when the batterers held positions of power within the church. Most of the women reported that their pastors focused on getting them to change, rather than their abusive partners.[7]

Spiritual Dilemmas

When people are in crisis, they usually rely on their basic beliefs about the world and their role in it. Those with strong religious convictions often hold beliefs and values that are based on principles of faith and religious doctrine. Crisis frequently affects such belief systems.[8] Battered women who are religious face a multitude of spiritual dilemmas, including a sense of abandonment by God and questions about the nature of suffering, the value of obedience, and the biblical justification for separation and divorce.[9] When they question their faith, they are trying to make sense of their suffering and find meaning for it in their lives. According to the Reverend Marie Fortune, founder and former executive director of the Faith/Trust Institute in Seattle, Washington, battered women's theological concerns "are to be seen as a healthy sign because they represent an effort to comprehend and contextualize the experience of family violence and thereby regain some control over their lives in the midst of crisis."[10]

For battered women of faith, religious concerns are often a priority and should be respected, or they will become obstacles that prevent the women from addressing their own safety and well-being. The manner in which communities of faith deal with the concerns of battered women will either jeopardize the women's lives or help them to transform their experiences. Theological questions cannot be met with simplistic answers and then dismissed. Efforts at intervention will be thwarted until the crisis of faith is acknowledged and addressed.[11]

Women may find simple explanations for their suffering insufficient. They may feel that their faith has failed them or that their God has abandoned them. In reality, it may be that the actions of their particular denomination have failed them. According to Fortune, many religious battered women receive such instructions as the following:[12]

◆ "Keep the commandments and everything will work out."

◆ "Pray more, pray harder."

◆ "Accept Jesus Christ as your Lord and Savior and everything will be fine."

◆ "Go to services every week."

◆ "Bring your husband to services."

Although principles such as these may be part of the fundamental teachings of religious faith, they do not effectively address the complexity of domestic violence. When offered as simple and complete answers to battered women's crises, these sorts of responses leave women vulnerable and set up a dynamic that actually blames women for their own suffering.

The way the Bible and other religious texts are interpreted by religious leaders to whom battered women turn for support and guidance is crucial. The misinterpretation and misuse of religious texts to support subordination of women, suffering as virtuous, forgiveness without justice, and divorce as a sin help to keep battered women in their abusive relationships.[13] According to Linda Osmundson, executive director of Community Action Stops Abuse, "Women with more conservative religious beliefs tend to stay in relationships longer, to work it out, even if it's to their detriment."[14] The misinterpretation of religious texts contributes to the guilt, self-blame, and suffering that battered women experience and serves as a rationalization for abusers. When batterers misinterpret religious writings, they are misusing the teachings to excuse or justify their abusive behaviors.

After careful study of Jewish and Christian scripture, Fortune has found that it is impossible to use scripture to justify family violence. Nor does the Qur'an support the abuse of wives. According to Sharifa Alkhateeb, director of the Peaceful Families Project, "Under no circumstances is violence against women encouraged or allowed. The holy Qur'an contains tens of verses extolling good treatment of women."[15] It is possible, however, to *misuse* scripture and other traditional religious literature for this purpose.[16] According to a statement released by the U.S. Conference of Catholic Bishops in 2002, "As bishops, we condemn the use of the Bible to support abusive behavior in any form. A correct reading of Scripture leads people to an understanding of the equal dignity of men and women and to relationships based on mutuality and love."[17]

It is not uncommon for women who seek help from their pastors, priests, rabbis, or imams to receive advice reflecting a theology of female suffering and submission. For example:[18]

◆ "Marriage is sacred. You must do whatever you can to hold it together."

◆ "Your husband is the head of your household. Obey him and he
won't need to resort to violence."

◆ "All of us must suffer. Offer up your suffering to Jesus/God/Allah,
and he will give you strength to endure."

That some communities of faith continue to misuse scripture to keep
women locked in abusive relationships is evident by the results of the Alsdurfs' survey of conservative Protestant clergy. Twenty-seven percent of the
pastors surveyed felt that if a woman submits to her husband, God will eventually honor her and either the abuse will stop or God will give her the
strength to endure it. According to the Alsdurfs, "[T]o take such a stance is to
acknowledge that the principle of wifely submission preempts other considera-
tions, such as that of a woman's safety. This was evident by the fact that pastors
who stressed wifely submission were also opposed to victims using certain protective legal and medical resources and were inclined to discount women's
reports of violence."[19]

Many communities of faith minimize the severity of violence reported by
women because of traditional attitudes that encourage the maintenance of
marriage at all costs. Pastors in the Alsdurfs' survey were asked to rate just
how intense marital violence would have to be to justify a woman's leaving.
One-third of the respondents felt that the abuse would have to be life threatening, and almost one-fifth believed that no amount of abuse would justify a
woman's leaving.[20]

Spiritual Abuse

Misusing scripture and other religious literature to support domestic violence
is a form of spiritual abuse, but it's not the only form that women of faith
might suffer. Melissa Martin, in her book *For Better or for Worse: A Blessing or
a Curse?* identifies a number of ways in which batterers intentionally misuse
their partners' faith to control them, including the following:[21]

◆ The abuser may not allow the survivor to pay tithes or offerings to
the church.

◆ The abuser may not allow the survivor to teach their children about
religious texts.

◆ The abuser may accuse the survivor of having an affair with the faith
leader or another key religious person.

◆ The abuser may not allow the survivor to read spiritual writings or
keep them in the home.

◆ The abuser may demand that the survivor read nothing but spiritual writings.

◆ The abuser may tell the survivor that God does not care about her.

◆ The abuser may tell the survivor that she is not a good Christian/Jew/Muslim.

Creating an Effective Pastoral Response to Domestic Violence

Communities of faith have the potential to be a source of direct and indirect support for battered women. To do so, they must begin to accept their responsibility to prevent, recognize, and intervene in cases of domestic violence. To create an effective response to domestic violence, religious leaders and their congregations must work together to evaluate their own attitudes, acknowledge and learn more about the problem, speak out against it, work with secular resources, and reach out to the community.

Conduct a Self-Evaluation

Self-evaluation is one of the first steps religious leaders need to take to address the issue of domestic violence. First, to become comfortable with the issue, religious leaders should examine their attitudes, feelings, and beliefs about domestic violence, battered women, and women in general.[22] Religious leaders must also examine their traditions and theologies to determine whether they are a source of comfort and support for all parishioners or oppressive to some. According to Rita-Lou Clarke, author of *Pastoral Care of Battered Women,* "We need to see that the Bible also speaks of healing for sufferers and forgiveness with repentance and reconciliation. We need to see that divorce can be an option for new life. These views can help to liberate a woman from the bondage of a battering relationship."[23]

Leaders should evaluate their understanding of domestic violence as well as their strengths and limitations for helping battered women. Many seminaries do not provide instruction regarding ministry in situations of family violence. Some seminarians are not even alerted that they will encounter family violence in their ministries. One Protestant minister explains that for too many years the need to understand the problem of domestic violence has been overshadowed by a belief in the need to maintain the marriage covenant. Religious leaders must begin to understand the dynamics of this issue if they are to effectively respond to battered women and their families.[24]

Many battered-women's programs offer training for volunteers. Religious leaders should try to attend these or other types of training offered by shelters, state coalitions against domestic violence, or the religious community. In addition, religious leaders should review and make use of some of the excellent publications that address the religious concerns of battered women (see Resources, at the back of the book).

Acknowledge and Address the Problem

Religious leaders can break the silence surrounding domestic violence by educating congregations about the realities of the issue and creating an atmosphere in which battered women feel a sense of belonging and support. When religious leaders communicate that it is acceptable to talk about violence in church, they are giving battered women a clear signal that it is safe to ask for help. Once battered women feel safe, they will begin to reach out to others for the comfort and assistance they so desperately need.

One way religious leaders can educate their congregations and create a safe environment for abused women is through relevant sermons and scripture readings. Addressing domestic violence and oppression from the pulpit sends a strong message to congregants. According to Dr. Jim Rigby, pastor of the St. Andrew's Presbyterian Church in Austin, Texas, the weekly sermon provides a "teachable moment" for men and women. He explains, "Religion is very important in helping to form people's views on things. We [religious leaders] play a role in that. The idea that domestic violence is a secret and should not be addressed is particularly harmful. There really isn't a sideline for us. We're teaching either positive or negative images. Our teachings will be either part of the abuse or part of the healing. Every time we address domestic violence in our sermons we're throwing out lifelines."

Several suggested sermon topics are listed below. In addition, a moment of silence or a candlelight service can be offered for victims of domestic violence, perhaps including testimony from a survivor on a topic such as "How God Helped Me Through My Crisis."

Suggested Sermon Topics in the Jewish Tradition

"And they shall be one flesh." (Genesis 2:24)

"Let none deal treacherously against the wife of his youth." (Malachi 2:15)

"He that troubleth his own house shall inherit the wind." (Proverbs 11:29)

"You should impose peace between them, and if the husband does not fulfill his part in maintaining the peace but rather continues to beat her and denigrate her, let him be excommunicated, and let him be forced by gentile authorities to give her a writ of divorce." (Rabbi Simhah)

Suggested Sermon Topics in the Christian Tradition

"Let the husband render unto the wife due benevolence and likewise also the wife with the husband." (1 Corinthians 7:3)

"He who loves his wife loves himself." (Ephesians 5:28)

"Husbands love your wives and be not bitter against them." (Colossians 3:19)

"If a house be divided against itself, that house cannot stand." (Mark 3:25)

Suggested Sermon Topics in the Islamic Tradition

"And among His Signs is this: He created for you mates from among yourselves, that ye may dwell in tranquility with them, and He has put love and mercy between your (hearts): verily in that are Signs for those who reflect." (Sura 30 Ayat 21)

"The Believers, men and women, are protectors one of another; they enjoin what is just, and forbid what is evil: they observe regular prayers, practice regular charity, and obey Allah and his Messenger. On them will Allah pour His mercy: for Allah is Exalted in power, Wise." (Sura 9 Ayat 71)

"Allah commands justice, the doing of good, and liberality to kith and kin, and He forbids all shameful deeds, and injustice and rebellion: He instructs you, that ye may receive admonition." (Sura 16 Ayat 90)

Religious leaders can also post fliers advertising such local resources as battered-women's shelters and adapt curricula dealing with domestic violence for Sunday school classes. Announcements can be made from the pulpit about local shelters and support groups for battered women and abusers. Speakers can be brought in from local shelters or seminaries to talk to youth groups, adult education classes, couples' groups, singles' groups, social groups, and women's groups. Religious leaders can support observance of National Domestic Violence Awareness Month (October) by including relevant articles in the church newsletter. The congregation can supply resources such as money, referral sources, clothes, food, and child care to families in crisis.[25]

Leaders should be alert for signs of abuse among parishioners, such as frequent church hopping, intermittent attendance, and very private couples who keep to themselves and rarely socialize or interact with church acquaintances or relatives.[26] They should also be aware that when women are pregnant they are at greater risk for intimate-partner violence, a fact that can be addressed in baptismal-preparation programs.[27] The issue of domestic violence can be raised in marriage-preparation sessions by questioning couples about how they handle disagreements and about their families' problem-solving patterns. Leaders can help couples learn how to increase justice and equality in their marriages.

Know about and Use Secular Resources

Religious leaders should familiarize themselves with community resources available to battered women, including talking to the local battered-women's shelter to learn about the services that are offered. The National Domestic Violence Hotline (see Resources) can provide the names and telephone numbers of community organizations willing to help battered women. When resources are available, it is advisable to refer battered women or their abusive partners to shelters or batterers' treatment programs. Staff and volunteers at these agencies are trained to deal with abuse and have the knowledge and experience to provide the needed support and advocacy. A religious leader's wise use of referrals comes from an awareness of his or her limitations and a clear understanding of what his or her role should be. Seldom do religious leaders have the training or time to provide the long-term advocacy that battered women or their abusive partners need. They can often be most effective by serving as support persons and advocates while the battered woman is getting specialized help.

Some leaders are hesitant to utilize secular resources in response to domestic violence. They often do not trust battered-women's advocates to be sensitive to the spiritual needs of their parishioners. Likewise, many battered-women's advocates are hesitant to trust religious leaders to know how to help battered women. Unfortunately, it is battered women who suffer most from this mutual mistrust. It can put them in a position of choosing either battered-women's services or pastoral support. An effective response develops when religious leaders and secular helpers reach out to each other as peers, share information, offer mutual training, serve on boards together, and provide services when referred by the other. Working together to meet the needs of battered women begins to build the mutual trust that is necessary for effective advocacy.[28]

Several years ago Joel Maiorano, a minister at a church in Austin, called me because concerned parents of a battered woman had just contacted him. Although Maiorano had attended a volunteer training class offered by the Center for Battered Women (now SafePlace) and was knowledgeable about domestic violence, he decided to refer the callers to me. I contacted the family members and was able to provide them with appropriate assistance. By working together, Maiorano and I found a way to address the spiritual, emotional, and informational needs of his acquaintances.

Support Community Outreach

Religious groups can participate in planning a coordinated community response to domestic violence and can take the lead in teaching that violence against women and children is morally wrong. Religious leaders can participate in community activities that discourage violent behavior and support battered-women's shelters. Church groups can be encouraged to support local shelters by volunteering and donating money or needed resources. Religious leaders should also encourage the formation of a committee or task force to educate the congregation about the problem and recruit volunteers for service.

Religious Leaders as Advocates for Battered Women

The very nature of ministry makes it difficult to spend more than a few sessions in serious counseling with a parishioner. Battered women are better served when religious leaders recommend resources that can provide the long-term advocacy abused women frequently need. Religious leaders can then continue to offer support to battered women as they struggle to make decisions about their lives. Although a leader's time with a battered woman may be limited, the quality of his or her efforts can make a substantial difference in the woman's life.

The Advocacy Wheel shown on page 263 is a helpful tool for anyone interested in helping a battered woman. In addition, the following ideas may be beneficial to religious leaders who are approached by battered women for help.

Listen and Believe

Most battered women are relieved when they feel it is safe to discuss their situation. Encourage the woman to openly share her story and her feelings. Try to listen without assigning blame or judging her. Be prepared to hear about and validate feelings of anger, shame, isolation, guilt, confusion, fear, powerlessness, and hopelessness.

Hearing horrific stories of abuse can be quite unsettling, and it may seem incomprehensible that a person could do such terrible acts to someone he supposedly loves. Do not deny or minimize what she is sharing with you. Being knowledgeable about domestic violence, knowing what to do, and not allowing personal feelings of anger, disbelief, or discomfort to interfere helps the listener to overcome the tendency to minimize. It is also helpful to remember that, in an attempt to make an intolerable situation seem more tolerable, many battered women actually minimize, rather than exaggerate, the abuse they suffer.[29]

Some women may hesitate to admit that they are being abused by their partners. Asking clear, direct questions in a sensitive and caring manner helps to create an environment in which a woman feels safer about discussing her situation. If you suspect that a woman is experiencing violence, the following questions may be useful:[30]

◆ Are you in a relationship in which you feel you are treated badly?

◆ Has your partner ever destroyed things that you cared about?

◆ Are you afraid of your partner when he gets angry?

◆ Has your partner ever physically hurt you or threatened you?

◆ Has your partner ever threatened or hurt your children?

Express your concern about the violence, and be very clear in communicating to the woman that she does not deserve to be beaten. Let her know that not only is domestic violence illegal; it is also a sin. Assure her that it is not her fault. Tell her that she is not alone in her situation and that she has your support and the support of her religious community.

Conduct a Safety Assessment

Safety is the first priority for battered women and their children. Ask the woman if she is safe, and encourage her to take the necessary steps to protect herself and her children. Offer to help her develop a safety plan in case violence reoccurs. A sample safety plan is outlined in Appendix II.[31]

Make Appropriate Referrals

The battered woman you are helping may find it difficult to assess her situation and to make decisions. You can help her to evaluate her personal strengths, resources, and support systems. Be aware that making decisions for her is less helpful than offering information and outlining options. Offer her the telephone numbers of local resources such as shelters or other safe locations, and brainstorm with her about the possibility of her attending a support group, getting counseling, obtaining legal counsel, or continuing her education and training.

Let her know that you support her decisions even if it means breaking up her family. Her safety and the safety of her children must be secured before work to preserve the family can begin.

Address Pastoral Concerns

A battered woman may struggle to understand her suffering in the context of her religious beliefs. She may believe that she deserves the abuse because of a previous sin or that suffering is the way to salvation. Recognize her inner conflict and be willing to discuss her religious questions. Stress that religious scripture does not condone or justify the abuse. Address her guilt by emphasizing that the responsibility for the abuse lies with the batterer.

Maintain a Connection

Stay in contact with the battered woman as she struggles with her situation. Acknowledge the danger she faces, and let her take the lead as to whether it is safe for you to contact her or whether she should contact you. Ask her how she is doing with the referrals you offered. Continue to reassure her of the ongoing support of her religious community.[32]

Guidelines for Crisis Counseling

There may be occasions when religious leaders receive a call from a woman who has just been beaten. This can be a very dangerous situation for everyone, and special precautions are required.

First, do not go to a home where violence is occurring. Doing so is extremely dangerous. Ask the woman if she is safe and if she would like you to call the police. If the violence is over, ask how she is. Does she need medical attention? Where are her children? Do her children need medical attention? When is her husband returning?

If she is in physical danger, encourage her to find a safe place for herself. Does she want to leave? Explore options available to her, including parents, friends, a church-family refuge, a motel, or a shelter. If the shelter is the only option, give her the telephone number. Whether she decides to leave or stay, encourage her to make contact with the nearest shelter for support and assistance.

Guidelines for Secular Helpers

213

Battered
Women and
Communities
of Faith

Secular advocates may encounter a battered woman who has religious questions and concerns. Marie Fortune's booklet *Keeping the Faith: Questions and Answers for the Abused Woman* is an excellent resource for both the advocate and the abused woman.[33] In addition, the following recommendations may be helpful:[34]

1. Acknowledge and pay attention to religious questions, comments, and references.

2. Respect any religious concerns the woman may have.

3. Affirm the concerns as appropriate and try to identify how important they are for the woman.

4. If you are uncomfortable or feel unqualified to pursue the discussion, refer the woman to a trusted religious leader who is willing to help her address her particular concerns.

5. If you are comfortable pursuing the conversation, emphasize the ways that her religious beliefs can be a resource for her. Assure her that religious scripture does not justify nor condone domestic violence.

Pitfalls Religious Leaders Should Avoid

Successful advocacy on behalf of battered women and their families means avoiding certain pitfalls. Listed below are some actions that religious leaders should not take:

1. Do not contact the batterer or disclose any information to him about the woman's discussions with you. You could endanger her life.

2. Do not suggest marriage counseling, mediation sessions, or communication workshops. These avenues will not stop the batterer's violence. Counseling to stop a batterer's violence must take place with a professional skilled in working with domestic-violence situations. Marriage counseling and other intervention strategies may be beneficial only after the batterer has received the treatment he needs.[35]

3. Do not interview a battered woman and her abusive partner as a couple or try to counsel the couple together to stop the batterer's violence. It is important to talk with the battered woman alone. Joint counseling often threatens her safety, and the batterer's presence may hinder her ability to openly discuss the abuse.[36]

4. Do not minimize what a battered woman shares with you. Assume that you are hearing only a part of her story.

5. Do not try to deal with the problem alone. Refer as often as you can to appropriate resources.

6. Do not be manipulated by a batterer's claim of a religious conversion experience. Such claims are common once batterers are arrested. An experience of religious conversion may be genuine, but should not be used as a reason to avoid the consequences of the batterer's violent behavior.[37]

7. Do not encourage premature reconciliation. Safety is a priority in domestic-violence situations. This may mean a marital separation. True reconciliation can occur only when certain conditions have been met. First, the woman must be safe. Next, the batterer must be held responsible for his violence, genuinely repent, and seek help for his abusive behavior. Acceptance of responsibility for the abuse and a firm commitment to change are crucial for authentic repentance. Even when the batterer has expressed regret, he must be encouraged to seek help to change his abusive behavior.[38]

Breaking the Silence: Religious Communities Address Domestic Violence

Although communities of faith have long ignored the problem of domestic violence, recent years have witnessed a change in this mindset. The Faith/Trust Institute (formerly the Center for the Prevention of Sexual and Domestic Violence), founded by the Reverend Marie Fortune, has made exemplary efforts to educate religious communities in the United States and Canada. An interreligious ministry, the institute develops educational programs for use at all levels of organized religion.[39] It also acts as a bridge between religious and secular communities, preparing and encouraging professionals from both to work cooperatively so that victims, offenders, and their families can receive thorough and meaningful assistance.

In 2001, Jewish Women International (JWI) introduced a long-term global strategy to end domestic abuse in the Jewish community. In recognition of the organization's work, the U.S. Department of Health and Human Services awarded it a three-year grant to help support three strategic efforts: education and training, an international conference on domestic abuse, and a national needs assessment.[40] In 2003 JWI convened the conference "Pursuing

Truth, Justice and Righteousness: A Call to Action: The First International Conference on Domestic Abuse in the Jewish Community." The outcome of the conference was a vision statement to inspire personal commitments to end domestic violence. A second international conference was held in March of 2005.[41] Other JWI efforts are listed below:[42]

◆ *Call to Action National Network:* Provides technical assistance and support to grassroots efforts to end domestic violence in the Jewish community via a series of facilitated conference calls

◆ *Embracing Justice: A Resource Guide for Rabbis on Domestic Abuse* and *Healing and Wholeness: A Resource Guide on Domestic Abuse in the Jewish Community:* Intended to help rabbis, professionals, and Jewish volunteers in their work to support battered women and their children

◆ *Domestic Abuse Clergy Task Force:* An effort to bring the leadership of the rabbinical community together on the issue of domestic violence in the Jewish community

◆ *Domestic Abuse Is Not Kosher:* Designed to heighten Orthodox women's awareness about domestic violence

In 2003 the Islamic Society of North America (ISNA) hosted its third annual Muslims Against Domestic Violence Conference, which brought together activists, imams, community leaders, and scholars to formulate an action plan to address the issue in the Muslim community. The ISNA website includes a forum for domestic violence that features, among other things, scholarly discussions regarding what the holy texts say about domestic violence.[43]

In the United States, the Catholic church has publicly taken a strong stand against domestic violence. A recent statement issued by the U.S. Conference of Catholic Bishops says, "In 1992 we spoke out against domestic violence. We called on the Christian community to work vigorously against it. Since then, many dioceses, parishes, and organizations have made domestic violence a priority issue. We commend and encourage these efforts.... In this update of our 1992 statement, we again express our desire to offer the Church's resources to both the women who are abused and the men who abuse."[44]

The Catholic diocese in Austin, Texas, has made an outstanding effort to address and prevent family violence. Working closely with the Center for Battered Women (now SafePlace), the Texas Council on Family Violence, and other domestic-violence organizations, the diocese developed a comprehensive educational manual, *Breaking the Silence: A Pastoral Response to Domestic*

Violence Against Women.[45] A valuable resource for both religious and secular helpers, the manual offers guidelines for preventing domestic violence as well as suggestions for preaching on the issue with sensitivity. It also explores how religious leaders can approach the topic in marriage- and baptism-preparation sessions. With the knowledgeable assistance of both secular and religious leaders, the diocese began offering workshops on domestic violence in 1995. According to Chris Attal, former director of parish social ministries in Austin, "Our first conference was so successful that we decided to offer a second one. Since then we continue to work with parishes on an individual basis, offering our support based on their specific needs and referring as often as possible."

In Austin, individual churches and parishioners have begun to reach out to battered women and their families. Cristo Rey Catholic Church, St. Catherine of Siena, St. Louis, and St. Paul's have each formed either a domestic-violence committee or an awareness program. At Cristo Rey, Father Larry Mattingly and parishioner Roy Gomez have developed a domestic-violence-awareness program. Gomez, whose daughter lost her life as a result of domestic violence, feels that educating people about the problem is their greatest challenge. "We have to rely on the church to condemn domestic violence from the pulpit," he says. He commends Father Mattingly's understanding of the issue and "the harm it does."

Gomez works closely with SafePlace to educate and assist battered women and their families. He has created an information center that features publications on domestic violence in both Spanish and English. He recruits speakers—survivors, family members, and battered-women's advocates—to address the congregation during mass. He runs ads in the church bulletin addressing domestic violence, listing his name and telephone number as a resource. And he gets calls. "Many of the women I talk to have heard of CBW [now SafePlace], but they seem to be more willing to reach out to another church member. They'll call me first and we work from there." Gomez, along with Father Mattingly and other members of the congregation, provide resources to battered women to help them stay safe and rebuild their lives.

Dottie Davis, a member of Austin's St. Paul's Catholic Church, also lost her daughter to domestic violence. In an effort to bring awareness about the issue to the congregation, Davis, in conjunction with Father Paul McCallum, director of parish social ministries Bernice Machala, and parishioner Leann Ross, began a series of awareness activities and provided assistance and advocacy to battered women. Sadly, Davis has passed away, but the work she started at St. Paul's continues. Domestic-violence materials are always available at the church, and every October Machala coordinates a "Purple Ribbon Campaign" to recognize and honor domestic-violence survivors. Machala has developed a strong relationship with SafePlace and other domestic-violence programs in the area. Not only does she refer survivors to SafePlace, but advocates at the center make referrals to her as well. Machala is pleased at the progress that has been made in breaking the silence about domestic violence, but she recognizes that there is still more work to be done. She says that one of the biggest challenges she and other religious advocates continue to face is "for the priests and congregations to accept that domestic violence does exist."

In 1999 advocates at St. William, St. Patrick, St. Helen, St. John Vianney, Cristo Rey, and St. Paul's Catholic Churches joined forces to form HOPE Ministries, which provides a variety of services to battered women and their children, including support, peer counseling, and information and referral.

The Austin Catholic community serves as an example of the positive impact religious groups can have on battered women and their families. From the U.S. Conference of Catholic Bishops to individual dioceses, priests, and parishioners, the Catholic community has demonstrated a willingness to address domestic violence and to work with secular advocates. Ultimately, their efforts contribute not only to the enhanced safety and well-being of battered women and their children, but also to a more loving and peaceful society. As Fortune so eloquently puts it, "It is time we began focusing on what is really important—and that is the promise that for each of us God wishes life in all its abundance. Saving the family means ending the violence that is destroying it."[46]

...12

Domestic Violence and the Military

Domestic violence will not be tolerated in the Department of Defense.... Domestic violence is an offense against the institutional values of the Military Services of the United States of America. Commanders at every level have a duty to take appropriate steps to prevent domestic violence, protect victims, and hold those who commit it accountable.

— *Paul Wolfowitz, deputy U.S. secretary of defense,*
November 2001 [1]

The United States Department of Defense is in the unique position of preserving national security. In 2002 there were approximately 3.3 million active-duty service members and their families stationed in the United States and abroad for this purpose. [2] As in the civilian population, survivors of domestic violence can be found in the military community. In 2001 more than eighteen thousand cases of spouse abuse involving military personnel were reported to the Department of Defense's (DoD's) Family Advocacy Program (FAP). [3] Among the branches of service, the Army consistently has shown the highest rates of domestic violence, followed by the Marines, Navy, and Air Force. [4] Demographic surveys indicate that survivors are predominantly female, slightly less than twenty-five years old, and are the civilian spouses of male active-duty personnel. Seventy-eight percent of abuse survivors in the military have children, and more than half have been married for two years or less. [5]

218

The DoD categorizes the severity of physical abuse into three levels: severe, moderate, and mild. But according to the National Coalition Against Domestic Violence, "The DoD severity definitions are inconsistent with commonly held 'characterizations' of domestic violence. A DoD prerequisite to be categorized as severe physical abuse is major physical injury requiring inpatient medical treatment or causing temporary or permanent disability or disfigurement. A strangulation case in the civilian community is considered very dangerous, whereas in the Department of Defense, it might be defined to be mild or moderate abuse. As a result 69% of domestic violence cases reported in FY99 were mild and only 6% were classified as severe."[6]

Seventy-five to 84 percent of alleged perpetrators of domestic violence in the military are honorably discharged. Although data are difficult to obtain, it appears that relatively few military personnel are prosecuted or administratively sanctioned on charges stemming from domestic violence. Fewer than 7 percent of spouse-abuse cases are adjudicated by court-martial.[7]

Historically, civilian and military response systems for dealing with such issues as domestic violence have operated independently from each other. This is changing. Awareness about domestic violence in the military is increasing, and civilian advocates are increasingly being asked to assist military survivors of domestic abuse. Fifty-six percent of U.S. military personnel and their families live off of military installations, making it more likely that they will contact civilian resources in times of crisis.[8] Colonel Martha Davis, the Air Force's chief of the Family Advocacy Program at Brooks Air Force Base, in Texas, says, "We can provide assistance to anyone who feels they are in a volatile relationship.... [I]t doesn't matter if they're married, single or divorced."[9] In reality, however, this is not a militarywide policy, and certain populations, such as unmarried partners, may not even have access to military response systems. Others may feel a strong need for confidentiality that is not possible on a military installation. The military's "don't ask, don't tell" policy for gays and lesbians may prevent gay and lesbian survivors from asking for military assistance. For all of these groups, civilian resources may be the best option.[10]

The Dynamics of Domestic Violence in the Military

The dynamics of domestic violence are the same in the military as they are in the civilian population. However, certain characteristics of military life can make some families more vulnerable, including a prior history of abuse, economic dependence of one partner on the other, constant mobility, and several other factors unique to the military community. This section examines these issues.

Prior History of Abuse

Among Navy recruits, 54 percent of women and 40 percent of men witnessed domestic violence within their families of origin prior to enlistment.[11] Thirty percent of active-duty military women report having experienced intimate-partner violence (physical or sexual assault) sometime in their life, and 22 percent report intimate-partner sexual assault during their military service.[12]

Economic Dependence

Military wives earn less and are less likely to be employed than their civilian counterparts, which can leave survivors economically dependent on their abusive partners.[13] In addition, the benefits of military employment (such as child care, housing assistance, and health care) may be jeopardized when a woman leaves an abusive partner, ultimately generating economic risks for the survivor and her children.

Mobility/Isolation

On average, military personnel are required to change locations about once every three years.[14] The constant relocation, often to unfamiliar countries, isolates survivors from established support networks.

Additional Risk Factors

A number of other special factors combine to make military families at risk for domestic abuse, including:

Age of perpetrators: The highest risk for committing domestic violence is concentrated between ages twenty and forty.[15] Seventy-six percent of active-duty military personnel are between ages seventeen and thirty-four.[16]

Cultural values: The military community expects service members to be held responsible for the behavior of their spouses and their children. As Judith Beals, author of *The Military Response to Victims of Domestic Violence: Tools for Civilian Advocates,* writes, "This cultural norm can be used as a rationale to exercise abusive power and control tactics with family members."[17]

Access to weapons: Many military personnel have had weapons training and exposure to combat. Access to weapons has been shown to be a significant risk factor in domestic-violence homicides.[18]

Barriers to Reporting

Military survivors experience many of the same barriers to reporting domestic violence as their civilian counterparts. Feelings of shame, isolation, fear of retaliation from the abusive partner, and economic concerns, to name just a few, work together to keep many military survivors from reaching out for help. In addition, two special factors—the lack of confidentiality and the fear of career consequences—play an important role in military survivors' willingness (or lack thereof) to disclose abuse.

Lack of Confidentiality

Currently, the only military personnel who are granted confidentiality in their communications are chaplains. (Military attorneys have confidentiality, but only within the context of an attorney/client relationship.) All other individuals within the military community, including physicians, therapists, advocates, and social workers, do not have the privilege of confidentiality in their communications with survivors of domestic abuse. In addition, all military personnel and civilians employed by the military are required to report suspected cases of domestic violence, regardless of the wishes of the survivor.[19]

Fear of Career Consequences

Many survivors fear reporting domestic violence because they believe the report will affect their husbands' chance for promotions and pay increases or will result in their husbands' discharge.[20] According to Beals, "[M]ilitary life, with its powerful control over the lives of service members, presents unique challenges for victims in need of help. Unlike the civilian world, where clear institutional boundaries exist between one's employer, doctor, judge, social worker and advocate, the military system is, for the most part, seamless."[21] Disclosing domestic abuse to a military advocate is basically the same as disclosing it to a perpetrator's employer. Beals notes that the risk for retaliation is "obvious, and it is frightening."[22]

Survivors who are in active-duty service face a similar, albeit somewhat reversed, situation. According to the DoD's *Final Report of the Study of Spousal Abuse in the Armed Forces,* active-duty survivors fear they will be perceived as "weak" and be proven unsuitable for career advancement. They say they are concerned that their own careers will become tarnished if they report the abuse they are experiencing.[23]

DoD Task Force on Domestic Violence

In 1999, a segment on the TV news program *60 Minutes* titled "The War at Home" highlighted the problem of domestic violence in the military. After analyzing Pentagon records from 1992 through 1996, reporter Ed Bradley said rates of domestic violence were as much as five times higher in military families than in civilian ones. The broadcast declared that the armed services were neglecting the problem and that very few perpetrators were being held accountable.[24]

Congressional reaction was swift. The Defense Task Force on Domestic Violence (DTFDV) was created in 2000 as part of the National Defense Authorization Act for Fiscal Year 2000. The statute required that the findings and recommendations of the DTFDV be submitted to the Secretary of Defense in a series of three annual reports, and that the secretary evaluate each report and forward the report and his evaluation to the Senate and House Committees on Armed Services.[25]

The DTFDV was created to help the Secretary of Defense prevent domestic abuse in the military and to better respond when it did occur. Specifically, the task force was directed to make recommendations to the Family Advocacy Program (FAP) that would[26]

- ◆ focus on preventing domestic violence in the military

- ◆ make DoD policies, practices, and programs more consistent and effective in providing safety for survivors and in promoting offender and program accountability

- ◆ provide military leaders with better tools for preventing and intervening in domestic violence

- ◆ improve coordination and communication between the DoD and the civilian community

The task force was made up of twenty-four members appointed by the Secretary of Defense, half of whom were senior military and civilian personnel from the Department of Defense, and half of whom were civilian experts from advocacy programs, the Department of Justice, and the Department of Health and Human Services. Initially Lieutenant General Jack Klimp and upon his retirement, Lieutenant General Garry Parks and Deborah D. Tucker, executive director of the National Center on Domestic and Sexual Violence, were appointed as co-chairs.[27]

In February 2001 the task force released its first report, which listed more than seventy-five recommendations.[28] Legislators gave Defense Secretary Donald Rumsfeld ninety days to review the report and send it to Capitol Hill, but it was stalled for many months, waiting for Rumsfeld's review. When the report was finally transmitted, in November, the Pentagon signed off on all but eleven of the task force's recommendations and promised to begin working on them immediately.[29] Subsequent reports followed in 2002 and 2003.

The final report, a culmination of three years of investigation into the domestic-violence policies of the DoD, synthesized findings from the previous two reports and made almost two hundred detailed recommendations. Co-

chair Deborah D. Tucker's accompanying statement said, in part, "This report
is the result of painstaking, difficult work to bring together two communities
that have had few formal ties in the past. Our mandate was urgent—to find
ways to protect victims of domestic violence in the military and in military
families, and to ensure that the military does much more to stop domestic
violence. If these recommendations are implemented with adequate resources
and continuing guidance from experts, they offer the promise that members
of military families will face fewer domestic assaults and homicides."[30]

Key points from the final report included the following:[31]

◆ Demand a culture shift that:
  - Does not tolerate domestic violence
  - Moves from victims holding offenders accountable to the
    system holding offenders accountable
  - Punishes criminal behavior
◆ Establish a Victim Advocate Program with Provisions for Confi-
  dentiality
◆ Implement Proposed Domestic Violence Intervention Process
  Model with the Following Protocols:
  - Victim Advocate Protocol
  - Commanding Officer's Protocol/Guidelines
  - Law Enforcement Protocol
  - Offender Intervention Protocol
◆ Separate Abuse Substantiation Decisions From Clinical Decisions
◆ Enhance System and Command Accountability and Include a
  Fatality Review Process
◆ Implement DoD-Wide Training and Prevention Programs
◆ Hold Offenders Accountable
◆ Strengthen Local Military and Civilian Community Collaboration
◆ Evaluate Results of Domestic Violence Prevention and Interven-
  tion Efforts

Speaking before the Subcommittee on Total Force House Armed Service
Committee of the U.S. House of Representatives, DTFDV co-chairs Lieutenant General Garry Parks and Deborah D. Tucker emphasized that all intervention programs should adhere to the following core principles:[32]

◆ Respond to the needs of victims and provide for their safety.
◆ Hold offenders accountable.

◆ Consider multicultural and cross-cultural factors.

◆ Consider the context of the violence and provide a measured response.

◆ Coordinate military and civilian response.

◆ Involve victims in monitoring domestic-violence services.

◆ Provide early intervention.

After the DTFDV filed its final report, members of Congress asked members of the task force if they wanted to continue the project beyond the 2003 deadline. Tucker explained in her testimony to the House Armed Services Committee the decision to decline their invitation for an extension and noted the alternative approach discussed with the Secretary of Defense in the Third Year Report Executive Summary to instead invite the group back after two years to determine for the Secretary of Defense and for Congress what he and his staff had accomplished.[33]

The DoD is now working to implement the final recommendations of the DTFDV. Of the 194 recommendations, the DoD has agreed with 147 and has agreed to study an additional 28. Of these 175 recommendations, 65 have been implemented, 91 are being staffed, and 19 are being further studied.[34]

As a direct result of the DTFDV recommendations the DoD has mandated the following actions:[35]

◆ Issue policy memoranda outlining domestic-abuse protocols for (1) victim advocates, (2) commanding officers, and (3) law enforcement.

◆ Issue a directive stating DoD policy regarding domestic abuse.

◆ Issue an instruction manual for responding to domestic abuse.

◆ Continue collaboration with Department of Justice grantees and civilian domestic-violence organizations.

◆ Provide training conferences for (1) commanding officers, (2) victim advocates, (3) law enforcement, and (4) chaplains.

◆ Continue research comparing rates of domestic violence in military and civilian populations.

◆ Evaluate Air Force FAP Case Review Committee process revision.

Some battered-women's advocates are skeptical about the DTFDV report and its potential to change the military's response to domestic violence. Christine Hansen, executive director of the Miles Foundation, a private nonprofit organization, reports having worked since 1996 with more than seven thousand survivors abused by military personnel. She explains that the problems with the military's response to survivors are deep and systemic and won't be easily solved.[36] The DoD has issued a "zero-tolerance policy" towards violence against women, including domestic violence, sexual assault, and sexual harassment. Unfortunately, according to Hansen, the message has not been clear and consistent throughout the armed forces.[37] Testifying in 2004 before the Personnel Subcommittee of the Senate Armed Services Committee, Hansen said, "The reestablishment of a zero tolerance policy is not a sufficient antidotal sign of progress. Victims remain fearful for their safety and privacy, as well as desire justice and social change."[38]

The DTFDV suggested that the secretary of defense invite the group back after two years for a follow-up evaluation. Deborah D. Tucker says, "We will reserve the right to say more at that time; we look forward to reconsidering things that weren't part of our initial recommendations and to bring new ideas we've encountered to the Department."[39]

Tragedy at Fort Bragg

In a tragic chain of events over a six-week period in June and July 2002, five domestic homicides occurred at Fort Bragg, an army base in North Carolina. On June 11 Sgt. 1st Class Rigoberto Nieves shot and killed his wife, Nancy, and then killed himself. Nieves had been serving in Afghanistan but had returned home before the murder to "resolve family problems." On June 29 Master Sgt. William Wright allegedly strangled his wife, Jennifer. Wright was charged with murder in July after leading investigators to his wife's body. He had been back from Afghanistan for approximately a month but had recently moved out of the family's home and was living in the Army barracks.

On July 9, Sgt. Cedric Ramon allegedly stabbed his estranged wife, Marilyn, at least fifty times and then set fire to her house. Ramon was charged with the murder. On July 19 Sgt. 1st Class Brandon Floyd shot and killed his wife and then killed himself in the family home. Floyd was a member of the anti-terrorism unit Delta Force and had returned from Afghanistan in January. On July 23 Joan Shannon allegedly shot her husband, Major David Shannon. She was charged with first-degree murder and conspiracy to commit murder.[40]

The Army conducted multiple investigations and interviewed military leaders, health professionals, military and civil law-enforcement authorities, and others. The Centers for Disease Control and Prevention worked with military behavioral-health and prevention-program experts and Army chaplains to explore the homicides and identify potential causal factors. The Army also conducted anonymous focus groups with soldiers, their spouses, military leaders, and health-care and social-service providers. *The Fort Bragg Epidemiologi-*

cal Consultation Report (EPICON Report) outlines the findings and includes recommendations on how to improve the Army's response to domestic violence at Fort Bragg and elsewhere.[41]

One key finding of the report states that the Army's "flawed model for behavioral health services" contributed to the homicides. Although there was "known marital distress" in all cases, there were no records of the soldiers' accessing military counseling services. Interviews and focus groups revealed that soldiers, their spouses, and others believed that seeking such services "is detrimental and often terminal, either directly or indirectly, to a soldier's career." The report further states that the Army's current model of delivering services for domestic violence is "counterproductive" because institutional attitudes discourage "early identification and therapeutic engagement."[42]

Outside experts found problems with the EPICON Report. Tiffany Carr, executive director of the Florida Coalition Against Domestic Violence, commented on one inherent flaw:

> This report suggests that the military is using a medical model to explain and treat domestic violence, rather than using an empowerment model and holding the abuser accountable for his own actions. The *EPICON Report* references the effects of the military lifestyle on family relationships and suggests that the stresses faced by military personnel contribute to relationship violence. However, it does not take into account the fact that thousands of members of the military are living under the same conditions, including combat conditions, as the soldiers who committed these homicides, and that these individuals have chosen not to take their stresses out on their significant others. Domestic violence is a conscious choice that the vast majority of military personnel have chosen not to make. Military leaders must be aware that being in combat does not create an abuser. Nor does being separated from a spouse for long periods of time. While these issues may exacerbate abusive behaviors that are already present, they do not cause these behaviors. The first step for addressing domestic violence within the military should include holding abusers accountable for their actions and not allowing excuses that remove personal fault.... [I]t should be a priority of domestic violence advocates to educate the military on domestic violence issues.[43]

In response to the tragic deaths at Fort Bragg, Robin Hayes, the district's representative in the U.S. Congress, sponsored the Armed Forces Domestic Security Act. The legislation, which was signed into law on December 2, 2002, provides that a civilian order of protection has the same force and effect on a military installation as it does within the jurisdiction of the court that issued the order. It closed a loophole that previously had prohibited the enforcement of civilian protection orders on military land. To date, a law mandating the reverse has not been put into effect; that is, military orders of protection have not been granted full faith and credit on civilian land. This 2002 legislation represents a major component of the protocol recommended by the DTFDV.[44]

The Military Response to Domestic Violence

The DoD has issued a directive for all branches of the military establishing guidelines for the appropriate response to domestic violence committed by or against active-duty personnel. Using the directive, each branch—the Army, the Marine Corps, the Air Force, and the Navy—has created its own regulations that describe its response in detail.[45] (The U.S. Coast Guard is part of the Department of Homeland Security; as such, it is not subject to the DoD directive. Neither is the National Guard or the Reserves, unless members have been called into active duty.[46]) Specific practices differ among the various branches of service, and even among installations. As with any institution, the protocols that guide the military response on a given installation may vary depending on the resources and informal relationships that exist, and on the extent to which collaborative relationships exist with the surrounding civilian community.[47]

The Responders

Survivors of domestic abuse will interact with any number of military personnel in their efforts to seek assistance. To understand the military response to domestic violence it is important to understand the various groups that are involved in the process.

Family Advocacy Program (FAP)

The DoD is mandated to establish policy and practices for the prevention of, response to, intervention in, and treatment of domestic violence. Each branch of service has established its own practices and programs, collectively referred to as the Family Advocacy Program, for the prevention, investigation, assessment, treatment, and monitoring of spouse abuse and child maltreatment. Within each branch the FAP is responsible for ensuring the survivor's safety and access to support and advocacy services, as well as ensuring that abusers receive appropriate intervention services. The FAP, which follows cases from the time they are reported until their closure, is a huge component of the military response to domestic violence. Responsibility for the FAP rests ultimately with the commander of each installation or his/her designated Family Advocacy Program Officer.[48]

Victim Advocates (VA)

Victim advocates help survivors navigate the military's complex legal and social-service systems. Not all military installations have victim advocates. On those that do, the VAs are typically assigned to the FAP; however, the Air Force has assigned advocates to the Judge Advocate General (JAG) office.[49] Unlike their civilian counterparts, military victim advocates do not have the privilege of confidentiality when working with survivors and their families.

Chaplains

Due to the privileged nature of communication between clergy and parishioner, a survivor may first seek assistance through the chaplain's office. Military chaplains receive a year of training in family-crisis intervention and are now being trained to avoid couples counseling in domestic violence situations. Current training encourages the use of support and pastoral counseling for survivors and referal to a certified batterer's intervention program for abusers.[50]

Military Police

If a domestic-violence incident occurs on a military installation, the military police may become involved. If a Memorandum of Understanding (MOU) exists between the military installation and civilian law enforcement, the military's law enforcement office will be contacted regarding an incident occurring off the military installation. The local law-enforcement agency may provide the military police with information related to the charges and/or arrest of military personnel. Deborah D. Tucker explains that joint training and MOUs between military law enforcement and their civilian counterparts have been strongly encouraged "to ensure that offenders are identified and the military can bring to bear its considerable persuasion on the offender to stop the violence."[51]

Military Criminal Investigative Organizations (MCIOs)

MCIOs are the military's trained investigative personnel. They conduct investigations into criminal activity—including, as necessary, cases of domestic violence—and provide security and protective services for the armed forces. The MCIOs include the Army Criminal Investigative Command (CID), the Naval Criminal Investigative Services (NCIS), the Air Force Office of Special Investigations (OSI), the Marine Corps Criminal Investigative Division (USMC CID), and the Defense Criminal Investigative Services (DCIS).[52]

The judge advocate general may conduct an investigation into a domestic-violence complaint. The JAG office provides legal counsel to the command office and may advise the command office during prosecution of a service member. Military-justice trial attorneys will provide counsel for both prosecution and defense during a court-martial.

Case Review Committee (CRC)

The CRC typically consists of both military personnel and civilian service providers. Its role in domestic-violence cases is to determine if abuse has occurred. The FAP counselor and VA present evidence to the committee, which "substantiates" the report. According to Christine Hansen, of the Miles Foundation, a "substantiated case" is one in which the "preponderance of available information indicates that abuse has occurred." Generally, low-level cases and those defined as "he said, she said" do not meet the standard.[53] If the case is not substantiated then it is closed, although services may still be offered. It is noteworthy that of the eighteen thousand cases of spouse abuse involving military personnel that were reported to FAP in 2001, more than ten thousand were substantiated.[54]

In cases where the CRC determines that a report of abuse is substantiated, most CRCs will rank the abuse as mild, moderate, or severe. The committee issues recommendations for treatment of the perpetrator and services for the survivor. Although the dangers of couples' counseling have been widely explored in domestic-violence literature, it is still among the recommendations made by some branches of service.

One key recommendation made by the Defense Task Force on Domestic Violence was the elimination of the CRC approach of substantiation/unsubstantiation in favor of the Domestic Violence Assessment and Intervention Team. The Team's role would be to support command in making timely interventions to ensure victim safety and to determine if a crime has been committed.[55]

Command

All service members report to a commanding officer, who is responsible for the training and general welfare of the members in his or her command. The commander may or may not be identified as the base/post commander. According to Hansen, "Commanders are well educated, highly trained and skilled in military protocols, combat tactics and assignment of men and machinery. However, commanders received limited training and introduction to FAPs."[56]

CRC recommendations are forwarded to the command office for review and implementation. The commander has total discretion over whether to concur, veto, alter, or delay the recommendations. He or she can order the service member to participate in an evaluation or a treatment program, or can court-martial the service member. The commander can also administer nonjudicial punishment, administratively separate the abuser from the service, or prosecute the abuser under the Uniform Code of Military Justice. If the commander chooses to court-martial the service member, then he or she serves as the convening authority during the proceedings.[57]

In situations where the perpetrator is a civilian spouse, the commander exercises little authority over the perpetrator except to bar him from the military installation. In such cases, the military can also turn the information over to civilian authorities.

Since the CRC process can take as long as 90 days, the immediate problems associated with victim safety may go unaddressed. According to Deborah D. Tucker, "the DTFDV strongly recommended that commanders be trained to recognize that domestic violence can involve many specific criminal acts and is not simply a personal problem for a couple, but a dangerous social pattern that can be stopped."[58]

The Response

The options available to a domestic-abuse survivor depend upon the branch of military involved. Some elements of the process common to all the branches include benefits entitlements, application of federal law (including the Violence Against Women Act), and the presence of a Family Advocacy Program (FAP), although the services provided by FAP differ from branch to branch.[59] Significant differences among the various branches can be found in the following areas:[60]

- ◆ Operating procedures for responding to domestic violence
- ◆ Delivery of services to survivors and their families
- ◆ Housing policies and procedures
- ◆ Types of prevention programs

The military response system to charges of domestic violence has three basic components. In phase I, a report of domestic violence is made. All suspected cases of domestic violence are required to be reported to either FAP, the military police, or the command. The unit that first receives the report is required to forward it to the other two. The report can originate through military or civilian law enforcement, health-care personnel housed on base, FAP, the survivor, the offender, the command, or other individuals such as coworkers, neighbors, or friends. Once the report is made the military response system is activated.[61]

FAP plays a crucial role in phase II. All domestic-violence reports are required to be investigated by either the military police, military investigators, command office, or FAP staff. Information obtained through these investigation and through the FAP's clinical assessment are then brought before a case review committee, which makes recommendations to the commander.[62]

In phase III, the military officially responds to the report. Depending on the severity of the abuse there are three basic outcomes:[63]

1. Protection for the survivor through such avenues as Military Protective Orders (MPOs), relocation, safety planning, etc.

2. Services for both survivor and perpetrator

3. Accountability for the perpetrator, including disciplinary action and prosecution under the Uniform Code of Military Justice (UCMJ)

Military Protective Orders (MPOs)

The MPO process is administrative rather than judicial. MPOs are issued by command and may direct service members to stay away from and refrain from contacting survivors. Other provisions of the MPO may include requiring a service member to move into government quarters and providing support to family members. MPOs are issued for indeterminate periods and are subject to review at the discretion of the command. Ex parte orders do not generally exceed ten days. A civilian perpetrator cannot be subject to an MPO.[64]

Firearms Possession

The Domestic Violence Offender Gun Ban (1996), also known as the Lautenberg Amendment to the Gun Control Act of 1968, bans military personnel who have perpetrated domestic abuse from possessing firearms. Those convicted of violating the ban face possible discharge, reassignment, or separation from the service. It is important to note, however, that a "conviction" does not include a summary court-martial conviction, imposition of nonjudicial punishment, deferred prosecutions, or similar alternative dispositions in a civilian court.[65]

Advocating for Survivors

In *The Military Response to Victims of Domestic Violence: Tools for Civilian Advocates,* Judith Beals offers a wealth of helpful information for civilian advocates working with survivors associated with the military. She writes, "The *only* way to become an effective advocate for military victims is to get to know your local military installation, how it operates, and who the players are.... Learn *everything* you can about military resources in your community."[66] To educate themselves about the military community's response to domestic violence, Beals recommends that advocates do the following:[67]

1. Visit the Family Advocacy Program. Ask FAP to conduct an in-service training for civilian domestic-violence staff in the community.

2. Review relevant websites and printed materials relating to the installation.

3. Find out if a Memorandum of Understanding (MOU) exists between military and civilian response systems in the community.

To better understand how collaborative relationships can be strengthened between civilian and military authorities, one study examined Anchorage, Alaska, and San Diego, California. The two cities were the first recipients of funds from the DoD under an incentive program intended to promote collaboration between military installations and their surrounding communities.[68] As a result of the study researchers made the following suggestions to improve collaboration between civilian domestic-violence programs and the military:[69]

◆ Civilian-military liaison positions can facilitate collaboration.

◆ Domestic-violence collaborations should be viewed as a high priority by both high-level military commands and civilian authorities.

◆ The cost of the program should not be seen as a barrier to participation in civilian batterer-intervention programs for military personnel who are required to attend.

◆ Providing community advocates with materials explaining both the services offered by the installation and victims' rights within the military would be helpful.

◆ Information about the military implications of the federal gun-control law might reduce confusion and inconsistency.

◆ Formal procedures for civilians to identify domestic-violence cases and notify the military can promote sharing of information.

◆ Agreements are needed to address victim confidentiality.

◆ Domestic-violence collaboration conferences and participation in domestic-violence council meetings can provide benefits.

♦ Training may be needed for both civilian and military personnel on domestic violence and the role of collaboration.

♦ Working through issues arising on installations that have shared civilian jurisdiction may require special attention.

In particular, the researchers found that "[c]ollaborative relationships can be strengthened by formalized memorandums of understanding (MOUs). Key here is the notion of 'formal' MOUs. Most of the interviewees noted that the existing relationships had begun informally and that such relationships needed to be formalized to ensure that they did not depend on individual personalities and relationships and thus [were not] jeopardized by turnover in personnel."[70]

Although the military has begun to make progress in its efforts to improve responses to survivors and perpetrators of domestic abuse, much more work is yet to be done. According to Deborah D. Tucker:

> We must all consider the ways in which our combined efforts can end violence against women in military *and* civilian families. I am confident that one profound difference the Task Force has made is that military officials no longer feel isolated from the battered women's movement. Today, they know many of us. They have seen the concern, the willingness to help, and the dismay that we felt upon realizing how different our respective approaches have been and how little we understood one another. The unfamiliarity, at least, is irrevocably changed.... We are one nation, not divisible into the two worlds of military and civilian. We are one people who must end violence in our homes, in our streets, and someday, in our world.[71]

... *13*

Creating a Community Response to Domestic Violence

We cannot have a healthier community unless we all work together to recognize our strengths, abilities, weaknesses, and needs to achieve the common goal of preventing family violence.

— *Caryl Clarke Colburn and Mike Denton, former co-chairs*
Travis County (Texas) Family Violence Task Force

Domestic violence is much more than an individual or family problem; it is a widespread community and societal problem. For thirty years the battered-women's movement has done a commendable job of advocating for battered women and children and increasing public awareness about domestic violence. However, increased community accountability and collaboration must become the standard if we are to realize our dream of a future without family violence.

Because individual communities are in the best position to understand their needs and resources, efforts to end family violence must be community driven. Communities are also in the best position to prioritize their needs with respect to family violence and to allocate increasingly scarce resources.

234

Community Accountability

235

Creating a
Community
Response to
Domestic
Violence

The ideal community response to domestic violence is one in which community opinion makes clear that domestic violence is unacceptable. A unified outlook will lead all social institutions to demand full accountability from batterers by applying appropriate consequences. Mike Jackson and David Garvin, with the Domestic Violence Institute of Michigan, have developed a Coordinated Community Action Model, which outlines the ideal institutional responses to domestic violence.[1] It appears below. Collectively, institutional responses can have a major impact on both the intervention in and prevention of domestic violence.

Ideal Institutional Responses to Domestic Violence

Employers will

1. make batterers' continuing employment conditional on their remaining nonviolent

2. actively intervene against stalking and harassment in the workplace

3. safeguard battered employees' employment and careers by providing flexible schedules and leaves of absence, and establishing enlightened personnel policies

4. provide employment security to battered employees

5. provide available resources to support and advocate for battered employees

The justice system will

1. adopt pro-arrest policies for batterers

2. charge and prosecute batterers in a manner that does not rely on the survivor's involvement

3. regularly disclose relevant statistics on the disposition of domestic-violence cases

4. devote training to the issue that is proportionate to the number of domestic-violence cases handled

5. vigorously enforce batterers' compliance with court mandates, and protect women and children's safety with custody, visitation, and injunctive orders

6. provide easily accessible and enforceable protection orders

The educational system will

1. support and educate teachers to recognize and respond to symptoms of domestic violence in students' lives
2. teach skills in violence prevention, promoting and honoring peace, conflict resolution, and communication
3. acknowledge gender bias in teaching materials and develop alternatives
4. require education about relationships at all levels
5. teach that it is the civic duty of all citizens to oppose oppression and to support those who are oppressed

The clergy will

1. routinely assess for domestic violence in premarital and pastoral counseling
2. seek out and maintain a relationship with the community's domestic-violence response system that emphasizes both learning and referral
3. speak out against domestic violence from the pulpit
4. oppose the use of biblical or theological justification for domestic violence
5. reject patriarchal dominance as a preferred social pattern

The media will

1. spotlight efforts that promote nonviolence
2. prioritize subject matter that celebrates peace and nonviolence
3. devote an equitable proportion of their product to covering the needs of battered women and their children
4. educate about the dynamics and consequences of violence rather than glorifying it
5. cease labeling domestic violence as "love gone sour," "a lover's quarrel," "a family spat," etc.
6. stop portraying the batterer's excuses and lies as if they were the truth.

Social-service providers will

1. design and deliver services that are responsive to the needs of battered women and their children

2. require staff to receive training on the etiology and dynamics of domestic violence

3. oppose the "pathologizing" of domestic-violence survivors and the exclusive control of the field by "degreed professionals"

4. shift the focus from "trying to keep the family together at all costs" to the safety of battered women and their children

5. utilize methods to help identify domestic violence

The health-care system will

1. develop and utilize safe and effective methods for identifying domestic violence

2. provide referral, education, and support services to battered women and their children

3. refrain from overly prescribing sedative drugs to battered women

4. utilize accountable documentation and reporting protocols for domestic violence

5. devote training to the issue that is proportionate to the number of domestic-violence cases handled

The government will

1. enact laws that define battering as criminal behavior

2. enact laws that allow courts to sentence repeat offenders with harsher consequences

3. adequately fund both battered-women's service agencies and violence-prevention education

4. commute the sentences of battered women who kill in self-defense

5. heavily tax the sale of weapons and pornography to subsidize prevention and intervention efforts against sexual and physical violence

Systems Advocacy

Working to create an effective community response to domestic violence can be thought of as systems advocacy. Systems advocacy is a companion to advocacy for individual survivors and their children. It includes two basic components: first, efforts to enhance various system responses to domestic violence, and, second, efforts to ensure that system policies and procedures are effective in their intent. Basically, systems advocates work to improve how "the system" responds to domestic violence. The next few sections look at some elements of systems advocacy.

As with other aspects of domestic-violence work, systems advocacy can be challenging and complex. According to Jill Davies, author of *Safety Planning with Battered Women,* "[A]dvocacy is by nature the work of compromise and negotiation. It involves balancing interests and the exercise of power and influence. Which interests are balanced, where the compromises are made, and how power and influence are exercised are [all] day-to-day and long-term questions for policy advocates."[2]

As advocates work toward enhancing community collaboration, it is important for them to understand the long-term implications of their efforts. As Davies puts it, "Ultimately, policy advocacy is a long-range safety-plan for all battered women, one that will be ongoing and ever-changing, but relentless in its movement forward."[3]

Enhancing Community Collaboration

In 1994 the American Medical Association invited a broad range of organizations to send representatives to the National Conference on Family Violence: Health and Justice. Results of the conference included recommendations for a better-coordinated, communitywide approach to reducing both the effects and incidence of family violence.[4]

One recommendation that came out of the conference suggested that individual communities should create special councils to coordinate efforts to end family violence at the local level. The councils should consist of representatives of all groups and agencies who deal with family violence. There should be no barriers to membership, and all interested parties, including the following, should be encouraged to join:

- ◆ Physicians
- ◆ Nurses, including clinical and school nurses
- ◆ Nurse practitioners
- ◆ Midwives
- ◆ Medical administrators
- ◆ Legislators
- ◆ Judges
- ◆ Formerly battered women

239

**Creating a
Community
Response to
Domestic
Violence**

◆ Advocates

◆ Law-enforcement officials

◆ Educators

◆ Social workers

◆ Clergy

◆ Pharmacists

◆ Substance-abuse counselors

◆ Mental-health providers

◆ Prosecutors

◆ Attorneys

◆ Probation and parole officials

◆ Corrections officials

◆ Researchers

◆ Community-based organizations

◆ Rehabilitated batterers

◆ Concerned community members

The family-violence councils should adopt the following general goals:

◆ To enhance coordination among hospitals, service agencies, police departments, and the courts at both the system and service levels

◆ To provide opportunities for the various disciplines to educate each other and to facilitate cross training

◆ To promote and evaluate interventions that have been found to be effective

◆ To improve the response to family violence in order to reduce its incidence

◆ To identify areas where interventions are known to work and need only to be coordinated, and to identify areas lacking effective programs and where new interventions must be developed

◆ To promote the development and support of intervention programs within hospitals and health-care systems

◆ To promote the development and replication of family-centered, community-based intervention programs

In addition to providing leadership for intervention and rehabilitation, family-violence councils are in an ideal position to address prevention, community education, assessment, and coverage by the media, and to work to integrate these activities. Specific strategies should include the following:

- Developing and revising policies and procedures for interagency coordination and cooperation at both the system and service levels

- Sponsoring conferences that focus on family violence in the community

- Promoting educational programs in primary and secondary schools

- Providing professional education

- Identifying intervention and rehabilitation methods within both the health-care and justice systems that have been effective in other disciplines and that can be applied to family violence

- Searching for cross-disciplinary approaches

Ann Jones, author of *Next Time She'll Be Dead: Battering and How to Stop It*, reminds us that a crucial element of a coordinated community approach is mutual accountability. Institutions within the community, she writes, "must build in to their design specific ways to monitor one another's work, collaborate on reviewing and revising programs, hold one another accountable for ineffective policies and practices, provide mutual support, and work to overcome institutionalized sexism, racism, and homophobia.... Every aspect of the coordinated community program must aim to protect victims and to hold offenders accountable."[5]

Models for a Coordinated Community Response

Barbara Hart, legal director with the Pennsylvania Coalition Against Domestic Violence, identifies several models that communities can utilize when trying to create a coordinated response to domestic violence.[6] The model recommended by the National Conference on Family Violence, Health and Justice is commonly referred to as a "domestic-violence task force," "coordinating council," or "coordinated community-response team." In addition to local councils, statewide councils also play an important role in improving the responses to domestic violence. In 1995 the National Council of Juvenile and Family Court Judges found that of forty-three state domestic-violence coalitions contacted, twenty-three participated in some form of statewide coordinating council. Although the councils varied somewhat in terms of structure and form, the study found that each council's statement of purpose included

241

Creating a
Community
Response to
Domestic
Violence

three major functions: assessment of the legal/justice and social systems involved, policy development, and planning.[7]

A second popular model is the "community-partnering" model. As Hart describes it, "In this model, the domestic violence program identifies a strategic plan for community action. Tasks are prioritized. The program partners with individuals and organizations in the community to work on the various initiatives in the plan. Work groups are established that are task specific and draw upon the expertise of members in the community.... From planning through execution, the work is collaborative with selected actors in the community. The domestic violence program orchestrates and oversees the work undertaken."[8]

A third model for a coordinated community response is known as a "community intervention project" (CIP). CIPs are nonprofit agencies that are external to the criminal-justice system and grounded in the battered-women's movement. One of the better-known CIPs is the Duluth Domestic Abuse Intervention Project (DAIP), which has served as a model in numerous communities in states including Minnesota, Colorado, California, Wisconsin, and Washington.[9] Like the community-partnering model, the CIP method establishes the core of activity within a grassroots organization. The CIP works with all segments of the justice system and the mental-health system to create an "effective deterrent to domestic violence, to safeguard battered women and children[,] and to align the community in efforts to end violence against women."[10] However, CIPs differ from community-partnering initiatives in that they also provide direct services to batterers.

The Travis County Family Violence Task Force

Community agencies continue to struggle to meet the demand for services that comes from battered women and their children. With few exceptions, current waiting lists are long. Domestic violence programs are often underfunded and understaffed, resulting in the cautious delivery of prevention-services and community education. According to Julia Spann, former associate director of SafePlace, in Austin, Texas, "It's clear that in order to impact the problem in a more comprehensive way, all service providers and community planners must cooperate and collaborate. Even though we desperately need new resources, we also need to ensure that [existing] services are being coordinated throughout the community."

The Austin community has historically been deeply concerned about domestic violence. This is evident from the grassroots formation in 1977 of the Center for Battered Women (now SafePlace), the first shelter for battered women and their children in the state, and the creation in 1981 of the first Austin/Travis County Family Violence Task Force (FVTF). The FVTF developed from the understanding that a significant impact on family violence could only be accomplished if service providers adopted a common vision and a united approach.

The FVTF serves as a good model for other communities. Organizations and individuals represented on the task force include the following:

- Adelante (a batterer's reeducation program)
- Association of Criminal Defense Lawyers
- Austin Child Guidance Center
- Austin Municipal Courts
- Austin Police Department—assault, patrol, and victim-service units
- Austin Stress Clinic (a batterer's reeducation program)
- Domestic Violence Survivors
- Legal Aid
- LifeWorks (a batterer's reeducation program)
- SafePlace
- Travis County Attorney's Office
- Travis County Community Supervision and Corrections Department (provides pre-trial services)
- Travis County Constable's Office, Precinct 5
- Travis County Counseling and Education Services
- Travis County Court at Law, No. 4
- Travis County District Attorney's Office
- Travis County Domestic Relations Office
- Travis County Sheriff's Office
- University of Texas at Austin Law School Domestic Violence Clinic
- Women's Advocacy Project (provides legal services)

The FVTF has had a tremendous impact on the Austin community. It has helped to educate sectors of the community about domestic violence and has effected legal, policy, and procedural changes at the legislative, criminal-justice, and law-enforcement levels. As a result of the task force's efforts, area agencies better understand each other's expertise so that services are provided by the most appropriate entity and duplication of services is avoided. This means a continuum of care is available to domestic-violence survivors, their families, and abusers.

243

Creating a
Community
Response to
Domestic
Violence

Listed below are some of the accomplishments attributed to the Travis County Family Violence Task Force:

1. Adoption of a pro-arrest policy, which states that police officers are expected (but not required) to make an arrest when they see signs of domestic assault

2. Filing of family-violence misdemeanors at the more serious Class A level instead of at Class C, meaning offenders are subject to harsher punishments

3. Establishment of mandated screening for batterers' counseling as a condition of personal recognizance bonds (*personal recognizance* means the offender is released upon posting little or no bond and is trusted to reappear on his court date, often under the conditions that he have a home address and a job)

4. Establishment of quality-control standards for batterers' intervention programs

5. Adoption of a "direct-file" policy, which requires the arresting officer, rather than the victim, to file charges against the offender

6. Implementation of procedures for law enforcement to request emergency protective orders on behalf of victims

7. Creation of a jail-based batterers' intervention program

8. Establishment of procedures to allow prosecutors to request increased police patrols in cases involving very angry abusers

9. Establishment of a policy whereby jail personnel routinely attempt to contact the victim to help insure her safety prior to an abuser's release

10. Creation of investigative techniques by prosecutors and law enforcement that are more sensitive to victims

11. An increased number of Austin Police Department Victim Service mobile crisis teams

12. Creation and implementation of Project Options, a supportive educational program for victims who request that charges against their offenders be dropped

13. Creation of a specialized criminal domestic-violence court in which participating officials receive cross training

14. Creation of the CourtWatch Program, in which volunteers are trained to observe legal proceedings affecting survivors and to report on both courtroom conditions and the legal process

15. Establishment of the periodic review of the content of batterers' intervention programs by formerly battered women

16. Increased cross training among system components

The FVTF has been involved in identifying the various kinds of services that should be in place, including (1) outreach and primary prevention, (2) intervention and treatment, (3) collaboration, and (4) policy change. These components encompass a systems approach to identifying those abused, helping people to be safe, intervening appropriately, reducing domestic violence, and ultimately fostering a healthier community.

The task force's activities currently focus largely on the justice system's response, but recent efforts to raise public awareness and to reach out to survivors indicate the beginning of a new era. "We really want to branch out," explains Gail Rice, director of community advocacy with SafePlace and part of the FVTF. Accordingly, the FVTF has created the psycho-educational program Showing Teens Other Paths (STOP), for young people ages fourteen to seventeen who are convicted in the juvenile system and who have a family history of domestic violence. In addition, FVTF members have been active in two substantive planning efforts: the Community Action Network Master Study and Master Plan for Austin/Travis County Health and Human Services, and the Criminal Justice Council Task Force Community Plan. Both efforts were launched in 1994, completed in 1995, and remain in place as working programs that are being refined, expanded, and enhanced to ensure a comprehensive approach to dealing with violence and victimization.

The SafePlace Transitional Housing Program

Advocates understand that domestic violence is a major cause of homelessness for women and their children. Recent studies confirm this connection. San Diego's Regional Task Force on the Homeless found that almost 50 percent of homeless women in San Diego are domestic violence survivors. A 2003 survey of Denver, Nashville, New Orleans, Phoenix, Norfolk, Portland, Salt Lake City, and Seattle reports that domestic violence is a primary cause of homelessness. A 2002 report on homelessness in New York City states that almost half of all homeless parents had been abused and 25 percent of all homeless parents were homeless as a direct result of domestic violence.[11] These statistics are substantiated by SafePlace and the Salvation Army, which together provided emergency shelter to 90 percent of all homeless families that received shelter in Austin in 1993. The mutual effort of these two organizations can be an excellent model for other communities attempting to address the need for transitional housing.

SafePlace has been a consistent participant in attempts to create a continuum of care for domestic-violence survivors in the Austin/Travis County metropolitan area. In the mid-1990s major social-service funders—including the City of Austin, Travis County, United Way, the State of Texas, the Austin Independent School District, and various local foundations—joined together to form the Community Action Network (CAN). CAN's functions are to develop a comprehensive assessment of social-service needs in the community, to evaluate the effectiveness of current social-service programs, to identify gaps in services, and to make recommendations concerning annual funding decisions. An outgrowth of CAN was the creation of the Homeless Coalition, which works to develop initiatives to address issues facing the homeless, to facilitate collaborative development of applications for funding, to create alliances among organizations, and to strengthen the collective effectiveness of social-service providers.

In 1994 the Center for Battered Women (now SafePlace), in collaboration with the Salvation Army, was awarded over $2 million in federal Department of Housing and Urban Development (HUD) funding under the transitional-housing component of the Supportive Housing Program. Their joint effort, the Transitional Housing Program, addresses a critical gap in the continuum of care for homeless families in Austin. Transitional housing, combined with other intensive support services, aims to move homeless families from emergency shelters to permanent housing and self-sufficiency. The pairing of SafePlace, a local agency serving battered women, with the Salvation Army, a national organization serving homeless people, represented an innovation in aiding battered women and their children.

Families served by both SafePlace and the Salvation Army encounter multiple problems and barriers that maintain their dependent and homeless status. A lack of affordable housing is a primary barrier. In addition, lack of job skills, unemployment, lack of child care, poor parenting skills, lack of confidence and self-esteem, and unresolved issues resulting from abusive relationships must all be addressed before a family can become independent. The Transitional Housing Program addresses these and numerous other obstacles that can prevent families from ending their homelessness. Initially, the two agencies address the families' safety, shelter, and emergency needs. Next, the families are moved into transitional housing that is owned and operated by SafePlace but shared by both agencies' clients. In addition, both the agencies

245

Creating a
Community
Response to
Domestic
Violence

participate with the Homeless Coalition to share other available transitional housing.

Services provided by SafePlace to participants in the transitional-housing program include outreach, assessment, case management, life-skills training, and counseling for women and children. SafePlace also collaborates with educational and social-service organizations to provide child care, substance-abuse services, mental-health services, specialized services for developmentally delayed children, and transportation. While shelters often offer a range of services to their clients, SafePlace's provision of therapeutic child care, focused on building parenting skills and developing healthier families, is an innovative addition that is easily replicated.

In 2001 SafePlace completed construction on fourteen new apartments, new community rooms, and a children's playscape at the Transitional Housing Apartment Community. The community room provides space for gatherings, holiday parties, training, and after-school tutoring; the playscape offers young children a safe and fun place to play. The expansion puts the total number of apartments at forty and allows SafePlace for the first time to offer transitional housing to women without children in the form of six new efficiency units.

Other SafePlace Collaborations

SafePlace's willingness to collaborate with the Salvation Army demonstrates the agency's belief in the need for a united response to domestic violence. The Transitional Housing Program is one in a long list of ventures between SafePlace and other entities intent on ending family violence. Some of SafePlace's other collaborations are listed below:

- ◆ *County attorney's office:* Two SafePlace legal advocates, housed at the county attorney's office, provide advocacy at court that is independent of the legal system. The goal of the joint effort is to address safety issues and to link battered women with support services.

- ◆ *District attorney's office:* A SafePlace legal advocate is also housed at the district attorney's office to assist in providing advocacy to survivors in criminal cases involving either domestic violence or sexual assault.

- ◆ *Austin Police Department (APD):* The SafePlace shelter has an agreement with APD Victim Services through which APD referrals are admitted to the shelter on a twenty-four-hour, as-needed basis, even if the shelter is full.

- ◆ *Family Violence Protection Team:* SafePlace has joined with the Austin Police Department, Travis County Sheriff's Office family-violence detectives, victim-services workers, and attorneys from Legal Aid, the county attorney's office, the district attorney's office, and the Women's Advocacy Program to provide an integrated approach to helping domestic-violence survivors. The goals of the project are to encourage the arrests of abusive partners, to increase the enforcement of protective orders, and to improve survivors' access to legal and supportive services.

247

Creating a
Community
Response to
Domestic
Violence

◆ *Texas Rural Legal Aid:* SafePlace partners with Legal Aid in the Civil Legal Assistance Program, which started in 1998 with a grant from the U.S. Department of Justice. Through the program Legal Aid assists domestic-violence survivors with their civil legal needs.

◆ *The University of Texas (UT) School of Law:* Through a grant from the U.S. Department of Justice, SafePlace partners with the UT School of Law's Domestic Violence Clinic to provide civil legal assistance for domestic-violence survivors and training specific to domestic violence for student lawyers.

◆ *Women's Advocacy Project:* Through a grant from the U.S. Department of Justice that funds the Civil Legal Assistance Program, SafePlace contracts with the Women's Advocacy Project to provide civil legal assistance to domestic-violence survivors.

◆ *Family Forward:* SafePlace, in partnership with Family Forward, offers "Safe Parenting," a domestic-violence and parenting-education program designed to prevent child abuse and domestic violence.

◆ *Austin Families:* Through a child-care voucher system, Austin Families assists families participating in the SafePlace Transitional Housing Program who choose not to use the SafePlace Child Development Center. Families who reside at the shelter or participate in the Passages Program (see below) also receive child-care subsidies through Austin Families.

◆ *Passages:* The Passages Program is a six-agency collaboration that provides intensive case-management services and financial assistance to the homeless. The program reimburses SafePlace for the salary and benefits of two case managers and provides financial assistance to participating clients for transitional housing.

◆ *Austin Independent School District (AISD):* SafePlace delivers a range of services to AISD schools (K–12), including individual counseling and support groups for students who have experienced or witnessed domestic violence, sexual abuse or assault, or dating violence; classroom presentations on sexual harassment and healthy relationships; and staff training for preventing bullying and sexual harassment.

◆ *University of Texas (UT) Mental Health and Counseling Services:* Safe-Place receives funding from UT to assist in the ongoing development of the campuswide Voices Against Violence Project, which includes prevention, education, and survivor services.

◆ *University of Texas (UT) Continuing and Extension Education/Distance Education Center:* SafePlace contracts with UT to operate an on-site charter school located at SafePlace. UT provides teacher salaries, teacher training, books and other educational materials, and student assessment services.

◆ *Deaf and Abused Women and Children Advocacy Services (DAWCAS):* SafePlace and DAWCAS are working together on a statewide project to provide videos in sign language explaining shelter rules and guide-lines. The agencies also work together on outreach education activities.

◆ *Saheli:* SafePlace and Saheli collaborate on outreach programs to the Asian and South Asian community about sustaining healthy relation-ships and preventing domestic violence.

Our ability to end family violence is directly related to our willingness, as in-dividuals and communities, to unite our voices and our efforts. Our society cannot afford to rely solely on the battered-women's movement to end this epidemic. While the movement has accomplished incredible feats, we need everyone's participation if we truly want to make our communities and our world more loving, peaceful places for women and children.

...*14*

Intervention Strategies for Battered Women and Their Children

GROWING

I am the fish which strikes forth into the great blue endless ocean.
My eyes are open and I am travelling ahead, strong and free.
My body, smooth and wet, is surging through waves
which splash and lull me on my endless journey.
Openness and freedom are my jewels—
Space is my reward.
Let lightness and airiness carry me on my journey.

— *P. M.G.*[1]

Intervention on behalf of battered women and their children takes place in a variety of arenas. The battered-women's movement has distinguished itself as a leader in the effort. Our experiences with battered women and, for many of us, our experiences as survivors have taught us that women have a variety of needs. First, and most important, battered women need to be safe. Advocates' understanding of this fact has given rise to the many shelters and safe-home networks (private residences opened to women in need by concerned citizens) that exist across the country. Second, battered women need information. They need to know about the resources and options available to them.

Third, battered women need material resources. Initially, they need a safe place in which to gather whatever material resources they have. If their own resources are limited or unavailable, they may need to access resources from the city or state. Battered women may need medical assistance, housing, food, clothing, transportation, or money. They may need child care, education, job training, jobs, or legal assistance. Some women may need to secretly relocate to another area to protect themselves from their abusive partners.

Battered women also need opportunities to break their isolation. They need opportunities to connect, to share, to be respected, and to heal. Two types of intervention that provide these opportunities are support groups and individual counseling.

Support Groups

Support groups for battered women, whether inside or outside the shelter setting, offer advantages that are different from those afforded by individual counseling and other services. Participating in groups is often the best way for women to gain support and information while reducing their sense of isolation. Women who feel isolated and powerless and who blame themselves for the abuse often benefit from exchanging information and expressing their feelings with other women in similar situations. And women who have begun to change their lives are impressive role models for new group members. In some groups women act as advocates for each other, and many eventually join the battered-women's movement.

Support groups for battered women are the direct offspring of the feminist ideas nurtured in the consciousness-raising groups of the 1960s and 1970s. Ginny NiCarthy, Karen Merriam, and Sandra Coffman, in their book *Talking It Out: A Guide to Groups for Abused Women,* outline these foundational ideas:[2]

- Women are the best experts on their own lives.

- Women are often safer relying on others who are like themselves.

- Women teach each other that their problems aren't individual, but are social, political, and shared by many others.

- Institutionalized sex roles are damaging to women, and the first step in changing them is to understand them.

- Individual women have power, and collectively their power can be great.

◆ The best place for women to look for emotional support and practical help is often from other women.

Most support groups have a facilitator to provide guidance, enhance the sense of safety, and enable each woman to contribute as much to the group as she is willing to. Many groups, such as those described by Ellen Pence, build on the work of the adult educator Paulo Freire, whose approach was based on a group process of critical reflection and transformative action.[3] The development of critical consciousness starts with recognition of the problem and moves on to analysis, action, and organization. In the Freirian model, the facilitator does not impart knowledge to passive participants but rather serves as a partner in a common search for insight about problems.[4] In support groups for battered women the facilitator helps women gain a critical consciousness about gender, power, and how violence operates in women's lives. According to Pence, "There is no greater challenge for any social movement than to live the vision of the change it seeks. A women's group does not merely prepare women for a future experience of empowerment or liberation. The group is itself an act of empowerment or liberation."[5]

Support groups are composed entirely of women, including the facilitator. The absence of men frees women to express feelings and thoughts they might suppress in a mixed group. This may be especially true for battered women, who have learned to fear men. If battered women are to benefit from a support group, they need to learn to trust again and to risk intimacy with others.

Support groups help women face the reality of what has happened to them, what might happen, and what their responsibilities are. They provide an opportunity for women to explore feelings and options previously unknown or denied and an environment in which they can make decisions with the support of other participants. As women begin to experience insights and revelations about their abuse, they may become fearful and retreat into an earlier stage of denial. Women who feel too threatened may decide not to return to the group, but the group experience may help them to take action at a later date.[6]

If possible, groups for battered women should be divided into two stages: a first stage for women in crisis or who are trying to get free from abusive relationships, and a second stage for women who have successfully escaped abusive relationships and are facing other life issues. Many communities do not have the luxury of providing groups for specific populations, such as battered women of color or lesbians. Still, every effort should be made to form groups of whatever type are most needed in the community. If specialized groups are not feasible, facilitators should try to incorporate information and ideas about different populations into the mixed groups (see Chapter 7).

Individual Counseling

In the 1970s Phyllis Chesler's critique of the ways in which traditional counseling reinforced the oppression of women led the way to alternative approaches to helping women.[7] Articles were published that discussed consciousness-raising groups as therapy for women, and soon the terms *feminism* and *feminist therapy* were being used in the psychotherapeutic context.[8]

Feminist therapy has several basic tenets. First, it is a wellness-based rather than a pathological-based approach. The counselor or advocate, instead of viewing battered women as psychologically impaired or "sick," approaches them with respect for their success in surviving. In her book *In Our Best Interest: A Process for Personal and Social Change,* Ellen Pence reminds advocates, "We must constantly be aware of the tremendous pressure to view women's oppression as a sickness rather than as a political, social and cultural condition."[9] Second, the feminist approach is based on the principles of individual choice and self-determination. Neither individual counselors nor the battered-women's movement knows what will work best for any particular woman. Instead, battered women themselves know what will work best for them.

Third, the role of the counselor is to provide support, to identify resources, to supply information, and, at times, to serve as an advocate for battered women. Fourth, the relationship between the counselor and the battered woman is characterized by equal power. The counselor's actions do not suggest that she is the expert; rather, they affirm the battered woman's power and competence to make decisions and to act. The counselor and the battered woman talk and work together to solve problems. This feature of feminist counseling stands in direct contrast to traditional psychotherapy, which operates from a hierarchical power structure in which the therapist knows best and directs the counseling process. Fifth, the techniques of counseling include the identification of battered women with other women, particularly other battered women, and consciousness-raising about institutionalized sexism.[10]

Individual counseling offers battered women a safe environment in which to connect with another woman and begin to explore their personal situations. According to Margaret Bassett, manager of the SafePlace Women's Shelter, individual counseling coupled with support groups can be doubly rewarding for women. "Women who participate in individual counseling seem to do better in the support groups," she says. "They seem to have a higher [degree of] self-awareness and are more willing and better able to focus on themselves instead of their abusive partners."

Intervention with Children of Battered Women

253

Intervention
Strategies
for Battered
Women
and Their
Children

Intervention with children of battered women is closely associated with the battered-women's movement. Intervention models specifically designed for children of battered women were developed throughout the 1980s as a response to the difficulties observed in children who had been exposed to domestic violence. As is the case with their abused mothers, intervention with children must be centered on the issue of their safety. Children who live with ongoing violence need to be protected from its direct and indirect consequences.

A major focus for shelter staff is to ensure that children and their needs do not become invisible. Children of battered women experience emotional trauma that requires an outlet for expression.[11] Residing in a shelter may present an ideal opportunity for children to share their feelings and to sense some safety and adult support. According to Melinda Cantu, shelter director at SafePlace, "Our work with these children is not to take away their feelings, but to help them understand them so that they may lead nonviolent, healthy lives. Basically, we're trying to work ourselves out of a job so that future generations will know what it means to live in peace and harmony."

Battered-women's shelters provide children with safety and support, but at the same time may be experienced by children as highly stressful environments. The needs of children in shelters are great and often require both crisis intervention and ongoing emotional support, medical attention, and interaction with educational systems and child-protection agencies. Shelter programs for children have become increasingly focused on children's crisis, their special needs at the time of admission to the shelter, and the development of more extensive programs to assist in their recovery.[12] Intervention typically consists of individual and group support and falls into four areas: children's programs, parenting intervention, protecting children from abuse, and academic assistance. The next four subsections examine each of these topics. After that, two more subsections take a look at some children's programs offered by SafePlace.

Children's Programs

Stopping the violence does not, by itself, create healing. Children need emotional support both during and after witnessing or experiencing violence. Many children of battered women are traumatized by the violence and require intensive short- or long-term individual therapy. Other children may have their needs met through small groups in which they can break the silence surrounding family violence.

One of the challenges facing shelter staff is providing meaningful services in a limited amount of time. Women and children often average only a week at a shelter, and some stay for only one or two nights. Many shelters have developed programs that are directed to specific age groups and have defined strategies, such as the following:[13]

♦ Techniques to deal with specific behaviors, such as aggression

♦ Play assessment and play therapy to encourage preschool-age children to express feelings about the violence

♦ Encouragement of teenagers to develop and act out plays about family violence to foster awareness, self-expression, and a sense of helping others

♦ Individual counseling for children, including very specific strategies to obtain a better understanding of the children's reaction to the current crisis and to prepare them for possible violence in the future

♦ Structured group counseling for children and teenagers to assist them in gaining peer support and a sense of not being alone with the problem

♦ Multifamily groups that include both women and children, that encourage mutual support within and among families in crisis, and that are open-ended enough to deal with the reality of a brief, time-limited intervention

One of the most widely used interventions for children of battered women is group counseling. Although most children require a great deal of individual attention from shelter staff, group programs are an essential service. Groups allow children an opportunity to learn that they are not alone in dealing with their crises and that other children have comparable life experiences. Children can learn helpful coping strategies from other survivors and from caring adults who lead the group. For many children group counseling is their first opportunity to openly discuss the issue of violence in their families. They are often anxious to share their thoughts and feelings and are sometimes surprised to hear about alternative ideas for dealing with family violence.

Most group-counseling programs involve sixty- to ninety-minute sessions that meet weekly for six to ten weeks. The number of sessions typically depends on the child's length of stay in the shelter. Participants range in age from one to sixteen, but most groups focus on ages four to thirteen. Groups are usually divided according to the children's developmental abilities, and many are small, involving only three to six children.[14]

Most programs have specific goals, including helping children to—

- ◆ define violence and responsibility for violence

255

Intervention
Strategies
for Battered
Women
and Their
Children

- ◆ express feelings, including anger

- ◆ improve communication, problem-solving, and cognitive-coping skills

- ◆ increase self-esteem

- ◆ develop social-support networks

- ◆ develop safety plans

- ◆ feel safe and develop trust during the group sessions

Programs achieve their goals through a variety of structured educational and play activities that include presentations, discussions, modeling, role-playing, art projects, homework assignments, and perhaps a family night during which children's activities take place either concurrent with a parents' program or with parent participation.[15]

Children's attendance at group sessions may raise uncomfortable issues for their mothers. It is important that group leaders maintain close contact with the mothers and prepare them for the issues that will be covered. Providing mothers with information and feedback both initially and on an ongoing basis is essential. Some group models suggest that mothers be part of the group and that parent-child relationships become a major focus.

According to Peter Jaffe, David Wolfe, and Susan Wilson, authors of *Children of Battered Women,* group-counseling programs may be best suited for children with mild to moderate behavioral problems. For children exposed to repeated acts of severe violence over many years, a group will address only a small proportion of their numerous concerns. These children may require more extensive, individual work.[16]

Dana Grasso Gillispie, director of child and adolescent counseling at Safe-Place, says the following about programs for children of battered women: "Through the use of various treatment modalities children are given a safe space to freely express their feelings regarding the abuse in their homes. It is critical to involve the parent and other appropriate family members in this process in order to address the family patterns and dynamics that may result from the abuse. In addition, involving the family helps to enhance and sustain the progress that the child achieves as a result of the counseling."

Parenting Intervention

Domestic violence often raises parenting challenges for mothers. Problematic relationships between mothers and children are not unusual, both because of the violence the children have witnessed and because the mothers are in crisis.

Children may miss their fathers and quickly forget or minimize the reasons why they came to the shelter. They may blame their mothers for displacing them from their homes and friends. At the same time, child rearing may be one of the few areas where battered women perceive they have control. Any parenting intervention with battered women needs to be respectful and to acknowledge their struggle to be the kind of parents they want to be.[17]

Through supportive counseling, parenting groups, and some parenting relief, shelter staff and other advocates can help mothers empower themselves to become more effective parents. Many battered women have had few role models for effective parenting because of their own childhood sexual and/or physical abuse. Some mothers residing in shelters may be unable to elevate their parenting skills without very specific educational programs that teach them new ways of relating to their children. Parenting groups for battered women can take place in or outside of a shelter.

Protecting Children

A major challenge faced by children's advocates at women's shelters is the protection of abused children and coordination of these efforts with child-protection agencies. All staff members of a domestic-violence program, but children's staff in particular, must be clear about the appropriate policies and procedures for reporting abuse and neglect and protecting children from further abuse. An appropriate response to child abuse includes protecting the children from further abuse while understanding the abuse in the context of woman battering. Intervention should help the women to empower themselves by highlighting their strengths and encouraging them to take control over their lives and their children's lives.[18]

In families in which the mother continues to reside with the batterer or returns to the batterer after staying in a shelter, realistic goals need to be formulated to assist the children in coping with ongoing violence. The focus should be on working with children to create a safety plan, both to increase their safety and to lessen the impact of the exposure to violence. Melinda Cantu, shelter director at SafePlace, recommends that advocates incorporate the following steps when creating a safety plan with children:

- ◆ Identify a safe adult in the neighborhood.
- ◆ Identify someone in the school system with whom they can talk.
- ◆ Call 911.
- ◆ Reach out to any adult with whom they have a trusting relationship.

According to Cantu, "Our primary goal in helping children create a safety plan is to make sure they get safe, then get help."

Academic Assistance

257

Intervention
Strategies
for Battered
Women
and Their
Children

After admission to a shelter, many children may not attend school because of the fear of the fathers kidnapping them. Others face the further disruption of relocating to a new school environment. In terms of children's educational requirements, a temporary stay at a shelter may present opportunities to identify remedial needs, offer individual support, and create some sense of routine and stability. Shelters may offer a variety of school services, including the following:[19]

- ◆ Liaison with the child's school to ensure that officials there are aware of the trauma and will help provide continuity in the child's education

- ◆ Specialized teachers on site to offer remedial assistance and help with reintegration into the school system after the crisis period

- ◆ Specialized classrooms in schools that have a close relationship with the shelter and are prepared for the unique demands on these students

The Family Tree Child Development Center

In 1999, in the wake of the kidnapping and murder of a survivor's child by her abusive partner, SafePlace staff initiated discussions about the possibility of providing on-site child care for survivors receiving services. With the generous financial support of a private donor and the assistance of professionals in the Austin child-care community, SafePlace opened the Family Tree Child Development Center (CDC) in 2001.

The center provides quality early-childhood education to children of survivors and staff. The program focuses on children's social, emotional, physical, and cognitive needs while working to maintain the safety and security of each child. Enrollment is open to children who are living in the family shelter, children of survivors in the transitional-housing program, and children of Safe-Place staff and board members.

SafePlace Educational Program

In conjunction with the founding of the CDC, SafePlace staff expressed a desire for the school-age children residing in the shelter to have the option of attending school on-site. Staff felt this would allow the children to be closer to their mothers and siblings, feel safer, and have their sometimes acute academic needs met before they made the transition to a new public school. As a result, the building constructed in 2001 accommodates both the CDC and school classrooms. The mission of the SafePlace Educational Program is to offer a safe and secure environment in which children coming from violent homes may flourish as a result of having positive experiences and more individualized attention.

The program encompasses two classrooms, one for kindergarten through second grade and the other for third through eighth grade. Class sizes are generally limited to eight to ten students. As a part of the University of Texas at Austin's Charter School, the program meets the state's educational requirements and receives state financial support, administrative support, and educational support. The university also provides a superintendent, a principal, academic counselors, curriculum specialists, and other staff.

The SafePlace Educational Program plays many important roles in the lives of the families it serves. It allows parents to build relationships with teachers so they can begin to view school as a resource for both themselves and their children. And it works to meet the educational needs of school-age children even while it addresses their safety and security needs and helps to end the isolation they may feel as a result of having lived in a violent home.

Safety and Empowerment for Battered Women and Their Children

Regardless of the form it takes, any action on behalf of battered women and their children should ensure their safety and help them to empower themselves. The key here is *helping them to empower themselves.* As advocates for battered women and their children, we must exercise care in our use of the word *empowerment.* The literal definition of *empower*—to grant power to another— presumes the existence of an agent who is doing the granting. If we claim to empower battered women, we claim to give them power, an attitude that negates the feminist philosophy of an egalitarian relationship between the advocate and the battered woman. If we are committed to providing services that are aimed at liberating battered women and their children, we must realize that any truly liberating experience for battered women is not a result of anyone granting them power.

We can, however, talk with women about power, how it operates, and its effects. We can help women develop strategies, and we can join with them to seize personal and political power. This is how we help women to empower themselves, and this is how we nurture the power of women as a group.[20]

The next chapter discusses how to advocate for battered women in a way that helps them to empower themselves.

...15

Advocacy and Empowerment for Battered Women

When we advocate for a survivor we're asking her to give 110 percent. We have to be willing to do the same.

— Andrea Edgerson, training and hotline coordinator
Los Angeles Commission on Assaults Against Women

One of the most common questions I'm asked in my classes and trainings is, "How can I help someone who is being abused?" Throughout this book I've tried to address that question. *Helping* a battered woman certainly comes with its own challenges. To *advocate* for a battered woman, however, both presents a deeper level of challenges and requires a more advanced set of helping skills.

Understanding Empowerment

Karen Stout and Beverly McPhail, in *Confronting Sexism and Violence Against Women,* point out that the commonly accepted definition of *empower* is to increase the control people have over their lives.[1] They expand the definition by saying that empowerment also refers to the development of a certain state of mind (e.g., feeling powerful, competent, worthy of esteem, etc.) and to the modification of structural conditions for the purposes of reallocating power (e.g., modifying the society's opportunity structure). Empowerment, they emphasize, is both a process and a goal, and it results in positive self-image, increased skills and information, greater control over one's life, and action.[2]

Empowerment has been described as occurring in levels. The first level, personal empowerment, focuses on ways in which individuals can develop feelings of personal power and self-efficacy. The second level, interpersonal empowerment, focuses on the development of specific skills that allow individuals to be more capable of influencing others in a range of settings, such as the family or the workplace. The third level, political empowerment, emphasizes the goals of social action and social change.[3]

For each of us, personal empowerment is a private journey that is uniquely our own. As advocates for battered women, however, we are in the privileged position of getting to travel with other women as they make that journey.

The Advocate's Role

A critical component of any program working to end violence against women is advocacy. To advocate means to speak and act for justice on behalf of oneself or another person or a cause. We become advocates for survivors of domestic abuse when we speak out against violence toward women, when we talk to women on a crisis hotline, when we accompany survivors to court, or when we discuss visitation rights with a worker from child-protective services. Advocates are a blend of counselor, educator, community organizer, and social change agent.

Effective advocacy can occur at two levels: the individual level and the systems level. Individual advocacy serves survivors in a variety of ways, including helping them navigate various systems they must deal with as a result of the abuse they have experienced. Systems advocacy seeks to interface with various systems within a given community to effect policy and procedural changes in order to improve the systems' response to survivors (see Chapter 13 for more about systems advocacy). According to Jill Davies, author of *Safety Planning with Battered Women,* advocates "can include staff or volunteers of a battered women's shelter or program, or medical, legal, social service, law enforcement[,] or other institutional systems that respond to domestic violence."[4] She explains that the context in which advocacy occurs will drive, to some extent, the role of the advocate.

Advocates work with survivors who have all kinds of challenges and needs. In the morning an advocate may discuss alcoholism with one survivor and in the afternoon speak with a caseworker from child-protective services regarding another survivor. While it is unrealistic to expect every advocate to be an expert in all areas, it is important to understand advocates' basic responsibilities to survivors. The Pennsylvania Coalition Against Rape has identified several responsibilities advocates have to rape survivors. The responsibilities, listed below, apply equally to advocates for domestic-violence survivors:[5]

◆ To serve as a liaison between survivors and systems

◆ To help facilitate survivors' decision making

◆ To inform survivors of their rights

◆ To help survivors by providing necessary information

◆ To accompany survivors as they move through systems

◆ To inform survivors of other available services

◆ To document services provided according to program requirements

◆ To reach out for assistance and support when necessary

Ultimately, the advocacy process seeks to (1) enhance the safety of battered women and their children, (2) hold abusers accountable, (3) ensure the responsiveness of community systems to the needs of battered women and their children, and (4) end domestic violence. If we are successful in our endeavors then we are closer to reaching our goal of safety and justice for battered women and their children.

Service-Defined Advocacy Versus Woman-Defined Advocacy

Davies identifies two basic types of advocacy, "service-defined" and "woman-defined." It is important to distinguish between the two. According to Davies, "When advocates focus exclusively on providing a service, whether or not it fits into a battered woman's risk analysis or safety plans, they are providing what we call service-defined advocacy. Although providing services is an essential part of the work of all domestic violence advocates, we stress that providing services should be distinguished from advocacy defined by services."[6]

Woman-defined advocacy, by contrast, works to build partnerships that "provide advocates with the opportunity to integrate their knowledge, resources, and advocacy into the woman's risk analysis and plans. This integration provides both the advocate and the battered woman with the best possible information on which to base further analysis and safety planning."[7]

Strength-Based Empowerment Strategies

Woman-defined advocacy follows a "strength-based" approach. Battered women, to the best of their abilities, use a variety of skills and strategies to survive and to deal with the violence in their lives. By acknowledging these strengths, advocates are better able to help battered women build on them to empower themselves. Don't automatically assume that a survivor is powerless. Remember, she has survived the abuse and in doing so has developed coping skills. Although some of her strategies may be less appropriate or less useful to her outside the context of domestic violence, they are helping to keep her alive right now. Acknowledge this fact and commend her for her determination and perseverance.

Create a partnership with the survivor by focusing on her strengths and offering her opportunities to build on them. Resist any temptation to simply do things for her. Coni Huntsman Stogner, manager of family advocacy at SafePlace, in Austin, Texas, says, "Sometimes advocates are so committed and so compassionate that they want to take on a survivor's problems rather than walking side by side with that person." In a true partnership an advocate will help the survivor explore ways in which she can do things for herself. Help her to see how she can transfer her strengths to other areas of her life. See Chapter 8 for a discussion of helping battered women as opposed to rescuing them.

Partnerships imply equality, or at the very least equity. Although an advocate may have information and resources that will be helpful to the survivor, the survivor has her own information, understanding, and resources as well. When all of these elements are combined, survivors can work to empower themselves rather than be passive recipients of another person's vision.

It is important to note that even as advocates work to create partnerships with battered women, our roles in these relationships do give us institutional power. Among our responsibilities are to avoid abusing this power and to be mindful of how we allow it to affect our relationships with the women we serve.

One of the most powerful steps a battered woman can take is to reach out for help when she needs it. The same applies for the advocates who work with battered women. Stogner says, "I've seen advocates that didn't want to talk to anyone about something that was bothering them because they thought people would think less of them as an advocate. The reality is that this isn't easy work. All advocates, no matter how long they've been doing this work, struggle with something at some point. We see terrible things and it's to be expected that something will bother us every now and then. When this happens reach out to someone you trust and talk to them about it."

Advocating for Battered Women

The Advocacy Wheel, located on the next page, makes several recommendations to guide advocacy efforts on behalf of battered women. The material below discusses the recommendations in detail. Taken together, the suggested

263

**Advocacy
and Empow-
erment for
Battered
Women**

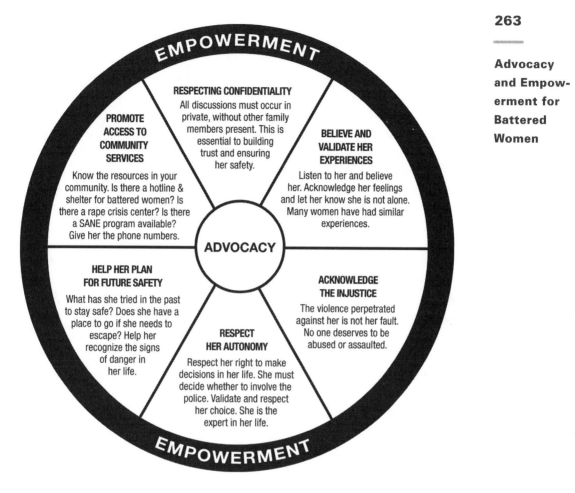

Advocacy Wheel

*Developed by Pathways of Courage, Inc., Women's and Children's Horizons, 1511-
56th St., Kenosha WI 53140, (262) 656-3500, modeled after the "Power and
Control and Equality Wheels" developed by the Domestic Abuse Intervention Project,
202 East Superior St., Duluth MN, (218) 722-2781, www.duluth-model.org.*

actions help to build a safe, supportive, and empowering foundation upon
which survivors and advocates can develop a respectful and effective partnership.

Respect Confidentiality

Domestic-violence shelters and programs have confidentiality policies that
govern what will and will not be disclosed about survivors both within and
outside the agency. Know, understand, and follow your agency's policy. Inter-
nally, information about specific survivors should be shared with other staff

members on a need-to-know basis only. Confidentiality serves as a major bridge between the survivor and the advocate and often helps the survivor to build trust toward the advocate. An advocate's failure to follow confidentiality policies not only disrespects a woman in crisis who has begun to trust the advocate, but may also place her life in serious danger.

One of the first steps an advocate needs to take is to inform survivors of the agency's confidentiality policy, including any limitations of the policy. For example, survivors need to know what will happen if they share information about child abuse, or if they are considering hurting themselves or someone else. In particular, many advocates struggle with the balance between advocating for battered women and being mandated to report cases of suspected or known child abuse. In states where "failure to protect" policies are in place, many service providers may be uncomfortable reporting child abuse knowing that the nonabusing parent may lose her child. However, if the batterer is also abusing the child then the advocate may feel the only thing she can do is report the abuse and risk revictimizing the survivor. In this type of situation it is possible to obey the law and still avoid revictimizing the survivor.

The process is as follows. Tell the survivor that, as a mandated reporter, you're required by law to report child abuse. Explain to the survivor that this doesn't have to be a negative process and it doesn't have to mean she'll lose her children. Ask the survivor if she would like to make the call and report the abuse. Explain that child-protective services may be more likely to work with the parent and not take her children away if she makes the call. At the same time, however, remember that you can't make guarantees. Ask her if she would like for you to stay with her for moral support while she makes the call.

If the survivor agrees to make the call and wants you there, then proceed accordingly. Explain to her that you'll be making a call later in the day to file the same report. If the survivor says she will make the call but doesn't want you around, then you can let her know that you respect her wishes but that at a particular time you'll be making a call to child-protective services to file a report. (You do, after all, need to make the report regardless of what the survivor does.) If the survivor refuses to make the call, then you'll need to inform her of your intention to file a report.

Regardless of the survivor's actions, you, as a supportive advocate, have offered her options and choices which, depending on her decision, may be the beginning steps toward her empowerment and the safety of her children.

Believe and Validate Her Experiences

Believe what the survivor tells you. Any deviation from accuracy in her story may be a result of her minimizing events rather than exaggerating them. Others frequently call the credibility of survivors into question, particularly if her abuser has any status in the community or if she has a history of substance use/abuse or mental illness.

Empathize with the survivor. Use active listening skills to communicate that you are interested and concerned. Spend more time listening than talking. When necessary, ask clarifying questions to make sure you understand what she is telling you. You may find it helpful to review the section in Chapter 8 on listening with love.

In addition, acknowledge her strength, courage, and determination. Point out the various resourceful ways in which she has tried to protect herself and her children, even if her actions have not been successful. Being heard, believed, and validated can be an extremely affirming experience for survivors.

Acknowledge the Injustice

Offer positive, affirming comments to help counter any hurtful, blaming messages she may have received. Say things like, "You are not to blame for what has happened to you; the abuse is not your fault," or, "You don't deserve to be hurt—not even by someone who tells you he/she loves you." Be mindful of the ways in which you may unintentionally use language that implies failure, weakness, or fault.

Respect Her Autonomy

Provide as many options and alternatives as possible to help facilitate her decision-making process. Rather than telling the survivor what to do, *ask* her what she wants to do. Support her right to make decisions about her life, even when you do not agree with those decisions. Remember that she is the expert on her own life. Resist the temptation to view leaving the abuser as the most appropriate action a battered woman can take. For many survivors, leaving makes sense only if it will help to reduce the overall risks that she and her children face. Remember, research has shown that the most dangerous time for survivors is when they leave.

Consider reframing your definition of a successful intervention. As Theresa Zubretsky and Colleen McGrath, both with the New York State Office for the Prevention of Domestic Violence, explain, "It is more helpful to assess the 'success' of our interventions based on what *we* do rather than what an individual battered woman does or doesn't do. Her decision of *inaction,* for example, may, in fact, be the best safety strategy for her at any given time. Her personal evaluation of the risks she faces may prevent her from taking actions that we determine necessary to protect the safety interests of the children involved."[8] If a survivor makes a decision that you feel places her in danger, it is possible to both support her and express your concerns. Zubretsky and McGrath write, "Regardless of her decisions, workers can continue to engage [a

265

Advocacy
and Empow-
erment for
Battered
Women

battered woman] in a supportive way, expressing concern for her safety and a willingness to continue seeking solutions that work to improve her and her children's safety."[9]

Tell the survivor that you respect and support her right to make her own decisions, but also say, "I am, however, very concerned about your safety. Have you thought about what you might do if the violence starts again or gets worse? Have you thought about creating a safety plan to help keep you and your children safe? Would you like me to help you work on a safety plan?"

Help Her Plan for Her Safety

In 1996 the American Psychological Association Presidential Task Force on Violence and the Family identified a number of strategies battered women use to try to keep themselves safe, including the following:[10]

- Calling the police
- Calling a shelter
- Leaving the home or scene
- Complying with the batterer's demands (even if only apparently or superficially)
- Talking to friends
- Hiding
- Avoiding the batterer
- Seeking professional help
- "Being nice" and not upsetting the batterer
- Keeping information from the batterer
- Avoiding conflict and keeping the peace
- "Walking on eggshells"
- Separating from or divorcing the batterer
- Fighting back with physical force
- Obtaining a gun or other weapon

A 2004 study examining women's survival strategies found that the most common tactics included trying to talk to the perpetrator about his violence, contacting the police, avoiding the perpetrator at certain times, and trying to end the relationship.[11] Research showed that none of these strategies were likely to make the situation better.

A safety plan is a way to help survivors protect themselves and their children against an abusive partner. Safety plans may help a survivor to become more aware of both her personal resources and those within the community. Most of all, a safety plan helps a survivor determine the steps she needs to take to protect herself and her children. Appendix II contains an example of a comprehensive safety plan that addresses such concerns as safety when leaving, safety during a violent incident, safety in the home or in public, and safety with a protective order.

It is important to remember that when it comes to knowing how the perpetrator might respond, the battered woman is the expert. Survivors engage in a number of behaviors in an attempt to keep themselves and their children safe and advocates can use this information to help survivors construct a personalized safety plan. With this in mind, the advocate should encourage the survivor to consider the following questions prior to completing the safety plan:

♦ What are some of the cues or behaviors that are present before a violent incident occurs?

♦ What have you done in the past to successfully protect yourself and your children?

♦ What can you do to increase your independence (e.g., opening a bank account in your name or taking classes to improve job skills)?

♦ What legal resources are available to you?

♦ What medical services are available to you?

♦ What social-service agencies are available to you?

Every survivor faces different risks and has varying levels of support and resources, a fact that will be reflected in individual safety plans. Thus, while there may be some similarity between safety plans, each will be as unique as the woman it is intended to protect. Furthermore, a woman's safety plan will change over time. Various factors impacting a safety plan include the success or failure of a particular strategy, the perpetrator's reaction to a specific strategy, and the information and resources provided by advocates and other responders.[12] Advocates have a responsibility to revisit a survivor's safety plan with her to help ensure that it is adequately modified and updated to reflect the survivor's ever-changing safety needs.

While each safety plan should be personalized to the woman's individual circumstances, a few characteristics should be common to every plan. According to Jill Davies, effective safety planning should try to reduce or eliminate

the full range of batterer-generated risks a woman faces, not just physical violence. A plan may include strategies for staying in and/or leaving the relationship and may encompass short-term and/or long-term time frames.[13]

The Texas Council on Family Violence provides a brief guide to help advocates as they work with survivors to create personal safety plans. Recommendations include the following:[14]

◆ Identify the issues or problems.

◆ Identify realistic actions the survivor could take to resolve the issues
or problems.

◆ Identify resources and options (both civilian and military, if applicable).

◆ Identify possible barriers to carrying out a plan of action.

◆ Brainstorm strategies for overcoming the barriers.

◆ Identify persons or organizations to assist in carrying out the plan of
safety.

◆ Identify how to monitor the outcome.

Danger Assessment

According to Barbara Hart, legal director of the Pennsylvania Coalition
Against Domestic Violence, assessment for dangerousness or lethality "attempts to identify those times and circumstances in which the batterer is most
likely to attempt injurious or lethal assaults. The purpose of dangerousness assessments in the context of domestic violence is to enhance the strategic construction of safety plans."[15] Lethality assessment is a complex and ongoing
process. As Hart notes, "It is not a tool for certain prediction but rather one
for risk assessment and safety planning or intervention in light of the appre-
hended risk."[16]

In 1985 Jacquelyn Campbell developed the Danger Assessment Tool. It
was revised in 1988 after being subjected to reliability and validity studies. Researchers have found that, despite certain limitations, the tool can, with some
reliability, identify women who may be at risk of being killed by their abusive
partners. The tool, which appears below, may assist advocates and survivors to
better understand the potential for danger and the level of risk survivors face.[17]

Danger Assessment

Several risk factors have been associated with increased risk of homicides (murders) of women and men in violent relationships. We cannot
predict what will happen in your case, but we would like you to be

aware of the danger of homicide in situations of abuse and for you to see how many of the risk factors apply to your situation.

Using the calendar, please mark the approximate dates during the past year when you were abused by your partner or ex-partner. Write on that date how bad the incident was according to the following scale:

1. Slapping, pushing; no injuries and/or lasting pain
2. Punching, kicking; bruises, cuts, and/or continuing pain
3. "Beating up"; severe contusions, burns, broken bones, miscarriage
4. Threat to use weapon; head injury, internal injury, permanent injury, miscarriage
5. Use of weapon; wounds from weapon

If any of the descriptions for the higher number apply, use the higher number.

Mark **Yes** or **No** for each of the following.

("He" refers to your husband, partner, ex-husband, ex-partner, or whoever is currently physically hurting you.)

Yes   No

____ ____   1. Has the physical violence increased in severity or frequency over the past year?

____ ____   2. Does he own a gun?

____ ____   3. Have you left him after living together during the past year?

3a. (If [you] have *never* lived with him, check here ___)

____ ____   4. Is he unemployed?

____ ____   5. Has he ever used a weapon against you or threatened you with a lethal weapon?

5a. (If yes, was the weapon a gun? ___)

____ ____   6. Does he threaten to kill you?

____ ____   7. Has he avoided being arrested for domestic violence?

____ ____   8. Do you have a child that is not his?

____ ____   9. Has he ever forced you to have sex when you did not wish to do so?

____ ____   10. Does he ever try to choke you?

____ ____ 11. Does he use illegal drugs? By drugs, I mean "uppers" or amphetamines, speed, angel dust, cocaine, "crack," street drugs, or mixtures.

____ ____ 12. Is he an alcoholic or problem drinker?

____ ____ 13. Does he control most or all of your daily activities? (For instance: does he tell you who you can be friends with, when you can see your family, how much money you can use, or when you can take the car?)

(If he tries, but you do not let him, check here ___)

____ ____ 14. Is he violently and constantly jealous of you? (For instance, does he say "If I can't have you no one can.")

____ ____ 15. Have you ever been beaten by him while you were pregnant?

(If you have never been pregnant by him, check here ___)

____ ____ 16. Has he ever threatened or tried to commit suicide?

____ ____ 17. Does he threaten to harm your children?

____ ____ 18. Do you believe he is capable of killing you?

____ ____ 19. Does he follow or spy on you, leave threatening notes or messages on [your] answering machine, destroy your property, or call when you don't want him to?

____ ____ 20. Have you ever threatened [to] or tried to commit suicide?

_____ **Total "Yes" answers**

Thank you. Please talk to your nurse, advocate[,] or counselor about what the Danger Assessment means in terms of your situation.

(Source: Jacquelyn Campbell, PhD, RN, FAAN. Copyright 2004 Johns Hopkins University, School of Nursing. Reprinted with permission.)

The first portion of the instrument measures the severity and frequency of battering. Campbell explains that when a woman uses the calendar to recall past violence she is being given the opportunity to reduce her denial and her minimization of the abuse.

The second part of the instrument measures risk factors associated with intimate partner homicide. The "cutoff" score for questions 1 through 15 of this assessment is 4. At this level there is a need for great caution and protective action. A score of 8 or more indicates that the survivor is in extreme danger and at risk of death.

It is important to note that in studies evaluating the reliability of this assessment, 83 percent of the women who were killed had scores of 4 or higher, but so did almost 40 percent of the women who were *not* killed. The research showed that only a score of 8 or 9 reliably identified those women who were killed, a finding indicating that advocates should use the assessment as a *guide* in the safety process rather than as a precise tool.[18]

Promote Access to Community Resources

Prior to sharing information with a survivor about community resources and services, it is helpful to know exactly what she may need. The only way an advocate can determine a survivor's needs for services is by asking. SafePlace has developed the following detailed questionnaire for this purpose, to be completed very early in the advocate-survivor partnership:

I. Medical Information

Do you need medical care?

Current injuries that need initial medical treatment:

Injuries from abuse that need follow-up care:

Injuries from previous abuse that need treatment:

Chronic medical condition(s):

Current medication(s):

Need prescription(s) filled? _____

Need dental care? _____

Need eye care? _____

Where do you get medical care?

Private doctor _____

Clinic _____

Hospital _____

No recent medical care _____

How do you pay for medical care?

Private insurance (for self or others) _____

Private insurance paid by someone else _____

Enrolled in Medical Assistance Program (MAP) _____

Enrolled in Medicare _____

Enrolled in Medicaid _____

II. Children's Needs

Medical:

Where do your children receive medical care?

How do you pay for their medical care?

Do they need immunizations? _____

Do you have their shot record(s)? _____

Are your children currently sick? _____

Do they have chronic medical condition(s)? _____

Are they on medication? _____

Do they need prescription(s) filled? _____

Do they need dental care? _____

Do they need eye care? _____

Education:

Do the children need to transfer schools? _____

Name of school children were attending: _____

In what grades? _____

Special education needs? _____

Child care: _____

Need day care? _____

Need after-school care? _____

Need full-day summer program? _____

Emotional:

How did the children react to leaving home and coming into the shelter? _____

How often did they witness the abuse? _____

Are they showing any behaviors that concern you?

Have any of your children living in the shelter been arrested or convicted of a crime? _____

[Explain "no spanking" policy. _____]

Parent's usual method of disciplining children? _____

Do the children have what they need to feel comfortable here?

Child abuse:

Explain the need to report child abuse to DPRS. _____

Physical abuse: _____

Sexual abuse: _____

Emotional abuse: _____

Abuse must be reported to DPRS (1-800-252-5400)

Report taken on ___/___/___ By: _____

III. Housing Information

Where were you living?

Previous address: _____

Were you renting? _____

Names on lease: _____

Do you own your home? _____

Names on title or mortgage: _____

Staying with friends or relatives? _____

Other: _____

Who lived in household?

Abusive partner: _____

Relationship to abusive partner: _____

Children: _____

Other adults: _____

Children's relationship to abusive partner: _____

Rental history:

Rent currently paid in full? _____

Need to terminate current lease? _____

Need to terminate utilities? _____

Current or pending eviction? _____

Previous eviction and date: _____

IV. Current Finances/Resources

Cash available: _____

Bank account(s) in your name: _____

Joint accounts: _____

V. Employment Information

Current job (name, phone, address of employer):

Work schedule/# hours weekly: _____

Salary (weekly, biweekly, or monthly): _____

Interested in looking for work? _____

Kind of work you are seeking? _____

Would you like GED or job training? _____

VI. Legal Information

Has a current protective order. It will expire on ____/____/____.

Needs a protective order for the following family members:

Charges filed on most recent assault. Case #: _____

Charges filed on previous assault. Date: _____/_____/_____

Would you like to file for divorce? _____

Would you like to file for custody and visitation? _____

Existing custody order for these children: _____

This order was granted by _____ County Court on _____/_____/_____.

Do you need to have the existing custody order amended?

Are there outstanding warrants for your arrest? _____

Are you currently on probation or parole? _____

Do you have a previous criminal history? _____

Outstanding warrants for abusive partner: _____

Previous arrests or convictions of abusive partner: _____

Current or prior arrests or convictions of any children residing here:

Any immigration issues? _____

Other legal issues? _____

VII. Current Resources

Do you have any of the following? (Highlight whatever applies.)

Education: High school diploma or GED

      Some college

      College graduate

Income: TANF*   Amount _____

 *Temporary Assistance for Needy Families

      Food stamps Amount _____

      Child support Amount _____

      SSI/Disability Amount _____

      Other income Amount _____

Medical: Medicaid For whom

      Clinic card For whom

      Private insurance For whom

Transportation:	Own car
	Bus system
	Friend
Children's resources:	Day care Where
	After-school care Where
	WIC
Documents:	Birth certificates For whom
	Social security cards For whom
	Current ID/DL

Other referrals made:

When discussing options it is important to explore a survivor's existing resources and support systems. According to Zubretsky and McGrath, "Many women may be wary of using the formal service system at all—because of past experiences, existing barriers, or cultural values, for example.... Many women are more comfortable asking a friend, family member, clergy person, or neighbor for assistance than they are requesting assistance from strangers. In addition, the formal service system does not provide all the answers to the myriad problems facing battered women."[19]

Locate, and refer survivors to, resources in their specific ethnic, racial, and religious communities. Remember that many survivors have had negative past experiences with systems that oppressed rather than served their best interests. Exhibit sensitivity to a survivor's decision not to trust a particular system out of fear of further victimization.

Ask the survivor if she would like to begin keeping a "personal resource guide": a notebook with all the names, phone numbers, addresses, and lengthy to-do lists that she will soon be compiling. If she agrees, help her to start and organize one.

Navigating the Systems

A key component in the advocacy role is to help survivors navigate the numerous systems they may encounter. The legal, health-care, social-service, child-protective, mental-health, and governmental systems all have their own policies and procedures. When referring a survivor to any of these groups it is helpful to be able to provide at least a basic idea of what she can expect to encounter. In addition, survivors need to know their rights and what a particular system expects from them.

One of the more challenging systems for advocates and survivors to navigate is the child-welfare system. According to Esta Soler, president of the Family Violence Prevention Fund (FVPF), "Victims of domestic violence often find the child welfare system confusing, frightening[,] and overwhelming. Domestic violence service providers need to know how to help women navigate the child protection system, because nothing is more important to a mother than ensuring that her child is safe and secure."[20] In *Advocacy Matters: Helping Mothers and Their Children Involved with the Child Protection System,* the FVPF identifies the following five strategies that advocates can use to assist domestic-abuse survivors who are also involved with the child-welfare system:[21]

1. Create safe spaces in which mothers can talk.

2. Define your roles and the actions you can take.

3. Develop a relationship with the CPS caseworker(s).

4. Learn as much as you can about laws, policies, and procedures.

5. Increase the accessibility of your program.

It is important to note that the same strategies, with minor revisions, can apply when working with any number of systems. The bottom line is that we cannot expect a survivor to successfully navigate any system without some background information on rights, responsibilities, and expectations, and in order to provide such information we must make the time to do our own investigative research.

Andrea Edgerson, training and hotline coordinator with the Los Angeles Commission on Assaults Against Women, points out that as advocates we are only as good as our word. She says, "Anything that you say you're going to do, then be sure and do it. And if you don't, then have a good reason to offer to the survivor. Anything less implies that an advocate is not invested and that [this particular action is] not crucial. We have to remember that survivors have timelines and everything is crucial for them."

Sometimes helping a survivor to navigate the system involves systems advocacy. The website for the Women's Justice Center explains that a systems' responses to domestic violence "cover the full range from excellent to atrocious and everything in between, even within an individual agency."[22] When a system fails to respond appropriately to survivors then they have fewer options available to themselves and their children. Whereas individual advocacy is crucial for the safety and well-being of a particular survivor, systems advocacy is necessary to bring justice to all survivors. For additional information about systems advocacy and strategies for developing a community response to domestic violence please see Chapter 13.

Appreciating Individuality

All survivors of domestic violence share the common experience of having a partner or ex-partner who uses some form(s) of abuse to try to control them. Beyond this fact, we must remember that every survivor is unique. According to Davies, "How each woman experiences that control, how she responds, what she fears, what options are available to her, what options she perceives to be available to her, and how the people she encounters will respond to her are unique to each woman. Understanding this uniqueness is essential for woman-defined advocacy."[23]

We can begin to appreciate survivors' diversity and individuality by really listening to them without presumptions, assumptions, or generalizations. When we do this we are "walking the advocacy talk." After all, if we tell a battered woman that she has every right to be treated with dignity and respect, what better way to illustrate our point than by doing just that?

...16

Intervention and Prevention Programs for Batterers

Violence against women will cease when men renounce the thinking and practice of dominance. We can begin to do this on an individual basis at home, at work, and in our community. When we begin to speak up, other men will listen and the seeds of change will be planted. I hope men will take the initiative and work with other men to confront sexism and violence, not to get approval from women, but because it is the right thing to do for women and men.

— *Michael Paymar, training coordinator, Duluth Domestic Abuse Intervention Projectand author of* Violent No More[1]

The first intervention programs for batterers were organized in the late 1970s by men who wanted to end violence against women. EMERGE, in Boston, and RAVEN (Rape and Violence End Now), in St. Louis, were two of the first programs to offer counseling and educational services for batterers. In their initial efforts to develop programs, organizers were careful to base their analyses of domestic violence on the experiences of battered women.[2] The safety of battered women and their children is the top priority of profeminist batterers' programs.

The first interagency batterers' intervention programs were organized by advocates in the newly emerging battered-women's movement. (Interagency programs exist within or grow out of larger, established programs.) They focused on changing the way the judicial system handled individual domestic-violence cases and usually included rehabilitation as an important part of a larger intervention strategy. Although the early programs valued education and counseling for men, such strategies were viewed as secondary to criminal-justice reform. The Domestic Abuse Intervention Project (DAIP), in Duluth, and the AMEND program, in Denver, fall into this category.[3]

Starting in the 1980s and continuing through today, batterers' intervention programs have spread across the United States. Various programs embrace various models, not all of which have the same feminist commitment to battered women as do some of the earlier ones. Although some intervention techniques may be similar to one another, different programs communicate very different messages to men about their responsibility for their violence.

Treatment Models

Most new programs are being started by mental-health centers through the efforts of private mental-health practitioners. The focuses of these programs vary tremendously. Some attempt to restore relationships by viewing violence as a symptom of a dysfunctional relationship. Others work exclusively with batterers on anger management, interpersonal communication skills, and stress reduction. Still others adapt the model used by such programs as EMERGE, RAVEN, AMEND, or the DAIP.[4] Several of the treatment approaches routinely give contradictory messages to men about why they batter and what they—or their partners—must do to stop the battering. From a feminist perspective some of the approaches actually collude with batterers by failing to make their violence the primary issue or by implicitly legitimizing men's excuses for violence.

In his in-depth analysis David Adams identifies five clinical approaches currently used with batterers: the insight model, the ventilation model, the interaction model, the cognitive-behavioral model, and the profeminist model.[5] Each of them is described in this section. Although many batterers' programs consider themselves eclectic, most are predominantly guided by one of these models.

The Insight Model

Although many variations exist within the insight model, the broad theme is that certain intrapsychic problems give rise to violent behavior, including poor impulse control, low frustration tolerance, dependency, fear of abandonment, fear of intimacy, underlying depression, and impaired ego functioning resulting from developmental trauma.

281

Intervention
and
Prevention
Programs for
Batterers

When underlying problems like insecurity are made the central focus of treatment, not only does therapy fail to confront the violence, but it also fails to confront the more immediate causes of the insecurity. Violence increases the man's feelings of insecurity since it also increases the risk that his partner will leave or grow distant from him. He typically reacts to these possibilities with more violence. In this way, violence is self-perpetuating unless it is directly confronted.

The Ventilation Model

Proponents of the ventilation model do not provide specialized interventions for batterers, primarily because violence is seen as a symptom of the core problem of emotional repression. Batterers and their partners are usually included in groups for couples or individuals that address repressed feelings and dishonest communication. Domestic violence is usually compared to miscommunication or "game playing," and distinctions between violent and nonviolent men are deemphasized or blurred.

In the ventilation approach participants are encouraged to "level with one another" while also being taught to "fight fairly." In some cases acts of "mock fighting," such as punching pillows or hitting one another with foam clubs, are practiced to facilitate the release of pent-up aggression. Encouragement to "fight fairly" while venting hostile feelings sends a dangerous, contradictory message to men about the acceptability of violent behavior. Ventilation therapy dangerously distorts men's understanding of growth and emotional maturity by selectively promoting certain forms of self-expression without confronting the violence itself.

The Interaction Model

The interaction model is similar to the ventilation approach in that treating both the batterer and his partner is considered essential for improving marital communication, resolving conflict, and ending violence. Couples participate either in couples' therapy or in specialized groups with other "violent couples." Most interaction therapists, however, do not consider ventilation to be an appropriate method of ending violence.

The goal of interaction therapy is for each partner to identify and change how he or she contributes to the problem. The tendency of the counselor to equalize responsibility for violence between the man and the woman is at the heart of the feminist criticism of the interaction model.

Couples' counseling gives ambiguous and contradictory messages to batterers about how much responsibility they should take for ending their violent behavior. In addition, although women are expected to be open about their feelings and report their partners' violence, doing any of these things places them in danger of continued abuse.

The Cognitive-Behavioral Model

The cognitive-behavioral approach (sometimes referred to as the psychoeducational approach) makes violence the primary focus of treatment. In addition, because violence is seen as having a dominating influence on marital interaction, abusive men are seen separately in specialized groups or in individual therapy to increase the opportunity for them to focus on their own behavior.

According to the cognitive-behavioral model, since violence is a learned behavior, nonviolence can similarly be learned. The psychoeducational therapist points out the damaging and self-defeating consequences of violence and teaches alternative behaviors. Since battering behavior is also seen as reflecting certain deficits in social skills, interpersonal-skills training is provided as an important element in helping men refrain from violence.

Although they share a philosophy that identifies the learning of skills as fundamental to change, psychoeducational programs vary in terms of which skills are emphasized. They also vary in how explicitly they address battering as an abuse-of-power issue or confront the sexist attitudes of participants. Psychoeducational programs that do not address sexism tend to view battering as a skills-deficit or stress-management problem. The majority of interventions are aimed at helping batterers better manage their anger, cope with stress, and improve communication skills.

The cognitive-behavioral model has offered many valuable insights and interventions for battering behavior. From a feminist perspective, however, its major weakness is that when interventions are too broadly aimed at reducing stress or improving interpersonal skills, the important power and control dimensions of domestic violence are minimized or ignored.

The Profeminist Model

Domestic violence is a controlling behavior that creates and maintains a power imbalance between the batterer and his partner. Such is the feminist insight that directs the profeminist approach to batterers' intervention programs. Therapeutic interventions that follow a profeminist model directly challenge the batterer's attempts to control his partner through the use of physical force and verbal and nonverbal intimidation. Compared to other models, the profeminist approach broadly defines violence as any act that causes a woman to do something she does not want to do, prevents her from doing something she wants to do, or causes her to be afraid.

283

Intervention
and
Prevention
Programs for
Batterers

The profeminist model, like the psychoeducational model, recognizes the need to provide basic education to batterers about caretaking and communication skills. However, it also sees the need to challenge the sexist expectations and controlling behaviors of batterers. Therefore, whereas the focus of early treatment is on the identification and elimination of violent and controlling behaviors, later interventions focus more on sexist expectations and attitudes.

Other Program Considerations

A batterer typically enters a treatment program for at least one of five reasons: his partner is threatening to leave; his partner has left; he has recently committed an abusive act and is feeling particularly remorseful; something was different about his last offense (for example, he reached relatively greater levels of violence or started hitting the children as well); various state or local authorities have become involved and ordered him to do so.[6] A batterer can be referred by any number of agencies and individuals, though state-sanctioned referrals usually carry more influence in providing the initial motivation to attend and in compelling men to stay in the program.

Although programs vary a great deal, the preferred format seems to be small groups of five to fifteen men, the leaders of which may be male, female, or both. Most programs are highly structured, focus on teaching behavior and attitude change, and last from ten to thirty-six sessions.[7] Most programs use standardized curricula in which a diverse group of men participate. There is, however, a shortage of culturally sensitive programs for men of color and for gay and lesbian batterers.

Approaches and treatment methods frequently become generic and standardized. Although generic methods may be effective with men of color or with gay and lesbian batterers, it is important to consider the race and culture of participants when designing intervention programs. Programs that are not sensitive to their particular population can be as ineffective as those that take a stereotypical approach to working with battered women and their children.[8] Battering-intervention programs should establish ways to respectfully account for cultural and racial differences while focusing on participants' personal responsibility and the unacceptability of domestic violence.

The Success of Batterers' Intervention Programs

"Do batterers' intervention programs really work?" That is one of the most frequent questions I hear in my presentations and workshops on domestic violence. Expecting a simple yes or no answer, audiences are often frustrated by my response. It seems the answer to the question depends upon a variety of factors, including whom you ask, the program's definition of success, and the manner in which the program is studied and evaluated. At best, evaluative research on batterers' treatment programs is both confusing and conflicting.

The way in which the term *success* is defined will greatly influence the degree to which intervention programs are perceived as effective. For example, does success mean that physical abuse is reduced rather than eliminated? Under this criterion, men could be considered successful participants if they have decreased their average violence from four beatings to two beatings a week, even if the decrease makes little difference to those who continue to receive or witness the abuse. Thankfully, most experts working with batterers agree that ending violent behavior is an important success criterion.[9] Furthermore, varying research designs and methodologies generate varying results, and low response rates and high dropout rates may lead to overly positive estimates of a program's effectiveness.[10]

In an evaluation conducted on four batterers' treatment programs in Pittsburgh, Dallas, Houston, and Denver, Edward Gondolf, professor of sociology at Indiana University of Pennsylvania and research director of the Mid-Atlantic Addiction Training Institute, assessed the reassault patterns among 840 batterers. The batterers and their partners were interviewed every three months for fifteen months after the initial intake. According to the survivors, 31 percent of the men reassaulted during the follow-up. Nearly half of the men who reassaulted did so within three months after the program intake. Voluntary participants were significantly more likely to reassault (44 percent), as were program dropouts (40 percent). Gondolf concludes by stating, "The 'well-established' batterer programs appear to contribute to a short-term cessation of assault in the majority of batterers. However, a small portion of the men are unaffected by or unresponsive to the intervention."[11]

The National Institute of Justice (NIJ) reports that over thirty-five evaluations have been published on batterer-intervention programs using quasiexperimental designs. These initial studies consistently found that programs were slightly effective. When more rigorous evaluations were undertaken, however, the results were inconsistent. The NIJ explains, "Most of the later studies found that treatment effects were limited to a small reduction in reoffending, although evidence indicates that for most participants (perhaps those already motivated to change), BIPs [Batterer Intervention Programs] may end the most violent and threatening behaviors. The results, however, remain inconclusive because of methodological flaws in these evaluations."[12]

285

Intervention
and
Prevention
Programs for
Batterers

Much of the controversy about the success of batterers' programs centers around the issue that many battered women continue to feel unsafe despite the fact that their partners eliminate the use of physical violence. Emotional abuse and other forms of manipulation may continue or even increase, often replacing physical violence while maintaining the system of power and control. Ending physical violence alone does not create true safety for women and children. Evaluations that are more sensitive to the perspectives of battered women may provide further insight into their safety concerns and thus help refine batterers' programs.[13]

Batterers' intervention programs are a relatively new approach to a widespread social problem, and it is simply too soon to be able to make a definitive determination regarding their effectiveness. The NIJ reports, "It is too early to abandon the concept. It is also too early to believe that we have all the answers."[14] Only through continued research and study will we be able to respond appropriately to questions regarding the effectiveness of such programs.

The Search for an Appropriate Model

Much debate has surrounded the question of which model is most effective, especially the issue of the appropriateness and importance of couples' counseling in batterers' programs. In response to the debate, an increasing number of states have set parameters regulating the structure and content of batterers' programs and the qualifications of providers offering them.[15] As of 2000, eight states (California, Colorado, Florida, Massachusetts, Oklahoma, Texas, Utah, and Washington) had enacted mandatory standards and legislation regulating batterers' programs. Nine states (Alabama, Connecticut, Iowa, Maine, Ohio, Illinois, Kentucky, Rhode Island, and Vermont) had enacted mandatory standards without legislation. Twelve states had voluntary standards, eight states had drafted standards, and eleven states were developing standards. Only three states had no standards at all.[16]

According to the guidelines set forth by the Texas Council on Family Violence and the Texas Department of Criminal Justice, traditional couples' counseling, family therapy, and mediation are inappropriate as the initial or primary intervention for batterers. Approaches that treat the batterer and partner together are considered detrimental for the following reasons:[17]

1. They tend to avoid fixing responsibility on the batterer and imply that the partner or the relationship is also to blame for the abuse.

2. They may perpetuate the abuse by giving the batterer a sense of support for his actions and placing the partner in the position of

286

━━━

**When
Violence
Begins
at Home**

disclosing information that the batterer may subsequently use against her.

3. They underestimate the real power imbalance between family members and leave the partner at a disadvantage.

There are no guarantees that any program will work. Much depends on the batterer's motivation and capacity for change. Some programs do, however, work better than others. The Texas Council on Family Violence offers the following guidelines for women whose partners are in a batterers' intervention and prevention program.

Your Safety Must Be the First Priority. The program should always assess your safety when communicating with you. It should never disclose, without your permission, information that you have provided. It should not misrepresent its ability to change your partner's behavior. Its definition of success should be the quality of your life and your children's lives, starting with safety.

The Program Needs to Last Long Enough. Change takes time. Programs should last at least eighteen weeks and require at least thirty-six hours of participation during that time, in addition to any individual sessions that may be scheduled for orientation or evaluation. The longer the program, the better the chances are that your partner will change. A year or longer in a program is preferable, although that is not always possible.

The Program Must Hold Him Accountable. The first step of accountability is that your partner take responsibility for choosing to use violence in the relationship. A program should recognize that his behavior is the problem and not allow him to use your behavior as an excuse. His violence is the problem, not you. Programs should also hold your partner accountable for attendance, participation, and complying with the group's rules.

The Curriculum Needs to Address the Root of the Problem. The content of the program should challenge your partner's underlying belief system that he has the right to control and dominate you. Programs that address only his anger, communications skills, and stress do not get to the root of his problem.

The Program Should Make No Demand on You to Participate. You are not the one with the problem. Some programs offer groups for partners of batterers. Your participation is entirely optional. Don't let anyone lead you to believe that your partner's success in the program is dependent upon your participation.

The Program Should Be Open to Your Input. If you initiate contact with the program to ask questions or give input you think may be useful, the program should welcome your participation. This is different from requiring you to participate. Also, if a program initiates contact with you to discuss your partner's behavior outside the program, you are not obligated to share information, especially if you feel it may create a risk of violence against you.

The Program Needs to Encourage Follow-Up Support. Completing a program does not guarantee that your partner will be nonviolent. Staying nonviolent can be a lifelong challenge. A program should promote self-help and social support beyond the duration of the program, in the form of such activities as community service and participation in self-help programs.[18]

Creating a Men's Movement

Regardless of the effectiveness of any batterers' intervention program, we must remember that the goal of most programs is to try within a relatively short period of time to counterbalance much of what men have learned over years of exposure to a sexist culture. According to Jeffrey Edleson, "What is needed... is a major social movement in which men take responsibility for their abuses of power, both large and small, and in which they join with a more mature women's movement. Many men would probably welcome a movement that would lessen their emotional isolation from each other and from their intimate partners; ironically, that very isolation among men is probably one factor that inhibits such change."[19]

Since the original publication of this book, numerous efforts have been made to create a men's movement to end violence against women. While it may be premature to claim the existence of a widespread men's nonviolence movement in this country, the efforts of a large number of male allies certainly indicate that we may well be on our way. In 2000, the Battering Intervention and Prevention Project of the Texas Council on Family Violence was reconceptualized as the Men's Nonviolence Project. According to its mission statement, the project "pursues safety and justice for women, works to hold men accountable for their violence and abuse, and strives to eradicate the sexism from which violence against women grows."[20] It offers technical assistance, training, and monitoring of the statewide programs that work with batters. It recognizes that men's violence against women will not end as a result of batterers' programs alone; social change must also occur. Accordingly, the project has coordinated a variety of events that address the root causes of men's violence against women. Below are just a few of its accomplishments:

◆ Held forums on Men's Work to End Violence Against Women

◆ Produced and distributed the statewide education video *Circle of Accountability*

◆ Coordinated the Men Make Choices/Hombres de Verdad Escogen community-awareness and action campaign

◆ Held statewide organizing meetings on the topic of "Building a Men's Movement"

At the national level, the Family Violence Prevention Fund has initiated the media campaign Coaching Boys into Men, which encourages men to teach boys that violence against women and girls is wrong. The FVPF partners with the National High School Athletic Coaches Association to encourage coaches to become active partners in this effort. The White Ribbon Campaign, one of the largest efforts in the world consisting of men working to end men's violence against women, is an educational organization that encourages reflection and discussion leading to personal and collective action among men. Wearing a white ribbon is a personal pledge never to commit, condone, or remain silent about violence against women. Other groups include the Founding Fathers Campaign (also a program of the Family Violence Prevention Fund), Men Against Sexual Violence (sponsored by the Pennsylvania Coalition Against Rape), and Men Can Stop Rape. All-male peer-education groups include One in Four, at the University of Virginia, and Men Against Sexual Assault, at the University of Texas at Austin.

Although the men's nonviolence groups listed in this chapter represent an important step in ending male violence against women, the work remains unfinished. In *Stopping Rape: A Challenge for Men,* Rus Ervin Funk discusses the importance of building and sustaining men's nonviolence groups. He writes, "Underlying much of what I say is a strong desire to see thousands of pro-feminist men's anti-rape and anti-violence groups develop across the continent and around the planet. I want to see men come together to discuss these issues, and to plan how to dismantle this system of domination and control that keeps men in a position as victimizer or threat. That is our, men's work. We are in a position to effectively counter the "male lobby" that continues to advocate the maintenance of male supremacy.... We have the ability to create a world where all women, children and men are safe from the threat of men's violence."[21]

...17

Loving Ourselves:
Self-Care for Helpers

Pleasure is the expression of the true self.

— *Gloria Steinem*[1]

There's a small child running down the hallway looking for his mother. Two women are arguing over who is going to do the dinner dishes. A new resident has just walked through the door. An advocate needs to use the van, but it has a flat tire—again. One of the children's advocates has just discovered a raccoon in the garbage can. Welcome to shelter life!

Working in the battered-women's movement can be incredibly rewarding, but it can also take a tremendous toll. The strain of dealing extensively with other human beings, particularly those in crisis, frequently creates a state of emotional exhaustion, frustration, and reduced personal accomplishment known as burnout. Burnout occurs when we give too much energy to others and don't conserve enough for ourselves.[2] Regrettably, the battered-women's movement loses a lot of good people to this insidious phenomenon. The connection between burnout and turnover is all too apparent: Two years is frequently cited as the first critical point at which burnout will lead people to quit the movement.[3] Susan Schechter, author of *Women and Male Violence: The Visions and Struggles of the Battered Women's Movement*, reflects, "It may well be that helping one battered woman after another for fifty hours a week[,] and realizing that violence is extensive and infinite, heightens burnout."[4]

Burnout appears to be a response to chronic stress rather than to occasional crisis. Emotional pressure brought on by working closely with people is a part of the daily routine of advocating for battered women. Over time, one's tolerance for this sort of stress erodes.[5] Overload is another risk factor for burnout. Too much information is pouring in and too many demands are being made on the helper, which can lead to her becoming overextended and feeling overwhelmed. People respond to this set of circumstances with emotional exhaustion. They feel drained, used up.

The risk for burnout is also high when helpers lack a sense of control over the care they are providing, which can be a consequence of having no input into how tasks are accomplished or no influence on policy decisions that affect their jobs. The loss of a sense of control can also arise when a person receives little or no support from coworkers or has no opportunity to get away from a stressful situation. Whatever the reason for it, perceiving that one has no control over important outcomes in one's job adds to the emotional strain of the helping relationship.[6]

In addition to external factors, internal factors play an important role in determining a person's susceptibility to burnout. Psychological characteristics like personal needs, motivation, self-esteem, and expressiveness, as well as basic physiological makeup, influence how someone handles external sources of emotional stress. This helps to explain why two different people will respond to the same stress in different ways.[7]

Fight or Flight

If we are to take care of ourselves effectively and avoid burnout, it is helpful to know exactly what happens to our bodies when we are placed in stressful situations. An individual's reactions are partly determined by the sensitivity of her sympathetic nervous system, which produces the fight-or-flight response to stress and excitement.

The human body, when it anticipates the necessity for fight or flight, begins to mobilize almost instantly, producing a biochemical chain reaction that stands at the very heart of the burnout process. It all starts in the hypothalamus, a bundle of nerve cells at the center of the brain that acts as a command post of sorts. In response to a situation perceived as threatening, messages (in the form of hormones) race from the hypothalamus to spread an alarm throughout the nervous system. Muscles tense; blood vessels constrict; the capillaries directly under the skin shut down. The hypothalamus also sends a hormone to the pituitary gland, located at the base of the brain, which responds by secreting its own hormones. These move through the bloodstream to stimulate the thyroid and adrenal glands to secrete hormones. Thyroid hormones increase the energy supply we need to cope physically with the stress. Adrenal hormones, which number about thirty, go to nearly every organ in the body.

This "chemical cascade" known as the automatic stress response causes the pulse rate and blood pressure to shoot up. The stomach and intestines stop the activity of digestion. The senses of hearing and smell grow more acute. Literally hundreds of other physical changes occur without our knowledge.[8] All types of stress stimulate the stress response, so our bodies experience this energy-draining mobilization again and again. It may happen once a day or dozens of times, depending on the amount of stress we experience and, to some extent, our body's ability to stay calm in the face of stress. And the stress response can be mobilized not only by actual stressors, but also by simply thinking about them.[9]

Repeated episodes of the fight-or-flight reaction can eventually be damaging to our bodies. If we constantly mobilize energy at the cost of energy storage, we will never store any surplus energy, leading us to experience fatigue more rapidly and risk developing a form of diabetes. The consequences of chronically overactivating the cardiovascular system are similarly damaging, and the repair and remodeling of bone and other tissues can be disrupted. A variety of reproductive disorders may ensue: In women, menstrual cycles can become irregular or cease entirely; in men, sperm count and testosterone levels may decline. In both sexes, interest in sexual behavior decreases. The immune system can become compromised, which can lead to the body's inability to resist a variety of diseases. Finally, certain brain functions can be damaged by overexposure to some of the hormones secreted during stress.[10]

The High Cost of Caring

Exposure to chronic stress can have devastating effects on those ill-prepared to take care of themselves. Although stress does not necessarily cause illness, it does make us more susceptible to physical, emotional, mental, and spiritual imbalance. Following is a list of some of the many symptoms of stress exhaustion.[11]

Physical Symptoms

Appetite change

Headaches

Tension

Fatigue

Insomnia

Colds

Muscle aches

Digestive upsets

Teeth grinding

Rash

Lower-back pain

Tension at the base of neck

Lowered sex drive

Increased alcohol, drug, or tobacco use

Mental Symptoms

Forgetfulness

Dulled senses

Poor concentration

Negative attitude

Confusion

Negative self-talk

Emotional Symptoms

Anxiety

Frustration

Nightmares

Irritability

Depression

Worrying

Discouragement

Joylessness

Isolation

Loneliness

Lashing out

Spiritual Symptoms

Emptiness

Loss of meaning

Loss of direction

Apathy

Cynicism

Burnout doesn't just suddenly overwhelm us; it is insidious, chipping away at our ability to resist it. In fact, there appear to be five recognizable stages leading toward burnout.[12] The first stage is a period of high energy and job satisfaction. It is, however, also a time when we use more energy than we realize. Our increased expenditure of energy sets us up for the second stage of burnout, when the energy drain is more visible and we start to experience inefficiency in our work. Fatigue and procrastination start to take their toll. If we don't stop to reenergize ourselves, we slip into the third stage. Symptoms that developed in the second stage become habitual, and new symptoms emerge, including chronic exhaustion and physical illness. Physical illness can occur in the form of a cold that lasts for months, for example, or a period when our immune system fails to work in our best interest.

Weakened by physical symptoms, we are now set up for the fourth stage. At this point, burnout dominates our lives. We may experience frustration, self-doubt, isolation, loss of enthusiasm, pessimism, and depression. One of the hallmarks of this stage is a change in the way helpers interact with others. Once emotional exhaustion sets in people often feel they are no longer able to give of themselves, so they try to put distance between themselves and others by emotionally detaching from them. While detachment may protect the helper from the strain of close involvement with others, it can also prevent any feelings from getting through. With increased detachment can come an attitude of indifference to others' needs and a disregard for their feelings, a response that frequently leads to depersonalization: The helper may begin to view people in more cynical and derogatory terms.[13] Feeling negatively about others can progress to the point where helpers develop a sense of inadequacy about their ability to relate to others, which may lead to feelings of failure. Many helpers who experience self-doubt begin to physically isolate themselves from others. Burnout can affect psychological well-being in another way, too. The person who feels emotionally exhausted is easily irritated. Even the most minor frustration can provoke an immediate response of anger.[14]

The fifth, and most destructive, stage witnesses individuals who can no longer function in their jobs. Some will seek counseling or therapy; others will change jobs, often to abandon any kind of work that brings them into stressful contact with other people. Regrettably, still others try to deal with burnout using alcohol or drugs. Recovery from this final stage of burnout is often a long, arduous process.

Balancing Our Lives

If you find yourself busily helping others, stop and ask yourself, "Am I treating myself as fairly and lovingly as I treat others?" If the answer is no, be careful. Waiting for someone other than yourself to take care of you may lead to burnout. Don't wait until your world is crumbling around you before you care for yourself. You don't need permission from others to do this; give yourself permission to take care of yourself. Each of us is valuable and warrants nurturing and love. To care for ourselves does not diminish the support and affection we have to share with others; it actually makes it sweeter. The bottom line is that we do not have to sacrifice ourselves in the pursuit of our passion.

Giving to others must be balanced with giving to ourselves. The concept of balance is probably the single most important factor in developing a lifestyle that can successfully support us over a long period of time. Balance means flexibility, the ability to make decisions from a wide variety of possibilities. To achieve some level of balance, we should attempt, in any twenty-four-hour period, to address our emotional, mental, spiritual, and physical needs. Think about your level of satisfaction in each of these areas. As long as you remind yourself daily of your need for balance, you probably won't stray too far from it.

The challenge of nurturing and maintaining balance can be helped by asking yourself certain questions (and doing so will ensure that at least your thinking is balanced). Consider the following:

- ◆ Do you usually get six to eight hours of quality sleep each night?
- ◆ Do you allow yourself time to touch nature each week, no matter how briefly?
- ◆ Do you get some kind of enjoyable exercise each week?
- ◆ Do you do something fun at least once a week?
- ◆ Are you happy with your sex life?
- ◆ Do you give and receive hugs on a regular basis?
- ◆ Do you have people whom you can honestly talk to and who will listen to you?
- ◆ Do you take reasonable risks and seek new experiences?
- ◆ Do you ask for what you need?
- ◆ Do you forgive yourself when you make a mistake?
- ◆ Do you reward yourself for your accomplishments?

- Do you trust yourself?
- Do you do things that give you a sense of purpose, meaning, and joy?
- Do you try to live in the moment?
- Do you laugh at least once a day?
- Do you make time for your friends?
- Do you make time for solitude?
- Do you make time for daily or weekly spiritual nourishment?

If the answer to any of these question is no, then you have identified an area where you may decide to hold an intent in your mind to create more balance. In some ways "holding an intent" can be just as effective as striving and straining to reach a goal. No matter what, though, it is important to be easy on yourself. You definitely want to avoid putting pressure on yourself and feeling guilty for some perceived inadequacy in an elsuive attempt to achieve "perfect balance."

Connecting with Ourselves

The first step toward balancing our lives occurs when we attempt to connect with ourselves. This is actually a lifelong quest. To begin it, we must at some point start to lovingly and honestly take a look at ourselves. In the process of introspection, we should examine who we are, what is meaningful for us, who we want to be, and how we can get there. Once we begin to address these issues, we can establish the path we want to follow. We all, at least to some extent, create our own lives.

Consider the following as you begin your introspective journey.

Self-Concept — Your sense of who you are and how you feel about yourself plays a crucial role in your relationship to yourself and others. Self-care means making a commitment to the creation of a loving and positive attitude toward yourself. This does not mean that you see yourself as perfect or deny your limitations. Instead, it means that you strive to see the positive and to encourage and accept yourself. To know and like yourself is crucial when giving of yourself to others.

Needs — A need is something we require for our well-being. Self-care begins with evaluating what we need, from ourselves and from others. We can then determine whether or not our basic needs are being met and work to fulfill them.

Listening to Yourself — Be sensitive to the emotional and physical signals your body gives you. Trust them and use them as guides along your journey.

Goals — Set goals for yourself that you actually have a reasonable chance of accomplishing. If a goal is virtually impossible, you are setting yourself up for failure. Breaking larger goals into tiny, manageable mini-goals is helpful.

Knowing Your Limits — Setting realistic goals requires that you recognize your limitations as well as your abilities. Failing to recognize your limitations ultimately means there will be discrepancies between your aspirations and your achievements. You are the best judge of the gap between your desire to do something and the personal energy and resources you possess and are willing to commit to it.[15]

Boundaries — Define and consciously set boundaries.[16] Be very clear with yourself and others about what you will and will not accept. Not being honest with others about your personal boundaries will leave you feeling betrayed and angry. Begin to gently but clearly tell the people in your life what your limits are. Remember, too, that you may change your boundaries at any time.

Seeking Help — Helping work frequently brings up personal issues that are not addressed in the workplace. Seeking help from a counselor, therapist, or support group often provides a safe environment for personal growth and enhances our longevity in the battered-women's movement.

Suggestions for Self-Care

This section suggests many strategies you can use to balance your life and address burnout. They can be used either after burnout has occurred or as a means of preventing it. Some of the suggestions may interest you; others may not. Choose the ones that are meaningful and enjoyable and reflect who you are. You can combine them to create your own personalized pathway, or you can reject them altogether. In any event, reading them can serve as a catalyst to the discovery of other strategies that will work for you.

Whatever your responses to these activities, trust them. We all innately know what will work best for us. Honor yourself and follow your inner wisdom. We must each find our own path and discover what is right for us. That is one of the beautiful aspects of the individual journey, which is as unique and precious as each individual. It is my hope that these suggestions help you create your own special pathway to self-care and self-discovery.

When at Work

Strategies to address burnout can be implemented at several levels, including the organizational level (see the last section of this chapter). The suggestions below are individual strategies you can use to take care of yourself while you're at work.

Choose your battles. We encounter human needs almost constantly throughout our day, and it is easy to get involved with every struggle to improve services and efforts on behalf of battered women and their children. One of the quickest ways to burnout, however, is trying to do too much and taking on too many tasks.[17] Carefully assess each situation to determine whether it is best for you to get involved or to let it go.

Take breaks. As difficult as it may be to get away from your work, try to take a break occasionally, if only for a few minutes.

Monitor your overtime. Keep track of your overtime and try to avoid letting it get the best of you.

Take time off. Try to take a real vacation every year. A real vacation is more than two or three days or a long weekend; it means one to two weeks.[18]

Take mental-health days. Instead of waiting until you have totally run yourself down emotionally and physically, take a mental-health day for rest, relaxation, or play. Try to resist any feelings of guilt for taking this time for yourself. Remember, you are using self-care techniques that will help prolong your involvement in the movement.

Personalize your environment. Furnish your office with personal objects and mementos to serve as reminders of who you are and of your connections, personal convictions, and life outside of work.[19]

Relax your body. The stress and anxiety we feel at work are often reflected in tired shoulders and a stiff neck, which ultimately lead to a heightened state of fatigue. The following exercises, which can easily be done at work, may help to relax your body:[20]

- ◆ Sit straight in your chair with feet flat on the floor. Lift arms above your head with elbows straight and palms facing each other. Reach upward until your rib cage lifts. Bend down from the waist, reaching your hands toward your ankles. Relax in the bent position. Repeat five times.

- ◆ Sit back in your chair with hands clasped behind your head. Lean forward and touch your right elbow to your left knee. Then touch your left elbow to your right knee. Return to the starting position and repeat five times.

Prioritize and delegate. If you feel overwhelmed by the tasks you need to finish, try to address your anxiety by prioritizing. List all of the tasks you need to do the next day. Can any of them be delegated? If yes, delegate them to the appropriate persons, along with a deadline. Can any be dealt with later in the week? Assign a priority date and time to each of these.

Visualize yourself completing your tasks. Barbara Mackoff, author of *Leaving the Office Behind,* suggests that visualization can be an effective means of addressing anxiety over unfinished tasks. Review each task on your list. After you read each one, close your eyes and imagine yourself finishing it. Visualize the best possible outcome. You can end your day with a picture of yourself completing tomorrow's work. Visualizing your success in completing tasks can offer relief from the pressures of unfinished business and can be a powerful tool in your successful transition from work to home.[21]

Leave work at work. Try to limit the amount of time you spend finishing job-related tasks at home.

Remember why you do this work. Remind yourself of the importance and value of the work you do. A loss of meaning and hope can be countered by celebrating your successes with coworkers, friends, and loved ones—and with yourself.[22]

Diet, Exercise, and Sleep

Taking physical care of ourselves allows us to perform at our finest. The following are some ways to help you be at your physical best.

Monitor your diet. Determine the most healthful diet for you and make sure you have the right foods available to follow it. You will be much less susceptible to stress if your body has the nutrients it needs.[23]

Get sufficient exercise. Try to get a reasonable amount of exercise. Start slowly, gradually increasing the length and intensity of the exercise you choose. Walking and swimming are gentle exercises that can be taken at your own pace and are therapeutic for mind as well as body. Once you reach a certain level of fitness, consider taking up more strenuous exercises such as jogging or low-impact aerobics.[24] Be sure to contact your physician before beginning any exercise regimen.

Get enough sleep. Most people require six to eight hours of sleep each night, but the quality of sleep is also crucial. Sleeping poorly and insomnia are frequently caused by an inability to relax. If you experience these problems, try doing things that are calming for you immediately before retiring, such as drinking a glass of warm milk, engaging in gentle stretching, relaxing in a warm bath, meditating, listening to soft music, or reading. Above all, try to clear your mind of the day's activities rather than focusing on them.[25]

Monitor your negative thoughts. If you find yourself unable to sleep because you are preoccupied with negative thoughts, try saying, *"Stop,"* either silently or aloud. It interrupts your negative self-talk and offers you the opportunity to redirect your thinking. Another way to relax and nurture a positive attitude about yourself is through affirmations. Affirmations provide a means of changing negative or punitive beliefs to more empowering and positive thoughts.[26] For example, you might tell yourself, "I am a valuable and loved person." Whatever affirmation you use should hold a special meaning for you.

Practice moderation. Moderate your use of substances like alcohol, tobacco, caffeine, and food, and your engagement in activities like sex, socializing, and work. Remember, balance is the key. Every day, ask yourself, "Am I doing too much of any one thing?"

Socializing and Solitude

Both solitude and socializing are necessary for addressing burnout. Wanting to get away from people is a common response when we are experiencing emotional overload. Occasional and healthy solitude, however, is not the same as isolation. The danger occurs when avoiding others turns into isolating oneself from one's support systems.

Take time for solitude. Insist on having at least thirty minutes each day in which you can be alone without interruption. A good time to do so is after everyone has gone to sleep or before everyone has awakened. Use your time to relax, read, meditate, walk, or just reflect.

Schedule escape. Read a novel in the bath, on the bus, or at lunchtime. See a movie. If your body can't go on a faraway adventure, at least your mind can.

Socialize. Cultivate and nurture close relationships. Have at least one friend with whom you are totally honest.

Join a group. Look around for a group of people with whom you can share an interest. If you can't find one, consider creating one of your own. Remember, however, the idea is not to increase your stress level, but to help reduce it. Ask yourself the following questions about the people you are considering spending your free time with:[27]

- Does having this group in your life make you feel more empowered and challenged than you otherwise would?
- Can you be honest inside the group?
- Do you feel accepted as you are?
- Does the group make you stretch and become better than you thought you could be?
- Is there a balance between what you're receiving from the group and what you're giving to it?

Everyday Fun

Don't underestimate the genuine pleasure that can come from the simple things in life. We would all do well to remember and emulate the way children have fun. Consider a few of the characteristics of children's play:[28]

- Children are curious and usually eager to try something at least once.
- Children smile and laugh a lot.
- Children are creative and innovative.
- Children learn enthusiastically.
- Children dream and imagine.
- Children seek out fun things to do or else find a way to have fun at what they are doing.
- Children jump from one interest to another, leaving an activity whenever they feel forced or become more interested in something else.
- Children are constantly growing, mentally and physically.

Play games. Take up crossword puzzles, backgammon, chess, pool, or any other game that you find relaxing and enjoyable.

Engage in leisure activities. Activities such as dancing, movies, frolicking with a pet, traveling, gardening, cooking, and reading help guard against stress buildup.

Nurture your creativity. Take up painting, drawing, pottery, sculpting, woodworking, weaving, or whatever lets your creative side come through.

Keep a journal. A private journal is a safe place for you to express your feelings, explore your world, and say whatever you want to say. Include the humorous stories as well as the painful ones.

Sing, hum, whistle. It doesn't matter if you can't carry a tune; embrace yourself and your world with the music of your spirit.[29]

Start a dream journal. Keep a journal by your bed and record your dreams. You may be surprised by what you learn from them.[30]

Laugh more. Laughter brightens faces, relaxes muscles, restores objectivity, and enhances hope. It also produces endorphins, the body's natural shield against pain.[31] At the same time, remember that if we laugh *at* people instead of *with* them, humor becomes cruel. Humor that disrespects others adds to the callousness of burnout.

Imagine the soundtrack of your life. Barbara Mackoff suggests that one of the easiest way to lighten your thoughts about work is to add an imaginary soundtrack to your recollections of the day.[32] As you review your workday, think of it as a movie or a television show that needs a musical score, and in your mind add songs and music that seem fitting. You don't need a large musical repertoire to do this, simply a willingness to see yourself with humor. You'll be surprised at the number of songs you can bring to mind that fit your everyday experiences.

Relaxation Techniques

One simple way you can begin to relax is by not rushing unnecessarily through life. To reduce your sense of urgency and lower your overall level of irritation, practice eating, drinking, and driving at a slower pace.[33]

Relaxation techniques such as the ones described in this section can help you create a sense of peace. The key to their effectiveness, however, is practice: It does not matter what you do as long as you actually do it. This means setting aside time to engage in the activity until it becomes second nature. At the same time, be aware that true relaxation arises from an attitude toward life rather than from a particular activity. Relaxation must engage the mind as well as the body.

If you are interested in learning more about these techniques or others, consider enrolling in a community-education class or visiting the library to find one of the many excellent books currently available on the topics of relaxation and stress reduction.

Meditation. Meditation helps to create a state of deep relaxation that is healing to the entire body. Set aside some time on a daily basis to sit quietly in your own space. You can also try meditating just before going to sleep to help you relax.[34]

Deep breathing. Deep-breathing techniques can have a major impact on feelings of stress and anxiety. They help to relax the entire body, strengthen muscles in the chest and abdomen, and heighten energy levels. A simple method is to sit or lie in a darkened room and concentrate on breathing in and out. At first it may be difficult to sit for any length of time, but with practice that will change. The beauty of this technique is that it can be used on the spot, in the middle of a stressful situation.[35]

Muscle relaxation. Muscle tension is frequently associated with high levels of stress. The following exercise will help you get in touch with areas of muscle tension and learn to release them. Lie on your back in a comfortable position. Allow your arms to rest at your sides, palms down. Inhale and exhale slowly and deeply. Clench your hands into fists and hold them tightly for fifteen seconds. As you do this, relax the rest of your body. Visualize your fists contracting, becoming tighter and tighter. Then let your hands relax, and visualize all your muscles becoming soft and relaxed. Now tense and relax the following parts of your body in this order: face, shoulders, arms, back, stomach, pelvis, legs, feet, and toes. Hold each part tensed for fifteen seconds, and then relax your whole body for thirty seconds before moving to the next part. Finish the exercise by shaking your hands and imagining any remaining tension flowing out of your fingertips.[36]

Visualization. Visualization can be an excellent destressing method. Susan Lark, author of *Anxiety and Stress: A Self-Help Program,* recommends visualization using colors. Color therapy has been shown to have a profound effect on health and well-being. Lark suggests visualizing the color blue to provide a calming and relaxing effect, since blue lessens the fight-or-flight response and calms such physiological functions as pulse rate, breathing, and perspiration.[37]

Yoga. Yoga is an excellent way to promote a deep sense of peace and calm. Unlike fast-paced aerobic exercise, yoga actually slows the pulse, heart rate, and breathing. Yoga exercises gently stretch every muscle in the body, relaxing tense muscles and improving their suppleness and flexibility. They also promote better circulation and oxygenation to tense and contracted areas throughout the body. The stress-reduction and physiological effects of yoga benefit all body systems.[38]

Tai chi. Tai chi, a Chinese system of gentle and soothing movements based on the martial arts, engages the mind, body, and spirit. It is far less physical than other martial arts and involves more of the senses. The slow movements, executed in a series of coordinated exercises, strengthen each part of the body.[39]

Hydrotherapy. For centuries people have used warm water as a way to calm themselves and relax their muscles. You can create your own home spa by adding soothing ingredients such as bath oils and salts to your bath water. While you're at it, try enriching your spa experience by adding candlelight and music.

Music. Music can have an incredibly relaxing effect on mind and body. Classical music and quiet music, such as that played over a background of sounds found in nature, are particularly good for relaxing. Music can have a pronounced effect on our physiological functions, slowing pulse and heart rate, lowering blood pressure, and decreasing levels of stress hormones.[40]

Massage. Gentle touching—from a trained massage therapist, your intimate partner, or even yourself—can be very relaxing. The kneading and stroking movements of a good massage soothe tense muscles, improve circulation, and induce a feeling of relaxation and well-being.[41]

Aromatherapy. Combine massage oils with flower and herbal extracts and you have aromatherapy, a relaxation technique designed to please the senses while treating the body. Scented oils, lotions, and bath products are excellent complements to massage or hydrotherapy. Making aromatherapy products yourself can be fun and relaxing, or they can be purchased ready-made.[42]

Reflexology. This is basically foot massage, but it is also much more. According to reflexology, the sole of the foot is a microcosm of the body as a whole—a certain area of the foot corresponds to the circulatory system, another point corresponds to the liver, etc.—and massaging these pressure points can treat the corresponding part of the body. Reflexology can help to increase circulation and relax tension.[43]

The Organization's Commitment to Its Staff Members' Self-Care

The self-care strategies explored up to now can be used by individuals to take care of themselves. The organization, however, also has a responsibility to help its staff minimize burnout.[44] First, it must recognize that people working in the battered-women's movement are at risk. Organizations should periodically examine their goals, structure, and division of labor. Providing workers with opportunities for job rotation promotes growth and continued enthusiasm. Understanding the effects of working with so much pain and violence is also crucial. An atmosphere that encourages paid staff and volunteers to openly discuss frustrations, pain, and anger contributes to their empowerment and longevity. Encouraging and respecting the self-care boundaries that workers have established for themselves should be standard. Providing adequate opportunities for time away from work will have positive long-term effects for both the individual and the organization.

Finally, opportunities for workers to learn more about their own self-care should be offered. The Texas Council on Family Violence and SafePlace have sponsored an inspirational and empowering self-care workshop called Healing the Healers. It helps workers explore their power as healers and teaches healthful, functional ways to address stress. According to workshop facilitator Lorena Monda, "It is crucial that we look at the things about our work which affect us individually and as a community of healers."

If we are to maintain credibility in voicing our philosophy of helping battered women to empower themselves, we must empower ourselves through self-care and self-discovery. As individuals, organizations, and a movement, we can support and encourage each other on this journey.

...18

The National Domestic
Violence Hotline

This is high-tech grassroots.

— *Sara Slater, former volunteer coordinator, Austin Center for Battered Women (now SafePlace), after touring the NDVH headquarters*

On February 21, 1996, President Bill Clinton announced the opening of the National Domestic Violence Hotline (NDVH), a project of the Texas Council on Family Violence. The NDVH connects individuals residing in all fifty states and all U.S. territories with services by way of a nationwide database developed and maintained at offices in Austin, Texas. The system stores up-to-date information on forty-five hundred family-violence service providers.[1] Hotline telephones are answered twenty-four hours a day, seven days a week by English- and Spanish-speaking advocates who provide support and information to battered women, their friends, their families, and other concerned individuals. Specific assistance includes the following:

◆ *Crisis intervention:* Helping callers identify problems and possible solutions, including making safety plans in an emergency

◆ *Information:* Sharing information about (1) resources that can provide assistance to individuals; (2) domestic violence, child abuse, and sexual assault; (3) intervention programs for batterers; and (4) working through the criminal-justice system and related issues

◆ *Referrals:* Making referrals to battered-women's shelters and programs, social-service agencies, legal programs, and other organizations willing to help

The NDVH is committed to meeting the needs of diverse communities. A toll-free TTY line is available for the deaf and hearing impaired, and access is provided to translators who speak 139 different languages. In addition, the NDVH distributes information in a variety of formats and languages.

History of the NDVH

The realization of a dream does not occur without dedication and effort. President Clinton's announcement represented more than three years of extensive planning and organizing to revive the NDVH. A national hotline for victims of domestic violence had previously existed, from September 1988 to January 1992, but a lack of funding had forced its closure. Calls to the hotline had reached approximately 10,000 per month, and once it closed those calls were going unanswered. Soon, the National Victim Center, which operates a nationwide information and referral service known as Infolink, began receiving calls from domestic-violence victims. In 1992 and 1993 Infolink broadcast its number following the airing of three television programs on the subject of domestic violence. At Infolink's request, staff of the Texas Council on Family Violence (TCFV) helped answer an astonishing 13,025 calls following the programs.

In November 1992, concerned about the future of the national hotline and other challenges facing the national battered-women's movement, Deborah D. Tucker, former TCFV executive director, and Ellen Rubenstein Fisher, former TCFV associate director, along with representatives from the National Coalition Against Domestic Violence, the Pennsylvania Coalition Against Domestic Violence, the National Women Abuse Prevention Project, the Domestic Violence Coalition on Public Policy, the Family Violence Prevention Fund, and other national leaders, joined together to discuss the future of the movement. Recognizing the TCFV's leadership capabilities, efficient organizational structure, and accomplishments, the group requested that the council consider opening and operating a national hotline for victims of domestic violence. Within a few months the TCFV had the support of both its staff and its board of directors to pursue the project. It began raising funds to assess feasibility and conduct research.

When the TCFV board of directors unanimously approved working to reestablish a national hotline, one board member became more than excited; she says she saw her destiny. Anna Belle Burleson, former hotline program director, says, "When we were discussing the creation of the NDVH, I said to myself, 'I want to be a part of this. This is what I want to do.'" So committed was she to seeing the NDVH get off the ground that she volunteered her time for seven months, including several months of full-time volunteering. She spent countless hours contacting coalitions across the United States seeking support for the NDVH.

Beginning in the winter of 1993, the TCFV began recruiting members for the hotline's professional advisory board and national development council. Members included national and regional leaders in the battered-women's movement and other public figures committed to domestic-violence prevention. The following summer the debut issue of *HotLines* newsletter was published to keep donors, supporters, and interested individuals and organizations informed of the project's progress.

On September 13, 1994, the Violence Against Women Act, which included five years of funding for a national hotline for victims of domestic violence, was signed into law by President Clinton as part of the crime bill. That same fall, the TCFV received unanimous support from all of the state domestic-violence coalitions, more than 650 local service providers, and 29 national domestic-violence organizations and other agencies to establish and operate the NDVH. A prototype computer and telecommunications system were installed.

The following spring the U.S. Department of Health and Human Services (HHS) announced its request for proposals for a grant to "operate a national, toll-free telephone hotline to provide information and assistance to victims of domestic violence." The TCFV submitted its proposal for the National Domestic Violence Hotline. In August 1995 Texas Congressman Lloyd Doggett announced that the TCFV had been awarded a $1 million grant by HHS to establish and operate the only nationwide domestic-violence hotline. Subject to the availability of funds, Congress authorized additional funds not to exceed $850,000 annually through fiscal year 1999 for the hotline's operation.

Staff were soon hired. They immediately set to work collecting information from more than two thousand domestic-violence service providers across the country to establish the hotline's comprehensive referral database. On December 18, 1995, the NDVH office opened in Austin, Texas. Advocates underwent an intensive four-week training on issues related to domestic violence and cultural sensitivity, and on computer and telecommunications equipment. The NDVH and SafePlace collaborated on a forty-hour training class for new volunteers.

The original annual operating cost of the National Domestic Violence Hotline was approximately $1.2 million. The Violence Against Women Act of 2000 reauthorized the NDVH at $2 million total for 2001 through 2005.[2] Money to match the federal funds must be raised each year from private sources across the country such as foundations, corporations, organizations, and individuals. The plan is to support the hotline through a broad-based mix of public and private funds.

The Texas Council on Family Violence

The National Domestic Violence Hotline is a direct result of the careful stewardship of the Texas Council on Family Violence, a nonprofit, statewide membership association representing seventy-seven shelters, nine nonresidential programs, twenty-seven batterers' intervention and prevention programs, and twenty special projects. TCFV was founded in 1978 by determined, visionary women who the year before had established the Austin Center for Battered Women (now SafePlace), the first shelter in Texas for battered women and their children. That the TCFV was chosen and supported in its effort to revive the NDVH is no surprise. The battered-women's movement in Texas has made tremendous progress, and the TCFV has played a significant leadership role. When the TCFV first advocated for state funding for battered-women's shelters in 1979, six shelters shared $200,000 from the state. In 2004 seventy-two shelters shared $4.4 million in state funding.

The TCFV provides support and assistance in a variety of ways. It responds each year to over five thousand requests for technical assistance; offers on-site consultation for family-violence programs across the state; sponsors innovative training opportunities throughout the year; coordinates an annual statewide family-violence conference; distributes tens of thousands of brochures and other printed items on a variety of subjects related to family violence; leads successful efforts to pass all of the laws proposed in the state legislature related to domestic violence (many of which have been used as models by other states); maintains extensive resource files and a lending library; sponsors summits for the business and faith communities; and creates public awareness that leads to social pressure and cultural values that forbid rather than support violence against women.

Although the TCFV is a statewide organization, its leadership over the years has extended to the national and international levels. It had a three-year contract with the U.S. Department of Defense to provide domestic-violence training to family-advocacy staff in all of the branches of the military. It has provided training, technical assistance, and public-education materials to battered-women's organizations in Peru, Argentina, Brazil, Spain, and Mexico. In conjunction with the Crime Victim Assistance Center of Monterrey, Mexico, it has copresented a domestic-violence conference in Monterrey and one in Mexico City.

TCFV staff serve in key leadership roles at the National Network to End Domestic Violence, which was formed specifically to advocate for passage of laws in Congress that impact battered women and their children. Two of the network's major successes to date have been the passage of the Violence Against Women Act in 1994 and 2000. Staff have also served on advisory boards for numerous organizations, including the National Coalition Against Domestic Violence, the National Resource Center on Domestic Violence, the National Network on Behalf of Immigrant Battered Women, and the Family Violence Prevention Fund's public-awareness campaign called "There's NO Excuse," sponsored by the National Advertising Council. TCFV staff members currently work with the American Corporate Alliance to End Partner Violence, Women's Law.org, and the Domestic Violence Resource Network.

NDVH: The Human Connection

Nestled among the computers and other high-tech equipment at the NDVH headquarters are signs of the movement's humanity. Pictures of smiling women, children, and men; teddy bears; and diverse symbols of spirituality watch over hotline advocates as they answer calls from women and children in pain and from loved ones concerned about them. Each small cubicle obviously represents someone's home and reflects the personality of its resident. As Ellen Rubenstein Fisher, former NDVH executive director, says, "This is the best of technology with a human voice."

Those human voices are reaching a lot of women. In fact, the numbers are staggering. During its first three months of operation NDVH staff answered more than twenty-four thousand calls. Today they answer an average of fifteen thousand calls each month. In August 2004 the hotline reached a milestone when one of its advocates answered the millionth call. Sheryl Cates, executive director of the TCFV and NDVH, says, "We are thankful that we can be here to help those who are being emotionally, sexually or physically abused by an intimate partner or those who are calling to find ways of helping someone they know who is being abused.... [I]t is so critical right now for people to know that there is a place to call for help to end the violence in their lives."[3] Sixty-two percent of women who call say it is the first call they've made for help. Cates says, "We want women to know there is hope; there is help; we want women to know they are not alone."

The NDVH has some powerful assistance in getting the word out about its services. According to assistant director Shaun Thompson, the hotline has "cooperative working relationships" with corporations like Lifetime Television for Women, Mary Kay, Inc., Jive Records, and The Body Shop. As a result, public-service announcements and a documentary have been aired, and many other public-awareness efforts have promoted the hotline.[4]

While the majority of calls NDVH receives are from battered women, a significant number come from family or friends of battered women. According to hotline advocate Diane Perez, "Calls from family members are often the hardest. Hearing Mom and Dad crying, really wanting to help their child and not knowing what to do. This can be really hard." Perez says the type of calls she receives varies from moment to moment. "I've gotten calls from women who were being beaten while they were on the phone with me, calls from batterers being abusive, and calls from women living underground who were lonely and just wanted someone to talk to who would understand. I've also gotten quite a few calls from children. Come to think of it, all of these calls, in some way or another, are difficult." Difficult is probably an understatement. Suicide, child abuse, incest, depression, rape, and torture are just a few of the issues hotline advocates deal with from callers every day. Their challenge is to help people who are in pain, afraid, confused, and in need.

The magic happens when they are able to help someone. According to one hotline advocate, "The most rewarding thing for me is when I've reached someone. We click and the caller really begins to understand. They know we're here for them no matter whether they stay or leave. You can hear the relief in their voice." Another advocate echoes these sentiments. "I can't tell you how many women I've talked to that told me I was the very first person they've ever talked to about this. They are so grateful for my help. I can't tell you how good that makes me feel."

The NDVH is committed to making sure that—whatever the need—women, children, and their families who need help are directed to where they can find it. It is through the NDVH's partnership with literally thousands of advocates across the United States that battered women can get the help they need as they consider their options and plan for a violence-free future. And what a future that can be. As a sign at the NDVH puts it, "Who knows what women can be when they are finally free to become themselves."

Conclusion

In June 2005 the U.S. Department of Justice Bureau of Justice Statistics (BJS) issued a report, *Family Violence Statistics,* that seemed to indicate that rates of family violence had declined by more than half between 1993 and 2002.[1] This claim left advocates perplexed and questioning the report's validity given that shelters continue to remain full and waiting lists long.

The National Network to End Domestic Violence (NNEDV) examined the BJS report and discovered a more complex dynamic than what was indicated. Family violence as defined by the BJS report included child abuse, and indeed, declines in the rate of child abuse during that period were much sharper than violence against spouses. Yet the definition *excluded* initmate-partner violence against heterosexual current or former girlfriends or boyfriends and against all same-sex partners. According to the NNEDV, "These data, therefore, provide an imprecise measure of the full scope of inti-mate partner abuse and the impact of programs designed to address it.... Based on the BJS data, family violence as a proportion of all violent victimi-zation has remained fairly stable over ther past ten years. While violent crime has declined sharply during this period, family violence has not. Moreover, family violence is declining at a slower rate than other violent crimes." [2]

Despite the limitations of the BJS report, NNEDV explains that intimate-partner abuse has apparently declined over the last ten years. These results are encouraging and speak to the need for continued funding, services, and re-search. As Del Martin wrote in the Foreword to this book, "There is hope."

Hope for a better future for battered women and their children drove the founding mothers of the battered-women's movement to spend limitless time, energy, and resources in pursuit of their vision. This hope remains alive today. Continued dedication to the movement's philosophy and mission, maintain-ing the certainty of what we have already learned, remaining open to asking questions, and working to further our understanding of the issues will com-bine to help ensure that the struggle to end domestic violence remains alive and well.

Appendix I
A History of Violence Against Women

If I want I may clean my shoes on you.

— *Wife batterer, 1934* [1]

Who knows, in the end the entire modern women's movement may be nothing but a revolt against the vicious thrashing of women, and its aim may be none other than the emancipation of woman from the cane.

— *Hedwig Dohm, nineteenth-century German feminist* [2]

Violence against women has its roots in a millennia-old patriarchal system that has historically viewed women as inherently inferior to men in the intellectual, spiritual, physical, sexual, and emotional realms. When misogynistic attitudes were at their height, during the Middle Ages, women were perceived as evil incarnate. The male tendency to devalue women and view them as property has led to a variety of cruel practices, including femicide, infanticide, rape, battering, torture, widow burning, veiling, footbinding, witch burning, chastity belts, clitoridectomies, and infibulation.[3] At the very heart of wife battering is the subordination of women to male control and authority, which has been institutionalized in the structure of the patriarchal family and supported by such societal institutions as economics, politics, religion, medicine, education, and culture.

In the Beginning...

Women have not always been subordinated by a patriarchal society. Ample archaeological evidence from the Paleolithic, Neolithic, and Bronze Ages supports the contention that women were once held in high esteem.[4] According to Frederick Engels, author of *The Origin of the Family, Private Property, and the State,* "It is one of the most absurd notions derived from eighteenth cen-

313

**Appendix I:
A History of
Violence
Against
Women**

tury enlightenment, that in the beginning of society woman was the slave of man."[5] Ancient wall paintings, cave sanctuaries, burial sites, and female figures of fertility goddesses depict women with dignity and signs of high status.[6] By far, most of the evidence consists of female figurines, discovered across Europe, the Mediterranean, and Eastern Asia, that emphasize breasts, hips, and buttocks. Approximately thirty thousand of these miniature sculptures in clay, marble, bone, copper, and gold have been excavated from some three thousand sites in southeastern Europe alone.[7] One of the reasons why women were so highly esteemed may be because lineage could be traced only through them. Early civilizations lived in extended families, making any knowledge of paternity impossible. Women were the only apparent parents. Women's power of creation resulted in their association with the divine.[8]

Gerda Lerner, author of *The Creation of Patriarchy,* believes that single-cause explanations for the rise of patriarchy are insufficient. She argues that it arose from a series of events occurring in several societies at different paces and different times, between approximately 3,100 and 600 B.C.E.[9] At some point during the agricultural revolution, egalitarian societies with a sexual division of labor developed into societies in which both the ownership of private property and the exchange of women based on incest taboos were common. The earlier societies were often matrilineal and matrilocal, but the later, surviving societies were predominantly patrilineal and patrilocal. The later, more complex societies contained a division of labor no longer based only on biological distinctions, but also on hierarchy and the power of some men over other men and all women. Numerous researchers have reported that this move coincided with the formation of archaic states.[10]

Susan Brownmiller, in her book *Against Our Will: Men, Women, and Rape,* reports that "Female fear of an open season of rape, and not a natural inclination toward monogamy, motherhood or love, was probably the single causative factor in the original subjugation of woman by man, the most important key to her historic dependence, her domestication by protective mating."[11] The price woman paid was a precious one, however. In trying to obtain security she relinquished much of her power. Those who assumed her protection, whether husband, father, brother, or uncle, began to perceive her as nothing more than chattel. The earliest permanent, protective monogamous relationships took the form of bride capture. A man took possession of a woman and staked a claim on her body by raping her. Bride capture was considered an acceptable means of acquiring women and existed in England as late as the fifteenth century.[12] A man's forcible extension of his boundaries to his mate and their children was the beginning of the concept of property and ownership.

The view of women as property is inherent in the very definition of the word *family,* which is derived from the Latin word *familia.* As Engels explains, "The word familia did not originally signify the composite idea of sentimentality and domestic strife in the present day philistine mind. Among the Romans it did not even apply in the beginning to the leading couple and its children, but to the slaves alone. Famulus means domestic slave and familia is the aggregate number of slaves belonging to one man.... The expression was invented by the Romans in order to designate a new social organism, the head of which had a wife, children and a number of slaves under his paternal authority and according to Roman law the right of life and death over all of them."[13]

Along with the notion of women as property was born the concept of male privilege, which asserted that a man was expected to protect his mate and that the primary purpose of his protection was to secure her faithfulness and the reliability of his paternal lineage. In assuming this responsibility, the man also became accountable for the woman's behavior, which he was expected to control by whatever means possible. According to Engels, "the women are delivered absolutely into the power of the men; in killing his wife, the husband simply exercises his right."[14]

Violence Against Women in the Archaic States

Ancient Babylonian and Mosaic laws provide the earliest written documentation that slavery, private property, and the subjugation of women were facts of life. The practice of buying one's wife became common.[15] According to Brownmiller, "A payment of money to the father of the house was a much more civilized and less dangerous way of acquiring a wife. And so the bride price was codified, at fifty pieces of silver."[16]

Women were no longer seen as equal human beings. Rather, their sexuality and reproductive potential became commodities to be exchanged or acquired for the service of families. Women were thus perceived to have less autonomy than men. While men belonged to a household or lineage, women belonged to the males who had acquired rights to them. The domestic subordination of women was the model out of which slavery evolved.

The development of slavery involved refinement of the concept that the permanent powerlessness of one group and total power of another were acceptable conditions of social interaction. Historical evidence suggests that the process of enslavement was first developed and perfected upon female war captives and reinforced by already known practices of the exchange and concubinage of women.[17] Lerner writes, "By experimenting with the enslavement of women and children, men learned to understand that all human beings have the potential for tolerating enslavement and they developed the techniques and forms of enslavement which would enable them to make of their absolute dominance a social institution."[18] By the time slavery had become widespread, the subordination of women was a historical fact.

The archaic states in the ancient Near East emerged in the second millennium B.C.E. from men's sexual dominance over women and the exploitation by some men of others. Male heads of household allocated the resources of society to their families the way the state allocated the resources of society to them. Husbands' control over their female kin and minor sons was vital and was reflected in the various Mesopotamian laws, especially in the great number of laws dealing with the regulation of female sexuality. Women in Mesopotamia depended on the males in their lives for any power they had; even women from the upper classes thought of themselves as dependent on the protection of a man. The daughters of the poor were sold into marriage or prostitution to advance the economic interests of their families. The daughters of men of property could command a bride price, paid by the family of the groom to the family of the bride, which frequently enabled the bride's family to secure more financially advantageous marriages for their sons, thus improving the family's economic position.[19]

As was the case in Mesopotamia and Israel, Greece of the eighth through fifth centuries B.C.E. was a thoroughly patriarchal society. Women's legal and social subordination was undisputed. The main function of wives was to produce male heirs and to supervise their husbands' households. Women were defined by the family and, within the family, by their relationship to the men of the group. The Greek philosopher Aristotle expresses the generally held view of women when he writes, "The male is by nature superior, and the female inferior; and the one rules, and the other is ruled; this principle, of necessity, extends to all mankind.... [T]he courage of a man is shown in commanding, of a woman in obeying."[20]

Laws rewarded and institutionalized women's dependence and subordination. All of these early cultures explicitly excluded women from the activities outside the family that were valued most. Powerful cultural messages reinforced the division of roles and activities and excluded women from government, philosophy, science, law, and in some cases religion.[21] Double standards prevailed for both divorce and adultery.[22]

In early Rome women fared little better. Every Roman family was autocratic.[23] The head of the household, whether father, grandfather, uncle, or slave owner, under the title of *paterfamilias,* occupied the position of absolute monarch. His authority, designated the *patria potestas,* extended to life-and-

315

Appendix I:
A History of
Violence
Against
Women

death decisions. A new recruit to the household, whether a newborn infant, a bride, a servant, or a slave, had to gain the formal acceptance of the paterfamilias. The newborn was laid before him. If he picked the child up, he or she was admitted into the family and given a name. If not, the child was "exposed," that is, abandoned with the chance that it might be rescued.[24]

Infanticide, especially of female children, was an accepted practice in early cultures. The decision over the fate of female infants was always made by the male head of household. Infants were rarely killed outright; instead, they were left on garbage heaps or in public places in the hope that a passerby might rescue them. Brothel owners collected infant girls and raised them to be prostitutes. In Rome there is ample evidence of the routine exposure of female infants. The Law of the Twelve Tables required a father to raise all his sons, but only one daughter. Written evidence in the early third century A.D. states that "there were far more males than females" among the Roman nobility of Augustus's era.[25] Outside of Greece and Rome, infanticide and exposure were condemned, but girls and women continued to be valued less than boys and men.[26] Early Roman husbands had the legal right to chastise, divorce, or kill their wives for engaging in behavior that they themselves engaged in. A woman could legally be beaten for drinking from the family wine cellar, attending public games without the husband's permission, or walking outdoors with her face uncovered.[27]

Although the earliest writings of Greece, Rome, and Israel justify female subordination, they are not misogynistic. This attitude came later, in the Greek poetry of the seventh and sixth centuries B.C.E., in the Roman satires and poetry of the first century A.D., and in the Jewish and Christian interpretations of the Old Testament from the second century B.C.E. to the third century A.D. That is when women began to be stigmatized as innately evil. The creation of woman was seen as punishment for man, and woman was identified as the enemy of both men and civilization. She was seen as the source of trouble and was equated with all things despised.[28] According to Euripides, "Terrible is the force of the waves of the sea, terrible the rush of river and the blasts of hot fire, terrible is poverty, and terrible are a thousand other things; but none is such a terrible evil as woman. No painter could adequately represent her: no language can describe her; but if she is the creation of any of the gods, let him know that he is a very great creator of evils and a foe to mortals."[29]

Such writings created the foundation for European culture. The works of many of the Greek philosophers, the laws of Rome, and the first five books of the Bible shaped the views of later generations and remained revered long after the Greeks, Romans, and Hebrews had ceased to dominate their regions.

They transmitted images, morals, and values grounded in the assumption that women were inferior and subordinate to men.[30]

317

Appendix I:
A History of
Violence
Against
Women

The Impact of Christianity

In the fourth century A.D., after struggling through three centuries of persecution and indifference, the Christian religion matured into a position of status and authority. As the barbarians and Romans mingled and adapted to each other, the Christian community aligned itself into history's first great church organization.

Church intellectuals created doctrines designed both to answer esoteric theological questions and to provide rules of conduct for everyday Christian life. St. Augustine and his fellow theologians were confronted by the marriage and family customs of the Roman and barbarian worlds. In several significant respects they shaped early church law to conform to a new perspective. The church soundly condemned abortion, infanticide, and contraception, including the rhythm method advocated by the Greek physician Hippocrates. In other areas, Christian teaching accepted existing custom or law.[31] The idea of original sin was used to subjugate women to the authority of the church, the state, and men.

Original sin was a misogynistic interpretation of other creation myths that predate the book of Genesis by at least seven thousand years.[32] It was reinforced by the philosophy of St. Augustine, who believed that only the church could absolve a person of original sin. It was an ingenious power play that kept people tied to the church with guarantees of forgiveness and eternal life. According to Jeanne Achterberg, author of *Woman as Healer,* "Women lost on all counts. In order to maintain the logic underlying the Church's hold on power, women's inherent sinfulness also had to be sustained. If there had been no evil temptress, no sin would exist, and the promised deliverance would wield no control over the masses. The doctrine of Original Sin was critical: any established church dependent on an economic power-base of unquestioned obedience would collapse if it were not considered the gateway to heaven by significant numbers of people."[33]

In St. Augustine's view, women assume a threefold role of temptress, wife, and mother. As temptress, woman is the instrument of the devil. As wife, she is the instrument of her husband, who oversees the peacefulness of the family. As mother, she is the instrument of God's creativity. This doctrine would later be used to justify wife beating. If women were inherently evil, they deserved to be beaten. According to St. Augustine, "And if any member of the family interrupts the domestic peace by disobedience, he is corrected either by word or blow, or some kind of just and legitimate punishment, such as society permits, that he may himself be the better for it and be readjusted to the family harmony from which he had dislocated himself."[34]

Women healers who tried to soothe the pangs of childbirth were severely punished because, according to the church, birth pains existed to remind women of their original sinful nature. Women began to see themselves as unclean and impure. They hid in shame, especially during menstruation, pregnancy, and childbirth. Women's role in creation became not a blessing but a curse.

The thirteenth-century church followed the leads of St. Paul and St. Augustine in solidifying its thinking about women. As a justification for the brutalization of women, the doctrine of original sin was expanded upon by the church fathers to demonstrate women's inferiority. *Summa Theologica,* the multivolume work written by St. Thomas Aquinas between 1266 and 1272, reflects official attitudes. It was destined to provide the Roman Catholic Church with its official theological and philosophical dogma for many centuries. According to Aquinas, "[W]oman is naturally subject to man, because in man the discretion of reason predominates."[35]

The Witch Craze

The period from the sixteenth to the eighteenth century illustrates the extent to which the church and state condoned and perpetuated the abuse, torture, and murder of women. The femicidal mania of the witch-hunt craze, which spanned from approximately 1560 to 1760, swept across Europe and even into the American colonies, resulting in thousands of executions, usually live burnings at the stake, in Germany, Italy, and other countries.[36] By far, the greatest number of crimes against women accused of being witches or heretics was committed in the Holy Roman Empire, which was centered in Germany. The second-heaviest concentration of European witch-hunts occurred in the French-speaking regions.[37]

Although exact numbers are unknown, researchers estimate that from two hundred thousand to ten million women were brutally tortured and killed as heretics and witches.[38] The majority of authority figures in witch trials were male, including the accusers, ministers, priests, constables, jailers, judges, doctors, witch prickers, torturers, jurors, executioners, and the courts of appeal. Women made up approximately 85 percent of those executed.[39]

The women accused and murdered were typically single women living alone, older women living alone (especially widows), healers, and midwives. Other women were accused because they were considered obnoxious, needy, deformed, or mentally disabled.[40] Many women were burned at the stake for threatening their husbands; talking back to a priest; stealing; prostitution; adultery; bearing a child out of wedlock; permitting sodomy; masturbation; lesbianism; child neglect; scolding and nagging; and miscarrying, even if the miscarriage was caused by a blow from a husband.[41]

"Wise women," such as healers and midwives, had been useful and popular members of society before 1550. By attacking the female-centered world of healing, the church cut at the very heart of female power. Anne Llewellyn Barstow, author of *Witchcraze,* writes, "The witch hunt records speak eloquently of the fear of the wise women that developed, especially in men. The role of healer, long respected and even seen as essential, became suspect."[42] Certain women were suspected of witchcraft not because they were powerless but precisely because they were seen to have a great deal of power. In the century preceding the beginning of the European witch craze, the field of medicine had become firmly established as a profession. Being in the medical profession required university training, thus making it easy to legally ban women from practicing. With few exceptions, universities were closed to women and licensing laws were established to prohibit all but university-trained doctors from practice.[43] Since women were not allowed to study medicine, it was widely accepted that the only way they could obtain the information needed for their skill was from the devil. The position of the church held that "if a woman dare to cure without having studied, she is a witch and must die."[44]

It is noteworthy that witch-hunting in Europe was a lucrative business. In most cases, the woman was required to pay the fees for the witch finder; her confinement; the activities of the torturers; the torture equipment; and the beer, meals, and banquets for the torturers, judges, clerics, and others involved in her arrest. According to Barstow, "Even more disturbing are the bizarre entertainments and banquets for the judges and priests that often preceded the executions—all of which had to be paid for by the family of the victim."[45] Because women in the Middle Ages were allowed to own property, the accused woman's estates were confiscated, and all the costs of her murder were charged to her heirs. If she was boiled in oil, a favorite means of death in France, the fees were particularly high.[46]

The witch-hunts were well-orchestrated campaigns that were initiated and executed by the church and the state. To Catholic and Protestant witch-hunters, the unquestioned authority on how to conduct a witch-hunt was the *Malleus Maleficarum,* written in the 1480s by the German Dominican friars Kramer and Sprenger. Using biblical, classical, and medieval sources, this misogynistic book explains that women were more likely to be witches be-

319

Appendix I:
A History of
Violence
Against
Women

cause they were more stupid, weak, superstitious, and fickle than men, and because they were sensual and insatiably carnal.[47] All of these stereotypes rendered women as less than human, thereby justifying the inhuman treatment inflicted upon them.

A woman could be arrested on the most minimal evidence. Finding a "devil's teat" on her body, said to be where animal familiars or demons could suckle, was sufficient to convict her and was one of the chief proofs of witchcraft.[48] Such spots, usually moles or other skin blemishes, were identified by the fact that they didn't bleed when pricked with a needle. (Modern researchers have discovered that many of the surviving "needles" used to test for witches were fake and simply retracted under pressure.[49]) About women who failed to pass the pricking test, Franciscan theologian Lodovico Maria Sinistrari wrote, "The Demon imprints on them some mark, especially on those whose constancy he suspects. That mark, moreover, is not always of the same shape or figure.... It is imprinted on the most hidden parts of the body... with women, it is usually on the breasts or the privy parts."[50] Although the searches were normally done by women, they were often witnessed by male court officials. In Scotland, however, the searcher, called the witch pricker, was always male.[51] Women were stripped and shaved and their genitals were probed for marks. When the witch's mark was found, as it usually was, the charges against the woman were considered validated.

The process in the secular courts for convicting someone of witchcraft followed methods used during the Inquisition. It was unnecessary to inform the accused of her crimes, and no defense was allowed. Communication with the accused was forbidden, and torture was repeatedly used. Promises of lighter torture were traded for the naming of accomplices, virtually assuring that more trials would ensue. Priests worked closely with the courts to obtain confessions. Officials sometimes went beyond what was prescribed by Inquisitional procedures. Women were often tortured even after conviction, and their bodies were repeatedly examined by the executioner. Two male guards were usually stationed in the cell with the woman, exposing her to the possibility of constant sexual harassment.[52]

The following is from a report of the first day's torture of a woman accused of witchcraft in Prossneck, Germany, in 1629:

> First, she was put on the "ladder," alcohol was thrown over her head and her hair was set fire. Strips of sulfur were placed under her arms and ignited. Then the torturer tied her hands behind her back and hoisted her to the ceiling, where she hung for four hours while he went to breakfast. On his return, he threw alcohol over her back and set fire to it. Placing heavy weights on her body, he jerked her up to the ceiling

again. Then he squeezed her thumbs and big toes in a vise, trussed her arms with a stick, and kept her hanging until she fainted. Then he whipped her with rawhide. Once more to the vises, and he went to lunch. After his lunch she was whipped until blood ran through her shift.[53]

321

Appendix I:
A History of
Violence
Against
Women

Performed on women by men, torture often had strong sexual angles. Sadistic experimentation and sexual advances were legal. When a woman was whipped, she was stripped to the waist, exposing her breasts to the public. When the executioner Jehan Minart of Cambrai prepared the condemned Aldegonde de Rue for the stake, he examined her mouth and *parties honeuses* (shameful parts). In another recorded incident, a priest applied hot fat repeatedly to an accused woman's eyes, armpits, thighs, elbows, the pit of her stomach, and *dans sa nature* (in her vagina).[54]

The ultimate form of torture was to be burned alive. According to Barstow, "[T]he most horrifying symbol of some men's power over all women and over some other men was public execution at the stake. That this ferocious type of punishment was commonly carried out on witches added to the sadistic nature of their treatment, compounding the sexual torture that many had already been subjected to. That this torture was carried out in the presence of large crowds often numbering in the thousands gave it a ritual meaning beyond that of simple punishment."[55]

In England the last official hanging of an accused witch took place in 1684, and in Germany the last burning at the stake of an accused witch occurred in 1775. The madness began to diminish when Christianity started to lose its stronghold on the governing bodies of Europe. Thus, this particular violence against women ended not because of changed attitudes about women, but because the power base of governments had shifted.[56]

It is easy to imagine the absolute horror women must have felt who lived during the era of the witch-hunts. Those accused found themselves essentially alone. With few exceptions husbands and families did not speak up for them and in many cases actually turned against them. Women learned that the safest route was to mind one's business and obey one's husband.

Domestic Violence in the Middle Ages

Medieval Europeans believed that a husband's right to beat his wife derived from God's command. Men were encouraged from the pulpit to beat their wives, and wives were encouraged to kiss the rod that beat them. A medieval theological manual, *Gratian's Decretum,* explains that "a man must castigate his wife and beat her for her correction, for the lord must punish his own."

The church approved these methods of keeping women in subjection and advised abused wives to try to win their husbands' goodwill through increased devotion and obedience.[57]

Family law also reinforced and promoted violence against women. Late-medieval law in Christian Saxony allowed a squire to whip any woman in his domain who displayed pride and self-respect, referred to in the statute as "immodesty."[58] The thirteenth-century French legal code *Customs of Beauvais* stated, "In a number of cases men may be excused for the injuries they inflict on their wives, nor should the law intervene. Provided he neither kills nor maims her, it is legal for a man to beat his wife when she wrongs him."[59] In sixteenth-century Russia, under Ivan the Terrible, the murder of one's wife was legal as long as it was done for disciplinary purposes. In fact, wife battering was so well accepted and so common that the Russian Church issued an edict titled the Household Ordinance, which outlined when and how best to beat one's wife. Samuel Collins, an English physician to Tsar Alexei from 1660 to 1669, described a Russian merchant who beat his wife with a whip two inches thick. Whipping her until he was exhausted, he then forced her into a smock dipped in brandy and set her on fire. She died in the flames, and the man went unpunished.[60]

In the following narrative the knight Geoffrey de la Tour de Landry educates his daughters about the consequences of women's "misbehavior":

> Here is an example to every good woman that she suffer and endure patiently, nor strive with her husband nor answer him before strangers, as did once a woman who did answer her husband before strangers with short words; and he smote her with his fist down to the earth; and with his foot he struck her in her visage and broke her nose, and all her life after she had her nose crooked, which so shent [spoiled] and disfigured her visage after, that she might not for shame show her face, it was so foul blemished. And this she had for her language that she was wont to say to her husband. And therefore the wife ought to suffer, and let the husband have the words, and to be master, for that is her duty.[61]

The matter of obedience dominates the manual composed by the Ménagier of Paris for his fifteen-year-old wife, which says that she should obey her husband's rules and act according to his desires rather than her own because his pleasure should come before hers. She should not contradict him or shame him in public because "it is the command of God that women should be subject to men ... and by good obedience a wise woman gains her husband's love and at the end hath what she would of him."[62]

323

Appendix I:
A History of
Violence
Against
Women

In Germanic village law, which was not replaced by Roman law until the sixteenth century, the right to administer corporal punishment was a part of the guardianship *(Munt)* of husband over wife.[63] In many regions the husband who did not observe the right to practice physical punishment was threatened with repercussions such as the following, described by Wilhelm Heinrich Riehl: "The men of the neighboring villages solemnly came in with an ass, upon which the woman was set, and she was driven around the town, so that the men according to God's commandment should remain the masters and keep the upper hand. The husband who had put up with it is punished as well as the wife who commits the outrage and only by the donation of an Ohm [137.4 liters] of beer to the allied communities could the guilty married couple buy their way free from the punishment."[64]

In an effort to maintain women's chastity many men during the Middle Ages performed infibulation on their wives, the practice of fastening together the labia majora by means of a ring, buckle, or padlock. As late as 1871, a European woman complained to her doctor that the weight of the padlock her husband had imposed on her was tearing the lips of her vulva and causing great pain and bleeding. The husband had bored holes in her labia through which he had inserted two metal rings, which he had drawn together and fastened securely with a padlock. A similar case involving a German immigrant couple was reported in New York in 1894 and another in Eastern Europe in 1906. According to Elizabeth Gould Davis, author of *The First Sex,* "This sort of thing was probably a great deal more common in Europe than is generally supposed, the few cases which have come to light having been discovered purely accidentally. The sewing up of the labia over the vaginal opening... also occurred spasmodically in Europe, though probably less frequently than the padlock type of infibulation."[65]

The surgical procedure Davis describes involves the removal of the clitoris, labia minora, and at least two-thirds of the labia majora. The raw edges are then sewn together, leaving a small opening for the flow of urine and menstrual fluid. The suturing is done so that the remaining skin of the labia majora will heal together and form a bridge of scar tissue over the vaginal opening. Incredibly, this horrific procedure is still practiced today in parts of Africa (including parts of Egypt), Iraq, Iran, and Latin America.[66]

In medieval Europe, infibulation was performed on women of the lower socioeconomic classes, but the chastity belt was used on women of the upper classes. Some resesearchers believe that the chastity belt, like the practice of infibulation, was brought from the East by the crusaders and became common in Europe during the thirteenth century. Others believe it was a product of the European Renaissance. The device consisted of an iron or silver corset with a tight-fitting metal bar that curved between the legs and had a narrow opening surrounded by rows of tiny, sharp teeth. The woman was locked into the instrument of torture, and her husband usually possessed the only key. Men were frequently gone to war for months or even years, leaving women to suffer from incredible infection and disease as a result of their inability to properly tend to their personal hygiene.[67] In colonial America the Pennsylvania Dutch settlers used a version of the chastity belt known as a day belt. As late as 1946 a man in Atlantic City, New Jersey, padlocked his wife into a chastity belt each day as he left for work. When he was eventually arrested for assault and battery, he stated that he had fashioned the belt in his spare time and used it on his wife to "keep her from running around."[68]

The "Common Scold"

Once I had a scolding wife
She wasn't very civil
I clapped a plaster on her mouth
And sent her to the Devil

— *"Haul Away Joe,"American whaling ballad* [69]

Instruments of torture and punishment were used in medieval England and afterward against women convicted as "scolds." Scolds, as defined by *Jacob's Law Dictionary,* were "troublesome and angry women, who, by their brawling and wrangling amongst their neighbors, break the public peace."[70] A scold was a crime that consisted basically of speaking one's mind, and it was a crime that could be committed only by a woman.

One of the punishments for scolding was a public ducking in a body of cold water, using a "ducking stool." A version of the ducking stool involved an armchair fastened with a type of axle to the ends of two beams held parallel to each other over a pond or river. The chair, swinging on the axis, remained in the horizontal position while the woman was raised up and down. Some ducking stools could be wheeled to and from the water; others were stationary. The woman was tied to the chair and plunged into the water, the number of times dependent upon her sentence. In some instances the ducking was carried to such an extreme that the woman died.[71]

Writing in 1780, Benjamin West, of Northamptonshire, England, describes the fate of the common scold:

There stands, my friend, in yonder pool,
An engine called the ducking-stool,

325

Appendix I:
A History of
Violence
Against
Women

By legal pow'r commanded down,
The joy and terror of the town,
If jarring females kindle strife,
Give language foul or lug the coif;
If noisy dames should once begin
To drive the house with horrid din,
Away, you cry, you'll grace the stool,
We'll teach you how your tongue to rule.
The fair offender fills the seat,
In sullen pomp, profoundly great,
Down in the deep the stool descends,
But here, at first, we miss our ends;
She mounts again, and rages more
Than ever vixen did before.
So, throwing water on the fire
Will make it but burn up the higher;
If so, my friend, pray let her take
A second turn into the lake,
And, rather than your patience lose,
Thrice and again repeat the dose.
No brawling wives, no furious wenches,
No fire so hot, but water quenches.
In Prior's skilful lines we see
For these another recipe:
A certain lady, we are told
(A lady, too, and yet a scold),
Was very much reliev'd you'll say
By water, yet a different way;
A mouthful of the same she'd take,
Sure not to scold, if not to speak.[72]

The latest recorded instance of the use of the ducking stool in England was in 1809, although it began to fall out of favor as early as the 1770s.[73]

Another instrument used to punish scolds was the brank or scold's bridle, an iron, cagelike frame that was placed over the head and had a mouthpiece that was either sharpened or covered with spikes. If the wearer attempted to move her tongue in any way, she was sure to be injured. The "scold," her head encaged in the brank, was led through the streets on a chain by a town official. In some towns it was the custom to chain the victim to a pillory, whipping post, or market cross. Some houses had a hook attached to the side of the fireplace. To punish his wife, a man could send for the town jailer to bring the brank and have her chained, wearing it, to the fireplace. There she remained until her husband instructed the jailer to release her.[74]

The Common Scold Law and the torturous devices used to punish its violators were brought from England to Connecticut by the Puritans and early settlers. From Connecticut they were carried into New Jersey and other colonies. A Virginia act of 1662 ordered each county to erect a pillory, stocks, a whipping post, and a ducking stool. Declaring that "brabling women often slander and scandalize their neighbors for which their poore husbands are often brought into chargeable and vexatious suites, and cast in greate damages," it stipulated that, if a husband refused to pay the damages for an act of slander by his wife, she was to be punished by ducking. If the offense was so weighty that it called for damages greater than five hundred pounds of tobacco, the wife was to be ducked one time for every five hundred pounds fined against her husband. Later acts of the Virginia and Maryland assemblies made it compulsory for counties to build ducking stools, and county court minutes show many court orders for the erection of such devices.[75]

It was not until 1967 that the Common Scold Law was declared obsolete in England by the Criminal Law Act. The last woman convicted in the United States under the scold laws was a journalist named Ann Royall in 1829. However, the last time a woman was *indicted* as a scold was in 1971 in New Jersey. At that time the law was still on the books, but the state's superior court threw the case out the following year.[76]

Riding the Stang

Traditional community sanctions did exist against unacceptable levels of domestic violence. The "punishments" included rituals of public shaming known as charivari, skimmington rides, riding the stang, rough music, or misrules and involved costumes, floats, dancing, singing, rude songs, and sometimes physical punishment. Common from the fifteenth through the nineteenth century, such punishments were also used on men who allowed themselves to become "henpecked."[77]

To begin the ceremony, a trumpeter blew his horn and the villagers gathered around him. A pole or ladder was obtained, and the wittiest man in the village was placed in a chair atop the ladder, raised shoulder high, and carried through the streets. In one hand he held a large key or stick and in the other a pan, which he banged together to lead the music and the crowd. Men, women, and children joined the jovial procession, beating pots and pans. Tin whistles, horns, and trumpets were blown. Every fifty yards approximately the procession stopped and the mounted man loudly spoke a rhyme such as the following:

327

**Appendix I:
A History of
Violence
Against
Women**

> Here we come with a ran, dan, dang:
> It's not for you, nor for me, we ride this stang;
> But for _____, whose wife he did bang.
> He banged her, he banged her, he banged her indeed:
> He banged her, poor creature, before she stood need.
> He took up neither tipstaff nor stower,
> But with his fist he knocked her backwards ower;
> He kicked her, he punched her, till he made her cry,
> And to finish all, he gave her a black eye.
> Now, all you good people that live in this row
> We would have you take warning, for this is our law:
> If any of you, your wives you do bang,
> We're sure, we're sure, to ride you the stang.[78]

The house of the wife beater was visited several times each night, and the proceedings were kept up three nights in succession. If the offense was considered a serious one, the batterer was burnt in effigy in front of his door. In some places the batterer was compelled to ride the stang himself. Such was the punishment for men accused of beating their wives.

Misogynistic Practices Across Cultures

The formalized oppression of women has been common among many different cultures around the world. Cultural differences may distinguish the character and means of subjection, but the tactics—insititutionalizing certain practices through popular culture, law, and religious or social tradition—remain the same. This section examines two practices that in the past were customary in other countries: footbinding and sati.

Footbinding

Footbinding began in tenth-century China as an innovation of palace dancers in the imperial harem. A symbol of gentility, bound feet were considered an asset in the marriage market. In effect, by preventing women from moving around easily, they reinforced women's oppression, because Chinese tradition dictated that a woman should not appear in public or be seen in the company of men.[79] The objective was to achieve what was known as a Golden Lotus, or a foot no longer than three inches.[80]

Manufacturing this deformity required the application around each foot of a bandage about two inches wide and ten feet long. One end was placed under the instep and pulled over the small toes to force the toes to curl inward and towards the sole. The large toe was left unbound. The bandage was then forcefully wrapped around the heel so that the heel and toes were drawn together. The process was repeated until the entire bandage had been applied.[81] The torture usually began for girls between ages five and seven.

Footbinding was an excruciatingly painful and crippling practice. A woman had to walk on the outside of her toes, which had been bent into the sole of her foot. Hard calluses formed and toenails grew into the skin. The feet became infected and bloody. Circulation was virtually stopped. Walking unassisted was almost impossible. To keep her balance, a woman would need to lean against a cane or a servant and take very short steps. She was actually falling with every step and catching herself with the next. According to Andrea Dworkin, author of *Woman Hating,* "Footbinding was a visible brand. Footbinding did not emphasize the differences between men and women—it created them, and they were then perpetuated in the name of morality. Footbinding functioned as the Cerberus of morality and ensured female chastity in a nation of women who literally could not 'run around.' Fidelity, and the legitimacy of children, could be reckoned on."[82]

Footbinding remained popular until it was outlawed after the 1911 revolution. By then, however, Chinese immigrants had brought the horrendous practice with them to the U.S. In 1904 a Chinese entrepreneur put a Chinese woman with bound feet on display at the St. Louis World's Fair.[83]

Sati

The original definition of the Sanskrit word *sati* (sometimes spelled *suttee*) meant a virtuous or pious woman. Indian tradition holds chastity, purity, and loyalty to the husband as the highest ideals for a woman. For a widow to voluntarily throw her body upon her husband's funeral pyre came to be considered an example of loyalty and devotion.[84] Hence, the word *sati* evolved to mean a woman who burned herself alive alongside the body of her deceased husband. Greek visitors to North India wrote accounts of sati as early as the fourth century B.C.E.[85] Evidence suggests that by 700 A.D. it was encouraged.[86] The importance of maintaining a woman's chastity was given as an excuse for endorsing the practice.

A widow was prohibited from burning herself on her husband's funeral pyre while she was menstruating (which was equated with uncleanness) or pregnant. If the husband's death occurred then, or when he was absent from home, some women would burn themselves with an article of his clothing or another personal effect. Typically, the widow or her eldest son was required to light the fire. On her way to the pyre, she would distribute money and jewelry to the onlookers. The richer she was, the more valuable the gifts. No woman who was unfaithful to her husband could be burnt. Sati did not *make* the woman virtuous; it proved that she had been virtuous all her life.[87]

Basically, widows had two choices. They could choose a painful but heroic death, or they could live, viewed as a sinner, in poverty and loneliness. Widows were not allowed to remarry. They were forbidden to turn to religious instruction, to hold jobs, or to maintain interests outside the home. For many women, sati became an escape from a seemingly bleak and hopeless future. The Widow Remarriage Act, passed in 1856, made it legal for widows to wed but did not readily eliminate the centuries of prejudice against widows' remarrying. Even today, remarriage is viewed less favorably for a widow than for a widower.[88]

Within Indian borders, the incidence of sati was subject to great regional variations. By the early nineteenth century, most satis occurred in the province of Bengal. From 1815 to 1828, Bengal officially recorded the occurrence of 7,941 sati rites. An 1829 study profiling Bengalese widows who burned themselves found that many came from impoverished families. According to Sakuntala Narasimhan, author of *Sati: Widow Burning in India*, "For many widows in the early nineteenth century, the virtue of becoming a sati lay in the deliverance that is promised from a life of certain misery."[89]

Sati was outlawed in British India in 1829. Nevertheless, cases continued to be reported long after that. By 1987, the Rajasthan Sati (Prevention) Act stated that an attempted sati was punishable with imprisonment ranging from one to five years and a fine of five thousand to twenty thousand rupees. For abetting a sati, directly or indirectly, one became subject to a death sentence or life imprisonment plus a fine.[90]

Domestic Violence in the American Colonies

Women in the American colonies were without political rights, and wives were generally considered legal nonentities. Single women, however, were considered fully competent for all the purposes of private law. As soon as a woman married, her legal existence was suspended or incorporated into that of her husband, who was regarded as her head and master.[91]

Addressing women in the late 1700s in his book *The Married Lady's Companion*, Samuel Jennings was to echo what generations of men before him had argued:

329

Appendix I:
A History of
Violence
Against
Women

It is in your interest to adapt yourself to your husband, whatever may be his peculiarities. Again, nature has made man the stronger, the consent of mankind has given him superiority over his wife, his inclination is, to claim his natural and acquired rights. He of course expects from you a degree of condescension, and he feels himself the more confident of the propriety of his claim, when he is informed, that St. Paul adds his authority to its support. "Wives submit yourselves unto your own husbands, as unto the Lord, for the husband is the head of his wife." In obedience then to this precept of the gospel, to the laws of custom and of nature, you ought to cultivate a cheerful and happy submission.[92]

Wife beating, although not a legal privilege, was an accepted right in the colonies. If the husband exceeded his legal prerogatives, the woman could take him to court. Many cases appear in the colonial records of a wife's appealing to the court for protection against her husband's battering. The justices usually ordered the husband to appear in court and promise his good behavior, but on occasion they fined him or imposed corporal punishment.

Still, judges recognized a husband's right to batter his wife. A Maryland court in 1681 expressed what appears to have been an orthodox opinion in a case involving Jane Bread, who complained to the court that she had been "grievously and manifestly threatened" by her husband with her life and with "mutilation of her members." The order instructed the sheriff to summon the husband and have him give bond not to do "any damage or evil" to his wife "otherwise than what to a husband, by cause of government and chastisement of his own wife, lawfully and reasonably belongeth."[93] Other evidence suggests that in some cases when a court was convinced that a woman's life was endangered by her abusive husband, it allowed her to live away from him and required him to furnish her a separate maintenance.

The acceptance of wife battering became a part of the American tradition through the borrowing of English common law by the colonists. (The only exception was in Massachusetts, where, in 1655, men convicted of beating their wives were fined a maximum of ten pounds and/or given corporal punishment.[94]) Under English common law the notion of chastisement in moderation prevailed, of which the "rule of thumb" is a good example. This law, which modified the weapons a man could legally use to beat his wife, was created as an example of compassionate reform. The old law authorized a husband to "chastise his wife with any reasonable instrument." The new law stipulated that the instrument must be "a rod not thicker than his thumb."[95] In 1765 Sir William Blackstone published the *Commentaries of the Law of England,* which provided the colonists with their primary source of information about English common law. Blackstone, who approved of chastisement, wrote, "For, as [the husband] is to answer for her misbehavior, the law thought it reasonable to intrust him with this power of chastisement, in the same moderation that a man is allowed to correct his apprentices or children."[96] Although Blackstone's work was quickly discredited in England, it was influential in the United States for the next hundred years. Not until the women's movement took hold in the 1800s was a serious challenge made to Blackstone's ideas concerning the legal status of women.[97]

331

**Appendix I:
A History of
Violence
Against
Women**

In 1824 the Mississippi Supreme Court became the first state to acknowledge a husband's right to beat his wife, and other states soon followed. By the 1870s, however, states began rejecting the legal justification of wife beating.[98] In 1871 both Alabama and Massachusetts rescinded the wife-beating privilege.[99] In 1874 the North Carolina Supreme Court disavowed a husband's right to beat his wife; however, the court also stated, "If no permanent injury has been inflicted, nor malice, cruelty nor dangerous violence shown by the husband, it is better to draw the curtain, shut out the public gaze and leave the parties to forget and forgive."[100] Twelve years later, as a result of this ruling, a lower court in North Carolina declared that a criminal indictment could not be brought against a husband unless the assault resulted in permanent injury, endangered life and limb, or was malicious beyond all reasonable bounds.

Between 1876 and 1906 bills to punish wife beaters with the whipping post were introduced in twelve states and the District of Columbia. The idea of whipping wife beaters originated in England during a period of public concern about armed robbery. It was believed that a man who battered his wife would also assault his neighbors or strangers. Well-known lawyers, judges, and other law-enforcement officials led the campaign, but opponents of the whipping post far outnumbered its supporters. Whipping-post bills were defeated in all states except Maryland in 1882, Delaware in 1901, and Oregon in 1905. Maryland's law provided a whipping of not more than forty lashes, a one-year jail term, or both.[101]

It was not until 1890 that the North Carolina Supreme Court eliminated the last remaining restrictions on a husband's liability and prohibited a man from committing even a minor assault against his wife.[102] By 1910 only eleven states still did not permit divorce by reason of cruelty by one spouse to the other.[103]

The Early Feminists

The popular eighteenth-century writer Jean-Jacques Rousseau was adamant in his belief that women were inferior and subordinate beings who should be nurtured for the sole purpose of serving men and providing them pleasure. He argued that women should be restricted to domestic chores and excluded from liberal education. Like others before him, Rousseau insisted that the patriarchal structure of the family was natural. In *Paternity and the Origin of Political Power*, he writes,

> In the family, it is clear, for several reasons which lie in its very nature, that the father ought to command. In the first place, the authority ought not to be equally divided between father and mother; the government must be single, and in every division of opinion there must be one preponderant voice to decide. Secondly, however lightly we may regard the disadvantages peculiar to women, yet, as they necessarily occasion intervals of inaction, this is a sufficient reason for excluding them from this supreme authority.... Besides, the husband ought to be able to superintend his wife's conduct, because it is of importance for him to be assured that the children, whom he is obligated to acknowledge and maintain, belong to no one but himself.[104]

In 1792 British writer Mary Wollstonecraft published *A Vindication of the Rights of Woman* as a rebuttal to Rousseau's popular work *Emile*.[105] Although an early disciple of Rousseau's egalitarian views, she objected to his assumption that man's nature and virtues differed from woman's, the essence of the distinction lying in the belief that women were deficient in reason. Since reason is the fundamental human characteristic, Wollstonecraft argued, to deny women a full measure of rationality amounts to denying their humanity. Ultimately, she explained, such beliefs and practices damaged not only women, but the family and society as well. Wollstonecraft urged equal rights for women, although she primarily addressed the problems of middle- and upper-class women.[106]

Wollstonecraft's book was one of the first sociopolitical manifestos demanding equal treatment for women. In the mid-1800s it became the bible for the early feminist movement in both England and the United States. The feminists supported Wollstonecraft's contention that women were not inherently inferior, but rather were victims of lifelong subjugation that was encouraged and perpetuated by social forces.[107]

It was out of a concern for others that American women found a concern for themselves. In the 1820s and 1830s, especially in New York, Pennsylvania, and New England, a spirit of reform was in the air. It started in the churches and was involved at first with such humanitarian issues as temperance, peace, capital punishment, and education. But the cause that most attracted these white, middle-class feminists was the antislavery movement. Their involvement gave them an opportunity to extend their lives beyond their roles as wives and mothers. They developed public-speaking and fund-raising skills, they learned how to distribute literature and how to call meetings, and they became adept in the use of the petition. In addition, they learned how to challenge male supremacy.[108]

Participation in the antislavery movement led white women to realize their own oppression and inequality. As a result of the frustrations caused by their awakening, they initiated the first organized efforts to change the conditions of their lives. Only when women decided to work together did the "women's movement" begin in the United States. This officially occurred in July 1848 in Seneca Falls, New York, with the first women's-rights meeting, organized by five women—Lucretia Mott, Martha C. Wright, Jane Hunt, Elizabeth Cady Stanton, and Mary Ann McClintock—to discuss "the social, civil and religious condition and rights of women."[109]

From that moment until well into the next century, reform became associated with women. Millions participated in a variety of causes or issues ranging from suffrage for women to legal and educational systems, employment, marriage, temperance, health, and birth control.[110] Early reformers included Lucy Stone, Susan B. Anthony, Carrie Chapman Catt, Harriet Tubman, Angelina and Sarah Grimké, Sojourner Truth, Ida B. Wells, Lucretia Mott, Mary Church Terrell, Margaret Sanger, Emma Goldman, Lucy Parsons, "Mother" Ella Reeve Bloor, Jane Addams, and "Mother" Mary Harris Jones.[111] Wendell Phillips, W. E. B. Du Bois, William Lloyd Garrison, and Frederick Douglass were some of the men who joined in these early reform movements.[112]

John Stuart Mill's *The Subjection of Women* was published in England in 1869, during the formative years of the feminist movement. Mill was one of the few men to actively call for equal rights for women and an end to their mistreatment by their husbands. He wrote, "The vilest malefactor has some wretched woman tied to him, against whom he can commit any atrocity except killing her, and, if tolerably cautious, can do that without much danger of the legal penalty."[113] Mill's analysis of the physical, psychological, and legal subjection of women proved highly controversial and helped to bring the issue to the attention of the British Parliament.[114]

British suffragist Frances Power Cobbe, an opponent of the whipping post, persuaded its supporters to instead favor a law protecting battered wives. Her bill, known as the Matrimonial Causes Act, provided a battered woman with legal separation from her husband, legal custody of her children, and an order requiring her husband to pay her and her children support. It was passed by the British Parliament in 1878.[115] In her campaign for the legislation Cobbe wrote, "The notion that a man's wife is his property ... is the fatal root of incalculable evil and misery. Every brutal-minded man, and many a man who in other relations of life is not brutal, entertains more or less vaguely the notion that his wife is his thing, and is ready to ask with indignation... of any one who interferes with his treatment of her, 'May I not do what I will with my own?' "[116]

Cobbe sent a copy of the bill to the American suffragist Lucy Stone, who introduced a similar one into the Massachusetts legislature in 1879. Opposition came from legislators who believed that its passage would make it too easy for women to secure legal separation and thus would create disharmony in the family. Stone made two more attempts to pass the bill, each of which failed.[117]

The Medical Solution

One of the effects of the murder of thousands of wise women during the witch craze was the virtual elimination of female healers and the creation of a new male medical profession. Since women had been barred from universities and the midwives had been murdered, it became the responsibility of male doctors to attend to women and their health. Between the late 1700s and the late 1800s, male midwives became identified by the name *gynecologist*.

A common diagnosis during this period was "female hysteria" or "female insanity," which encompassed a vast array of physical and emotional symptoms including fits, fainting, vomiting, choking, sobbing, laughing, and paralysis.[118] Not only did the management of female hysteria play a major role in the work of leading English, American, French, and German physicians; it also became the starting point for psychoanalysis.[119]

British doctor Isaac Baker Brown practiced clitoridectomy, a particularly brutal and extreme surgery, to cure female hysteria. A respected member of the Obstetrical Society of London, Brown became convinced that female hysteria was caused by masturbation and that the surgical removal of the clitoris would stop the disease. Brown conducted the surgery in his private clinic in London from 1859 to 1866. In the 1860s he began to expand the practice to include removal of the labia. As he grew more confident, he operated on patients as young as ten and even on women with eye problems. He operated on five women whose "madness" consisted of their wish to take advantage of the new Divorce Act of 1857 and found that in each case the patient returned humbly to her husband. Brown was most certain of clitoridectomy as a cure for nymphomania, for he had never seen a recurrence of the disease after surgery. In 1867 Brown was expelled from the Obstetrical Society, primarily because his patients had complained of being tricked and coerced into the treatment. Some had been threatened that if they refused to undergo surgery, their condition would worsen and they would become hopelessly insane.[120]

Clitoridectomy was enthusiastically accepted as a cure for female masturbation by some American gynecologists. In the 1860s Dr. Isaac Ray and his contemporaries proclaimed that women were susceptible to hysteria, insanity, and criminal impulses by reason of their sexual organs. In 1873 Dr. Robert Battey began the practice of "female castration," the removal of the ovaries to cure insanity. For the next several decades ovariectomy became the gynecological craze. Doctors claimed the surgery elevated the moral sense of women, making them orderly, industrious, and "cleanly."[121]

Although middle- and upper-middle-class women suffered most from these medical practices, pioneering work in gynecological surgery had been performed by Marion Sims on black female slaves, whom he kept for the sole purpose of surgical experimentation. Sims moved to New York City, where he continued his experiments on impoverished Irish women in the wards of the New York Women's Hospital.[122]

Doctors noticed that hysteria was likely to appear in young women who were especially rebellious. Dr. F. C. Skey observed that his hysterical patients were likely to be more independent and assertive than "normal" women. Other doctors also had seen a high percentage of unconventional women, such as artists and writers. From these observations, they concluded that rebelliousness could produce nervous disorders such as hysteria. Elaine Showalter, writing in *The Female Malady: Women, Madness, and English Culture,* explains that "during an era when patriarchal culture felt itself to be under attack by its rebellious daughters, one obvious defense was to label women campaigning for access to the universities, the professions, and the vote as mentally disturbed, and of all the nervous disorders … hysteria was the most strongly identified with the feminist movement."[123]

When the symptoms of hysteria became widespread among men, the notion of a "talking cure" finally entered English medicine. It was not feminism that initiated a new era of psychiatric practice, but rather the recharacterizing and renaming of female hysteria during World War I as "shell shock." Gradually, psychologists and medical personnel came to agree that the real cause of shell shock was the emotional disturbance created by chronic conditions of fear, tension, horror, disgust, and grief, and that the neurosis triggered by the malady was an escape from an intolerable situation.[124]

Societies for the Prevention of Cruelty to Children

In the United States the earliest attempts to confront domestic violence occurred in the 1870s with the founding of societies for the prevention of cruelty to children, the first social agencies devoted to family-violence problems. Originally focused only on child abuse, the agencies were soon drawn into other forms of family violence. By the end of the decade, there were thirty-four such societies in the United States.[125]

335

Appendix I:
A History of
Violence
Against
Women

From about 1875 to 1910, family-violence agencies were part of the general reform movement, which was heavily influenced by feminism.[126] Caseworkers tried to reform men who neglected or abused their families. They heckled, threatened, and cajoled. They made frequent home visits, surprise visits, and visits to employers and relatives, and they pursued men who failed to support their familes for money.

Societies for the prevention of cruelty to children originally tried to avoid intervention between husbands and wives, but their clients virtually dragged them into wife-abuse issues. Few battered women kept their problems to themselves. Many asked close neighbors, landladies, and relatives to provide child care, credit, food, places to stay, or money so they could maintain their own households. Battered women turned to child-welfare agencies when their informal networks could not protect them. Caseworkers tried to help battered women secure monetary assistance, safety, or housing. They also helped to increase public awareness of domestic violence. Another reason why battered women turned to child-protection agencies was because of the inadequacy of police protection. Police officers may have urged abusive husbands to moderate their violence and to sober up, but they frequently also identified with them, sympathized with their frustrations, and trivialized their assaults. They often removed men from their homes for a while to calm them, and they sometimes threatened men with arrest and jail.[127]

During the 1920s and 1930s, the women's movement shrank in size and effectiveness. The reform spirit, with its discontent and insistence on change, was at odds with the national mood. So was the women's movement. Since the turn of the century women had begun to gain more personal freedom; consequently they had less interest in collective activities and social reform.[128]

During the Progressive era, from about 1910 to 1930, efforts to curb family violence were absorbed into programs that relied heavily on state regulation. Social work was becoming professionalized and "scientific," and middle-class "experts" replaced upper-class reform workers as the group who set standards for family life. Social workers downplayed wife beating as a form of family violence. Feminist outcries against drunken, brutal men were seen as moralistic and unscientific. Instead, marital violence was portrayed as mutual, resulting from environmental stress, lack of education, or lack of "mental hygiene." Women began to be blamed for much of the abuse they suffered.

One of the major guiding principles of Depression-era social work was the defense of the "conventional" nuclear family. Family-violence agencies continued to deemphasize wife battering as a significant problem. Women were consistently held responsible for the treatment of children and the general mood of the family; men were not. The standard treatments for family

337

**Appendix I:
A History of
Violence
Against
Women**

violence were reconciliation and economic aid. The very meaning of the concept of family violence had shifted. It was seen as resulting from extrafamilial causes. Indeed, violence altogether was deemphasized, and the societies for the prevention of cruelty to children devoted themselves almost exclusively to child neglect.[129] The issues of violence against women, women's poverty, and women's overall frustrations were submerged in the troubles of the whole nation. As the country began to recuperate from the Depression, people turned their attention and energies toward Europe and Asia. From 1930 to 1945, and during the decade after the war, the women's movement was silent.[130]

Women's protests about wife beating escalated just as feminism was at an ebb. Records from child-protection societies after the 1930s indicate that the majority of women clients complained directly about their abusive husbands. Women continued to allege child abuse to get help from the agencies, but during the investigations they tended to protest more strongly about their own abuse. Through the 1940s and 1950s social workers were no longer reluctant to inquire into the roots of family conflict, but a focus on psychiatric categories and profamily values now dominated their approach. The most notorious example of psychiatry's influence on family-violence work was in the blaming of wives for their husbands' abuse. According to Linda Gordon, author of *Heroes of Their Own Lives,* "The 'nagging wife' of traditional patriarchal folklore was now transformed into a woman of complex mental ailments: failure to accept her own femininity and attempting to compete with her husband; frustration as a result of her own frigidity; a need to control resulting from her own sexual repression; masochism. These neuroses required diagnosis and treatment by professionals.... Moreover, these neuroses indicated treatment not of the assailant but of the victim."[131]

The 1940s and 50s mark a low point in the public awareness of domestic violence. The notion of defending and maintaining the conventional family prevailed. Until the revival of feminism and the establishment of battered-women's shelters in the 1970s, victims of domestic violence had three basic resources, none of them fully adequate: their individual survival strategies; the help of relatives, friends, and neighbors; and the child-welfare agencies. Although a woman's survival strategies may have kept her alive, they did not guarantee that she would live violence free. Friends and relatives were often intimidated by abusive husbands and by the sanctity of marriage. And child-welfare agencies did not represent the interests of battered women.

The Reemergence of Feminism

True emancipation... begins in woman's soul. History tells us that every oppressed class gain[s] true liberation from its masters through its own efforts. It is necessary that woman learn that lesson, that she realize that her freedom will reach as far as her power to achieve her freedom reaches.

— Emma Goldman, early twentieth-century feminist [132]

The renewed focus on and redefining of domestic violence in the 1960s and 1970s resulted from women's involvement with the civil-rights, antiwar, anti-rape, student, and women's movements. From their experiences in reform efforts, these activist women, like the feminists of the nineteenth century, became aware of their own oppression and inequality. Once again, their concern with the needs of others led to a concern for themselves.

The era's movements all challenged family norms, but in different ways. Critical questions were raised about the sanctity of family privacy, the privileged position of the male head of the family, and the importance of family togetherness at any price. A widespread spirit of protest allowed child abuse and wife beating to again be exposed. Linda Gordon writes, "Defining wife-beating as a social problem, not merely a phenomenon of particular violent individuals or relationships, was one of the great achievements of feminism. Women always resisted battering, but in the last hundred years they began to resist it politically and ideologically, with considerable success."[133]

Radical feminism had its roots in the civil-rights movement of the 1950s and 1960s. After leaving the South, many of the young women who'd worked for civil rights returned to their colleges and universities, where they later demonstrated against the war in Vietnam and joined groups associated with the new left. Examining the origins of feminism, Sara Evans, in her book *Personal Politics,* outlines the following preconditions for an insurgent revolt:[134]

1. Social spaces within which members of an oppressed group can develop an independent sense of worth in contrast to their received definitions as second-class or inferior citizens

2. Role models of people breaking out of patterns of passivity

3. An ideology that can explain the sources of oppression, justify revolt, and provide a vision of a qualitatively different future

4. A threat to the newfound sense of self that forces a confrontation with the inherited cultural definitions

5. A communication or friendship network through which a new interpretation can spread, activating the insurgent consciousness into a social movement

As more and more women participated in the various reform movements, these conditions were nurtured. When women in the Student Non-Violent Coordinating Committee (SNCC) and Students for a Democratic Society (SDS) voiced their concerns regarding the unequal treatment of men and women within their ranks, they were either ignored or laughed at. Taking literally the admonition to "look to your own oppression," many women made their final break with the new left in 1967 when they declared that feminism was their first priority.[135]

339

Appendix I:
A History of
Violence
Against
Women

Feminism soon developed two major branches. One was the women's-rights movement, exemplified by groups like the National Organization for Women (NOW), founded in 1966 to focus on legal inequalities and gaining access to the rights and opportunities held by men.[136] The other branch was the women's-liberation movement, which was embodied in radical feminist groups working on such issues as abortion, women's schools, day care, and prisoners' rights. The activists in the women's-liberation movement believed that the campaigns waged by the more moderate groups such as NOW were important; however, radical feminists wanted more. Crucial to the women's-liberation movement was the rejection of middle-class standards and lifestyles and a focus on such personal issues as the unequal gender division of labor and women's lack of control over their bodies, sexuality, and lives. Radical feminists urged a transformed society in which neither women nor men would be assigned or restricted to roles based on their sex.[137] Their demands went beyond equal rights to a demand for equality of power.

Radical feminists agreed that their first task was to awaken women by helping them explore their own experiences and how those experiences conformed to assigned social roles. The instinctive sharing of personal experience soon became a political instrument called consciousness-raising.[138] Feminists met in small consciousness-raising groups to talk about their backgrounds, their experiences, and their feelings. Very quickly they discovered that the problems they thought were uniquely their own were actually common to other women. In their book *A History of Women in America* Carol Hymowitz and Michaele Weissman write, "The idea that the personal is political was the most important insight of modern feminism. It led to the understanding that women were a caste or class, linked together by their sex. Regardless of the many differences among groups of women—class, race, age, education, life style—all women were subject to sexism."[139] Consciousness-raising groups inspired not only an analysis of personal experiences, but a thorough critique of both internal and external oppression.

Soon the radical ideas and cooperative forms of the women's-liberation movement were reshaping the more conservative, tightly structured women's-rights branch of the movement. Within a few years NOW had strengthened its positions on such issues as abortion and lesbianism and had considerably changed its style. In several cities NOW became the primary instigator of new consciousness-raising groups.[140]

By 1970 consciousness-raising groups had become the heart of the women's-liberation movement. Their format reflected the movement's grassroots origins and style. Groups developed wherever several women decided to meet and talk about their experiences. Common use of words like *sexism, chauvinism, oppression,* and *liberation* grew out of the phenomenon. The idea that women could make political changes through personal testimony became a reality. Women began to transform their lives in ways that would not only impact their families, friends, and coworkers, but also literally change the country.[141]

Sisterhood Is Powerful: The Birth of the Battered-Women's Movement

Prior to the revival of feminism, women occasionally organized efforts against battering, both in the United States and internationally. In 1875 Martha McWhirter opened a shelter in Belton, Texas, for battered women and women whose husbands spent the crop money on Saturday-night drinking binges. The shelter became so prosperous that the group donated money for Belton civic causes and thrived well into the 1890s.[142] In 1916 Rokeya Sakhawat Hossain organized the Muslim Women's Association to offer assistance to widows and shelter for battered women in Calcutta's slums. Following the Russian Revolution, women in villages near the Caspian Sea set up special community centers to provide assistance to women, which soon became shelters for those escaping battering husbands. A shelter was established in the Hupeh province of China by one of the many women's unions created during the Nationalist Revolution to assist women who were trying to divorce abusive husbands.[143]

Religious organizations in the United States sheltered battered women long before the movement mobilized in the 1970s. Closely allied with Al-Anon, programs like Rainbow Retreat, in Phoenix, Arizona, and Haven House, in Pasadena, California, sheltered women abused by alcoholic husbands as early as the 1960s.[144] In most cases, however, battered women had nowhere to go. Shelters were almost nonexistent, and medical, social-service, and law-enforcement agencies rarely provided battered women with the kind of support they needed.

Worldwide, women stopped hiding the violence in their lives and started helping each other during the 1970s. The British battered-women's movement, which began a few years before the movement in the United States, was led by Erin Pizzey, who founded the first shelter in England, Chiswick Women's Aid, in 1971.[145] Demonstrating a relentless determination in the battle to secure shelters for battered women, Pizzey brought international attention to the problem in her groundbreaking work, *Scream Quietly or the Neighbors Will Hear*.[146]

Women everywhere began to tell their stories. As they tore down the walls of isolation and shame, it became apparent that an epidemic of violence against women flourished worldwide. Not only were women living with daily threats to their lives, but little was being done to guarantee their safety. Outraged at society's failure to address this problem, activists began to take matters into their own hands. In Amsterdam, six women grew tired of waiting for social services to aid battered women. In September 1974 they occupied an abandoned house and established the shelter Blijf van m'n Lijf (Hands off My Body). That same year feminists in Sydney, Australia, took over two abandoned houses and refused to move out. The houses became Elsie, shelters for battered women. Feminists in Glasgow, Scotland, converted a three-bedroom apartment into the shelter Interval House. Across the Atlantic Ocean, Transition House opened in Vancouver, British Columbia. On November 2, 1979, Danish feminists stormed the dilapidated Danner House and demanded that the nineteenth-century palace be used to shelter women in need. After battling with the government, the women finally gained the right to the building. Even before renovations began, battered women and their children were streaming through the doors.

Thereafter, wherever women began to speak the truth of what happened in the privacy of their homes, they discovered other women willing to unite with them in their pain. Crisis centers opened in Berlin and Barcelona, in Bogota and Tokyo. Battered women sought the help of their sisters in New Delhi and Jerusalem. In Thailand, in 1981, Kanitha Wichiencharoen, an active member of the Women Lawyers' Association, founded that country's first shelter for battered women when she turned her home into a refuge. In 1989 Zimbabwe opened its first counseling service for survivors of rape and battering, in the city of Harare.[147]

The Battered-Women's Movement in the United States

Inspired by the feminist and antirape movements' analysis of male violence against women as a social and political issue, battered women in the United States began to speak out. The feminist assertion that women had the right to control their own bodies and lives resulted in the founding of women's hotlines and crisis centers, services that provided a way for battered women to reach out for help. The recognition of women's right to verbalize their pain without blame created an environment in which discussing violence was less shameful.

Formerly battered women and women who had witnessed violence in their families of origin were among the first to reach out to battered women. Whatever specific political label, if any, these women used, they brought a heartfelt commitment to the movement. Their experiences and strength were the forces that started the movement. Like their sisters who continue the work today, they were determined and persistent change agents who saw themselves as improving the world for women, children, and their communities.[148] According to Susan Schechter, author of *Women and Male Violence: The Visions and Struggles of the Battered Women's Movement,* "Far from being monolithic or homogeneous, the battered women's movement incorporates differences among women in ideology, class, race, ethnicity, education, skill and knowledge level[,] and sexual preference. The fight against battering, like those waged against other forms of male domination, bonds together diverse groups of women."[149]

In St. Paul, Minnesota, in 1972, members of the Women's Advocates Collective started a legal-information telephone service. They were surprised when most of the calls came from battered women. Advocates decided to provide shelter in their own homes, and for the next two years battered women and their children slept on their living-room floors. Finally, in October 1974, the group opened a shelter.[150] In the mid-seventies the Women's Center South, in Pittsburgh, evolved into a shelter for battered women. In Boston, Chris Womendez and Cherie Jimenez opened up their five-room apartment as a refuge for battered women and named it Transition House. For a time they supported the shelter, themselves, and two children on their welfare checks and small contributions from friends.[151] In Austin, Texas, a grassroots coalition of women opened the Center for Battered Women in 1977. They quickly discovered the magnitude of the problem and realized they lacked enough space. Three years later the CBW was adopted by the Austin Association of Homebuilders, who constructed the first shelter in the United States specifically designed for battered women and their children.[152] Equally important were the movement's roles in heightening community awareness about domestic violence and in promoting changes in the criminal-justice system and other institutions.[153]

Operating on shoestring budgets, battered-women's advocates began formal programs around the United States. Where only a handful of such programs existed in the mid-1970s, today there are more than two thousand shelters, hotlines, and safe-home networks nationwide.[154] Individual programs may differ in philosophy and approach, but all share the conviction that no one deserves to be beaten and that battered women need special resources to end the violence in their lives. Programs vary in size, services offered, and sources and levels of funding. Their most critical functions include crisis intervention and providing for the safety of battered women and their children. Most programs operate twenty-four-hour hotlines. Typical shelter services include legal, economic, housing, and medical advocacy; court accompaniment; education and job-training assistance; support groups for residents and non-residents; and child care and counseling programs for children. Some shelters operate separate programs for abusive men.[155]

Although the growth in the number of battered-women's programs over the last thirty years has been remarkable, many communities still have minimal or no services available. Programs are often inadequately funded and must turn away as many women as they help. Most rely heavily on donations and the ongoing grassroots efforts of volunteers. Community support, an essential component of a successful shelter program, can be difficult to generate since many communities still refuse to acknowledge the existence of domestic violence. In addition, advocates often struggle against the widely held misconception that shelters try to break up families, even though it is actually the violence that destroys families. Most shelters operate from a philosophy of supported self-help: Women are given the opportunity to explore their options and resources in a safe environment that helps them empower themselves to make their own decisions.

Gaining National Attention

Long before the battered-women's movement gained national recognition, activists wrote and distributed cutting-edge literature on domestic violence. In 1976 Betsy Warrior's invaluable directory *Working on Wife Abuse* and Del Martin's *Battered Wives* were first published. Martin's book, which proved to be a major source of information and validation for the movement, legitimized the view held by many activists that violence against wives is deeply rooted in sexism.[156] That same year, NOW announced the formation of a task force, co-chaired by Martin, to examine the problem of battering.

The first national conference on domestic violence, held in Milwaukee and sponsored by the Milwaukee Task Force on Battered Women, took place in 1976.[157] Since then literally hundreds of conferences have been organized, some serving as political and educational forums for activists in the movement and others reaching out to educate the community. In all kinds of settings, grassroots service providers have found one another, shared information,

343

Appendix I:
A History of
Violence
Against
Women

worked on problems, and, through mutual support, lessened the pain and frustration of the work of service delivery and organizing.

Although providing shelter for abused women is a top priority of the battered-women's movement, activists have organized in other ways too. In some cities, women representing a variety of agencies form coalitions. In 1976 Pennsylvania established the first state coalition against domestic violence. State coalitions, as the primary vehicles for lobbying and organizing efforts, sponsor workshops, produce educational materials, lobby legislators and policy makers, and provide support services for shelters and advocates. As a result of their capacity to mobilize hundreds of women in lobbying efforts, state coalitions often prove their strength in legislative campaigns.

In 1977 the National Communications Network for the Elimination of Violence Against Women (NCN) published the first national newsletter on battered women. The following year, NCN merged with the Feminist Alliance Against Rape to publish *Aegis: The Magazine on Ending Violence Against Women*, a grassroots feminist forum on rape, battering, and other issues of violence affecting women.[158] *Aegis* filled many needs. It alleviated women's sense of isolation and offered inspiration. It provided insight and direction so that women could define their community as national rather than local. It offered information and resources about legislation, and it printed political articles that provided the focal points for local, state, and regional discussions.[159]

The idea of establishing a national coalition started to become a reality when, on July 20, 1977, the first White House meeting on domestic abuse opened with the testimony of battered women, followed by carefully prepared statements from twelve advocates. The advocates offered suggestions about how specific federal agencies and legislation could be improved. Although no substantial decisions were made, advocates used the meeting to build trust and support among an ever-increasing number of grassroots activists. That November, the International Women's Year conference, held in Houston, provided the next opportunity for groups from all over the United States to organize themselves. A caucus on battered women met and reaffirmed the goal of developing a national feminist coalition based in local, autonomous grassroots programs.[160]

In 1978 the United States Commission on Civil Rights held "A Consultation on Battered Women," in Washington, D.C., which brought together hundreds of activists to clarify and define the needs of battered women and their children. One result of the proceedings was the publication of *Battered Women: Issues of Public Policy*, which consolidated more than seven hundred pages of written and oral testimony.[161] Even more, however, the event legitimized the needs of battered women, educated federal agencies about the problem of domestic violence, and introduced the agencies to a new constituency. A movement had been born and was now being recognized.

During the 1978 proceedings in Washington the goal of creating a nationwide coalition was realized with the formation of the National Coalition Against Domestic Violence (NCADV), a grassroots organization that serves as the voice of the battered-women's movement at the national level. NCADV, currently the only national organization of shelter and service programs for battered women, established the vision and philosophy that guided the development of hundreds of local programs and state coalitions.[162] Today NCADV continues in its efforts to build coalitions at the local, state, regional, and national levels; to offer support for the provision of safe homes and shelter programs; to educate the public about domestic abuse; to provide technical assistance; and to develop public policy. In 1980 a dream came true when six hundred women from forty-nine states traveled to Washington for the first official NCADV membership conference.[163] The event gained federal recognition of critical issues facing battered women and witnessed the birth of several state coalitions.

On April 27, 1979, President Carter created the Interdepartmental Committee on Domestic Violence, composed of representatives from twelve federal agencies and staff from the Office on Domestic Violence (ODV), formed on the same day. Many in the battered-women's movement supported the establishment of the Office on Domestic Violence as a potential federal advocate for battered women. During its brief existence, ODV staff worked with activists to develop lobbying strategies for the passage of federal legislation favorable to battered women. The collaboration was short-lived, however. After the 1980 election of President Reagan, the ODV was dismantled.[164]

As the movement continued to gain momentum, so did public awareness of the problem of domestic violence. As a result of grassroots lobbying efforts, the Family Violence Prevention and Services Act, which earmarked federal funding for programs serving victims of domestic violence, was passed in 1984. The next year the U.S. Surgeon General issued a report identifying domestic violence as a major health problem.[165] In 1987 NCADV established the first national toll-free domestic-violence hotline. The hotline closed in 1992; however, because of the unrelenting efforts of the Texas Council on Family Violence, the National Domestic Violence Hotline received federal funding and reopened in 1996. September 2004 marked the tenth anniversary of the Violence Against Women Act (VAWA), landmark legislation that authorized nearly $5 billion for a variety of programs and services, including shelters, child-abuse services, rape prevention, judicial training, community programs, youth education, and campus-assault programs. The VAWA of

345

**Appendix I:
A History of
Violence
Against
Women**

2000 reauthorized critical grant programs created by the original VAWA, established new programs, and strengthened federal law against domestic violence.[166]

Many other changes that have occurred in the last thirty years can be attributed to the battered-women's movement, including improved data collection about domestic violence, laws in all fifty states that identify domestic violence as a criminal act, enhanced availability of civil protection orders, increased reporting of domestic-violence cases in police departments and hospitals, and recognition of the problem at a national level. Although much has been accomplished, there is still more work to be done. Sheltering battered women and their children, effecting systematic changes, educating the community about domestic violence, and promoting victims' rights remain ongoing challenges. The incredible people who make up this movement are ready for the task and continue to unselfishly share of themselves, their time, their energy, and their money to assure that no woman or child need ever cry out in fear and pain.

Appendix II
A Personalized Safety Plan

This safety plan was developed by Barbara Hart and Jane Stuehling with the Pennsylvania Coalition Against Domestic Violence (PCADV) and is widely used by domestic-violence advocates. A safety plan is a way to help survivors protect themselves and their children against an abusive partner. Safety plans may help a survivor to become more aware of both her personal resources and those within the community. Most of all, a safety plan helps a survivor determine the steps she needs to take to protect herself and her children.

Prior to reviewing this safety plan with a survivor, it may be helpful to review the information about safety planning in Chapter 15, "Advocacy and Empowerment for Battered Women."

Name: _____

Date: _____

Review dates: _____

The following steps represent my plan for increasing my safety and preparing in advance for the possibility of further violence. Although I do not have control over my partner's violence, I do have a choice about how to respond to him/her and how to best get myself and my children to safety.

Step 1: Safety During a Violent Incident

Women cannot always avoid violent incidents. In order to increase safety, battered women may use a variety of strategies.

I can use some or all of the following strategies:

A. If I decide to leave, I will _____

_____

_____.

(Practice how to get out safely. What doors, windows, elevators, stairwells, or fire escapes would you use?)

B. I can keep my purse and car keys ready and put them _____ _____ (name the place) in order to leave quickly.

C. I can tell _____ about the violence and request that they call the police if they hear suspicious noises coming from my house.
I can also tell _____ about the violence and request that they call the police if they hear suspicious noises coming from my house.

D. I can teach my children how to use the telephone to contact the police and the fire department.

E. I will use _____ as my code word with my children or my friends so they can call for help.

F. If I have to leave my home, I will go to _____. (Decide where to go even if you don't think there will be a next time.) If I cannot go to the location above, then I can go to _____ or _____.

G. I can also teach some of these strategies to some/all of my children.

H. When I expect we are going to have an argument, I will try to move to a space that presents the lowest risk, such as

_____.

(Try to avoid arguments in the bathroom, in the garage, in the kitchen, near weapons, or in rooms without access to an outside door.)

I. I will use my judgment and intuition. If the situation is very serious, I can give my partner what he/she wants to calm him/her down. I have to protect myself until I/we are out of danger.

Step 2: Safety when Preparing to Leave

Battered women frequently leave the residence they share with the battering partner. Leaving must be done with a careful plan in order to increase safety. Batterers often strike back when they believe that a battered woman is leaving a relationship.

I can use some or all of the following safety strategies:

A. I will leave money and an extra set of keys with _____ so I can leave quickly.

B. I will keep copies of important documents or keys at
_____.

C. I will open a savings account by _____ (date),
to increase my independence.

D. Others things I can do to increase my independence include:
_____

_____

_____.

E. The domestic-violence program's hotline number is
_____. I can seek shelter by calling this hotline.

F. I can keep change for phone calls on me at all times. I understand
that if I use my telephone credit card or my cell phone, the following month's bill will show my batterer the numbers I called after I
left. To keep my telephone communications confidential, either I
must use pay phones, or I can ask a friend to permit me to use
their telephone credit card for a limited time when I first leave.

G. I will check with _____
and _____ to see who
would be able to let me stay with them or lend me some money.

H. I can leave extra clothes with _____.

I. I will sit down and review my safety plan every _____
(how often?) in order to plan the safest way to leave the residence.
_____ (name of domestic-violence
advocate or friend) has agreed to help me review this plan.

J. I will rehearse my escape plan and, as appropriate, practice it with
my children.

Step 3: Safety in My Own Residence

If a woman doesn't live with her batterer, there are many things she can do to
increase her safety in her residence. It may be impossible to do everything at
once, but safety measures can be added step by step.

Safety measures I can use include the following:

A. I can change the locks on my doors and windows as soon as possible.

B. I can replace wooden doors with steel/metal doors.

C. I can install security systems, including additional locks, window
bars, poles to wedge against doors, an electronic system, etc.

D. I can purchase rope ladders to be used for escape from second-floor windows.

E. I can install smoke detectors and purchase fire extinguishers for each floor in my house/apartment.

F. I can install a motion-sensitive lighting system outside that will light up when a person gets close to my house.

G. I will teach my children how to use the telephone to make a collect call to me and to _____ (friend/minister/other) in the event that my partner takes the children.

H. I will tell people who take care of my children who has permission to pick up my children; I will make clear that my partner is not permitted to do so. The people I will inform about pick-up permission include:

School _____

Day-care staff _____

Babysitter _____

Sunday school teacher _____

Teacher _____

Others _____

I. I can inform _____ (neighbor), _____ (pastor), and _____ (friend) that my partner no longer resides with me and that they should call the police if they see him near my residence.

Step 4: Safety with a Protection Order

Many batterers obey protection orders, but one can never be sure who will obey them and who will violate them. I recognize that I may need to ask the police and the courts to enforce my protection order.

The following are some steps I can take to help the enforcement of my protection order:

A. I will keep my protection order at _____ (location). (Always keep it on or near your person. If you change purses, that's the first thing that should go in.)

B. I will give my protection order to police departments in the community where I work, in the communities where I usually visit family or friends, and in the community where I live.

C. There should be a county registry of protection orders that all police departments can call to confirm a protection order. I can check to make sure that my order is in the registry. The telephone number for the county registry of protection orders is

_____.

D. For further safety, if I often visit other counties, I might file my protection order with the court in those counties. I will register my protection order in the following counties: _____,
_____, and _____.

E. I can call the local domestic-violence program if I am not sure about item B, C, or D above, or if I have some problem with my protection order.

F. I will inform my employer, my minister, my closest friend, and _____ that I have a protection order in effect.

G. If my partner destroys my protection order, I can get another copy from the courthouse located at _____.

H. If my partner violates the protection order, I can call the police and report a violation, contact my attorney, call my advocate, and/or advise the court of the violation.

I. If the police do not help, I can contact my advocate or attorney and will file a complaint with the chief of the police department.

J. I can also file a private criminal complaint with the district judge in the jurisdiction where the violation occurred or with the district attorney. I can charge my battering partner with a violation of the protection order and all the crimes that he commits in violating the order. I can call the domestic-violence advocate to help me with this.

Step 5: Safety on the Job and in Public

Each battered woman must decide if and when she will tell others that her partner has battered her and that she may be at continued risk. Friends, family, and coworkers can help to protect women. Each woman should consider carefully who to invite to help secure her safety.

I might do any or all of the following:

A. I can inform my boss, the security supervisor, and _____ _____ at work of my situation.

B. I can ask _____ to help screen my telephone calls at work.

C. When leaving work, I can

_____.

D. When driving home, if problems occur, I can

_____.

E. If I use public transit, I can

_____.

F. I can shop at different grocery stores and malls and shop during different hours from those I used when residing with my battering partner.

G. I can use a different bank and take care of my banking at hours different from those I used when residing with my battering partner.

H. I can also _____

_____

_____

_____

Step 6: Safety and Drug or Alcohol Use

Most people in this culture use alcohol. Many use mood-altering drugs. Much of this use is legal and some is not. The legal outcomes of using illegal drugs can be very hard on a battered woman; they may hurt her relationship with her children and may put her at a disadvantage in legal actions with her battering partner. Therefore, women should carefully consider the potential cost of using illegal drugs. In addition, the use of alcohol or other drugs can reduce a woman's awareness and her ability to act quickly to protect herself from her battering partner. Furthermore, the use of alcohol or other drugs by the batterer may give him/her an excuse to use violence. In consideration of all these factors, a woman needs to make specific safety plans if she or the batterer uses alcohol or other drugs.

If drug or alcohol use has occurred in my relationship with the battering partner, I can enhance my safety by doing some or all of the following:

A. If I am going to use, I can do so in a safe place and with people who understand the risk of violence and are committed to my safety.

B. I can also _____.

C. If my partner is using, I can _____.

D. I can also _____

_____.

E. To safeguard my children, I can _____

and _____.

Step 7: Safety and My Emotional Health

The experience of being battered and verbally degraded by one's partner is usually exhausting and emotionally draining. After leaving an abusive relationship, the process of building a new life for oneself takes much courage and incredible energy.

To conserve my emotional energy and resources and to avoid hard emotional times, I can do some of the following:

A. If I feel down and ready to return to a potentially abusive situation, I can _____

_____

B. When I have to communicate with my partner in person or by telephone, I can _____

_____

C. I can try to use "I can..." statements with myself and to be assertive with others.

D. I can tell myself "_____"
whenever I feel others are trying to control or abuse me.

E. I can read _____
to help me feel stronger.

F. I can call _____ and _____
for support.

G. Other things I can do to help me feel stronger are

_____,

and _____.

H. I can attend workshops and support groups at the domestic-violence program or _____ or
_____ to gain
support and strengthen my relationships with other people.

Step 8: Items to Take when Leaving

When women leave abusive partners, it is important to take certain items with them. In addition, it may be a good idea to give an extra copy of papers and an extra set of clothing to a friend in case you have to leave quickly.

Items with asterisks on the following list are the most important things to take. If there is time, I might also take the other items, or store them outside the home. If I store items outside the home, it might be best to place them in one location, so I can grab them quickly if I have to leave in a hurry. When I leave, I should take:

— Identification for myself*

— Children's birth certificates*

— My birth certificate*

— Social Security cards*

— School and vaccination records*

— Money*

— Checkbook, ATM (automatic teller machine) card*

— Credit cards*

— Keys to house/car/office*

— Driver's license and vehicle registration*

— Medications*

— Welfare identification

— Work permits

— Green card

— Passport(s)

— Divorce papers

— Medical records for all family members

— Lease/rental agreement, house deed, mortgage-payment book

— Bank books

— Insurance papers

— Small objects I can sell

— Address book

— Pictures

— Jewelry

— Children's favorite toys and/or blankets

— Items of special sentimental value

— Telephone numbers I need to know:

Police department near my home _____

Police department near my children's school _____

Police department near work _____

Battered-women's program _____

County registry of protection orders _____

Work number _____

Supervisor's home number _____

Minister _____

Other _____

(Source: Developed by Barbara Hart and Jane Stuehling, Pennsylvania Coalition Against Domestic Violence (PCADV), 524 McKnight Street, Reading, PA 19601, 1992.)

**Appendix II:
A Personal-
ized Safety
Plan**

Appendix III
Diagrama de Igualdad y
Diagrama del Poder y Control

SIN VIOLENCIA

NEGOCIACIÓN JUSTA
• Ante un conflicto, buscar soluciones convenientes para ambas partes. • Aceptar cambios. • Estar dispuesto a llegar a un acuerdo.

CONDUCTA NO AMENAZANTE
• Actuar y hablar de manera que ella se sienta segura y cómoda al hacer sus cosas y al expresarse.

ECONOMÍA COMPARTIDA
• Tomar juntos las decisiones económicas. • Asegurar que los acuerdos económicos beneficien a los dos.

RESPETO
• Escucharla sin juzgarla. • Apoyarla y comprenderla. • Valorar sus opiniones.

IGUALDAD

RESPONSABILIDAD COMPARTIDA
• Llegar a un acuerdo para una justa distribución de las tareas de la casa. • Tomar juntos las decisiones familiares.

CONFIANZA Y APOYO
• Apoyarla en sus metas en la vida. • Respetarle sus sentimientos, amigo(a)s, actividades, y opiniones.

ASUMIR LA RESPONSABILIDAD PATERNA
• Compartir las responsabilidades de la crianza. • Ser un modelo de conducta para sus hijo(a)s, actuando positivamente y sin violencia.

HONESTIDAD Y RESPONSABILIDAD
• Aceptar responsabilidad por sus acciones. • Reconocer y aceptar que actuó violentamente en el pasado. • Reconocer que estaba equivocado. • Comunicarse abiertamente y con la verdad.

SIN VIOLENCIA

Diagrama de Igualdad
Domestic Abuse Prevention Project, 202 East Superior St., Duluth MN 55802, (218) 722-2781, www.duluth-model.org.

A Spanish-language version of the Power and Control Wheel has been included in the second edition of the book for the benefit of advocates who work with Spanish speaking women.

357

**Appendix III:
Diagrama de
Igualdad y
Diagrama del
Poder y
Control**

Diagrama del Poder y Control

*Domestic Abuse Prevention Project, 202 East Superior St., Duluth MN 55802, (218)
722-2781, www.duluth-model.org.*

Notes

Chapter 1: The Dynamics of Abusive Relationships

1. American Psychological Association Presidential Task Force on Violence and the Family, *Violence and the Family* (Washington, DC: American Psychological Association, 1996), 19.
2. U.S. Department of Justice, *Intimate Partner Violence, 1993–2001* (Washington, DC: Office of Justice Programs, Bureau of Justice Statistics, February 2003).
3. National Domestic Violence Hotline, "National Statistics," no date. Retrieved June 13, 2004, from http://www.ndvh.org.
4. U.S. Department of Justice, *Violence by Intimates: Analysis of Data on Crimes by Current or Former Spouses, Boyfriends, and Girlfriends* (Washington, DC: Office of Justice Programs, Bureau of Justice Statistics, March 1998).
5. Gelles, R.J., *Intimate Violence in Families* (Thousand Oaks, CA: Sage Publications, 1997).
6. Gelles, R.J., 93.
7. Currie, D.H., "Violent Men or Violent Women? Whose Definition Counts?" in Bergen, R.K. (ed.), *Issues in Intimate Violence* (Thousand Oaks, CA: Sage Publications, 1998).
8. Ibid.
9. Walker, L., *The Battered Woman* (New York: Harper and Row, 1979), 21.
10. National Woman Abuse Prevention Project, *Domestic Violence Fact Sheet: Men Who Batter* (Washington, DC: no date).
11. American Psychological Association Presidential Task Force on Violence and the Family, 21.
12. Gondolf, E.W., "MCMI-III Results for Batterer Program Participants in Four Cities: Less 'Pathological' than Expected," *Journal of Family Violence* 14:1 (1999): 1–17.
13. American Psychological Association Presidential Task Force on Violence and the Family, 82.
14. Herman, J., *Trauma and Recovery* (New York: BasicBooks, 1992), 74–95.
15. Pence, E., *In Our Best Interest: A Process for Personal and Social Change* (Duluth: Minnesota Program Development, 1987).
16. Pence, E. and Paymar, M., *Education Groups for Men Who Batter: The Duluth Model* (New York: Springer Publishing Company, 1993), 2.

17. See Gelles, R.J., for a discussion of the various theoretical positions on domestic violence.
18. Gelles, R.J., 132.
19. Ibid., 132–39.
20. Ibid., 139.
21. Graham, D.L., Rawlings, E., and Rimini, N., "Survivors of Terror: Battered Women, Hostages and the Stockholm Syndrome," in Yllo, K., and Bogard, M. (eds.), *Feminist Perspectives on Wife Abuse* (Newbury Park, CA: Sage Publications, 1988), 217–33.
22. Rich, A., *On Lies, Secrets, and Silence* (New York: W.W. Norton and Company, 1979), 122. See also Pence, E., 1987.
23. Ferraro, K.J., "Rationalizing Violence: How Battered Women Stay," *Victimology* 8 (1983): 203–12.
24. Dutton, M.A., "Critique of the 'Battered Women Syndrome' Model," January 1997. Retrieved from the National Electronic Network on Violence Against Women, www.vawnet.org. See also Walker, L.E., "Battered Women and Learned Helplessness," *Victimology: An International Journal* 2:3/4 (1977–1978): 525–34.
25. Ibid.
26. Ibid.
27. Gondolf, E., and Fisher, E., *Battered Women as Survivors: An Alternative to Treating Learned Helplessness* (Boston, MA: Lexington Books, 1988), 91–93.
28. Walker, L., 1979, 49–61.
29. National Coalition Against Domestic Violence, "Predictors of Domestic Violence." Adapted from work by AMEND, Lenore Walker, Lydia Walker, and Jennifer Baker Fleming. Retrieved May 2, 2004, from http://www.ncadv.org/problem/predictors.htm.
30. U.S. Department of Justice, 2003.
31. American Psychological Association Presidential Task Force on Violence and the Family, 39.
32. National Woman Abuse Prevention Project, *Domestic Violence Fact Sheet: The Lethality of Domestic Violence* (Washington, DC: no date).

Chapter 2: The Effects of Family Violence on Children

1. Edleson, J.L., and Beeman, S.K., "Responding to the Co-occurrence of Child Maltreatment and Adult Domestic Violence in Hennepin County," 2000. Retrieved April 2, 2004, from http://www.mincava.umn.edu.
2. Bancroft, R.L., "The Connection Between Batterers and Child Sexual Abuse Perpetrators," 1997. Retrieved June 12, 2004, from http://www.mincava.umn.edu.
3. Ibid.
4. Edleson, J.L., Mbilinyi, L.F., Shetty, S., *Parenting in the Context of Domestic Violence* (San Francisco, CA: Judicial Council of California, Administrative Office of the Courts, Center for Families, Children and the Courts, March 2003), 10.

5. National Coalition Against Domestic Violence, *Fact Sheet* (Washington, DC: National Coalition Against Domestic Violence, 1993).

6. Martin, D., *Battered Wives* (Volcano, CA: Volcano Press, 1981), 22–24.

7. Doyne, S., Bowermaster, J., and Meloy, R., "Custody Disputes Involving Domestic Violence: Making Children's Needs a Priority," *Juvenile and Family Court Journal* 50:2 (1999). See also National Coalition Against Domestic Violence.

8. Straus, M., "Children as Witnesses to Marital Violence: A Risk Factor for Lifelong Problems among a Nationally Representative Sample of American Men and Women." Paper presented at the Ross Roundtable on Children and Violence, Washington, DC, September, 1991. See also Carlson, B.E., "Children's Observations of Interparental Violence," in Roberts, A.R. (ed.), *Battered Women and Their Families* (New York: Springer, 1984), 147–67.

9. Edleson, J.L., et al., 2003, 6.

10. See Bancroft, L., and Silverman, J., *The Batterer as Parent* (Thousand Oaks, CA: Sage Publications, 2002).

11. Edleson, J.L., et al., 2003, 8.

12. Edleson, J.L., "Problems Associated with Children's Witnessing of Domestic Violence," April 1999, 3. Retrieved July 3, 2004, from http://www.vawnet .org.

13. Bancroft, L., "The Batterer as a Parent," *Synergy* (newsletter of the National Council of Juvenile and Family Court Judges) 6:1 (Winter 2002): 6–8.

14. Bancroft, L., and Silverman, J., 2002.

15. Edleson, J.L., et al., 2003, 14.

16. Van Horn, P., and Lieberman, A., *Domestic Violence and Parenting: A Review of the Literature* (San Francisco: Judicial Council of California, Administrative Office of the Courts, Center for Families, Children and the Courts, 2002).

17. Edleson, J.L., et al., 2003, 14.

18. Fleury, R.E., Sullivan, C.M., and Bybee, D.I., "When Ending the Relationship Does Not End the Violence," *Violence Against Women* 6 (2000): 1363–83.

19. Holden, G.W., et al., "Parenting Behavior and Beliefs of Battered Women," in Holden, G.W., Geffner, R., and Jouriles, E.N. (eds.), *Children Exposed to Marital Violence: Theory, Research, and Applied Issues* (Washington, DC: American Psychological Association, 1998), 185–222.

20. Stark, E., and Flitcraft, A., "Women and Children at Risk: A Feminist Perspective on Child Abuse," in Bergen, R.K. (ed.), *Issues in Intimate Violence* (Thousand Oaks, CA: Sage Publications, 1998), 30.

21. See Jacobs, M.S., "Requiring Battered Women [to] Die: Murder Liability for Mothers Under Failure to Protect Statutes," *Journal of Criminal Law and Criminology* 88, no. 2 (Winter, 1998): 579–661. See also Schechter, S., and Edleson, J.L., "In the Best Interest of Women and Children: A Call for Collaboration Between Child Welfare and Domestic Violence Constituencies," 1994. Retrieved February 21, 2004, from http://www.mincava.umn.edu.

22. Goodman, E.J., "Battered Women and Their Fight to Keep Their Children," GothamGazette.com, January 2004. Retrieved April 21, 2004, from

http://www.gothamgazette.com/article/law/20040128/13/855.

23. Ibid.

24. Ibid.

25. Family Violence Prevention Fund, "Ruling May Help New York Battered Mothers Keep Their Children," *News Flash,* October 28, 2004.

26. Schechter, S., and Edleson, J.L.

27 Jaffe, P.G., Wolfe, D.A., and Wilson, S.K., *Children of Battered Women* (Newbury Park, CA: Sage Publications, 1990), 26–42. See also Groves, B.M., "Mental Health Services for Children Who Witness Domestic Violence," *Future of Children* 9:3 (1999): 122–132. Retrieved March 24, 2004, from http://www.futureofchildren.org; Kolbo, J., Blakely, E., and Engleman, D., "Children Who Witness Domestic Violence: A Review of Empirical Literature," *Journal of Interpersonal Violence* 11:2 (1996): 281–93.

28. Jaffe, P.G., et al., 1990, 28–29. See also Edleson, J.L., 1999.

29. Sroufe, L.A., and Fleeson, J., "Attachment and the Construction of Relationships," in Hartup, W.W., and Rubin, Z. (eds.), *Relationships and Development* (Hillsdale, NJ: Lawrence Erlbaum, 1986), 51–72.

30. Wolfe, D.A., et al., "Child Witnesses to Violence Between Parents: Critical Issues in Behavioral and Social Adjustment," *Journal of Abnormal Child Psychology* 14:1 (1986): 95–104.

31. Hughes, H.M., "Research with Children in Shelters: Implications for Clinical Services," *Children Today* (1986), 21–25.

32. Hyde, M., *Cry Softly! The Story of Child Abuse* (Philadelphia, PA: The Westminister Press, 1986), 28–29.

33. Jaffe, P.G., et al., 1990, 27–31.

34. Chamberlain, P., and Reid, J., "Differences in Risk Factors and Adjustments for Male and Female Delinquents in Treatment and Foster Care," *Journal of Child and Family Studies* 3:1 (1994): 23–39.

35. Wolfe, D.A., et al., "Strategies to Address Violence in the Lives of High Risk Youth," in Peled, E., Jaffe, P.G., and Edleson, J.L. (eds.), *Ending the Cycle of Violence: Community Responses to Children of Battered Women* (New York: Sage Publications, 1995).

36. American Psychiatric Association, *Diagnostic and Statistical Manual of Mental Disorders DSM-IV,* 4th edition (Washington, DC: American Psychiatric Association, 1994).

37. Grych, J.H., et al., "Patterns of Adjustment among Children of Battered Women," *Journal of Consulting and Clinical Psychology* 68 (2000): 84–94.

38. Edleson, J.L., et al., 2003, 16. See also Garmezy, N., "Stressors in Childhood," in Garmezy, N., and Rutter, M. (eds.), *Stress, Coping and Development in Children* (New York: McGraw Hill, 1983), 43–84.

39. Hess, R.D., and Camara, K.A., "Post-divorce Family Relationships as Mediating Factors in the Consequences of Divorce for Children," *Journal of Social Issues* 35 (1979): 79–96.

40. Kurdek, L.A., "An Integrative Perspective on Children's Divorce Adjustment," *American Psychologist* 36 (1981): 856–66.

Chapter 3: Teen Dating Violence

1. From *In Touch with Teens: A Relationship Violence Prevention Curriculum for Youth Ages 12–19* (Los Angeles, CA: Los Angeles Commission on Assaults Against Women, 1993, 1995). "Eddie's Got a Fast Car" is reprinted with permission.

2. Levy, B. (ed.), *Dating Violence: Young Women in Danger* (Seattle, WA: Seal Press, 1991), 3.

3. Silverman, J.G., et al., "Dating Violence Against Adolescent Girls and Associated Substance Use, Unhealthy Weight Control, Sexual Risk Behavior, Pregnancy, and Suicidality," *JAMA: Journal of the American Medical Association* 286:5 (2001): 572–79.

4. Levy, B. (ed.), 4.

5. Kanin, E.J., "Male Aggression in Dating-Courtship Relations," *Journal of Sociology* 63 (1957): 197–204.

6. Henton, J., et al., "Romance and Violence in Dating Relationships," *Journal of Family Issues* 4 (1983): 467–82. See also Laner, M.R., and Thompson, J., "Abuse and Aggression in Courting Couples," *Deviant Behavior* 3 (1982): 229–44.

7. Cate, R.M., et al., "Premarital Abuse: A Social Psychological Perspective," *Journal of Family Issues* 3 (1982): 79–91. See also Henton, J., et al.

8. Peacock, D., and Rothman, E., *Working with Young Men Who Batter: Current Strategies and New Directions,* National Resource Center on Domestic Violence, November 2001, 5. Retrieved June 22, 2004, from http://www.vawnet.org.

9. Ibid., p. 2.

10. Malamuth, N.M., "Rape Proclivity among Males," *Journal of Social Issues* 37:4 (1981): 138–57.

11. Sugarman, D.B., and Hotaling, G.T., "Dating Violence: A Review of Contextual and Risk Factors," in Levy, B. (ed.), 106–7.

12. Dutton, D.G., "Wife Assaulter's Explanation for Assault: The Neutralization of Self-Punishment," *Canadian Journal of Behavioral Science* 18:4 (1986): 381–90.

13. Levy, B. (ed.), 8–9.

14. Nicarthy, G., *Getting Free* (Seattle, WA: Seal Press, 1986), 269.

15. Giggans, P.O., "Youth in Jeopardy," *Livewire* 4:1 (Fall 1992): 1.

16. NiCarthy, G., "Addictive Love and Abuse: A Course for Teenage Women," in Levy, B. (ed.), 241–43.

17. Johnson, S.A., *When "I Love You" Turns Violent: Abuse in Dating Relationships* (Far Hills, NJ: New Horizon Press, 1993), 75–83.

18. Kessner, E., "Sweetheart Murders: When Teen Boyfriends Turn into Killers," *Redbook,* March 1988, 130–89.

19. Gamache, D., "Domination and Control: The Social Context of Dating Violence," in Levy, B. (ed.), 76–77.

20. Makepeace, J.M., "Courtship Violence among College Students," *Family Relations* 30 (1981): 97–102. See also Roscoe, B., and Callahan, J.E., "Adolescents Self Report of Violence in Families and Dating Relations," *Adolescence* 20 (1985): 545–53; and Roscoe, B., and Kelsey, T., "Dating Violence among High School Students," *Psychology* 23:1 (1986): 53–59.

21. Lane, K.E., and Gwartney-Gibbs, P.A., "Violence in the Context of Dating and Sex," *Journal of Family Issues* 6:1 (1985): 45–59.

22. Levy, B. (ed.), 9.

23. Fisher, G.J., "College Student Attitudes Toward Forcible Date Rape," *Archives of Sexual Behavior* 15:6 (1986): 457–67.

24. Miller, B., and Marshall, J., "Coercive Sex on the University Campus," *Journal of College Student Personnel* 28:1 (1987): 38–47.

25. Levy, B. (ed.), 4–5.

26. Gamache, D., 74.

27. Pirog-Good, M.A., and Stets, J.E., "The Help-Seeking Behavior of Physically and Sexually Abused College Students," in Pirog-Good, M.A., and Stets, J.E. (eds.), *Violence in Dating Relationships: Emerging Social Issues* (New York: Praeger Publishers, 1989), 108–25. See also Henton, J., et al.; Makepeace, J.M., 1981; Stets, J.E., and Pirog-Good, M.A., "Patterns of Physical and Sexual Abuse for Men and Women in Dating Relationships: A Descriptive Analysis," *Journal of Family Violence* 4:1 (1989): 63–76.

28. Levy, B. (ed.), 5.

29. McFarlane, J., "Battering in Pregnancy: The Tip of the Iceberg," *Women and Health* 15:3 (1989): 69–84. See also Campbell, J., "Nursing Assessment for Risk of Homicide with Battered Women," *Advances in Nursing Science* 8:4 (1986): 36–51.

30. McFarlane, J., "Violence During Teen Pregnancy: Health Consequences for Mother and Child," in Levy, B. (ed.), 136–37. See also Stark, E., and Flitcraft, A., *Women at Risk: Domestic Violence and Women's Health* (Thousand Oaks, CA: Sage Publications, 1996), 17.

31. Bullock, L., and McFarlane, J., "A Program to Prevent Battering of Pregnant Students," *Response* 11:1 (1988): 18–19.

32. Stark, E., and Flitcraft, A., 11 and 204. See also McFarlane, J., 137–41.

33. White, E.C., *Chain Chain Change: For Black Women Dealing with Physical and Emotional Abuse* (Seattle, WA: Seal Press, 1985).

34. White, E.C., "The Abused Black Woman: Challenging a Legacy of Pain," in Levy, B. (ed.), 85–86.

35. Levy, B. (ed.), 6–7.

36. Yoshihama, M., Parekh, A., and Boyington, D., "Dating Violence in Asian/Pacific Communities," in Levy, B. (ed.), 192.

37. Symonds, M., "Victims of Violence: Psychological Effects and After-Effects," *American Journal of Psychoanalysis* 35 (1975): 19–26.

38. Yoshihama, M., et al., 188–93.

39. Ibid., 189–90.

40. Levy, B., and Lobel, K., "Lesbian Teens in Abusive Relationships," in Levy, B. (ed.), 205–6.

41. Ibid., 206–7.

42. Rickert, V.I., and Wiemann, C.M., "Date Rape among Adolescents and Young Adults," *Journal of Pediatric Adolescent Gynecology* 11:4 (1998): 167–75.

43. Fisher, B., Cullen, F.T., and Turner, M.G., *The Sexual Victimization of College Women* (Washington, DC: Office of Justice Programs, U.S. Department of Justice, December 2000), 17.

44. Schwartz, R.H., Milteer, R., and LeBeau, M.A., "Drug Facilitated Sexual Assault," *Southern Medical Journal* 93:6 (June 2000): 558–61.

45. Ibid.

46. Hensley, L.G., "Drug-Facilitated Sexual Assault on Campus: Challenges and Interventions," *Journal of College Counseling* 5 (Fall 2002): 175–81.

47. The National Institute on Drug Abuse, *Club Drugs* (Washington, DC: National Institutes of Health, U.S. Department of Health and Human Services, January 2004).

48. Schwartz, R.H., et al., 558–61.

49. The National Institute on Drug Abuse, 1–3.

50. Schwartz, R.H., et al., 558–61.

51. The National Women's Health Information Center, *Date Rape Drugs* (Washington, DC: Office on Women's Health, U.S. Department of Health and Human Services, no date).

52. Roscoe, B., and Callahan, J.E., 545–53. See also Lane, K.E., and Gwartney-Gibbs, P.A., 45–59.

53. Henton, J., et al., 467–82. See also Makepeace, J.M., "Gender Differences in Courtship Violence Victimization," *Family Relations* 35 (1986): 383–88.

54. National Victim Center and Crime Victims Research and Treatment Center, *Rape in America: A Report to the Nation* (Arlington, VA: National Victim Center and Crime Victims Research and Treatment Center, April 1992).

55. Steketee, M.S.S., and Foa, E.B., "Rape Victims: Post-Traumatic Stress Responses and Their Treatment," *Journal of Anxiety Disorders* 1 (1987), 69–86.

56. Gallers, J., and Lawrence, K.J., "Overcoming Post-Traumatic Stress Disorder in Adolescent Date Rape Survivors," in Levy, B. (ed.), 172.

57. Ibid., 174.

58. Ibid., 173–74.

59. Sousa, C., Bancroft, L., and German, T., *Preventing Teen Dating Violence: Three Session Curriculum for Teaching Adolescents* (Cambridge, MA: Dating Intervention Project, 1989).

60. Texas Council on Family Violence and the Bridge Over Troubled Waters, *Dating Violence: An Anti-Victimization Program* (Austin, TX, no date). See also Johnson, S.A., 175–76.

61. Schechter, S., *Guidelines for Mental Health Practitioners in Domestic Violence* (Denver, CO: National Coalition Against Domestic Violence, 1987).

62. Nicarthy, G., 1986, 274–75.

63. Bartels, D., *What Teens Do and Don't Need from Adults and Peers* (Austin, TX: Austin Center for Battered Women, no date).

64. Levy, B. (ed.), 7.

65. Sugarman, D.B., and Hotaling, G.T., 116–17.

66. Peacock, D., and Rothman, E., 3.

67. Ibid.

68. See Levy, B., "Support Groups: Empowerment for Young Women Abused in Dating Relationships," in Levy, B. (ed.), 232–39.

69. See Rosenbluth, B., *Expect Respect: A Support Group Curriculum for Safe and Healthy Relationships* (Austin, TX: SafePlace, 1995–2004 editions).

Chapter 4: The Intimate Relationship Between Substance Abuse and Domestic Violence

1. Gelles, R.J., "Alcohol and Other Drugs Are Associated with Violence—They Are Not Its Cause," in Gelles, R.J., and Loseke, D.R. (eds.), *Current Controversies on Family Violence* (Newbury Park, CA: Sage Publications, 1993), 184.

2. Byles, J.A., "Violence, Alcohol Problems and Other Problems in the Disintegrating Family," *Journal of Studies on Alcohol* 39 (1978): 551–53. See also Coleman, D.H., and Straus, M.A., "Alcohol Abuse and Family Violence," in Gottheil, E., et al. (eds.), *Alcohol, Drug Abuse and Aggression* (Springfield, IL: Charles C. Thomas, 1983), 104–24; Leonard, K.E., et al., "Patterns of Alcohol Use and Physically Aggressive Behavior," *Journal of Studies on Alcohol* 46 (1985): 279–82; Kaufman Kantor, G., and Straus, M.A., "Substance Abuse as a Precipitant of Wife Abuse Victimization," *American Journal of Alcohol Abuse* 15 (1989): 173–89; Martin, S.E., "The Epidemiology of Alcohol-Related Interpersonal Violence," *Alcohol Health and Research World* 16 (1992): 230–37.

3. Roy, M., "Four Thousand Partners in Violence: A Trend Analysis," in Roy, M. (ed.), *The Abusive Partner: An Analysis of Domestic Battering* (New York: Van Nostrand Reinhold, 1982), 17–35. See also Rosenbaum, A., and O'Leary, K.D., "Marital Violence: Characteristics of Abusive Couples," *Journal of Consulting and Clinical Psychology* 49 (1981): 63–71; Browne, A., *When Battered Women Kill* (New York: The Free Press, 1987), 12–71; Fagan, J.A., Stewart, D.K., and Hansen, K.V., "Violent Men or Violent Husbands: Background Factors and Situational Correlates," in Finkelhor, D., et al. (eds.), *The Dark Side of Families* (Beverly Hills, CA: Sage Publications, 1983), 49–67; Gondolf, E.W., and Fisher, E.R., *Battered Women as Survivors: An Alternative to Treating Learned Helplessness* (Lexington, MA: Lexington Books, 1988), 6–7; Eberle, P., "Alcohol Abusers and Non-Users: A Discriminant Analysis of Differences Between Two Subgroups of Batterers," *Journal of Health and Social Behavior* 23:3 (September 1982): 260–71; Fitch, F., and Papantonio, A., "Men Who Batter: Some Pertinent Characteristics," *Journal of Nervous and Mental Diseases* 171:3 (March 1983): 190–92.

4. Browne, A., 12–73. See also Eberle, P., 260–71; Flanzer, J.P., "Alcohol and Family Violence: Double Trouble," in Roy, M. (ed.), 136–41; Fagan, J.A., et al., 49–67.

5. Fitch, F., et al., 190–92. See also Browne, A., 12–71.

6. Miller, M.M., and Potter-Efron, R.T., "Aggression and Violence Associated with Substance Abuse," in Potter-Efron, R.T., and Potter-Efron, P.S. (eds.), *Aggression, Family Violence and Chemical Dependency* (New York: Haworth Press, 1990), 1–36. See also Gelles, R.J., and Straus, M.A., *Intimate Violence* (New York: Simon and Schuster, 1988), 46–48.

7. Gelles, R.J., 1993, 187–88. See also Nicholi, A., "The Non-Therapeutic Use of Psychoactive Drugs," *New England Journal of Medicine* 308 (1983): 925–33; Taylor, S., and Leonard, K.E., "Alcohol and Human Physical Aggression," in Green, R., and Donnerstein, E. (eds.), *Aggression: Theoretical and Empirical Reviews,* vol. 2 (New York: Academic Press, 1983), 77–111.

8. Martin, D., *Battered Wives* (Volcano, CA: Volcano Press, 1981), 57.

9. Gondolf, E.W., "Alcohol Abuse, Wife Assault and Power Needs," in *The Relationship Between Substance Abuse and Domestic Violence,* compiled by the Texas Council on Family Violence, Austin, TX, July, 1994, 42–43. See also Gelles, R.J., and Straus, M.A., 45–46.

10. See MacAndrew, C., and Edgerton, R.B., *Drunken Comportment: A Social Explanation* (Chicago, IL: Aldine, 1969).

11. Lang, A.R., et al., "Effects of Alcohol on Aggression in Male Social Drinkers," *Journal of Abnormal Psychology* 84 (1975): 508–18.

12. Bard, M., and Zacker, J., "Assaultiveness and Alcohol Use in Family Disputes," *Criminology* 12 (1974): 281–92.

13. See Flanzer, J.P., "Alcohol and Other Drugs Are Key Causal Agents of Violence," in Gelles, R.J., and Loseke, D.R. (eds.), 171–79.

14. Martin, D., p. 57. See also Browne, A., 73.

15. Gondolf, E.W., 40.

16. Zubretsky, T.M., and Digirolamo, K.M., "Adult Domestic Violence: The Alcohol Connection," *Violence Update* 4:7 (March 1994): 1–2.

17. Gondolf, E.W., 40.

18. Lemle, R., and Mishkind, M., "Alcohol and Masculinity," *Journal of Substance Abuse Treatment* 6 (1989): 213–22. See also Lisansky Gomberg, E.S., "Learned Helplessness, Depression and Alcohol Problems of Women," in Russianoff, P. (ed.), *Women in Crisis* (New York: Human Science Press, 1981), 41–42.

19. American Psychological Association Presidential Task Force on Violence and the Family, *Violence and the Family* (Washington, DC: American Psychological Association, 1996), 38.

20. Gelles, R.J., 1993, 194.

21. Stark, E., and Flitcraft, A., *Women at Risk: Domestic Violence and Women's Health* (Thousand Oaks, CA: Sage Publications, 1996), 8–18 and 162–63. See also Gelles, R.J., and Straus, M.A., 136–37.

22. National Woman Abuse Prevention Project, *Domestic Violence Factsheet: Alcohol Abuse and Domestic Violence* (Washington, DC, no date).

23. DiMona, L., and Herndon, C. (eds.), *The 1995 Information Please Women's Sourcebook* (Boston, MA: Houghton Mifflin Company, 1994), 204. See also

Texas Commission on Alcohol and Drug Abuse, *New View* (Austin, TX, September 1992), 4–5.

24. National Council on Alcoholism, Inc., *Alcoholism and Alcohol-Related Problems Among Women* (Washington, DC, December 1985). See also DiMona, L., and Herndon, C., 203–4.

25. Lisansky Gomberg, E.S., 41–42. See also National Institute on Drug Abuse (NIDA), *Women and Drug Abuse* (Rockville, MD, March 1994), 2.

26. National Woman Abuse Prevention Project. See also Stark, E., and Flitcraft, A., 185; Thorne-Finch, R., *Ending the Silence* (Toronto, Canada: University of Toronto Press, 1992), 41.

27. Herman, J.L., *Trauma and Recovery* (New York: Basic Books, 1992), 42–5.

28. Friedman, C., "Alcohol and Other Drug Abuse in the Lives of Battered Women and Their Children," *NCADV Voice, Special Edition: Chemical Dependency, Co-Dependency and Battered Women* (Summer 1988), 16.

29. Stark, E., and Flitcraft, A., 95–102. See also Jones, A., *Next Time She'll Be Dead* (Boston, MA: Beacon Press, 1994), 145–52.

30. Herman, J.L., 78. See also NIDA, 2.

31. Beckman, L., and Amaro, H., "Patterns of Women's Use of Alcohol Treatment Agencies," in Wilsnack, S., and Beckman, L. (eds.), *Alcohol Problems in Women* (New York: Guilford Press, 1984), 342. See also Zubretsky, T.M., and Digirolamo, K.M., 3.

32. Herman, J.L., 161.

33. Haven House and the Alcoholism Center for Women, *Double Jeopardy: A Two Day Training for Those Working in the Alcohol or Domestic Violence Fields,* California State University, Los Angeles, CA, March 20–21, 1987, 17–24.

34. Ibid., 1–14. See also Black, C., *It Will Never Happen To Me* (New York: Ballantine Books, 1981), 149–51.

35. Black, C., 150.

36. Grusznski, R.J., and Carrillo, T., "Who Completes Batterer's Treatment Groups?: An Empirical Investigation," *Journal of Family Violence* 3 (1988): 141–50. See also Cocozzelli, C., and Hudson, C., "Recent Advances in Alcoholism Diagnosis and Treatment Assessment Research: Implications for Practice," *Social Science Review* 37 (1989): 533–52.

37. Battered-women's advocates may want to attend an AA, NA, or Al-Anon meeting. It would also be helpful to become familiar with AA's Twelve Steps and Twelve Traditions. Likewise, substance-abuse counselors may want to read more about the battered-women's movement and the philosophies upon which it is based. Several excellent books about battered women are listed throughout this book. A good introductory reference is Del Martin's *Battered Wives.*

38. See Alcoholics Anonymous World Services, Inc., *Alcoholics Anonymous* (New York: Alcoholics Anonyomous, 1976).

39. Gondolf, E.W., 48.

40. Ibid., 49–50.

41. Ibid., 49.

42. Black, C., 163.

43. See Al-Anon Family Group Headquarters, Inc., *Al-Anon Family Groups* (New York: Al-Anon Family Groups, 1986).

44. Zubretsky, T.M., and Digirolamo, K.M., 3.

45. Texas Council on Family Violence, *Points to Remember in Working with Battered Women,* Austin, TX, no date.

46. DiMona, L., and Herndon, C., 204.

47. Blume, S., "Women, Alcohol and Drugs," in Miller, N.S. (ed.), *Comprehensive Handbook of Drug and Alcohol Addiction* (New York: Marcel Dekker, Inc., 1991), 147–77.

48. Austin Women's Addiction Referral and Education Center (AWARE), *Things to Ponder,* Austin, TX, no date.

49. Zubretsky, T.M., and Digirolamo, K.M., 3.

50. Amaro, H., Beckman, L., and Mays, V., "A Comparison of Black and White Women Entering Alcoholism Treatment," *Journal of Studies on Alcohol* 48 (1987): 220–28.

51. AWARE.

52. DiMona, L., and Herndon, C., 203.

53. NIDA, 3.

54. National Council on Alcoholism, Inc.

55. See Unterberger, G., "Twelve Steps for Women Alcoholics," *The Christian Century,* December 6, 1989, 1150–52. See also Clemmons, P., "Feminists, Spirituality, and the Twelve Steps of Alcoholics Anonymous," *Women and Therapy* 11:2 (1991): 97–109.

Chapter 5: Battered Women and the Legal System

1. Buzawa, E.S., and Buzawa, C.G., *Domestic Violence: The Criminal Justice Response* (Thousand Oaks, CA: Sage Publications, 1996), 243.

2. Texas Council on Family Violence, *Working Together for Change: Battered Women's Advocates and the Criminal Justice System,* Austin, TX, 1994, Section III, 2.

3. Buzawa, E.S., and Buzawa, C.G., 155.

4. Sherman, L., and Beck, R., "The Specific Deterrent Effects of Arrest for Domestic Assault, " *American Sociological Review* 49 (1984): 261–72.

5. Binder, A., and Meeker, J.W., "Experiments as Reforms," *Journal of Criminal Justice* 18 (1998): 348.

6. Koss, M.P., "Blame, Shame, and Community: Justice Responses to Violence Against Women," Minnesota Center Against Violence and Abuse, 2000. Retrieved May 27, 2004, from http://www.mincava.umn.edu/documents/koss/koss.html.

7. Mills, L.G., *Insult to Injury: Rethinking Our Responses to Intimate Abuse* (Princeton, NJ: Princeton University Press, 2003), 37.

8. See Buzawa, E.S., and Buzawa, C.G; Mills, L.G.; Hart, B.J., "Domestic Violence Intervention System: A Model for Response to Woman Abuse," Minnesota Center Against Violence and Abuse, no date, retrieved October 10,

2001, from http://www.mincava.umn.edu/hart/dvinter.htm. See also Koss, M.P. and Ho, T.N., "Domestic Violence in a Southern City: The Effects of a Mandatory Arrest Policy on Male-Versus-Female Aggravated Assault Incidents," *American Journal of Criminal Justice* 25:1 (2000): 107–118.

9. Hart, B.J.

10. Koss, M.P.

11. Dunford, F.W., "The Measurement of Recidivism in Cases of Spousal Assault," *Journal of Criminal Law and Criminology* 83 (1992): 122–3.

12. Mills, L.G., 38.

13. Smith, A., "Domestic Violence Laws: The Voices of Battered Women," *Violence and Victims* 16 (2001): 102.

14. Mills, L.G., 39.

15. State of Connecticut, *Summary of Family Violence Arrest Incidents in Connecticut 1987–1997,* Office of Policy and Management Statistical Analysis Center, 1998.

16. Dasgupta, S.D., "Towards an Understanding of Women's Use of Non-Lethal Violence in Intimate Heterosexual Relationships," Violence Against Women Online Resources, February 2001. Retrieved January 19, 2004, from http://www.umn.edu/documents/vawnet/towards/towards.html.

17. Hirschel, D., and Buzawa, E., "Understanding the Context of Dual Arrest with Directions for Future Research," *Violence Against Women* 8:12 (December 2002): 1449–73).

18. Henning, K., and Feder, L., "A Comparison of Men and Women Arrested for Domestic Violence: Who Presents the Greater Threat?" *Journal of Family Violence* 19:2 (April 2004): 69–80).

19. Ibid, 77–78.

20. House, E., *When Women Use Force: An Advocacy Guide to Understanding the Issue and Conducting an Assessment with Individuals Who Have Used Force to Determine Their Eligibility for Services from a Domestic Violence Agency* (Ann Arbor, MI: Domestic Violence Project/SAFE House, no date).

21. Dasgupta, S.D., 5.

22. House, E., 4.

23. Dasgupta, S.D., 8.

24. Hirschel, D., and Buzawa, E., 1450.

25. House, E., 4.

26. Henning, K., and Feder, L., 78.

27. House, E., 5–11.

28. Deller Ross, S., et al., *The Rights of Women: The Basic ACLU Guide to Women's Rights,* Carbondale, IL: Southern Illinois University Press, 1993, p. 155.

29. U.S. Department of Justice, *Increasing Your Safety: Full Faith and Credit for Protection Orders* (Washington, DC, no date), 3.

30. Office of Victims of Crime, "Enforcement of Protective Orders," Legal Series Bulletin #4, 2002. Available from http://www.ojp.usdoj.gov/ovc/publications/bulletins/legalseries/bulletin4/1.html.

31. Deller Ross, S., et al., 156. See also Finn, P., and Colson, S., *Civil Protection Orders: Legislation, Current Court Practice and Enforcement* (Washington, DC: National Institute of Justice, Office of Justice Programs, U.S. Department of Justice, March 1990), v–1; Buzawa, E.S., and Buzawa, C.G., 188.

32. Deller Ross, S., et al., 156.

33. Finn, P., and Colson, S., 2–3.

34. Ibid., 3.

35. Ibid., 15.

36. Ibid., 2.

37. Newmark, L., and Harrell, A., "Study on Civil Protection Orders," *NCADV Voice,* Winter 1994, 16–17.

38. Nickum, L.L., "The Protective Order Experience," *The River,* Summer/Fall 1994, 5.

39. National Institute of Justice, *Legal Interventions in Family Violence: Research Findings and Policy Implications,* Washington, DC, 1998.

40. Office of Victims of Crime, 2.

41. Finn, P., and Colson, S., 2.

42. Office of Victims of Crime, 3.

43. Finn, P., and Colson, S., 15.

44. Nickum, L.L., 5.

45. Finn, P., and Colson, S., 63.

46. Ibid., 49.

47. Office of Victims of Crime.

48. Finn, P., and Colson, S., 4.

49. U.S. Department of Justice.

50. Lardner, G., "The Stalking Game," *The Washington Post,* June 2, 1996.

51. Office of Victims of Crime, p. 1.

52. National Institute of Justice, *Domestic Violence, Stalking, and Antistalking Legislation: Annual Report to Congress,* Washington, DC: Office of Justice Programs, U.S. Department of Justice, March 1996, p. 1.

53. Ibid., p. 9.

54. Ibid., pp. 6–7.

55. Ibid., p. 6.

56. Herman, K., "Anti-Stalking Law Rejected by State Court," *The Austin American Statesman,* September 12, 1996, A1.

57. National Institute of Justice, 1996, 4.

58. Ibid., B-2.

59. Walls, L.F., "Stalked!" *NCADV Voice,* Winter 1994, 2–5.

60. Stalking Resource Center, "Stalking Behavior and Incidence Log," no date. Retreived February 5, 2004, from the website of the National Center for Victims of Crime, http://www.ncvc.org.

61. Deller Ross, S., et al., 157–58.

62. Schechter, S., and Edelson, J.L., *Effective Intervention in Domestic Violence and Child Maltreatment Cases: Guidelines for Policy and Practice: Recommendations*

from the National Council of Juvenile and Family Court Judges (Reno, NV: Family Violence Department, University of Nevada, June 1999).

63. Deller Ross, S., et al., 158–59.
64. Ibid., 160.
65. National Council of Juvenile and Family Court Judges, *Family Violence: Improving Court Practice* (Pub. #28) (1990).
66. Deller Ross, S., et al., 160–61.
67. Ibid., 161. See also Robson, R., *Lesbian (Out)Law: Survival under the Rule of Law* (Ithaca, NY: Firebrand Books, 1992), 157–67.

Chapter 6: Living Underground

1. Bryant, D., in Casey, K. (ed.), *The Promise of a New Day: A Book of Daily Meditations* (Center City, MN: Hazelden Educational Materials, 1992).
2. See, for example, Culligan, J., *When in Doubt Check Him Out: A Woman's Survival Guide for the '90s* (Miami, FL: Hallmark Press, 1993).
3. Girdner, L.K., and Hoff, P.M., *Obstacles to the Recovery and Return of Parentally Abducted Children: Research Summary* (Washington, DC: Office of Juvenile Justice and Delinquency Prevention, Office of Justice Programs, U.S. Department of Justice, March 1994), 4.
4. "Getting New Social Security Numbers for Battered Women," *Domestic Violence Report,* April/May 1997, 52.
5. National Center on Women and Family Law, Inc., *Battered Women: Procedure for Change of Name and Social Security Number* (New York, National Center on Women and Family Law, Inc., 1995), 1.
6. "Getting New Social Security Numbers for Battered Women."
7. Social Security Administration, "SSA Provides Assistance to Victims of Domestic Violence." no date. Retrieved June 16, 2004, from http://www .ssa.gov/pressoffice/domestic_fact.html.
8. "Getting New Social Security Numbers for Battered Women."
9. National Coalition Against Domestic Violence, "Social Security Information," no date. Retrieved May 2, 2004, from http://www.ncadv.org/public policy/ssnumber.htm.
10. Ibid.
11. Ibid.
12. Ibid.
13. Privacy Rights Clearinghouse, "Fact Sheet 14: Are You Being Stalked? Tips for Protection," June 2001. Retrieved October 11, 2004, from http://www .privacyrights.org/fs/fs14-stk.htm.
14. Culligan, J., 2–35.
15 Privacy Rights Clearinghouse. See also Culligan, J., 51–73.
16. National Network to End Domestic Violence, *Web Wise Women* (Washington, DC: National Network to End Domestic Violence, March 2003).
17. Privacy Rights Clearinghouse.
18. Ibid.

19. Ibid.
20. Ibid.
21. National Network to End Domestic Violence.
22. Ibid.
23. Ibid.
24. Ibid. See also Privacy Rights Clearinghouse.

Chapter 7: The Oppression That Binds: Barriers to Living Violence Free

1. Lorde, A., "An Open Letter to Mary Daly," in Lorde, A., *Sister Outsider* (Freedom, CA: The Crossing Press, 1984), 70.
2. See Pence, E., *In Our Best Interest: A Process for Personal and Social Change,* (Duluth, MN: Minnesota Program Development, Inc., 1987).
3. Comas-Díaz, L., and Greene, B., "Overview: An Ethnocultural Mosaic," in Comas-Díaz, L., and Greene, B. (eds.), *Women of Color: Integrating Ethnic and Gender Identities in Psychotherapy* (New York: Guilford Press, 1994), 7.
4. White, E.C., *Chain Chain Change: For Black Women Dealing with Physical and Emotional Abuse* (Seattle, WA: The Seal Press, 1985), 20–1.
5. Ibid., 61–62.
6. Ibid., 63–65.
7. Ibid., 25.
8. Greene, B., "African American Women," in Comas-Díaz, L., and Greene, B. (eds.), 15.
9. White, E.C., 44.
10. Zambrano, M.M., *Mejor Sola Que Mal Acompañada: For the Latina in an Abusive Relationship* (Seattle, WA: The Seal Press, 1985), 226.
11. Ibid., 225–27.
12. Ibid., 227.
13. Ibid., 131.
14. Lum, J., "Battered Asian Women," *Rice,* March 1988, 50–52.
15. Ibid.
16. Ibid.
17. Das Dasgupta, S., and Warrier, S., *In Visible Terms: Domestic Violence in the Asian Indian Context* (Bloomfield, NJ: Manavi, 1995), 3.
18. Ibid., 11–12.
19. Ibid., 7–8.
20. DasGupta, K., "Asian Indian Women: Guidelines for Community Intervention in the Event of Abuse," *Family Violence and Sexual Assault Bulletin* 9:4 (1993): 27–28.
21. Das Dasgupta, S., and Warrier, S., 20.
22. DasGupta, K., 26.
23. Ibid., 27–28.

24. Chester, B., et al., "Grandmother Dishonored: Violence Against Women by Male Partners in American Indian Communities," *Violence and Victims* 9:3 (1994): 249–58.

25. Ibid.

26. Mousseau, M., and Artichoker, K., "Domestic Violence Is Not Lakota/ Dakota Tradition," (Pierre, SD: South Dakota Coalition Against Domestic Violence and Sexual Assault and Project Medicine Wheel, no date), 2.

27. Chester, B., et al., 249–58.

28. Ibid.

29. Mousseau, M., and Artichoker, K., 3.

30. Chester, B., et al., 249–58.

31. Ibid.

32. Family Violence Prevention Fund, *The Facts on Immigrant Women and Domestic Violence* (San Francisco, CA: Family Violence Prevention Fund, no date).

33. New York City Department of Health and Mental Hygeine, "Femicide in New York City: 1995–2002," October 2003. Retrieved June 13, 2004 from http://www.ci.nyc.ny.us/html/doh/html/public/press04/prl45-1022.html.

34. Anderson, M., "A License to Abuse: The Impact of Conditional Status on Female Immigrants," *Yale Law Journal* 102 (2000).

35. Orloff, L., et al., "With No Place to Turn: Improving Advocacy for Battered Immigrant Women," *Family Law Quarterly* 29:2 (1995): 313.

36. State Bar of Texas, *Violence Against Women Act (VAWA): Implications for Battered Immigrant Spouses and Children* (Austin, TX: State Bar of Texas, 1995), 9.

37. Family Violence Prevention Fund, "Background on Laws Affecting Battered Immigrant Women," no date. Retrieved October 11, 2004 from http://endabuse.org/programs/printable/display.php3?DocID=320.

38. Ibid.

39. State Bar of Texas, 2.

40. Family Violence Prevention Fund, "Ashcroft Fails to Decide Key Immigration Case," *NewsFlash!*, January 25, 2005.

41. State Bar of Texas, 3–4.

42. See Department of Human Services Family Violence Advisory Committee, *Survey on Undocumented Battered Women* (Austin, TX: Texas Department of Human Services, 1992).

43. Nyakabwa, K., and Harvey, C.D.H., "Adaptation to Canada: The Case of Black Immigrant Women," in Dhruvarajan, V. (ed.), *Women and Well-Being* (Montreal, Canada: McGill-Queen's University Press, 1990), 143.

44. State Bar of Texas, 4–5.

45. Nyakabwa, K., and Harvey, C.D.H., 144.

46. Renzetti, C.M., *Violent Betrayal: Partner Abuse in Lesbian Relationships* (Newbury Park, CA: Sage Publications, 1992), 115.

47. Pharr, S., "Two Workshops on Homophobia," in Lobel, K. (ed.), for the National Coaltion Against Domestic Violence Lesbian Task Force, *Naming the Violence: Speaking Out about Lesbian Battering* (Seattle, WA: The Seal Press, 1986), 204.

48. Pharr, S., *Homophobia: A Weapon of Sexism* (Inverness, CA: Chardon Press, 1988), 1.

49. Hart, B., "Lesbian Battering: An Examination," in Lobel, K. (ed.), 183–85.

50. Benowitz, M., "How Homophobia Affects Lesbians' Response to Violence in Lesbian Relationships," in Lobel, K. (ed.), 199.

51. Renzetti, C.M., 131.

52. Hammond, N., "Lesbian Victims and the Reluctance to Identify Abuse," in Lobel, K. (ed.), 194.

53. Renzetti, C.M., 127.

54. Ibid., 123.

55. United States Senate Special Committee on Aging, the American Association of Retired Persons, the Federal Council on the Aging, and the United States Administration on Aging, *Aging America: Trends and Projections* (Washington, DC: United States Department of Health and Human Services, 1991), xix.

56. Vinton, L., "Abused Older Women: Battered Women or Abused Elders?" in Women's Initiatives, American Association of Retired Persons, *Abused Elders or Older Battered Women?* (Washington, DC: AARP, 1992), 51.

57. Pillemer, K.A., and Finkelhor, D., "The Prevalence of Elder Abuse: A Random Sample Survey," *The Gerontological Society of America* 28:1 (1988): 51–57.

58. Breckman, R.S., and Adelman, R.D., *Strategies for Helping Victims of Elder Mistreatment* (Newbury Park, CA: Sage Publications, 1988), 29.

59. See Brandl, B., *Older Battered Women in Milwaukee* (Milwaukee: Community Care Organization of Milwaukee, Milwaukee Foundation, Wisconsin Coalition Against Domestic Violence, 1991).

60. Brandl, B., "Older Abused/Battered Women: An Invisible Population," *Wisconsin Coalition Against Domestic Violence Newsletter* 14:3 (1995): 7–8.

61. Ibid., 7.

62. Mixon, P., "Older Battered Women: The Forgotten Victims," *The River,* newsletter of the Texas Council on Family Violence, Winter 1995, 3.

63. United States Senate Special Committee on Aging, et al., 1991, xx–xxi.

64. Brandl, B., 1995, 8.

65. Mixon, P., 3.

66. Women's Initiative, American Association of Retired Persons, 16.

67. Brandl, B., 1995, 8.

68. Ibid., 8–9.

69. Adams, C.J., and Engle-Rowbottom, M., "A Commentary on Violence Against Women and Children in Rural Areas," in Fortune, M.M., *Violence in the Family: A Workshop Curriculum for Clergy and Other Helpers* (Cleveland, OH: The Pilgrim Press, 1991), 170.

70. Graveline, M.J., "Threats to Rural Women's Well-Being: A Group Response," in Dhruvarajan, V. (ed.), 173.

71. Adams, C.J., and Engle-Rowbottom, M., 169.

72. Ibid., 166–67.

73. Graveline, M.J., 171–72.

74. Ibid., 171.

75. Adams, C.J., and Engle-Rowbottom, M., 168–69.

76. Ibid., 167.

77. Krueger-Pelka, F., "Abuse: A Hidden Epidemic," *Mainstream,* March 1988.

78. Young, M.E., et al., "Prevalence of Abuse of Women with Physical Disabilities," *Archives of Physical Medicine and Rehabilitation* 78 (1997). Retrieved November 8, 2004, from http://www.bcm.edu/crowd/abuse_women/1PREVLNC.htm.

79. Ibid.

80. Schwartz, M., Abramson, W., and Kamper, H.A., *A National Survey on the Accessibility of Domestic Violence and Sexual Assault Services to Women with Disabilities,* unpublished data (Austin, TX: SafePlace, 2004).

81. Interview with Wendie Abramson, director of Disability Services ASAP at SafePlace, Austin, TX, November 2004.

82. Nosek, M.A., and Howland, C.A., "Abuse and Women with Disabilities," February 1998, 1–9. Retrieved September 23, 2004 from http://www.vaw.umn.edu/documents/vawnet/disab/disab.pdf.

83. Melling, L., *Abuse in the Deaf Community* (Washington DC: Center for Women Policy Studies, 1984).

84. Ibid.

85. Ibid.

86. Krueger-Pelka, F., "Abuse: A Hidden Epidemic," *Mainstream,* March 1988.

87. Nosek, M.A., and Howland, C.A.

88. Schwartz, M., et al.

89. Center for Research on Women with Disabilities, *Facts about Programs Delivering Battered Women's Services to Women with Disabilities* (Houston, TX: Center for Research on Women with Disabilities, 2000).

90. Donovan, S., "What Can We Do to Help?" *The River,* newsletter of the Texas Council on Family Violence (TCFV), Winter 1995, 5.

91. Ibid.

92. Osthoff, S., "When Battered Women Become Defendants: Should We Advocate?" *NCADV Voice,* Winter 1989, 6–7.

93. "National Estimates and Facts about Domestic Violence," *NCADV Voice,* Winter 1989, 12.

94. Ibid.

95. Donovan, S., "A View from the Inside," *The River,* newsletter of the TCFV, Winter 1995, 7.

96. "National Estimates and Facts about Domestic Violence."

97. Edwards, L., "My Story," *The River,* newsletter of the TCFV, Winter 1995, 6.

98. "National Estimates and Facts about Domestic Violence."

99. DuBow, T., "Getting the 'Inside' Story Out," *NCADV Voice*, Winter 1989, 8.

100. Ibid.

101. "National Estimates and Facts about Domestic Violence."

102. Wardlow, B., "Why Clemency Now?" *The River*, newsletter of the TCFV, Winter 1995, 7.

Chapter 8: For Friends, Family, and Loved Ones: When Someone You Know Is Being Hurt

1. Gelles, R.J., and Straus, M., *Intimate Violence* (New York: Simon and Schuster, 1988), 156–59. See also Gondolf, E.W., and Fisher, E.R., *Battered Women as Survivors: An Alternative to Treating Learned Helplessness* (Lexington, MA: Lexington Books, 1988), 28–31.

2. Herman, J.L., *Trauma and Recovery* (New York: Basic Books, 1992), 61.

3. American Psychological Association Presidential Task Force on Violence and the Family, *Violence and the Family* (Washington, DC: American Psychological Association, 1996), 38.

4. Texas Council on Family Violence, *What a Battered Woman Faces If She Leaves* (Austin, TX, Texas Council on Family Violence, no date). See also Browne, A., *When Battered Women Kill* (New York: The Free Press, 1987), 109–30.

5. Herman, J.L., 142–43.

6. Schechter, S., *Women and Male Violence: The Visions and Struggles of the Battered Women's Movement* (Boston, MA: South End Press, 1982), 253.

7. McEvoy, A.W., and Brookings, J.B., *Helping Battered Women: A Volunteer's Handbook for Assisting Victims of Marital Violence* (Holmes Beach, FL: Learning Publications, Inc., 1982), 9.

8. Jones, A., *Next Time She'll Be Dead: Battering and How to Stop It* (Boston, MA: Beacon Press, 1994), 234.

9. McEvoy, A.W., and Brookings, J.B., 10.

10. Rice, G., *Some Ideas on Helping a Battered Woman* (Austin, TX: Austin Center for Battered Women, no date).

11. Ellin, J., *Listening Helpfully: How to Develop Your Counseling Skills* (London: Souvenir Press, 1994), 104–5.

12. Clarke, R.L., *Pastoral Care of Battered Women* (Philadelphia, PA: The Westminster Press, 1986), 98–99.

13. Herman, J.L., 162.

14. Rice, G.

15. Texas Department of Human Services in cooperation with the Texas Council on Family Violence, *Counseling Battered Women* (Austin, TX: Texas Department of Human Services in cooperation with the Texas Council on Family Violence, no date).

16. Ellin, J., 40–51.

17. Small, J., *Becoming Naturally Therapeutic: A Return to the True Essence of Helping* (New York: Bantam Books, 1989), 27–30.

18. McEvoy, A.W., and Brookings, J.B., 12.

19. Texas Council on Family Violence, *Five Things to Say to a Victim Who Is Not Ready to Leave Her Abuser* (Austin, TX: Texas Council on Family Violence, no date).

20. Johnson, S.A., *When "I Love You" Turns Violent: Emotional and Physical Abuse in Dating Relationships* (Far Hills, NJ: New Horizon Press, 1993), 33.

21. Ibid., 169–70. See also Browne, A., 42–54; Walker, L., *The Battered Woman* (New York: Harper and Row, 1979), 223–24; Jones, A., and Schechter, S., *When Loves Goes Wrong* (New York: HarperCollins, 1992), 300–1.

22. Jones, A., 236.

23. Austin Center for Battered Women, *Warning Signs of Abuse* (Austin, TX: Austin Center for Battered Women, no date).

Chapter 9: Domestic Violence and the Workplace

1. Family Violence Prevention Fund, *57 Percent of Corporate Leaders Believe Domestic Violence Is a Major Social Problem According to Survey by Liz Claiborne*, San Francisco, CA, September 30, 1994.

2. Texas Council on Family Violence (TCFV), *Workplace Domestic Violence,* (Austin, TX, no date).

3. EDK Associates for the Body Shop, *The Many Faces of Domestic Violence and Its Impact on the WorkPlace* (New York: EDK Associates, 1997).

4. U.S. Department of Health and Human Services, National Center for Injury Prevention and Control, *Costs of Intimate Partner Violence Against Women in the United States* (Atlanta, GA: Centers for Disease Control and Prevention, March 2003).

5. TCFV, *Workplace Domestic Violence.*

6. McFarlane, J., et al., "Indicators of Intimate Partner Violence in Women's Employment: Implications for Workplace Action," *AAOHN Journal* 48:5 (2000): 215.

7. See Stark, E., and Flitcraft, A., *Women at Risk: Domestic Violence and Women's Health* (Thousand Oaks, CA: Sage Publications, 1996).

8. U.S. Department of Justice, Bureau of Justice Statistics, *Intimate Partner Violence 1993–2001,* NCJ197838, February 2003, 1.

9. TCFV, *Workplace Domestic Violence.*

10. Texas Council on Family Violence (TCFV), *What a Battered Woman Faces If She Leaves,* Austin, TX, no date.

11. Ibid.

12. National Conference of State Legislatures, "Analysis of the Personal Responsibility and Work Opportunity Reconciliation Act of 1996," no date. Retrieved February 26, 2005, from http://www.ncsl.org/statefed/hr3734.htm.

13. Ibid.

14. Ibid.

15. Ibid.

16. Tjaden, P., and Thoennes, N., *Prevalence, Incidence, and Consequences of Violence Against Women: Findings from the National Violence Against Women Study* (Washington DC: National Institute of Justice and the Centers for Disease Control and Prevention, November 1998).

17. Lyon, E., "Welfare and Domestic Violence Against Women: Lessons from Research," National Electronic Network on Violence Against Women, August 2002. Retrieved February 5, 2005, from http://www.vawnet.com.

18. Ibid.

19. United States General Accounting Office, Report to Congressional Committees, *Domestic Violence: Prevalence and Implications for Employment among Welfare Recipients,* Washington DC, November 1998.

20. Ibid.

21. Brush, L., "Battering, Traumatic Stress, and Welfare-to-Work Transition," *Violence Against Women* 6 (2000): 1039–65.

22. Moore, T., and Selkowe, V., *Domestic Violence Victims in Transition from Welfare to Work: Barriers to Self-Sufficiency and the W-2 Response,* report by the Institute for Wisconsin's Future to the Joyce Foundation of Chicago, 1999.

23. Raphael, J., and Haennicke, S., *Keeping Battered Women Safe Through the Welfare-to-Work Journey: How Are We Doing?* (Chicago, IL: Taylor Institute, 1999).

24. Moore, T., and Selkowe, V.

25. Griswold, E., Pearson, J., and Thoennes, N., "New Directions for Child Support Agencies when Domestic Violence Is an Issue: Preliminary Findings from Three Demonstration Projects," *Policy and Practice* 58 (2000): 29–36.

26. Levin, R., "The Reality of Implementing a Welfare-to-Work Program for Domestic Violence Victims and Survivors in Collaboration with the TANF Department," *Violence Against Women* 7 (2001): 211–21.

27. Lyon, E.

28. Patrice Tanaka and Company, Inc., News Release, *Corporate Leaders See Domestic Violence as a Major Problem That Affects Their Employees According to Benchmark Survey by Liz Claiborne, Inc.,* October 16, 2002.

29. Ibid. See also Roper Starch Worldwide Inc., *Addressing Domestic Violence: A Corporate Response,* prepared for Liz Claiborne, Inc., New York, August 1994.

30. Family Violence Prevention Fund, 1994.

31. Corporate Alliance to End Partner Violence, "Our Purpose," no date. Retrieved January 15, 2005, from http://www.caepv.org.

32. Polaroid Corporation, *Polaroid Corporation and the Domestic Violence Issue,* Cambridge, MA, no date.

33. Family Violence Prevention Fund, "Strategic Employer Responses to Domestic Violence: Verizon Wireless," no date. Retrieved January 19, 2005, from http://www.endabuse.org.

34. Ibid.

35. Family Violence Prevention Fund, "Working to End Domestic Violence: American Workplaces Respond to an Epidemic," no date. Retrieved January 19, 2005, from http://www.endabuse.org.

36. Family Violence Prevention Fund, 1994.

37. See Scholder, A. (ed.), *Critical Condition: Women on the Edge of Violence* (San Francisco, CA: City Lights Books, 1993).

38. Liz Claiborne, Inc., "Love Is Not Abuse Timeline," no date. Retrieved January 20, 2005, from www.lizclaiborne.com.

39. Liz Claiborne, Inc., *Liz Claiborne Women's Work Program Fact Sheet 1991–1995,* New York, no date.

40. Family Violence Prevention Fund, "Strategic Employer Responses to Domestic Violence: Liz Claiborne, Inc."

41. Ibid.

42. Texas Council on Family Violence, "Ending Workplace Violence: A Notable Trend," *The River,* Spring 2004, 1–3.

43. National Institute for Occupational Safety and Health, *Preventing Homicide in the Workplace,* Cincinnati, OH, September 1993, 3.

44. Roper Starch Worldwide Inc.

45. See Moskey, S.T., *Domestic Violence Policy Checklists for the Workplace: A Guide for Employers* (Cape Elizabeth, ME: Kettle Cove Press, 1996).

46. Family Violence Prevention Fund, *The Workplace Responds to Domestic Violence: A Resource Guide for Employers, Unions and Advocates,* San Francisco, CA, 2000, 4–5.

47. Minor, M., *Preventing Workplace Violence: Positive Management Strategies* (Menlo Park, CA: Crisp Publications, 1995), 21–22.

48. Moskey, S.T., 2.

49. Ibid., 4–6.

50. Family Violence Prevention Fund, *Domestic Violence: A Workplace Security Problem,* San Francisco, CA, no date.

51. Kelley, S.J., "Making Sense of Violence in the Workplace," *Risk Management* 42:10 (October 1995): 50–57. See also Mattman, J.W., "What's Growing in the Corporate Culture?" *Security Management* 39:11 (November 1995): 42–46.

52. Kelley, S.J., 50–57.

53. Moskey, S.T., 18–19.

54. Minor, M., 25.

55. Roper Starch Worldwide Inc.

56. Hardeman, J., *Intervention Strategies* (Cambridge, MA: Polaroid Corp., no date).

Chapter 10: Battered Women's Health: The Response of the Medical Community

1. Jones, A., *Next Time She'll Be Dead: Battering and How to Stop It* (Boston, MA: Beacon Press, 1994), 148.

2. National Institute of Justice and Centers for Disease Control and Prevention, *Prevalence, Incidence, and Consequences of Violence Against Women: Findings*

from the National Violence Against Women Survey (Washington, DC: National Institute of Justice and Centers for Disease Control and Prevention, 1998).

3. U.S. Department of Justice, Bureau of Justice Statistics, *Violence Related Injuries Treated in Hospital Emergency Departments: Special Report* (Washington, DC: U.S. Department of Justice, 1997).

4. Gondolf, E., and Fisher, E., *Battered Women as Survivors: An Alternative to Treating Learned Helplessness* (Lexington, MA: Lexington Books, 1988), 29–30.

5. Stark, E., and Flitcraft, A., "Spouse Abuse," in Last, J.M. (ed.), *Maxcy-Rosenau: Public Health and Preventive Medicine* (New York: Appleton-Century-Crofts, 1991), 1040–43.

6. U.S. Department of Health and Human Services and the National Center for Injury Prevention and Control, *Costs of Intimate Partner Violence Against Women in the United States,* Atlanta, GA: Centers for Disease Control and Prevention, March 2003.

7. Ulrich, Y.C., et al., "Medical Care Utilization Patterns in Women with Diagnosed Domestic Violence," *American Journal of Preventive Medicine* 24:1 (2003): 9–15.

8. Helton, A.S., and Snodgrass, F.G., "Battering During Pregnancy: Intervention Strategies," *Birth* 14 (1987), 142–47. See also Rath, G.D., Jarratt, L.G., and Leonardson, G., "Rate of Domestic Violence Against Adult Women by Male Partners," *Journal of the American Board of Family Practice* 2 (1989): 227–33; Hamberger, L.K., Saunders, D., and Harvey, M., "Prevalence of Domestic Violence in Community Practice and Rate of Physician Inquiry," *Family Medicine* 24 (1986): 283–87.

9. Browne, A., *When Battered Women Kill* (New York: The Free Press, 1987), 69.

10. Walker, L., *The Battered Woman* (New York: Harper and Row, 1979), 196–99.

11. Browne, A., 69. See also Stark, E., and Flitcraft, A., *Women at Risk: Domestic Violence and Women's Health* (Thousand Oaks, CA: Sage Publications, 1996), 17.

12. Stark, E., and Flitcraft, A., 1991, 1040–43. See also Collins, K.S., et al., *Health Concerns Across a Woman's Lifespan: The Commonwealth Fund 1998 Survey of Women's Health,* The Commonwealth Fund, 1999. Retrieved June 21, 2005, from http://www.cmwf.org/usr_doc/Healthconcerns_survey report.pdf.

13. Gelles, R.J., and Straus, M.A., *Intimate Violence* (New York: Simon and Schuster, 1988), 136–37.

14. Stark, E., and Flitcraft, A., 1996, 162–63. See also Gelles, R.J., and Straus, M.A., 136–37.

15. Collins, K., et al. See also Stark, E., and Flitcraft, A., 1996, 8–18, 162–63.

16. Gelles, R.J., and Straus, M.A., 132–33.

17. Stark, E., and Flitcraft, A., 1996, 196. See also Flitcraft, A.H., et al., "American Medical Association Diagnostic and Treatment Guidelines on Domestic

Violence," in *Strengthening the Health Care Response to Domestic Violence,* prepared by the Family Violence Prevention Fund's Health Resource Center on Domestic Violence, 1:1 (Summer 1993).

18. Currie, D., "Women's Liberation and Women's Mental Health: Towards a Political Economy of Eating Disorders," in Dhruvarajan, V. (ed.), *Women and Well-Being* (Montreal, Canada: McGill-Queens University Press, 1990), 32–33.

19. Acosta, K.S., "Abuse During Pregnancy," *Fit Pregnancy* 10:5 (January 2004): 14–16.

20. Stark, E., and Flitcraft, A., 1996, 11–17. See also McFarlane, J., "Violence During Teen Pregnancy: Health Consequences for Mother and Child," in Levy, B. (ed.), *Dating Violence: Young Women in Danger* (Seattle, WA: Seal Press, 1991), 136–37.

21. American Medical Association Council on Scientific Affairs, "Violence Against Women: Relevance for Medical Practitioners," *JAMA: Journal of the American Medical Association* 267 (1992): 3184–89.

22. Acosta, K.S., 14.

23. Thorne-Finch, R., *Ending the Silence: The Origins and Treatment of Male Violence Against Women* (Toronto, Canada: University of Toronto Press, 1992), 42–44.

24. Jones, A., 87.

25. Flitcraft, A.H., et al., 1993. See also Stark, E., and Flitcraft, A., 1996, 204.

26. "Motherhood Cut Short: When Pregnancy Ends in Murder," January 26, 2005. Retrieved January 26, 2005, from http://courttv.com/trials/peterson/090304_pregnantmurder_ctv.html.

27. Ibid.

28. See Renker, P.R., "Keep a Blank Face. I Need to Tell You What Has Been Happening to Me: Teens' Stories of Abuse and Violence Before and During Pregnancy," *The American Journal of Maternal/Child Nursing* 27:2 (March–April 2002): 109–16; Huth-Bocks, A.C., Levendosky, A.A., and Bogat, G.A., "The Effects of Domestic Violence During Pregnancy on Maternal and Infant Health," *Violence and Victims* 17:2 (April 2002): 169–85; Jasinski, J.L., "Pregnancy and Violence Against Women: An Analysis of Longitudinal Data," *Journal of Interpersonal Violence* 16:7 (July 2001): 712–33; Jasinski, J.L., "Pregnancy and Domestic Violence: A Review of the Literature," *Trauma, Violence, and Abuse* 5:1 (January 2004): 47–64; Borowsky, I.W., and Ireland, M., "Parental Screening for Intimate Partner Violence by Pediatricians and Family Physicians," *Pediatrics* 110:3 (September 2000): 509–16.

29. "Unborn Victims of Violence Act Passes in the House," Feminist Daily News Wire, April 27, 2001, Feminist Majority Foundation. Retrieved May 25, 2004, from http://www.feminist.org/news/newsbyte/printnews.asp?id=5469.

30. "Unborn Victims of Violence Act," statement of Juley Fulcher, Esq., Public Policy Director, National Coalition Against Domestic Violence, before the Subcommittee on the Constitution Committee on the House Judiciary, FDCH Congressional Testimony, July 8, 2003.

31. Ibid.

32. Doyle, M., "Laci, Conner Bill Is Law," *Bee Washington Bureau,* April 2, 2004. Retrieved January 26, 2005, from http://www.modbee.com/reports/peterson/trial/v-print/story/8380973p-9215282c.html.

33. "Eleanor Smeal, Feminist Majority President, Decries Senate Move," Feminist Daily News Wire, March 25, 2004, Feminist Majority Foundation. Retrieved May 25, 2004, from http://www.feminist.org/news/newsbyte/printnews .asp?id=8361. See also "Bush Signs Bill Undermining Abortion Rights," Feminist Daily News Wire, April 2, 2004, Feminist Majority Foundation. Retrieved May 25, 2004, from http://www.feminist.org/news/newsbyte/printnews.asp?id=8372.

34. Family Violence Prevention Fund, "Health Alert: Medical Care System's Response to Domestic Violence," in *Strengthening the Health Care Response to Domestic Violence* 1:1 (Summer 1993).

35. Stark, E., and Flitcraft, A., 1996, 9.

36. Warshaw, C., "Limitations of the Medical Model in the Care of Battered Women," *Gender and Society* 3 (1989): 506–17.

37. Stark, E., and Flitcraft, A., 1996, 20–23.

38. Ibid., 13.

39. Waitzkin, H., "Information Giving in Medical Care," *Journal of Health and Social Behavior* 26 (1985), 81–101. See also Stark, E., and Flitcraft, A., 1996, 16–17.

40. Stark, E., and Flitcraft, A., 1996, 16–18.

41. Ibid., 202. See also Buel, S.M., "Family Violence: Practical Recommendations for Physicians and the Medical Community," *Women's Health Issues* 5:4 (Winter 1995): 158–72.

42. Jones, A., p. 147. See also Campbell, J., "Nurses Have Been Saying It," *NCADV Voice,* Winter 1994, 5–7; Stark, E., and Flitcraft, A., 1996, 216.

43. Salber, P.R., "Domestic Violence: How to Ask the Right Questions and Recognize Abuse," in *Strengthening the Health Care Response to Domestic Violence* (Summer, 1993). See also Buel, S.M., 1995, 158–72; Flitcraft, A., "Project SAFE: Domestic Violence Education for Practicing Physicians," *Women's Health Issues* 5:4 (Winter 1995): 183–88; Stark, E., and Flitcraft, A., 1996, 216.

44. Buel, S.M., 158–72.

45. Texas Medical Association, *Domestic Violence: Start the Healing Now,* Austin, TX, no date, 1–2.

46. Flitcraft, A., 1995, 183–88. See also Buel, S.M., 158–72.

47. Alpert, E.J., et al., "Family Violence Curricula in U.S. Medical Schools," *American Journal of Preventive Medicine* 14:4 (May 1998): 273–82.

48. Flitcraft, A.H., et al., Summer, 1993.

49. Family Violence Prevention Fund, *Preventing Domestic Violence: Clinical Guidelines on Routine Screening,* San Francisco, CA, October 1999.

50. Texas Medical Association, 19.

51. Ibid., 9–12. See also Flitcraft, A.H., et al., Summer, 1993; Salber, P.R., no date.

52. Texas Medical Association, 16.

53. Stark, E., "Discharge Planning with Battered Women," in *Strengthening the Health Care Response to Domestic Violence,* prepared by the Family Violence Prevention Fund's Health Resource Center on Domestic Violence, San Francisco, CA, no date.

54. Flitcraft, A.H., et al., no date. See also Salber, P.R., no date.

55. Ibid.

56. Stark, E., no date.

57. Rounsaville, B.J., and Weissman, M., "Battered Women: A Medical Problem Requiring Detection," *International Journal of Psychiatry in Medicine* 8:2 (1977–1978): 191–202.

58. Salber, P.R., no date.

59. See National Coalition Against Domestic Violence, *NCADV Voice,* Winter 1994, 19.

60. U.S. Preventive Services Task Force, "Screening for Family and Intimate Partner Violence: Recommendation Statement," *Annals of Internal Medicine* 140:5 (March 2004): 382–86. See also Chamberlain, L., "The USPSTF Recommendation on Intimate Partner Violence: What We Can Learn from It and What Can We Do about It," *Family Violence Prevention and Health Practice* 1 (January 2005). Retrieved February 1, 2005, from http://www.jfvphp.org.

61. Chamberlain, L.

62. The Family Violence Prevention Fund's Research Committee, *The Family Violence Prevention Fund's Review of the U.S. Preventive Services Task Force Draft Recommendation and Rationale Statement on Screening for Family Violence* (San Francisco. CA: Family Violence Prevention Fund, no date).

63. Nelson, J.C., and Johnston, C., "Letter to the Editor," *Annals of Internal Medicine* 141:1 (July 2004), 81.

64. Flitcraft, A., 1995, 183–88. See also Schechter, S., with Gary, L.T., *Health Care Services for Battered Women and Their Abused Children: A Manual about AWAKE* (Boston, MA: Children's Hospital, 1992); Hadley, S.M., et al., "WomanKind: An Innovative Model of Health Care Response to Domestic Abuse," *Women's Health Issues* 5:4 (Winter 1995): 189–98.

65. Family Violence Prevention Fund, "Model Programs on Health Care and Domestic Violence." no date. Retrieved January 27, 2005, from http://endabuse .org/programs/printable/display.php3?DocID=35.

66. Ibid.

67. Achterberg, J., *Woman as Healer* (Boston, MA: Shambhala, 1991), 204.

Chapter 11: Battered Women and Communities of Faith

1. United States Conference of Catholic Bishops, "When I Call for Help: A Pastoral Response to Domestic Violence Against Women," tenth anniversary edition, A Statement of the U.S. Catholic Bishops, November 12, 2002. Retrieved October 18, 2004, from http://www.usccb.org/laity/help.shtml.

2. Jewish Women International, *JWI's Needs Assessment: A Portrait of Domestic Abuse in the Jewish Community,* Washington, DC, May 2004, p. 2.

3. Halsey, P., "Women in Crisis: Out There or In Here?" *Response,* June 1981, 5.

4. Alkhateeb, S., "Ending Domestic Violence in Muslim Families," Islamic Society of North America, no date. Retrieved October 19, 2004, from http://www.isna.net/services/dv.

5. Alsdurf, J., and Alsdurf, P., *Battered into Submission: The Tragedy of Wife Abuse in the Christian Home* (Downers Grove, IL: InterVarsity Press, 1989), 153.

6. Ibid., p. 77.

7. Ibid., p. 23.

8. Herman, J.L., *Trauma and Recovery* (New York: Basic Books, 1992), 51–52.

9. Clarke, R.L., *Pastoral Care of Battered Women* (Philadelphia, PA: The Westminister Press, 1986), 61–85; Fortune, M.M., "Ministry in Response to Violence in the Family: Pastoral and Prophetic," in Fortune, M.M., *Violence in the Family: A Workshop Curriculum for Clergy and Other Helpers* (Cleveland, OH: The Pilgrim Press, 1991), 198–99. See also Fortune, M.M., "The Transformation of Suffering: A Biblical and Theological Perspective," in Brown, J.C., and Bohn, C.R. (eds.), *Christianity, Patriarchy, and Abuse* (New York: The Pilgrim Press, 1990), 139–47.

10. Fortune, M.M., "A Commentary on Religious Issues in Family Violence," in Fortune, M.M., *Violence in the Family: A Workshop Curriculum for Clergy and Other Helpers,* 137–38.

11. Fortune, M.M., *Sexual Violence: The Unmentionable Sin* (New York: The Pilgrim Press, 1983), 191–93.

12. Fortune, M.M., "A Commentary on Religious Issues in Family Violence," 138–39.

13. Clarke, R.L., 1986, 61–85. See also Fortune, M.M., *Keeping the Faith: Questions and Answers for the Abused Woman* (San Francisco, CA: Harper, 1987).

14. Childress, S., "9/11's Hidden Toll: Muslim-American Women Are Quietly Coping with a Tragic Side Effects of the Attacks—A Surge in Domestic Violence," *Newsweek,* August 4, 2003. Retrieved October 18, 2004, from http://www.keepmedia.com/jsp/article_detail_print.jsp.

15. Alkhateeb, S.

16. Fortune, M.M., "A Commentary on Religious Issues in Family Violence," 138.

17. United States Conference of Catholic Bishops.

18. Bohn, C.R., "Dominion to Rule: The Roots and Consequences of a Theology of Ownership," in Brown, J.C., and Bohn, C.R. (eds.), *Christianity, Patriarchy and Abuse* (New York: The Pilgrim Press, 1990), 107.

19. Alsdurf, J., and Alsdurf, P., 156.

20. Ibid., 157–58.

21. Martin, M., *For Better or for Worse: A Blessing or a Curse?* (Phoenix, AZ: ACS Press, 1999), 14.

22. Fortune, M.M., 1983, 128–29.

23. Clarke, R.L., 62.

24. Fortune, M.M., "Ministry in Response to Violence in the Family: Pastoral and Prophetic," 193.
25. Alsdurf, J., and Alsdurf, P., 130–31.
26. Clarke, R.L., 91–92.
27. Ibid., 88–89. See also Fortune, M.M., 1983, 131–33.
28. Texas Department of Human Services, *Family Violence and the Clergy*, Austin, TX, November 1990, 6. See also Clarke, R.L., 96–101.
29. Salber, P.R., "Domestic Violence: How to Ask the Right Questions and Recognize Abuse," in *Strengthening the Health Care Response to Domestic Violence*, prepared by the Family Violence Prevention Fund's Health Resource Center on Domestic Violence, San Francisco, CA, no date.
30. Texas Department of Human Services, 7.
31. Clarke, R.L., 97.
32. Ibid., 101–2.
33. See Fortune, M.M., *Keeping the Faith: Questions and Answers for the Abused Woman* (San Francisco, CA: Harper, 1987).
34. Fortune, M.M., "A Commentary on Religious Issues in Family Violence," 140.
35. Clarke, R.L., 97. See also Fortune, M.M., 1987, 85.
36. Texas Department of Human Services, 6.
37. Fortune, M.M., "Forgiveness: The Last Step," in Fortune, M.M., *Violence in the Family: A Workshop Curriculum for Clergy and Other Helpers*, 177.
38. Canadian Conference of Catholic Bishops' Permanent Council on Violence Against Women, *To Live Without Fear*, June 13, 1991 in Diocese of Austin, *Breaking the Silence: A Pastoral Response to Domestic Violence Against Women*, Austin, Texas, 1995.
39. Center for the Prevention of Sexual and Domestic Violence (now the Faith-Trust Institute), *1994–1995 Annual Report*, Seattle, WA.
40. Jewish Women International, 6.
41. Ibid.
42. Ibid.
43. Website of the Islamic Society of North America, http://www.isna.net.
44. United States Conference of Catholic Bishops.
45. See Diocese of Austin, *Breaking the Silence: A Pastoral Response to Domestic Violence Against Women*, Austin, TX, 1995.
46. Fortune, M.M., "Saving the Family: When Is Covenant Broken?" in Fortune, M.M., *Violence in the Family: A Workshop Curriculum for Clergy and Other Helpers*, 241.

Chapter 12: Domestic Violence and the Military

1. Memorandum from Deputy Secretary of Defense Paul Wolfowitz, Washington, DC, November 2001.
2. Defense Manpower Data Center, Washington, DC: U.S. Department of Defense, 2002.

3. U.S. Department of Defense, Family Advocacy Program Report, *Child and Spouse Abuse Data* (FY97–01), Washington, DC, no date.

4. Caliber Associates for the Department of Defense, *The Final Report on the Study of Spousal Abuse in the Armed Forces,* Washington, DC, 1996.

5. Miles Foundation, "Interpersonal Violence Associated with the Military: Facts and Findings," no date. Retrieved May 2, 2004, from http://members .aol.com/milesfdn/myhomepage.

6. National Coalition Against Domestic Violence, *Domestic Violence in the Military,* Washington, DC, no date.

7. Miles Foundation.

8. Beals, J., "The Military Response to Victims of Domestic Violence: Tools for Civilian Advocates," Battered Women's Justice Project, June 2003, 4–7. Retrieved February 2, 2005, from http://www.bwjp.org.

9. EMediaMillWorks, Inc., "Program Helps Prevent, Deal with Domestic Violence," Washington, DC, September 23, 2002. Retrieved March 4, 2005, from FDCH Regulatory Intelligence Database, Item 32W4083112681.

10. Beals, J., 4–7.

11. Merrill, H., et al., *Maltreatment Histories of U.S. Navy Basic Trainees: Prevalence of Abusive Behaviors for the 4th Quarter of 1994 and the 2nd Quarter of 1996,* NHRC Report No. 97-2, San Diego, CA: Naval Health Research Center, 1997.

12. Campbell, J.C., et al., "Intimate Partner Violence and Abuse among Active Duty Military Women," *Violence Against Women* 9:9 (2003): 1072–92.

13. Hosek, J., et al., *Married to the Military: The Employment and Earnings of Military Wives Compared with Civilian Wives* (Santa Monica, CA: RAND, 2002).

14. Beals, J., 1.

15. Defense Manpower Data Center, U.S. Department of Defense, Washington, DC, 1999. See also FBI, *Crime in the United States,* Washington, DC, 1996.

16. Ibid. See also U.S. Census Data, 1998.

17. Beals, J., 8.

18. Campbell, J., et al., *Risk Factors for Femicide in Abusive Relationships: Results from a Multi-Site Case Control Study,* Washington, DC: National Institute of Justice, RO1#DA/AA1156, 2002.

19. Hansen, C., "A Considerable Service: An Advocate's Introduction to Domestic Violence and the Military," *Domestic Violence Report* 6:4 (April/May 2001): 49–64. See also Beals, J., 9.

20. National Advisory Council on Violence Against Women and the Violence Against Women Office, "The Role of the U.S. Military in Preventing and Responding to Violence Against Women," in *Toolkit to End Violence Against Women,* no date. Retrieved January 22, 2004, from http://toolkit.ncjrs.org/ default.htm.

21. Beals, J., 4.

22. Ibid.

23. Caliber Associates, *The Final Report of the Study of Spousal Abuse in the Armed Forces*, (Washington, DC: Department of Defense, 1996).

24. Radutsky, M., Nelson, T. (producers), Bradley, E. (reporter), "The War at Home," *60 Minutes*, CBS News, January 17, 1999.

25. Defense Task Force on Domestic Violence, "Compilation of Reports 2001–2003," no date. Retrieved February 11, 2005, from http://www.dtic .mil/domesticviolence/reports/start.pdf.

26. Defense Task Force on Domestic Violence, no date. Retrieved January 13, 2005, from http://www.dtic.mil/domesticviolence/body.htm.

27. Ibid. Interview with Deborah D. Tucker, April 1, 2005, Austin, Texas.

28. Taylor, L., "The Defense Department Takes Aim at Domestic Violence," *Government Executive,* March 2002. Retrieved May 21, 2004, from http://www.dtic.mil/domesticviolence/news-execdod.htm.

29. Ibid.

30. Family Violence Prevention Fund, "The Defense Task Force on Domestic Violence Reports," no date. Retrieved February 11, 2005, from http://end abuse.org.

31. Statement by Lieutenant General Garry L. Parks and Ms. Deborah D.Tucker, co-chairs of the Defense Task Force on Domestic Violence, before the Subcommittee on Total Force House Armed Service Committee, United States House of Representatives, Concerning Domestic Violence, March 19, 2003. Retrieved March 6, 2005, from http://armedservices.house.gov/openingstate mentsandpressreleases/108thcongress/03-03-19parks.htm.

32. Ibid.

33. Tucker, D., "My Three Years in the Military: The Department of Defense Task Force on Domestic Violence," *Notice* 1:1 (Summer 2003). Available from http://www.ncdsv.org/images/DT_story_NOTICE_Summer_03.pdf. Interview with Deborah D. Tucker, April 1, 2005, Austin, Texas.

34. Molino, J., "Implementation of Defense Task Force on Domestic Violence (DTFDV) Recommendations," Washington, DC: Congressional Women's Caucus, May 13, 2004. Retrieved March 3, 2005, from http://www.ncdsv .org/images/ImplementationDTFDVRecsMolino.pdf.

35. Ibid.

36. Taylor, L, 1–8.

37. Hansen, C, 60.

38. Prepared Statement of Christine Hansen, executive director, The Miles Foundation, Personnel Subcommittee, Senate Armed Services Committee, February 25, 2004. Retrieved March 4, 2005, from http://www.globalsecurity.org/ military/library/congress/2004_hr/040225-hansen.pdf.

39. Tucker, D, 4–5.

40. Family Violence Prevention Fund, "Fort Bragg Domestic Homicide Review," November 12, 2002. Retrieved March 4, 2005, from http://endabuse.org/ programs/printable/display.php3?NewsFlashID=387.

41. Ibid.

42. Ibid.

43. Carr, T., "Military and Political Leaders Take Action to Save Lives in the Aftermath of Fort Bragg Homicides," *Florida Voice,* Florida Coalition Against Domestic Violence, Spring 2003.
44. Ibid, 1–2. See also Tucker, D., 5.
45. Beals, 13.
46. Ibid.
47. Ibid, 4.
48. Hansen, C., 60–61.
49. Ibid, 61.
50. Ibid, 61. Interview with Deborah D. Tucker, April 1, 2005, Austin, Texas.
51. Ibid, 61. Interview with Deborah D. Tucker, April 1, 2005, Austin, Texas.
52. Ibid, 61.
53. Ibid, 61.
54. Beals, J., 8.
55. Ibid., 31. Interview with Deborah D. Tucker, April 1, 2005, Austin, Texas.
56. Hansen, C, 61–62.
57. Ibid, 61–62.
58. Interview with Deborah D. Tucker, April 1, 2005, Austin, Texas.
59. Beals, J., 14.
60. Ibid.
61. Ibid., 15.
62. Ibid.
63. Ibid.
64. Hansen, C., 62.
65. Ibid, 63.
66. Beals, J., 5.
67. Ibid.
68. RAND, "Suggestions for Improving Military-Civilian Domestic Violence Collaborations," Santa Monica, CA, 2003. Retrieved March 3, 2005, from http://www.rand.org.
69. Ibid.
70. Ibid.
71. Tucker, D., 5.

Chapter 13: Creating a Community Response to Domestic Violence

1. Jackson, M., and Garvin, D., "Coordinated Community Action Model," 2003. Retrieved October 15, 2004, from http://www.mincava.umn.edu/documents/ccam/ccam.html. Inspired and adapted from the "Power and Control Wheel" developed by the Domestic Abuse Intervention Project, Duluth, MN.
2. Davies, J., *Safety Planning with Battered Women: Complex Lives/Difficult Choices* (Thousand Oaks, CA: Sage Publications, 1998), 146–47.
3. Ibid., 164.

4. See Witwer, M.B., and Crawford, C.A., *A Coordinated Approach to Reducing Family Violence: Conference Highlights,* Washington, DC: United States Department of Justice, Office of Justice Programs, National Institute of Justice, October 1995.

5. Jones, A., *Next Time She'll Be Dead: Battering and How to Stop It* (Boston, MA: Beacon Press, 1994), 213–14.

6. Hart, B.J., "Coordinated Community Approaches to Domestic Violence," presented at the Strategic Planning Workshop on Violence Against Women, National Institute of Justice, Washington, DC, March 31, 1995. Retrieved January 23, 2004 from http://www.mincava.umn.edu/documents/hart/nij.shtml.

7. Shepard, M., "Evaluating Coordinated Community Responses to Domestic Violence," April 1999. Retrieved June 14, 2004, from http://www.mincava.umn.edu.

8. Hart, B.J, 3.

9. Shepard, M., 2

10. Hart, B.J., 3–4.

11. American Civil Liberties Union, Women's Rights Project, "Domestic Violence and Homelessness," October 26, 2004. Retrieved May 16, 2005, from http://www.aclu.org/Files/OpenFile.cfm?id=16884; See also Velsor-Friedrich, B., "Homeless Children and Their Families, Part I: The Changing Picture," *Journal of Pediatric Nursing* 8 (1993): 122.

Chapter 14: Intervention Strategies for Battered Women and Their Children

1. P.M.G., "Growing," in *Northern Ireland Women's Aid Federation* (Belfast, Northern Ireland: The Foam Sprite, 1993).

2. NiCarthy, G., Merriam, K., and Coffman, S., *Talking It Out: A Guide to Groups for Abused Women* (Seattle, WA: Seal Press, 1984), 25–26.

3. See Pence, E., *In Our Best Interest: A Process for Personal and Social Change* (Duluth, MN: Minnesota Program Development, 1987).

4. See Freire, P., *Pedagogy of the Oppressed* (New York: Continuum, 1970). See also Freire, P., *Education for Critical Consciousness* (New York: Continuum, 1973).

5. Pence, E., 20.

6. NiCarthy, G., et al., 27–29.

7. See Chesler, P., *Women and Madness* (Garden City, NY: Doubleday, 1972).

8. Whalen, M., *Counseling to End Violence Against Women: A Subversive Model* (Thousand Oaks, CA: Sage Publications, 1996), 31.

9. Pence, E., 5.

10. Whalen, M., 51–52.

11. Jaffe, P.G., Wolfe, D.A., and Wilson, S.K., *Children of Battered Women* (Newbury Park, CA: Sage Publications, 1990), 96–97.

12. Ibid., 86.

13. Ibid., 98.
14. Edleson, J.L., and Peled, E., "Small Group Intervention with Children of Battered Women," *Violence Update* 4:9 (May 1994): 1.
15. Ibid., 2.
16. Jaffe, P.G., et al., 89.
17. Peled, E., " 'Secondary' Victims No More: Refocusing Intervention with Children," in Edleson, J.L., and Eisikovits, Z.C. (eds.), *Future Interventions with Battered Women and Their Families* (Thousand Oaks, CA: Sage Publications, 1996), 145–47.
18. Ibid., 144.
19. Jaffe, P.G., et al., 99.
20. For a discussion of empowerment as depoliticization see Mann, B., "Working with Battered Women: Radical Education or Therapy" in Pence, E., 104–55.

Chapter 15: Advocacy and Empowerment for Battered Women

1. Stout, K.D., and McPhail, B., *Confronting Sexism and Violence Against Women: A Challenge for Social Work* (New York: Longman, 1998), 63.
2. Ibid.
3. Ibid.
4. Davies, J., *Safety Planning with Battered Women: Complex Lives/Difficult Choices* (Thousand Oaks, CA: Sage Publications, 1998), 2.
5. Pennsylvania Coalition Against Rape, *The Trainer's Toolbox*, Chapter 9, no date.
6. Davies, J., 1998, 6.
7. Ibid.
8. Zubretsky, T.M., and McGrath, C., "A Framework for Intervention with Survivors of Domestic Violence," no date. Retrieved July 19, 2000, from http://www.serve.com/zone/profinfo/intvsurv.html.
9. Ibid.
10. American Psychological Association Presidential Task Force on Violence and the Family, *Violence and the Family* (Washington, DC: American Psychological Association, 1996), 36.
11. Goodkind, J.B., Sullivan, C.M., and Bybee, D.J., "A Contextual Analysis of Battered Women's Safety Planning," *Violence Against Women* 10:5 (May 2004): 514–33.
12. Davies, J., *Safety Planning* (Hartford, CT: Greater Hartford Legal Assistance, 1997).
13. Ibid.
14. Texas Council on Family Violence, *Advocacy Based Safety Planning*, Austin, TX, no date.
15. Hart, B.J., "Lethality and Dangerousness Assessments," *Violence Update* 4:10 (June 1994): 7–8. Distributed by the National Resource Center on Domestic Violence, June 30, 1995.
16. Ibid., 7–8.

17. Campbell, J., *Assessing Dangerousness* (Newbury Park, CA: Sage Publications, 1995). See also Campbell, J.C., Webster, D., Koziol-McLain, J., Block, C.R., Campbell, D.W., Curry, M.A., Gary, F., Sachs, C.U., Sharps, P.W., Ulrich, Y., Wilt, S., Manganello, J., Schollenberger, J., Xu, X., and Frye, V., "Risk Factors for Femicide in Abusive Relationships: Results from a Multi-Site Case Control Study," *American Journal of Public Health,* in press.

18. Campbell, J.C., et al., "Assessing Risk Factors for Intimate Partner Homicide," *NIJ Journal* 250, no date: 15–19.

19. Zubretsky, T.M., and McGrath, C., 1–8.

20. Family Violence Prevention Fund, "New Resources Help Domestic Violence Service Providers Navigate Child Welfare System," *NewsFlash!* 2003.

21. Family Violence Prevention Fund, "Advocacy Matters: Helping Mothers and Their Children Involved with the Child Protection System," November 21, 2003. Retrieved November 21, 2003, from http://www.fvpf.org.

22. Women's Justice Center, "Tips for Social Workers, Counselors, Health Workers, Teachers, Clergy, and Others Helping Victims of Rape, Domestic Violence, and Child Abuse," 2000. Retrieved December, 2004, from http://www.justicewomen.com.

23. Davies, J., 1998, 41.

Chapter 16: Intervention and Prevention Programs for Batterers

1. Paymar, M., *Violent No More: Helping Men End Domestic Abuse* (Alameda, CA: Hunter House, 1993), 26.

2. Schechter, S., *Women and Male Violence: The Visions and Struggles of the Battered Women's Movement* (Boston, MA: South End Press, 1982), 261–62.

3. Ritmeester, T., "Batterers' Programs, Battered Women's Movement, and Issues of Accountability," in Pence, E., and Paymar, M., *Education Groups for Men Who Batter: The Duluth Model* (New York: Springer Publishing Company, 1993), 169.

4. Ibid., 171.

5. See Adams, D., "Treatment Models of Men Who Batter: A Profeminist Analysis," in Yllo, K., and Bograd, M. (eds.), *Feminist Perspectives on Wife Abuse* (Thousand Oaks, CA: Sage Publications, 1988), 176–99.

6. Thorne-Finch, R., *Ending the Silence: The Origins and Treatment of Male Violence Against Women* (Toronto, Canada: University of Toronto Press, 1992), 138–39.

7. Eisikovits, Z.C., and Edleson, J.L., "Intervening with Men Who Batter: A Critical Review of the Literature," *Social Service Review* 63 (1989): 384–414.

8. See Williams, O.J., "Ethnically Sensitive Practice to Enhance Treatment Participation of African American Men Who Batter," *Families in Society: The Journal of Contemporary Human Services* (December 1992): 588–95.

9. Edleson, J.L., "Controversy and Change in Batterers' Programs," in Edleson, J.L., and Eisikovits, Z.C. (eds.), *Future Interventions with Battered Women and Their Families* (Thousand Oaks, CA: Sage Publications, 1996), 156.

10. National Institute of Justice, *Batterer Intervention Programs: Where Do We Go from Here?* (Washington, DC: U.S. Department of Justice, Office of Justice Programs, June 2003), 23. Retrieved June 14, 2004, from http://www.ojp .usdoj.gov/nij.

11. Gondolf, E.W., "Patterns of Reassault in Batterer Programs," *Violence and Victims* 12:4 (Winter 1997): 373–87.

12. National Institute of Justice, 2.

13. Edleson, J.L., 164–65. See also Petrik, N.D., et al., "The Reduction of Male Abusiveness as a Result of Treatment: Reality or Myth?" *Journal of Family Violence* 9:4 (1994): 307–8.

14. National Institute of Justice, 27.

15. See Texas Department of Criminal Justice, Community Justice Assistance Division, and the Texas Council on Family Violence, *Battering Intervention and Prevention Project Guidelines,* Austin, TX, December 1, 1999.

16. Herman, M., *Knowledge and Information Services: The State of U.S. Batterer Program Standards* (Arlington, VA: The National Center for State Courts, 2000).

17. Texas Department of Criminal Justice, 5.

18. Texas Council on Family Violence, *Is He Really Going to Change This Time?* Austin, TX, August 1995.

19. Edleson, J.L., 162.

20. Texas Council on Family Violence, "Men's Nonviolence Project," no date. Retrieved November 2, 2004, from http://www.tcfv.org/mens_non-violence.htm.

21. Funk, R.E., *Stopping Rape: A Challenge For Men* (Philadelphia, PA: New Society Publishers, 1993), 129.

Chapter 17: Loving Ourselves: Self-Care for Helpers

1. Steinem, G., *Revolution from Within: A Book of Self-Esteem* (Boston, MA: Little, Brown and Company, 1992), 283.

2. Corrigan, M., "Burnout: How to Spot It and Protect Yourself Against It," *The Journal of Volunteer Administration* (Spring 1994): 24–31.

3. Maslach, C., *Burnout: The Cost of Caring* (New York: Prentice Hall Press, 2003), 81.

4. Schechter, S., *Women and Male Violence: The Visions and Struggles of the Battered Women's Movement* (Boston, MA: South End Press, 1982), 293.

5. Maslach, C., 11.

6. Ibid., 38–40.

7. Veninga, R.L., and Spradley, J.P., *The Work/Stress Connection: How to Cope with Job Burnout* (Boston, MA: Little, Brown and Company, 1981), 28–35. See also Maslach, C., 57.

8. Veninga, R.L., and Spradley, J.P., 20–21.

9. Sapolsky, R.M., *Why Zebras Don't Get Ulcers: A Guide to Stress, Stress-Related Diseases and Coping* (New York: Owl Books, 2004), 8.

10. Ibid., 13–14.

11. Fronk, R., *Creating a Lifestyle You Can Live With* (New Kensington, PA: Whitaker House, 1988).
12. Veninga, R.L., and Spradley, J.P., 39–73.
13. Maslach, C., 4.
14. Ibid., 75–76.
15. Ibid., 64–65.
16. Pearlman, L.A., and Saakvitne, K.W., *Trauma and the Therapist* (New York: W.W. Norton and Company, 1995), 386.
17. Veninga, R.L., and Spradley, J.P., 253–54.
18. Pearlman, L.A., and Saakvitne, K.W., 393.
19. Ibid., 390.
20. Mackoff, B., *Leaving the Office Behind* (New York: Dell Publishing Company, 1984), 59.
21. Ibid., 23.
22. Pearlman, L.A., and Saakvitne, K.W., 390–91.
23. See Lark, S.M., *Anxiety and Stress: A Self-Help Program* (Los Altos, CA: Westchester Publishing Company, 1993).
24. Saunders, C., *Women and Stress* (New York: HarperCollins, 1991), 10–11.
25. Ibid., 65.
26. See Lark, S.M., 171–74.
27. Steinem, G., 180.
28. McGee-Cooper, A., *You Don't Have to Go Home from Work Exhausted* (New York: Bantam Books, 1992).
29. See Steinem, G., 175–76.
30. See Reed, H., *Dream Solutions: Using Your Dreams to Change Your Life* (San Rafael, CA: New World Library, 1991).
31. See Steinem, G., 173–75.
32. Mackoff, B., 36.
33. Witkin-Lanoil, G., *The Female Stress Syndrome* (New York: New Market Press, 1988), 129.
34. See Lark, S.M., 161–64.
35. Saunders, C., 19. See also Lark, S.M., 177–84.
36. Lark, S.M., 164–66.
37. Ibid., 169–71.
38. Ibid., 201–17.
39. Saunders, C., 253–54.
40. Lark, S.M., 175.
41. Saunders, C., 260.
42. See Wildwood, C., *Creative Aromatherapy* (San Francisco, CA: Thorsons, 1993).
43. Saunders, C., 261.
44. See Schechter, S., 294.

Chapter 18: The National Domestic Violence Hotline

1. National Domestic Violence Hotline, Press Release, Austin, TX, November 29, 2001.
2. "The Violence Against Women Act of 2000 (VAWA 2000)," Washington, DC: Office of Justice Programs, United States Department of Justice, no date. Retrieved October 7, 2004, from http://www.ojp.usdoj.gov/vawo/laws/vawa_summary2.htm.
3. National Domestic Violence Hotline.
4. Ibid.

Appendix I: A History of Violence Against Women

1. Gordon, L., *Heroes of Their Own Lives: The Politics and History of Family Violence* (New York: Penguin Books, 1988), 250.
2. Janssen-Jurreit, M., *Sexism: The Male Monopoly on History and Thought* (New York: Farrar, Straus and Giroux, 1982), 223.
3. See Daly, M., *Gyn/Ecology: The Metaethics of Radical Feminism* (Boston, MA: Beacon Press, 1978), 109–313. See also McAllister, P., *This River of Courage: Generations of Women's Resistance and Action* (Philadelphia, PA: New Society Publishers, 1991), 149–61; Lightfoot-Klein, H., *Prisoners of Ritual: An Odyssey into Female Genital Circumcision in Africa* (New York: Harrington Park Press, 1989); Narasimhan, S., *Sati: Widow Burning in India* (New York: Anchor Books, 1990).
4. Johnson, B., *Lady of the Beasts: Ancient Images of the Goddess and Her Sacred Animals* (San Francisco, CA: HarperCollins, 1988), 3.
5. Engels, F., "The Origin of the Family, Private Property and the State" (Chicago, IL: C.H. Kerr and Co., 1902), in Agonito, R.(ed.), *History of Ideas on Woman,* (New York: Perigee Books, 1977), 274.
6. Lerner, G., *The Creation of Patriarchy* (New York: Oxford University Press, 1986), 31.
7. Ibid., 39, 125–47. See also Janssen-Jurreit, M., 70–71; Johnson, B.; Eisler, R., *The Chalice and the Blade* (San Francisco, CA: Harper and Row, 1987), 2–28.
8. Chevillard, N., and Sebastien, L., "The Dawn of Lineage Societies," in Coontz, S., and Henderson, P. (eds.), *Women's Work, Men's Property: The Origins of Gender and Class* (London: Verso, 1986), 101. See also Martin, D., *Battered Wives* (Volcano, CA: Volcano Press, 1981), 25; Johnson, B., 348–49.
9. Lerner, G., 8.
10. Ibid., 53.
11. Brownmiller, S., *Against Our Will: Men, Women and Rape* (New York: Simon and Schuster, 1975), 16–19.
12. Ibid., 17. See also Engels, F., 273–74; Scott, G.R., *Curious Customs of Sex and Marriage* (London: Senate, 1995), 53–57 (orig. pub. 1953).
13. Engels, F., 279–80.
14. Ibid., 280.

15. Mill, J.S., *The Subjection of Women* (Arlington Heights, IL: AHM Publishing Corp., 1980), 29 (orig. pub. 1869).

16. Brownmiller, S., 18. See also Scott, G.R., 64–69.

17. Lerner, G., 77–213.

18. Ibid., 81–100.

19. Ibid., 212–16.

20. Aristotle, "The Differences Between Men and Women" (Oxford, England: Claredon Press, 1912), in Agonito, R., 51–54.

21. Anderson, B.S., and Zinsser, J.P., *A History of Their Own: Women in Europe from Prehistory to the Present,* vol. I (New York: Harper and Row, 1988), 31.

22. Donaldson, J., *Woman: Her Position and Influence in Ancient Greece and Rome, and Among the Early Christians* (New York: Longmans, Green and Co., 1907), 87–88. See also Gies, F., and Gies, J., *Women in the Middle Ages* (New York: Barnes and Noble Books, 1978), 13.

23. Dobash, R.E., and Dobash, R.P., *Violence Against Wives: A Case Against the Patriarchy* (New York: Free Press, 1979), 34–40.

24. Gies, F., and Gies, J., *Marriage and the Family in the Middle Ages* (New York: Harper and Row, 1987), 18–19.

25. Ibid., 27. See also Scott, G.R., 145–50.

26. Anderson, B.S., and Zinsser, J.P., 30–31. See also Janssen-Jurreit, M., 261.

27. Dobash, R.E., and Dobash, R.P., 37.

28. Anderson, B.S., and Zinsser, J.P., 23–49.

29. Donaldson, J., 10.

30. Anderson, B.S., and Zinsser, J.P., 15–23.

31. Gies, F., and Gies, J.,1987, 37–41. See also Donaldson, J., 188–90.

32. Achterberg, J., *Woman as Healer* (Boston, MA: Shambhala, 1991), 66. See also Davidson, T., "Wifebeating: A Recurring Phenomenon Throughout History," in Roy, M. (ed.), *Battered Women: A Psychosociological Study of Domestic Violence* (New York: Van Nostrand Reinhold Co., 1977), 6–10.

33. Achterberg, J., 66–68.

34. Augustine, "Woman as Auxiliary and Subject to Man" (Edinburgh, Scotland: T. & T. Clark, 1871), in Agonito, R., 79.

35. Aquinas, T., "Woman as Derived Being" (London: R. and T. Washbourne, 1912), in Agonito, R., 85.

36. Barstow, A.L., *Witchcraze* (San Francisco, CA: Pandora, 1994), 21.

37. Achterberg, J., 85–86. See also Barstow, A.L., 58–69.

38. Barstow, A.L., 20–21.

39. Ehrenreich, B., and English, D., 8. See also Barstow, A.L., 142.

40. Achterberg, J., 88.

41. Davis, E.G., *The First Sex* (New York: Penguin Books, 1979), 257.

42. Barstow, A.L., 109.

43. Ehrenreich, B., and English, D., 15–19.

44. Achterberg, J., 81.

45. Barstow, A.L., 54.

46. Achterberg, J., 84.

47. Ehrenreich, B., and English, D., 9. See also Barstow, A.L., 62–63, 171–72; Williams, S.R., and Adelman, P.W., *Riding the Nightmare: Women and Witchcraft from the Old World to Colonial Salem* (New York: HarperPerennial, 1992), 35–45.

48. Barstow, A.L., 129–30. See also Williams, S.R., and Adelman, P.W., 83.

49. Achterberg, 84.

50. Sinistrari, L.M., *Demoniality* (New York: Dover Publications, 1989), 10 (orig. pub. London: The Fortune Press, 1927). See also Williams, S.R., and Adelman, P.W., 99.

51. Barstow, A.L., 129–30.

52. Ibid., 54. See also Williams, S.R., and Adelman, P.W., 19.

53. Achterberg, J., 83.

54. Barstow, A.L., 131.

55. Ibid., 143. See also Williams, S.R., and Adelman, P.W., 62.

56. Achterberg, J., 98.

57. Davis, E.G., 252–55. See also Dutton, D.G., *The Domestic Assault of Women* (Vancouver, Canada: UBC Press, 1995), 19.

58. Ibid., 253.

59. Gies, F., and Gies, J., 1978, 46.

60. Martin, D., 30.

61. Janssen-Jurreit, M., 225.

62. Tuchman, B.W., *A Distant Mirror* (New York: Ballantine Books, 1978), 213–14.

63. Janssen-Jurreit, M., 225.

64. Ibid., 227.

65. Davis, E.G., 163–65. See also Dingwall, E.J., *The Girdle of Chastity: A History of the Chastity Belt* (New York: Dorset Press, 1992), 2–4.

66. Janssen-Jurreit, M., 243–54. See also Daly, M., 153–70; Lightfoot-Klein, H.

67. Davis, E.G., 165–66. See also Scott, G.R., 132–33; Dingwall, E.J., 4–91.

68. Scott, G.R., 133.

69. Luria, G., and Tiger, V., *Everywoman* (New York: Random House, 1976), 15.

70. Adams, A., *An Uncommon Scold* (New York: Simon and Schuster, 1989), 9.

71. Andrews, W., *Old Time Punishments* (New York: Dorsett Press, 1991), 1–4 (orig. pub. 1890).

72. Ibid., 13–14.

73. Ibid., 22–35.

74. Ibid., 38–42.

75. Spruill, J.C., *Women's Life and Work in the Southern Colonies* (New York: W.W. Norton and Co., 1972), 330–31.

76. Adams, A., 9–12.

77. Gordon, L., 279. See also Davidson, T., 12–13; Scott, G.R., 151–52.

78. Andrews, W., 180–81.

79. Dubois, E.C., and Ruiz, V.L., *Unequal Sisters: A Multi-Cultural Read in U.S. Women's History* (New York: Routledge, 1990), 197.
80. Dworkin, A., *Woman Hating* (New York: Plume, 1974), 96–97.
81. Levy, H.S., *Chinese Footbinding: The History of a Curious Erotic Custom* (New York: W. Rawls, 1966), 25–26.
82. Dworkin, A., 101–3.
83. Dubois, E.C., and Ruiz, V.L., 197.
84. Narashimhan, S., 11.
85. Stein, D.K., "Women to Burn: Suttee as a Normative Institution," in Radford, H., and Russell, D.E.H. (eds.), *Femicide: The Politics of Woman Killing* (New York: Twayne Publishers, 1992), 62.
86. Narashimhan, S., 18.
87. Stein, D.K., 63.
88. Narashimhan, S., 43.
89. Ibid., 52–53.
90. Ibid., 61–73.
91. Spruill, J.C., 340–41. See also Hymowitz, C., and Weissman, M., *A History of Women in America* (New York: Bantam Books, 1978), 22–23.
92. Jennings, S., "Proper Conduct of the Wife Towards Her Husband" (New York: Lorenzo Dow, 1808), in Cott, N.F. (ed.), *Root of Bitterness* (New York: E.P. Dutton, 1972), 113.
93. Spruill, J.C., 341–43.
94. Stacey, W.A., and Shupe, A., *The Family Secret: Domestic Violence in America* (Boston, MA: Beacon Press, 1983), 12.
95. Martin, D., 31. See also Stacey, W.A., and Shupe, A., 12–13.
96. Davidson, T., 18–19.
97. Hymowitz, C., and Weissman, M., 25.
98. Stacey, W.A., and Shupe, A., 13. See also Davidson, T., 4.
99. Davidson, T., 19.
100. Martin, D., 32.
101. Pleck, E., "The Whipping Post for Wife Beaters, 1876–1906," in Moch, L.P., and Stark, G.D. (eds.), *Essays on the Family and Historical Change* (College Station, TX: Texas A&M University Press, 1983), 127–29.
102. Martin, D., 32.
103. Stacey, W.A., and Shupe, A., 13.
104. Rousseau, J.J., "Paternity and the Origin of Political Power" (London: J.M. Dent and Sons, Ltd., 1913), in Agonito, R., 119.
105. See Wollstonecraft, M., *A Vindication of the Rights of Woman,* New York: Everyman's Library, 1992 (orig. pub. London: J. Johnson, 1792); See Rousseau, J.J., *Emile* (New York: Barron's Educational Series, Inc., 1964) (orig. Eng. trans. pub. 1768).
106. Agonito, R., 145–146.
107. Hymowitz, C., and Weissman, M., 76–77.

108. Davis, A., *Women, Race and Class* (New York: Vintage Books, 1981), 39. See also Hymowitz, C., and Weissman, M., 79.

109. Papachristou, J., *Women Together* (New York: Alfred A. Knopf, 1976), 23.

110. Hymowitz, C., and Weissman, M., 218–20.

111. Davis, A., 144–71. See also Hymowitz, C., and Weissman, M., 79–114, 218–63.

112. Papachristou, J., 29.

113. Mill, J.S., 34.

114. Agonito, R., pp. 223–24. See also Davidson, T., pp. 16–17.

115. Pleck, E., p. 142.

116. Cobbe, F.P., "Wife Torture in England" (orig. pub. London, 1878), in Radford, J., and Russell, D.E.H. (eds.), 47. See also Stark, E., and Flitcraft, A., *Women at Risk* (Thousand Oaks, CA: Sage Publications, 1996), 43–45.

117. Pleck, E., 142–43.

118. Showalter, E., *The Female Malady: Women, Madness, and English Culture* (New York: Penguin Books, 1985), 129.

119. See Masson, J.M., *A Dark Science* (New York: Farrar, Straus and Giroux, 1986).

120. Showalter, E., 74–78.

121. Daly, M., 224–28.

122. Ehrenreich, B., and English, D., *For Her Own Good: 150 Years of the Experts' Advice to Women* (New York: Doubleday, 1978), 123–25.

123. Showalter, E., 145.

124. Ibid., 164–70.

125. Gordon, L., 27, 115.

126. Ibid., 19.

127. Ibid., 252–81. See also Feldberg, M., "Police Discretion and Family Disturbances: Some Historical and Contemporary Reflections," in Newberger, E.H., and Bourne, R. (eds.), *Unhappy Families* (Littleton, MA: PGS Publishing, 1985).

128. Papachristou, J., 196–97.

129. Gordon, L., 20–23.

130. Papachristou, J., 212.

131. Gordon, L., 23.

132. Goldman, E., *The Traffic in Women and Other Essays on Feminism* (Ojai, CA: Times Change Press, 1970), 14 (orig. pub. New York: Mother Earth Publishing, 1917).

133. Gordon, L., 251.

134. Evans, S., *Personal Politics* (New York: Vintage Books, 1979), 219–20.

135. Hymowitz, C., and Weissman, M., 347–49.

136. Cohen, M., *The Sisterhood* (New York: Fawcett Columbine, 1988), 390–91.

137. Hymowitz, C., and Weissman, M., 349.

138. Evans, S., 214–16.

139. Hymowitz, C., and Weissman, M., 350.

140. Evans, S., 215, 130.
141. Hymowitz, C., and Weissman, M., 351–55. See also Cohen, M., 175–76.
142. Texas Council on Family Violence, *Working Together for Change,* Austin, TX, 1992, 5.
143. McAllister, P., 132–51.
144. Schechter, S., *Women and Male Violence: The Visions and Struggles of the Battered Women's Movement* (Boston, MA: South End Press, 1982), 5.
145. Ibid., 154.
146. See Pizzey, E., *Scream Quietly or the Neighbors Will Hear* (Short Hills, NJ: Ridley Enlow Publishers, 1974).
147. McAllister, P., 134–35.
148. Schechter, S., 29–51.
149. Ibid., 258.
150. McAllister, P., 133–34. See also Schechter, S., 62–63.
151. Schechter, S., 56–57.
152. Austin Center for Battered Women, *History of the Austin Center for Battered Women,* Austin, TX, no date.
153. National Woman Abuse Prevention Project (NWAPP), *Domestic Violence Factsheet: The Battered Women's/Shelter Movement,* Washington, DC, no date.
154. National Coalition Against Domestic Violence (NCADV), "Summary of Organization's History," Denver, CO, no date. Retrieved October 17, 2004, from http://www.ncadv.org/about.htm.
155. NWAPP, *Domestic Violence Factsheet: The Battered Women's/Shelter Movement.*
156. See Martin, D.
157. NWAPP, *Domestic Violence Factsheet: Highlights of Major Events of the Battered Women's Movement,* Washington, DC, no date.
158. Ibid.
159. Schechter, S., 133–35.
160. Ibid., 136–37.
161. See United States Commission on Civil Rights, *Battered Women: Issues of Public Policy,* Washington, DC, January 30–31, 1978.
162. NWAPP, *Domestic Violence Factsheet: Highlights of Major Events of the Battered Women's Movement.*
163. Schechter, S., 192–95.
164. Ibid., 143.
165. NWAPP, *Domestic Violence Factsheet: Highlights of Major Events of the Battered Women's Movement.*
166. "The Violence Against Women Act of 2000 (VAWA 2000)," Office of Justice Programs, United States Department of Justice, Washington, DC, no date. Retrieved October 7, 2004, from http://www.ojp.usdoj.gov/vawo/laws/vawa_summary2.htm.

Conclusion

1. Durose, C.W.H., Langan, P.A., Motivans, M., Rantala, R.R., and Schmitt, E.L., "Family Violence Statistics," Washington, DC: U.S. Department of Jus-

tice, Bureau of Justice Statistics, 2005. Retrieved August 21, 2005, from www.ojp.usdoj.gov/bjs/abstract/fvs.htm.

2. National Network to End Domestic Violence, "Talking Points in Response to *Family Violence Statistics, a Report of the Bureau of Justice Statistics, U.S. Department of Justice* (Released June 2005)," Washington, DC: National Network to End Domestic Violence, 2005.

Resources

State Domestic-Violence Coalitions

Alabama	(334) 832-4842
Alaska	(907) 586-3650
Arizona	(602) 279-2900
Arkansas	(800) 269-4668
	(501) 907-5612
California	
– Statewide California Coalition for Battered Women	(562) 981-1202
– California Alliance Against Domestic Violence	(916) 444-7163
Colorado	(303) 831-9632
Connecticut	(860) 282-7899
Delaware	(302) 658-2958
District of Columbia	(202) 299-1181
Florida	(850) 425-2749
Georgia	(404) 209-0280
Hawaii	(808) 832-9316
Idaho	(208) 384-0419
Illinois	(217) 789-2830
Indiana	(317) 917-3685
Iowa	(515) 244-8028
Kansas	(785) 232-9784
Kentucky	(502) 695-2444
Louisiana	(225) 752-1296
Maine	(207) 941-1194
Maryland	(301) 352-4574
Massachusetts	(617) 248-0922
Michigan	(517) 347-7000
Minnesota	(612) 646-6177
Mississippi	(601) 981-9196
Missouri	(573) 634-4161
Montana	(406) 443-7794
Nebraska	(402) 476-6256
Nevada	(775) 828-1115
New Hampshire	(603) 224-8893
New Jersey	(609) 584-8107
New Mexico	(505) 246-9240
New York	(518) 482-5465
North Carolina	(919) 956-9124
North Dakota	(701) 255-6240
Ohio	
– Ohio Domestic Violence Network	(614) 781-9651
– Action Ohio Coalition for Battered Women	(614) 221-1255
Oklahoma	(405) 524-0700
Oregon	(503) 365-9644
Pennsylvania	(717) 545-6400
Puerto Rico	(787) 721-7676
Rhode Island	(401) 467-9940
South Carolina	(803) 256-2900
South Dakota	(605) 945-0869
Tennessee	(615) 386-9406
Texas	(512) 794-1133
U.S. Virgin Islands	(340) 773-9272
Utah	(801) 521-5544
Vermont	(802) 223-1302
Virginia	(757) 221-0990
Washington	
– Olympia office	(360) 586-1022
– Seattle office	(260) 389-2515
West Virginia	(304) 965-3552
Wisconsin	(608) 255-0539
Wyoming	(307) 755-5481

General Resources on Domestic Violence

Domestic-Violence Reading Material

Bograd, Michele, and Kersti Yllo, eds. *Feminist Perspectives on Wife Abuse.* Newbury Park, CA: Sage Publications, 1988.

Brown, Sandra L. *How to Spot a Dangerous Man.* Alameda, CA: Hunter House, 2005.

Brownmiller, Susan. *Against Our Will: Men, Women and Rape.* New York: Simon and Schuster, 1975.

Cole, Johnnetta B., ed. *All American Women: Lines That Divide, Ties That Bind.* New York: The Free Press, 1986.

Evans, Patricia. *The Verbally Abusive Relationship: How to Recognize It and How to Respond.* Holbrook, MA: Bob Adams, 1992.

Ferrato, Donna. *Living with the Enemy.* New York: Aperture Publishing Co., 1991.

Finkelhor, David, and Kersti Yllo. *License to Rape: Sexual Abuse of Wives.* New York: Holt, Rinehart and Winston, 1985.

Fisher, Ellen, and Edward Gondolf. *Battered Women as Survivors: An Alternative to Treating Learned Helplessness.* Lexington, MA: D.C. Heath and Co./Lexington Books, 1988.

Gondolf, Edward. *Man Against Woman: What Every Woman Should Know about Violent Men.* Bradenton, FL: Human Services Institute, 1989.

Hale, Katherine, and M'Liss Switzer. *Called to Account.* Seattle, WA: Seal Press, 1987.

Jayne, Pamela. *Ditch That Jerk! Dealing with Men Who Control and Hurt Women.* Alameda, CA: Hunter House, 2000.

Johnson, Scott. *When "I Love You" Turns Violent: Emotional and Physical Abuse in Dating Relationships.* Far Hills, NJ: New Horizon Press, 1993.

Jones, Ann. *Next Time, She'll Be Dead: Battering and How to Stop It.* Boston, MA: Beacon Press, 1994.

Jones, Ann, and Susan Schechter. *When Love Goes Wrong: Strategies for Women with Controlling Partners.* New York: HarperCollins Publishers, 1992.

Lissette, Andrea, and Richard Kraus. *Free Yourself from an Abusive Relationship.* Alameda, CA: Hunter House, 2000.

Martin, Del. *Battered Wives.* New York: Pocket Books, 1983.

NiCarthy, Ginny. *The Ones Who Got Away: Women Who Left Abusive Partners.* Seattle, WA: Seal Press, 1987.

Pence, Ellen. *In Our Best Interest: A Process for Personal and Social Change.* Duluth: Minnesota Program Development, 1987.

Pizzey, Erin. *Scream Quietly or the Neighbors Will Hear.* Short Hills, NJ: Ridley Enslow Publishers, 1977.

Schechter, Susan. *Women and Male Violence: The Visions and Struggles of the Battered Women's Movement.* Boston, MA: South End Press, 1982.

Walker, Lenore. *The Battered Woman.* New York: Harper and Row, 1979.

Weiss, Elaine (ed.). *Surviving Domestic Violence: Voices of Women Who Broke Free.* Scottsdale, AZ: Agreka Books, 2000.

Center for Nonviolence
235 W. Creighton Ave.
Fort Wayne IN 46807
(260) 456-4112
Website: www.centerfor
nonviolence.com

Centers for Disease Control and
Prevention
1600 Clifton Rd.
Atlanta GA 30333
(800) 311-3435
(404) 639-3534
Website: www.cdc.gov

Community United Against Violence
160 14th St.
San Francisco CA 94103
(415) 777-5500
Website: www.cuav.org

Commission for Prevention of Violence
Against Women
915 Cedar St.
Santa Cruz CA 95060
(831) 420-6298
Website: www.ci.santa-cruz.ca.us/
cm/cpvaw/cpvaw.html

Faith/Trust Institute
2400 N. 45th St., #10
Seattle WA 98103
(206) 634-1903
Website: www.faithtrustinstitute.org

Family Violence Prevention Fund
383 Rhode Island St., Suite 304
San Francisco CA 94103
(415) 252-8900
(800) 585-4889, TTY
Website: http://endabuse.org

Minnesota Center Against Violence and
Abuse (MINCAVA)
University of Minnesota School of
Social Work
105 Peters Hall

1404 Gortner Ave.
St. Paul MN 55108
(612) 624-0721
Website: www.mincava.umn.edu

National Center for Victims of Crime
2000 M St. NW, Suite 480
Washington DC 20036
(202) 467-8700
(800) FYI-CALL (394-2255) (victim
assistance)
(800) 211-7996, TTY (victim assistance)
Website: www.ncvc.org

National Clearinghouse for the Defense
of Battered Women
125 S. 9th St., Suite 302
Philadelphia PA 19107
(215) 351-0010

National Clearinghouse on Domestic
Violence
PO Box 2309
Rockville MD 20852

National Coalition Against Domestic
Violence (Public Policy Office)
1633 Q St. NW, Suite 210
Washington DC 20009
(202) 745-1211

National Coalition Against Domestic
Violence (Membership Office)
PO Box 18749
Denver CO 80218
(303) 839-1852
(303) 839-8459, TTY
Website: www.ncadv.org

National Domestic Violence Hotline
PO Box 161810
Austin TX 78716
(800) 799-SAFE (7233)
(800) 787-3224, TTY
Website: www.ndvh.org

National Online Resource Center on
Violence Against Women
6400 Flank Dr., Suite 1300
Harrisburg PA 17112-2778
(800) 537-2238
(717) 545-6400
(800) 553-2508, TTY
(717) 545-9456, fax
Website: www.vawnet.org

National Resource Center on Domestic
Violence
Pennsylvania Coalition Against Domes-
tic Violence
6400 Flank Dr., Suite 1300
Harrisburg PA 17112
(800) 537-2238
Website: www.nrcdv.org

National Violence Against Women
Prevention Research Center
(a program sponsored by the Centers
for Disease Control and Prevention)
(843) 792-2945
Website: www.musc.edu/vawprevention

Office on Violence Against Women
U.S. Department of Justice
Website: www.ojp.usdoj.gov/vawo

PrePARE (Protection, Awareness,
Response, Empowerment)
147 W. 25th St., 8th Fl.
New York NY 10001
(800) 442-7273
(212) 225-0505
Website: www.prepareinc.com

Project for Research on Welfare, Work,
and Domestic Violence
University of Michigan School of Social
Work
1080 South University Ave.
Ann Arbor MI 48109-1106
Website: www.ssw.umich.edu/trapped

The Purple Ribbon Project
PO Box 159
Swanzey NH 03469
(603) 357-1050
Website: www.purpleribbonproject.com

SafePlace
PO Box 19454
Austin TX 78760
(512) 267-SAFE (7233)
(512) 967-9616, TTY
Website: www.austin-safeplace.org

Silent Witness National Initiative
20 Second St. NE, Suite 1101
Minneapolis MN 55413
(612) 623-0999
Website: www.silentwitness.net

Standing Together Against Rape
(STAR)
1057 W. Firewood Ln., #230
Anchorage AK 99503
(907) 276-RAPE (7273)
Website: www.star.ak.org

Violence Against Women Online
Resources
Website: www.vaw.umn.edu

Women Against a Violent Environment
(WAVE)
PO Box 93196
Rochester NY 14692
(585) 234-7019
Website: www.rochesternow.org

Women's Crisis Center—Defensa de
Mujeres
233 E. Lake Ave., Suite 326
Watsonville CA 95076
(831) 722-4532
Website: www.wcs-ddm.org

Resources Related to Families and Children

Reading Material Related to Families and Children

Alson, Sheila, and Gayle B. Burnett. *Peace in Everyday Relationships: Resolving Conflicts in Your Personal and Work Life*. Alameda, CA: Hunter House, 2003.

Bancroft, L., and J. Silverman. *The Batterer as Parent*. Thousand Oaks, CA: Sage, 2002.

Brandwein, Ruth A. *Battered Women, Children and Welfare Reform: The Ties That Bind*. Thousand Oaks, CA: Sage, 1999.

Crompton, Vickie, and Ellen Zelda Kessner. *Saving Beauty from the Beast: How to Protect Your Daughter from an Unhealthy Relationship*. New York: Little, Brown, 2003.

Faber, Adele, and Elaine Mazlish. *How to Talk So Kids Will Listen and Listen So Kids Will Talk*. New York: Avon Books, 1980.

Garbarino, James, Edna Guttman, and Janis Wilson Seeley. *The Psychologically Battered Child*. San Francisco, CA: Jossey-Bass Publishers, 1986.

Jaffe, P., D. Wolfe, and S. Wilson. *Children of Battered Women*. Newbury Park, CA: Sage, 1990.

Johnson, Kendall. *Trauma in the Lives of Children: Crisis and Stress Management Techniques for Counselors, Teachers, and Other Professionals*, 2nd edition. Alameda, CA: Hunter House, 1998.

Johnson, Scott A. *Man to Man: When Your Partner Says No—Pressured Sex and Date Rape*. Orwell, VT: Safer Society Press, no date.

Johnson, Scott A. *When "I Love You" Turns Violent: Emotional and Physical Abuse in Dating Relationships*. Far Hills, NJ: New Horizon Press, 1993.

Johnston, Janet R. *High Conflict and Violent Parents in Family Court: Findings on Children's Adjustment, and Proposed Guidelines for the Resolution of Custody and Visitation Disputes*. Corte Madera, CA: Center for the Family in Transition, 1992. 5725 Paradise Dr., Building B, #300, Corte Madera CA 94925.

Justice, Blair, and Rita Justice. *The Abusing Family*. New York: Human Science Press, no date.

Kaufman, Bobbie, and Agnes Wohl. *Silent Screams and Hidden Cries: An Interpretation of Artwork by Children from Violent Homes*. New York: Brunner-Mazel Publishers, 1985.

Kivel, Paul. *Boys Will Be Men: Raising Our Sons for Courage, Caring and Community*. Gabriola Island, BC, Canada: New Society Publishers, 1999.

Kosof, Anna. *Incest: Families in Crisis*. New York: Franklin Watts, 1985.

Levy, Barrie, and Patricia Occhiuzzo Giggans. *What Parents Need to Know about Dating Violence*. Seattle, WA: Seal Press, 1995.

McDermott, Judith, and Frances Wells Burck. *Children of Domestic Violence: A Guide for Moms*. New City, NY: Rockland Family Shelter, 1990.

Miedzian, M. *Boys Will Be Boys: Breaking the Link Between Masculinity and Violence*. New York: Anchor Books, 1991.

Mones, Paul A. *When a Child Kills: Abused Children Who Kill Their Parents*. New York: Pocket Books, 1991.

Muller, Ann. *Parents Matter: Parents' Relationships with Lesbian Daughters and Gay Sons.* Tallahassee, FL: Naiad Press, 1987.

National Resource Center on Domestic Violence, *Children Exposed to Intimate Partner Violence: An Information Packet.* March 2002. Available from National Resource Center on Domestic Violence, 6400 Flank Dr., Suite 1300, Harrisburg PA 17112-2791, (800) 537-2238.

A Parent's Handbook: How to Talk to Your Children about Developing Healthy Relationships. Available from Liz Claiborne, Inc., http://www.aboutourkids.org/aboutour/publications/Liz%20Claiborne%20Handbook.pdf.

Peled, E., P.G. Jaffe, and J.L. Edleson (eds.). *Ending the Cycle of Violence: Community Responses to Children of Battered Women.* Thousand Oaks, CA: Sage, 1995.

Rafkin, Louise, ed. *Different Daughters: A Book by Mothers of Lesbians.* Pittsburgh, PA: Cleis Press, 1987.

Schwartz, Pepper. *Peer Marriage: How Love Between Equals Really Works.* New York: Free Press, 1994.

Warren, Andrea, and Jay Wiedenkeller. *Everybody's Doing It: How to Survive Your Teenagers' Sex Life (and Help Them Survive It Too).* New York: Penguin Books, 1993.

Wolfe, David A., et al. *Alternatives to Violence: Empowering Youth to Develop Healthy Relationships.* Thousand Oaks, CA: Sage Publications, 1996.

Children's Reading Material

Bernstein, Sharon. *A Family That Fights* (4–12 years). Morton Grove, IL: Albert Whitman, 1991. (847) 581-0033.

Davis, Diane. *Something Is Wrong at My House* (3–10 years). Seattle, WA: Parenting Press, 1993. (800) 992-6657, http://www.parentingpress.com.

Deaton, Wendy. *I Saw It Happen: A Child's Workbook about Witnessing Violence.* Alameda, CA: Hunter House, 1998.

Deaton, Wendy, and Kendall Johnson. *Living With My Family: A Child's Workbook about Violence in the Home.* Alameda, CA: Hunter House, 1991.

Deaton, Wendy, and Kendall Johnson. *No More Hurt: A Child's Workbook about Recovering from Abuse.* Alameda, CA: Hunter House, 1991.

Kivel, Paul, with illustrations by Nancy Gorrell. *I Can Make My World a Safer Place: A Kid's Book about Stopping Violence.* Alameda, CA: Hunter House, 2001.

Paris, Susan. *Mommy and Daddy Are Fighting* (4–8 years). Seattle, WA: Seal Press, 1986. (206) 283-7844, http://www.sealpress.com.

The Rape and Abuse Crisis Center of Fargo-Moorhead. *I Wish the Hitting Would Stop* (6–14 years). Fargo, ND: Red Flag Green Flag Resources. (800) 627-3675, http://www.redflaggreenflag.com.

Trottier, Maxine. *A Safe Place* (5–9 years). Morton Grove, IL: Albert Whitman, 1997. (800) 962-1141, http://www.childswork.com.

Winn, Christine, and David Walsh. *Clover's Secret* (4–8 years). Minneapolis, MN: Fairview Press, 1996. (612) 672-4980, http://fairview press.org.

Teens' Reading Material

Abner, Allison, and Linda Villarosa. *Finding Our Way: The Teen Girl's Survival Guide.* New York: Harper Perennial, 1996.

Bass, Ellen, and Kate Kaufman. *Free Your Mind: The Book for Gay, Lesbian, and Bisexual Youth and Their Allies.* New York: Harper Collins, 1996.

Borhek, Mary. *Coming Out to Parents: A Two Way Survival Guide for Lesbians and Gay Men and Their Parents.* Cleveland, OH: Pilgrim Press, 1993.

Dee, Catherine. *The Girls' Guide to Life: How to Take Charge of the Issues That Affect You.* New York: Little, Brown, 1997.

Gittelsohn, Roland B. *Love in Your Life: A Jewish View of Teenage Sexuality.* New York: UAHC Press, 1991.

Hipp, Earl. *Feed Your Head: Some Excellent Stuff on Being Yourself.* Center City, MN: Hazelden, 1991.

Kuklin, Susan G.P. *Speaking Out: Teenagers Take on Race, Sex, and Identity.* New York: Putnam's Sons, 1993.

Levy, Barrie. *In Love and in Danger: A Teen's Guide to Breaking Free of Abusive Relationships.* Seattle, WA: Seal Press, 1993.

NiCarthy, Ginny. *Assertion Skills for Young Women.* Seattle, WA: New Directions for Young Women, 1981.

Parrot, Andrea. *Sexual Assault on Campus.* Lexington, MA: Lexington Books, 1993.

Silverstein, Herma. *Date Abuse.* Hillside, NJ: Enslow Publishers, 1994.

Curricula Related to Families and Children

Bridge over Troubled Waters, Inc., and Texas Council on Family Violence. *Dating Violence: An Anti-Victimization Program.* Austin: Texas Council on Family Violence and Bridge Over Troubled Waters, Inc., 1990.

Cantor, Ralph, with Paul Kivel, Allan Creighton, and Oakland Men's Project. *Days of Respect: Organizing a School-Wide Violence Prevention Program.* Alameda, CA: Hunter House, 1997.

Creighton, Allan, and Paul Kivel, Battered Women's Alternatives, with Oakland Men's Project. *Helping Teens Stop Violence: A Practical Guide for Counselors, Educators, and Parents.* Alameda, CA: Hunter House, 1990.

Creighton, Allan, and Paul Kivel. *Young Men's Work: Stopping Violence and Building Community.* Center City, MN: Hazelden, 1995.

FaithTrust Institute. *Love—All That and More: A Video Series and Six-Session Curriculum on Healthy Relationships.* Seattle, WA: FaithTrust Institute, 2000. Available from http://www.faithtrustinstitute.org.

Harris, Cathy A., and Toby B. Simon. *Sex Without Consent, Volume I: A Peer Education Training Manual for Secondary Schools.* Holmes Beach, FL: Learning Publications, 1993.

Kivel, Paul. *Young Men's Work.* Center City, MN: Hazelden Educational Materials, 1994.

Kivel, Paul, and Allan Creighton. *Making the Peace: A 15-Session Violence Prevention Curriculum for Young People.* Alameda, CA: Hunter House, 1997.

Los Angeles Commission on Assaults Against Women (LACAAW). *In Touch with Teens: A Relationship Violence Prevention Curriculum.* Los Angeles, CA: LACAAW, 1993. Available from http://www .lacaaw.org.

Men Can Stop Rape. *Visible Allies: Engaging Men in Preventing Sexism and Sexual Violence.* Washington DC: Men Can Stop Rape, 1997. Available from http://www.mencan stoprape.org.

Men for Change. *Healthy Relationships: A Violence-Prevention Curriculum.* Halifax, Canada: Men for Change, 1992. Box 33005, Quinpool Postal Outlet, Halifax, Nova Scotia, Canada B3L 4T6. Available from http://www.m4c.ns.ca/order.html.

Myhand, Nell, and Paul Kivel. *Young Women's Lives: Building Self-Awareness for Life.* Center City, MN: Hazelden, 1998.

Rosenbluth, Barri. *Expect Respect: A Support Group Curriculum Manual for Safe and Healthy Relationships,* 3rd edition. Austin, TX: SafePlace, 2002. To read or download a replication manual for the Expect Respect Program, published by the National Resource Center on Domestic Violence. Available from http://www.vawnet.org.

Stein, Nan, and Dominic Cappello. *Gender Violence/Gender Justice: An Interdisciplinary Teaching Guide for Teachers of English Literature, Social Studies, Psychology, Health, Peer Counseling, and Family and Consumer Sciences (Grades 7–12).* Wellesley, MA: Wellesley College Center for Research on Women, 1999. Available from http://www .wellesley.edu/WCW/crwsub.html.

Stein, Nan, and Lisa Sjostrom. *Flirting or Hurting? A Teacher's Guide on Student-to-Student Sexual Harassment in Schools (Grades 6–12).* Wellesley, MA: Wellesley College Center for Research on Women, 1994. Available from http://www.wellesley .edu/WCW/crwsub.html.

Tobin, Pnina, and Sue Levinson Kessner. *Keeping Kids Safe: A Child Sexual Abuse Prevention Manual.* Alameda. CA: Hunter House, 2002.

Vasquez, Hugh, M. Nell Myhand, and Allan Creighton, with Todos Institute. *Making Allies, Making Friends: A Curriculum for Making the Peace in Middle School.* Alameda, CA: Hunter House, 2003.

Voelkel-Haugen, Rebecca, and Marie M. Fortune. *Sexual Abuse Prevention: A Course of Study for Teenagers.* Cleveland, OH: The United Church Press, 1996.

Videos Related to Families and Children

Flirting or Hurting? GPN, PO Box 80669, Lincoln NE 68501-0669, (800) 228-4630, http://gpn .unl.edu.

It Ain't Love. Olmos Productions, 18034 Ventura Blvd., Encino CA 91319, (310) 557-7010.

Let's Get Real. Women's Education Media, 2180 Bryant, Suite 203, San Francisco CA 94110, (800) 405-3322. Available from http://www.womedia.org.

Love—All That and More. FaithTrust Institute, 2400 N 45th St. #10, Seattle WA 98103, (206) 634-1903. Available from http://www.faithtrust institute.org.

Tough Guise. Media Education Foundation. Available from http://www .mediaed.org.

Twisted Love: Dating Violence Exposed. In the Mix Thirteen/WNET. Available from http://www.pbs.org/ inthemix/shows/show_dating _violence.html.

Young Asians Rising/Breaking Down Violence Against Women. Asian Domestic Violence Prevention Collaborative, Nihonmachi Legal Outreach, (415) 567-6255. Available from http://www.youngaznlife.org.

Resource Agencies Related to Families and Children

Center for the Study of Anorexia and Bulimia
1841 Broadway, 4th Fl.
New York NY 10023
(212) 333-3444
Website: www.icpnyc.org/centerforthe studyofanorexiabulemia/

Child Welfare League of America
440 First St. NW, 3rd Fl.
Washington DC 20001
(202) 638-2952
Website: www.cwla.org

Children's Defense Fund
25 E St. NW
Washington DC 20001

(202) 628-8787
Website: www.childrensdefense.org

Committee for Mother and Child Rights
Rt 1 Box 256-A
Clear Brook VA 22624
(703) 722-3652

Family Violence Prevention Fund
383 Rhode Island St., Suite 304
San Francisco CA 94103
(800) 313-1310
(415) 252-8900
(800) 595-4889, TTY
Website: http://endabuse.org

National Association of Mothers Centers
64 Division Ave.
Levittown NY 11756
(800) 645-3828
(516) 520-2929
Website: www.motherscenter.org

National Clearinghouse on Child Abuse and Neglect
330 C St. SW
Washington DC 20447
(800) 394-3366
Website: http://nccanch.acf.hhs.gov

National Clearinghouse on Marital and Date Rape
2325 Oak St.
Berkeley CA 94708
(510) 524-1582
Website: http://members.aol.com/ ncmdr/

National Organization for Victim Assistance
510 King St., Suite 424
Alexandria VA 22314
(703) 535-NOVA (6682)
Website: www.trynova.org

National Organization of Single Mothers
Website: www.singlemothers.org

National Center for Victims of Crime
2000 M St. NW, Suite 480
Washington DC 20036
(202) 467-8700
(800) FYI-CALL (394-2255) (victim assistance)
(800) 211-7996, TTY (victim assistance)
Website: www.ncvc.org

Parents, Families, and Friends of Lesbians and Gays (PFLAG)
1726 M St. NW, Suite 400
Washington DC 20036
(202) 467-8180
Website: www.pflag.org

Resource Center on Child Custody and Child Protection
National Council of Juvenile and Family Court Judges
PO Box 8970
Reno NV 89507
(800) 52-PEACE (527-3223)

Young Women's Project
1328 Florida Ave. NW, Suite 2000
Washington DC 20009
(202) 332-3399
Website: www.youngwomens project.org

Resources on Sexual Abuse

Sexual-Abuse Reading Material

Bass, Ellen, and Laura Davis. *The Courage to Heal: A Guide for Women Survivors of Child Sexual Abuse.* New York: Harper and Row, 1988.

Blume, Sue E. *Secret Survivors: Uncovering Incest and Its Aftereffects in*

Women. New York: Ballantine Books, 1990.

Crewdson, John. *Silence Betrayed: Sexual Abuse of Children in America.* Boston, MA: Little, Brown, 1988.

Finkelhor, David. *Sexually Victimized Children.* New York: Free Press, 1979.

Hunter, Mic. *Abused Boys: The Neglected Victims of Sexual Abuse.* New York: Fawcett Columbine, 1990.

Ledray, Linda E. *Recovering from Rape.* New York: Henry Holt and Company, 1994.

Woititz, Janet. *Healing Your Sexual Self.* Deerfield Beach, FL: Health Communications, 1989.

Sexual-Abuse Resource Agencies

FaithTrust Institute
2400 N. 45th St., #10
Seattle WA 98103
(206) 634-1903
Website: www.faithtrustinstitute.org

National Center for Redress of Incest and Sexual Abuse
1858 Park Rd. NW
Washington DC 20010
(202) 667-1160

National Clearinghouse on Child Abuse and Neglect Information
330 C St. SW
Washington DC 20447
(800) 394-3366
Website: http://nccanch.acf.hhs.gov

RAINN: Rape, Abuse and Incest National Network
635-B Pennsylvania Ave. SE
Washington DC 20003
(800) 656-HOPE (4673)
Website: www.rainn.org

Resources for Substance Abuse and Recovery

Reading Material on Substance Abuse and Recovery

Al-Anon Family Groups. *Al-Anon Faces Alcoholism.* New York: Al-Anon Family Groups, 1986.

Alcoholics Anonymous World Services. *Alcoholics Anonymous.* New York: Alcoholics Anonymous World Services, 1976.

Beckman, Linda, and Sharon Wilsnack, eds. *Alcohol Problems in Women.* New York: Guilford Press, 1984.

Black, Claudia. *It Will Never Happen to Me.* New York: Ballantine Books, 1981.

Fleeman, William. *The Pathways to Sobriety Workbook.* Alameda, CA: Hunter House, 2004.

Flitcraft, Anne, and Evan Stark. *Women at Risk: Domestic Violence and Women's Health.* Thousand Oaks, CA: Sage Publications, 1996.

Klesges, Robert C., and Margaret DeBon. *How Women Can Finally Stop Smoking.* Alameda, CA: Hunter House, 1994.

Potter-Efron, P.S., and R.T. Potter-Efron, eds. *Aggression, Family Violence, and Chemical Dependency.* New York: Haworth Press, 1990.

Robertson, Nan. *Getting Better: Inside Alcoholics Anonymous.* New York: William Morrow and Company, 1988.

Russianoff, Penelope, ed. *Women in Crisis.* New York: Human Science Press, 1981.

Sandmaier, Marian. *The Invisible Alcoholics: Women and Alcohol Abuse in America.* New York: McGraw Hill, 1980.

Schaef, Anne Wilson. *Co-Dependence: Misunderstood, Mistreated.* Minneapolis, MN: Winston Press, 1986.

Swallow, Jean, ed. *Out from Under: Sober Dykes and Our Friends.* San Francisco, CA: Spinsters Ink, 1983.

Woodside, Migs. *Children of Alcoholics* (booklet). Available from State of New York: Division of Alcoholism and Alcohol Abuse, 1994 Washington Ave., Albany NY, 12210.

Newsletters on Substance Abuse and Recovery

The Healing Woman
PO Box 3038
Moss Beach CA 94038
(415) 728-0339

Sobering Thoughts
PO Box 618
Quakertown PA 18951
(800) 333-1606
(215) 536-8026

Women's Recovery Network
PO Box 1145
New Albany IN 47150

Cross-Training Material Related to Substance Abuse and Recovery

Haven House and the Alcoholism Center for Women. *Double Jeopardy.* Available from ACW, 1147 S. Alvarado, Los Angeles CA 90006.

Wright, Janet. *Chemical Dependency and Violence: Working with Dually Affected Families.* Available from Wisconsin Clearinghouse, 1954 E. Washington Ave., Madison WI 53704.

Resource Agencies for Substance Abuse and Recovery

Coalition on Alcohol and Drug Dependent Women and Their Children
National Council on Alcoholism and Drug Dependence
2333 Whitehorse-Mercerville Rd., Suite J
Hamilton NJ 08619
(609) 689-0599
Website: www.ncaddnj.org

The Galano Club
Recovery and Social Club for Gay, Lesbian, Bisexual, and Transexual People
315 W. Court St.
Milwaukee WI 53212
(414) 276-6936
Website: http://my.execpc.com/~reva

National Clearinghouse for Alcohol and Drug Information
5635 Fishers Ln., MSC 9304
Bethesda MD 20892
(301) 468-2600
Website: www.niaaa.nih.gov

Woman to Woman
Retreat for Women in Recovery
PO Box 30344
Sea Island GA 31561
Website: www.gacoast.com/recovery/w2w.html

WomanFocus
69 Linwood Ave.
Buffalo NY 14209
(716) 884-3256
Website: www2.pcom.net/pre

Women in Transition
21 S. 12th St., 6th Fl.
Philadelphia PA 19107
(215) 564-5301
Website: www.womenintransition inc.org

Women for Sobriety
PO Box 618
Quakertown PA 18951
(800) 333-1606
(215) 536-8026
Website: www.womenforsobriety.org

Legal Resources

Reading Material on Legal Issues

Anderson, Ken. *Texas Crime Victims Handbook.* Georgetown, TX: Georgetown Press, 1995.

Browne, Angela. *When Battered Women Kill.* New York: The Free Press, 1987.

Buzawa, Carl G., and Eve S. Buzawa. *Domestic Violence: The Criminal Justice Response.* Thousand Oaks, CA: Sage Publications, 1996.

Ellis, Deborah A., Isabelle Katz Pinzler, Susan Deller Ross, and Kary L. Moss. *The Rights of Women: The Basic ACLU Guide to Women's Rights.* Carbondale, IL: Southern Illinois University Press, 1993.

Geller, Gloria. *Justice for Women Victims and Survivors of Abuse.* Regina, Canada: Social Administration Research Unit Faculty of Social Work, University of Regina, 1991.

Jones, Ann. *Women Who Kill.* New York: Holt, Rinehart and Winston, 1980.

Kuehl, Sheila James, and Lisa G. Lerman. *Mediator's Response to Abusive Men and Battered Women.* Washington, DC: National Woman Abuse Prevention Project, 1988. 2000 P St. NW, #508, Washington DC 20036.

Lardner, George, Jr. *The Stalking of Kristin.* New York: Atlantic Monthly Press, 1996.

Pence, Ellen. *The Justice System's Response to Domestic Violence Assault Cases.* Duluth, MN: Minnesota Program Development, 1985.

Project to Develop a Model Antistalking Code for States. Washington, DC: National Criminal Justice Association, Department of Justice, National Institute of Justice, 1993.

Richie, Beth E. *Compelled to Crime: The Gender Entrapment of Battered Black Women.* New York: Routledge, 1996.

Robson, Ruthann. *Lesbian (Out)Law: Survival under the Rule of Law.* Ithaca, NY: Firebrand Books, 1992.

Violent Crime Control and Law Enforcement Act of 1994, Public Law 103-322. Available from http://usinfo.org/usia/usinfo.state.gov/usa/infousa/laws/majorlaw/h3355_en.htm.

Walker, Lenore E. *Terrifying Love: Why Battered Women Kill and How Society Responds.* New York: Harper Perennial, 1989.

Working Together for Change: Battered Women's Advocates and the Criminal Justice System. Austin, TX: Texas Council on Family Violence, 1994. 8701 North Mopac Expwy., Suite 450, Austin TX 78759.

Resource Agencies for Legal Issues

AARP Legal Counsel for the Elderly
601 E. St. NW, 4th Fl.
Washington DC 20049
(888) OUR-AARP 687-2277
(202) 434-2120
Website: www.aarp.org

American Civil Liberties Union (ACLU)
125 Broad St., 18th Fl.

New York NY 10004
Website: www.aclu.org

Aid to Incarcerated Mothers
434 Massachusetts Ave.
Boston MA 02118
(617) 536-0058
Website: www.catalogueforphilanthropy.org/ma/2003/aid_incarcerated_908.htm

American Bar Association Commission on Domestic Violence
740 15th St. NW
Washington DC 20005-1019
(202) 622-1000
Website: www.abanet.org/domviol/home.html

The American Prosecutors Research Institute's National Center for the Prosecution of Violence Against Women
99 Canal Center Plaza, Suite 510
Alexandria VA 22314
(703) 549-4253
Website: www.ndaa-apri.org/apri/programs/vawa/vaw_home.html

Custody Action for Lesbian Mothers
PO Box 281
Narberth PA 19072
(215) 667-7508

Indian Law Support Center
Native American Rights Fund
1506 Broadway
Boulder CO 80302
(303) 447-8760
Website: www.narf.org

Lambda Legal Defense and Education Fund
120 Wall St., Suite 1500
New York NY 10005
(212) 809-8585
Website: www.lambdalegal.org

Legal Momentum (formerly NOW
Legal Defense and Education Fund)
395 Hudson St.
New York NY 10014
(212) 925-6635
Website: www.legalmomentum.org

Legal Services for Prisoners with Children
1540 Market St., Suite 490
San Francisco CA 94102
(415) 255-7036
Website:
http://prisonerswithchildren.org

Migrant Legal Action Program
1001 Connecticut Ave. NW, Suite 915
Washington DC 20036
(202) 775-7780
Website: www.mlap.org

National Bar Association
Black Elderly Legal Assistance Project
1225 11th St. NW
Washington DC 20001
(202) 842-3900

National Center for Lesbian Rights
870 Market St., Suite 370
San Francisco CA 94102
(415) 392-6257
Website: www.nclrights.org

National Center for Victims of Crime
2000 M St. NW, Suite 480
Washington DC 20036
(202) 467-8700
(800) FYI-CALL (394-2255) (victim
assistance)
(800) 211-7996, TTY (victim assistance)
Website: www.ncvc.org

National Clearinghouse for the Defense
of Battered Women
125 S. 9th St., Suite 302
Philadelphia PA 19107
(800) 903-0111, ext. 3

(215) 351-0010
Website: www.bwjp.org

National Council on Juvenile and
Family Court Judges
PO Box 8970
Reno NV 89507
(775) 784-6012
Website: www.ncjfcj.org

National Criminal Justice Reference
Service
PO Box 6000
Rockville MD 20849
(800) 851-3420
(301) 519-5500
(877) 712-9272, TTY
Website: www.ncjrs.org

National Domestic Violence Hotline
PO Box 161810
Austin TX 78716
(800) 799-SAFE (7233) (hotline)
(800) 787-3224, TTY
Website: www.ndvh.org

National Immigration Law Center
3435 Wilshire Blvd, Suite 2850
Los Angeles CA 90010
(213) 639-3900
Website: www.nilc.org

National Legal Center for the Medically
Dependent and Disabled
7 South 6th St., Suite 208
Terre Haute IN 47807
(812) 238-0769

National Women's Law Center
11 Dupont Circle NW, #800
Washington DC 20036
(202) 588-5180
Website: www.nwlc.org

WomensLaw.org
150 Court St., 2nd Fl.
Brooklyn NY 11201
Website: www.womenslaw.org

Women's Law Project
125 S. 9th St., Suite 300
Philadelphia PA 19107
(215) 928-9801
Website: www.womenslawproject.org

Women's Prison Association
110 Second Ave.
New York NY 10003
(212) 674-1163
Website: www.wpaonline.org

Resource Agencies Related to Living Underground

Equifax (credit agency)
PO Box 740241
Atlanta GA 30374-0241
(800) 685-1111
Website: www.equifax.com

Experian (credit agency)
PO Box 2002
Allen TX 75002
(888) 397-3742
Website: www.experian.com

Transunion (credit agency)
PO Box 390
Springfield PA 19064
(800) 888-4213
Website: www.transunion.com

National Domestic Violence Hotline
PO Box 161810
Austin TX 78716
(800) 799-SAFE (7233), hotline
(800) 787-3224, TTY
Website: www.ndvh.org

National Center for Victims of Crime
2000 M St. NW, Suite 480
Washington DC 20036
(202) 467-8700
(800) FYI-CALL (394-2255) (victim assistance)
(800) 211-7996, TTY (victim assistance)
Website: www.ncvc.org

Resources for Women of Color

Reading Material for Women of Color

Allen, Paula Gunn. *The Sacred Hoop: Recovering the Feminine in American Indian Traditions.* Boston, MA: Beacon Press, 1992.

Angelou, Maya. *I Know Why the Caged Bird Sings.* New York: Bantam Books, 1969.

Agtuca, Jacqueline R. *A Community Secret: For the Filipina in an Abusive Relationship.* Seattle, WA: Seal Press, 1994.

Balzer, Roma, Genevieve James, Liz LaPraire, Tina Olson, Sandra L. Goodsky, and Eileen Hudon. *Full Circle: Coming Back to Where We Began.* Duluth: Minnesota Program Development, 1994.

Bataille, Gretchen M., and Kathleen Mullen-Sands. *American Indian Women.* Lincoln: University of Nebraska Press, 1984.

Bumiller, Elisabeth. *May You Be the Mother of a Hundred Sons: A Journey among the Women of India.* New York: Fawcett Columbine, 1990.

Cornwell, Anita. *Black Lesbian in White America.* Tallahassee, FL: Naiad Press, 1983.

Dasgupta, Shamita Das, and Sujata Warrier. *In Visible Terms: Domestic Violence in the Asian Indian Context.* Bloomfield, NJ: Manavi, 1995. PO Box 614, Bloomfield NJ 07003.

hooks, bell. *Ain't I a Woman? Black Women and Feminism.* Boston, MA: South End Press, 1981.

Hungry Wolf, Beverly. *The Ways of My Grandmother.* New York: Quill, 1982.

Jelin, Elizabeth, ed. *Women and Social Change in Latin America.* Atlantic Highlands, NJ: Zed Books, 1990.

Levinson, David. *Family Violence in Cross Cultural Perspective.* Newbury Park, CA: Sage Publications, 1989.

Moraga, Cherríe, and Gloria Anzaldúa, eds. *This Bridge Called My Back: Writings by Radical Women of Color.* New York: Kitchen Table: Women of Color Press, 1983.

Mousseau, Marlin, and Karen Artichoker. *Domestic Violence Is Not Lakota/Dakota Tradition.* Pierre, SD: South Dakota Coalition Against Domestic Violence and Sexual Assault Project, 1997.

Narasimhan, Sakuntala. *Sati: Widow Burning in India.* New York: Doubleday, 1990.

Ratti, R. *A Lotus of Another Color: An Unfolding of the South Asian Gay and Lesbian Experience.* Los Angeles, CA: Alyson Publications, 1993.

Richie, Beth E. *Compelled to Crime: The Gender Entrapment of Battered Black Women.* New York: Routledge, 1996.

Tsuchida, Nobuya, ed. *Asian and Pacific American Experiences: Women's Perspectives.* Minneapolis: University of Minnesota Press, 1982.

Walker, Alice. *Possessing the Secret of Joy.* New York: Harcourt Brace Jovanovich, 1992.

West, C., *Violence in the Lives of Black Women: Battered, Black and Blue.* Binghamton, NY: Haworth Press, 2003.

White, Evelyn C. *Chain Chain Change: For Black Women Dealing with Physical and Emotional Abuse.* Seattle, WA: The Seal Press, 1985.

Zambrano, Myrna M. *Mejor sola que mal acompañada: For the Latina in an Abusive Relationship.* Seattle, WA: The Seal Press, 1985.

Zambrano, Myrna. *No más: Guía para la mujer golpeada.* Seattle, WA: The Seal Press, 1996.

Resource Agencies for Women of Color

American Indian Law Center, Inc.
PO Box 4456 Station A
Albuquerque NM 87196
(505) 277-5462

Asian American Legal Defense and Education Fund
99 Hudson St., 12th Fl.
New York NY 10013
(212) 966-5932
Website: www.aaldef.org

Asian and Pacific Islander Institute on Domestic Violence
450 Sutter St., Suite 600
San Francisco CA 94108
(415) 954-9988, ext. 315
Website: www.apiahf.org/apidv institute/default.htm

Asian-Indian Women in America
150-38 Union Tpke., #11J
Flushing NY 11367
(718) 591-6511

Asian Task Force Against Domestic Violence
PO Box 120108
Boston MA 02112
(617) 338-2355
Website: www.atask.org

BIHA: Black Indian Hispanic Asian Women in Action
1830 James Ave. North

Minneapolis MN 55417
(612) 521-2986
Website: www.biha.org

Cambodian Women for Progress
8102 Bonair Ct.
Silver Springs MD 20910
(301) 386-0202

Indigenous Women's Network
13621 FM 2769
Austin Texas 78726
(512) 258-3880
Website: www.indigenouswomen.org

Institute on Domestic Violence in the
African American Community
University of Minnesota School of
Social Work
290 Peters Hall
1404 Gortner Ave.
St. Paul MN 55108-6142
(877) NID-VAAC (643-8222)
Website: www.dvinstitute.org

Manavi (advocates for battered Asian
women)
PO Box 614
Bloomfield NJ 07003
(908) 687-2662
Website: www.research.att.com/~krish
nas/manavi/resource.htm

Mending the Sacred Hoop S.T.O.P.
Violence Against Indian Women Technical Assistance Project
202 E. Superior St.
Duluth MN 55802
(218) 722-2781
Website: www.msh-ta.org

Mexican American Women's National
Association
1201 16th St. NW, Suite 230
Washington DC 20036
(202) 223-3440

National Association of Cuban-
American Women
320 E. 43rd St.
New York NY 10017
(212) 573-5000

National Council of Negro Women
633 Pennsylvania Ave. NW
Washington DC 20004
(202) 737-0120
Website: www.ncnw.org

National Institute for Women of Color
3101 20th St. NW, #702
Washington DC 20001
(202) 828-0735
Website: www.womenofcolorday.com

National Political Congress of Black
Women
8484 Georgia Ave., Suite 420
Silver Springs MD 20910
(301) 562-8000
Website: www.npcbw.org

Native American Circle
PO Box 149
Avery TX 75554
(866) 622-3872
(903) 684-3365
Website: www.nativeamericancircle.org

Organization of Pan Asian American
Women
PO Box 39128
Washington DC 20016
(202) 659-9370

Revolutionary Sisters of Color
PO Box 191021
Roxbury MA 02119
(617) 445-3432

Sacred Circle
722 St. Joseph St.
Rapid City SD 57701
(877) RED-ROAD (733-7623)
E-mail: scircle@sacred-circle.com

Saheli (advocates for battered Asian women)
PO Box 3665
Austin TX 78764
(512) 703-8745
Website: www.saheli-austin.org

Resources for Immigrant Women

Reading Material for Immigrant Women

Abraham, Margaret. *Speaking the Unspeakable: Marital Violence among South Asian Immigrants in the United States.* Piscataway, NJ: Rutgers University Press, 2000.

Misra, Mamata, Indira Chakravorty, Kanti C. Shah, Vandana Agarawal, and Varada Pandit. *You Can! A Guide for the Immigrant Woman to Live Independently in the U.S.* Austin, TX: Saheli, 2000. Available from http://www.saheli-austin.org.

Seller, Maxine. *Immigrant Women.* Philadelphia, PA: Temple University Press, 1981.

The State Bar of Texas. *Violence Against Women Act (VAWA): Implications for Battered Immigrant Spouses and Children.* Austin, TX: The State Bar of Texas, 1995. 1414 Colorado, Austin TX 78701.

Volpp, Leti. *Working with Battered Immigrant Women: A Handbook to Make Services Accessible.* San Francisco, CA: Family Violence Prevention Fund, 1995. Available from http://www.fvpf.org.

Resource Agencies for Immigrant Women

Advocates for Immigrant Women
3094 Kaloaluiki St.

Honolulu HI 96822
(808) 988-6026

Casa de Esperanza
PO Box 75177
St. Paul MN 55175
(612) 772-1611 (crisis line)
(612) 646-3014

Legal Momentum's Immigrant Women Program
1522 K St. NW, Suite 550
Washington DC 20005
(202) 326-0040
E-mail: iwp@legalmomentum.org
Website: www.legalmomentum.org

Maitri
234 East Gish Rd., #200
San Jose CA 95112
(888) 8-MAITRI (862-4874) (hotline)
(408) 436-8393 / 436-8398
Website: www.maitri.org

Narika
PO Box 14014
Berkeley CA 94712
(800) 215-7308
(510) 540-0754
Website: www.narika.org

National Immigration Law Center
3435 Wilshire Blvd, Suite 2850
Los Angeles CA 90010
(213) 639-3900
Website: www.nilc.org

National Network to End Violence Against Immigrant Women
Website: www.immigrantwomenetwork.org

Organización en California de Líderes Campesinas (Farmworker Women's Leadership Network)
611 S. Rebecca St.
Pomona CA 91766
(909) 865-7776

Political Asylum Project of Austin
(PAPA)
1715 East 6th, Suite 206
Austin TX 78702
(512) 478-0546

Refugee Women's Alliance Domestic
Violence Program
4008 Martin Luther King Jr. Way S.
Seattle WA 98108
(206) 721-0243
Website: www.rewa.org

Saheli
PO Box 3665
Austin TX 78764
(512) 703-8745
Website: www.saheli-austin.org

Resources for Lesbians and Gays

Reading Material for Lesbians and Gays

Berzon, Betty. *Permanent Partners:
Building Gay and Lesbian Relationships That Last.* New York: Plume,
1990.

Blumenfeld, Warren J. *Homophobia:
How We All Pay the Price.* Boston,
MA: Beacon Press, 1992.

Girshick, Lori B. *Woman-to-Woman
Sexual Violence: Does She Call It
Rape?* Boston, MA: Northeastern
University Press, 2002.

Island, David, and Patrick Letellier.
*Men Who Beat the Men Who Love
Them: Battered Gay Men and Domes-
tic Violence.* Binghampton, NY:
Harrington Park Press, 1991.

Lesbian Battering Intervention Project.
*Confronting Lesbian Battering: A
Manual for the Battered Women's
Movement.* St. Paul: Minnesota
Coalition for Battered Women,
1990.

Lobel, Kerry, ed. *Naming the Violence:
Speaking Out about Lesbian Battering.* Seattle, WA: Seal Press, 1986.

Pharr, Suzanne. *Homophobia: A Weapon
of Sexism.* Inverness, CA: Chardon
Press, 1988.

Renzetti, Claire M. *Violent Betrayal:
Partner Abuse in Lesbian Relationships.* Newbury Park, CA: Sage Publications, 1992.

Taylor, Joelle, and Tracey Chandler. *Lesbians Talk Violent Relationships.*
London: Scarlet Press, 1995.

Resource Agencies for Lesbians and Gays

Custody Action for Lesbian Mothers
PO Box 281
Narbeth PA 19072
(215) 667-7508

Human Rights Campaign Fund Federal
Advocacy Network
1640 Rhode Island Ave. NW
Washington DC 20036
(800) 777-4723
(202) 628-4160
(202) 216-1572, TTY
Website: www.hrc.org

Lambda Legal Defense and Education
Fund
120 Wall St., Suite 1500
New York NY 10005
(212) 809-8585
Website: www.lambdalegal.org

Lavender Families Resource Network
PO Box 21567
Seattle WA 98111
(206) 325-2643

Lesbian Support Services
PO Box 7164
Santa Rosa CA 95407

National Gay and Lesbian Task Force
1325 Massachusetts Ave. NW, Suite 600
Washington DC 20005
(202) 393-5177
Website: www.thetaskforce.org

The Northwest Network of Bi, Trans, Lesbian and Gay Survivors of Abuse
PO Box 20398
Seattle WA 98102
(206) 568-7777
(206) 517-9670, TTY
Website: www.nwnetwork.org

Resources for Older Women

Older Women's Reading Material

AARP Women's Initiative. *Abused Elders or Older Battered Women: Report on the AARP Forum.* Washington, DC: AARP, 1992.

Adelman, Ronald D., and Risa S. Breckman. *Strategies for Helping Victims of Elder Mistreatment.* Newbury Park, CA: Sage Publications, 1988.

American Association of Retired Persons (AARP). *Spouse/Partner Abuse in Later Life: Resource Guide for Service Providers.* Washington, DC: AARP, no date. AARP Women's Initiative, 601 E. St. NW, Washington DC 20049.

The Boston Women's Health Collective. *Ourselves Growing Older.* Boston, MA: The Boston Women's Health Collective, 1987.

Chaney, Elsa M., ed. *Empowering Older Women: Cross-Cultural Views.* Washington, DC: AARP, 1990. AARP Women's Initiative, 601 E Street NW, Washington DC 20049.

The Committee on the Status of Women. *STOP Violence Against Women: A Report and Recommendations from the Committee on the Status of Women.* New York: Episcopal Church Center, 1994.

Decalmer, Peter, and Frank Glendenning, eds. *The Mistreatment of Elderly People.* Newbury Park, CA: Sage Publications, 1993.

Goldman Institute on Aging. *Serving the Older Battered Woman: A Conference Planning Guide.* San Francisco, CA: San Francisco Consortium for Elder Abuse Prevention, 1997.

Goodman, Jane, and Elinor B. Waters. *Empowering Older Adults.* San Francisco, CA: Jossey-Bass Publishers, 1990.

Martz, Sandra, ed. *When I Am an Old Woman I Shall Wear Purple.* Watsonville, CA: Papier-Mache Press, 1987.

Nerenberg, Lisa. *Older Battered Women: Integrating Aging and Domestic Violence.* Washington, DC: National Center on Elder Abuse, 1996.

Older Women's League. *Ending Violence Against Midlife and Older Women.* Washington, DC: Older Women's League, 1994.

Rosenthal, Evelyn R., ed. *Women, Aging, and Ageism.* Binghampton, NY: Harrington Park Press, 1990.

Vinton, L. "Battered Women's Shelters and Older Women: The Florida Experience," *Journal of Family Violence* (January 1992): 63–71.

Older Women's Resource Agencies

AARP Women's Initiative
601 E St. NW
Washington DC 20049
(888) OUR-AARP (687-2277)
Website: www.aarp.org

National Center on Elder Abuse
1201 15th St. NW, Suite 350
Washington DC 20005
(202) 898-2586
Website: www.elderabusecenter.org

Older Women's League
1750 New York Ave. NW, Suite 350
Washington DC 20006
(202) 783-6686
Website: www.owl-national.org

The Wisconsin Coalition Against
Domestic Violence
National Clearinghouse on Abuse in
Later Life (NCALL)
Website: www.ncall.us

Resources for Women with Disabilities

Reading Material for Women with Disabilities

Akers, D.K. *Balancing the Power: Creating a Crisis Center Accessible to People with Disabilities*. Austin, TX: Safe-Place, 2005.

The Alliance for Technology Access. *Computer Resources for People with Disabilities,* 4th ed. Alameda, CA: Hunter House, 2004.

Charlton, J.I. *Nothing About Us Without Us: Disability, Oppression and Empowerment*. Berkeley: University of California Press, 1998.

Finger, Anne. *Past Due: A Story of Disability, Pregnancy, and Birth*. Seattle, WA: The Seal Press, 1990.

Hillyer, B. *Feminism and Disability.* Norman, OK: University of Oklahoma Press, 1993.

Hoog, C. "Model Protocol on Safety Planning for Domestic Violence Victims with Disabilities." Abused Deaf People's Advocacy Services for the Washington State Coalition Against Domestic Violence, 2003. Available from http://www.wscadv .org/projects/disability_protocols .htm.

Hughes, Celia. *Stop the Violence, Break the Silence Training Guide: Building Bridges between Domestic Violence and Sexual Assault Agencies, Disability Service Agencies, People with Disabilities, Families, and Caregivers.* Abramson, W.H. (ed.). Austin, TX: Disability Services ASAP (A Safety Awareness Program), SafePlace, 2003.

Rousso, Harilyn, with Susan Gusher O'Malley and Mary Severance. *Disabled, Female, and Proud.* Westport, CT: Bergin and Garvey, 1993

Sobsey, Dick. *Violence and Abuse in the Lives of People with Disabilities: The End of Silent Acceptance?* Baltimore, MD: Paul H. Brooks, 1994.

Wisseman, K.B. "You're My Pretty Bird in a Cage: Disability, Domestic Violence, and Survival" (electronic version), *Impact* (Fall 2000). Available from http://ici.umn.edu/products/ impact/133/over1.html.

Resource Agencies for Women with Disabilities

American Speech-Language-Hearing Association
10801 Rockville Pike
Rockville MD 20852
(800) 638-8255
(301) 897-5700, TTY
Website: www.asha.org

Center for Research on Women with Disabilities
3440 Richmond Ave., Suite B
Houston TX 77046

(800) 44-CROWD (442-7693)
Website: www.bcm.edu/crowd/

Deaf Abused Women and Children
Advocacy Services (DAWCAS)
PO Box 19454
Austin TX 78760
(512) 386-6172, TTY
Relay Services: 711
Website: www.dawcas.org

Disability Services ASAP (A Safety
Awareness Program)
SafePlace
PO Box 19454
Austin TX 78760
(512) 267-SAFE (7233), hotline
(512) 927-9616, TTY
Website: www.austin-safeplace.org

Disabled Women's Alliance
510 16th St., Suite 100
Oakland CA 94612
(510) 251-4355

Domestic Violence Initiative/Women
with Disabilities
PO Box 300535
Denver CO 80203
(303) 839-5510

National Clearinghouse on Women and
Girls with Disabilities
114 E. 32nd St.
New York NY 10016
(212) 725-1803

The Wisconsin Coalition Against
Domestic Violence (WCADV)
Website: www.wcadv.org

Helpers' Resources

Helpers' Reading Material

Dass, Ram, and Mirabai Bush. *Compassion in Action: Setting Out on the Path of Service.* New York: Bell Tower, 1992.

Ellin, Jeanne. *Listening Helpfully: How to Develop Your Counseling Skills.* London: Souvenir Press, 1994.

Evans, Patricia. *The Verbally Abusive Relationship.* Holbrook, MA: Bob Adams, 1992.

Herman, Judith. *Trauma and Recovery.* New York: BasicBooks, 1992.

Jackson, Donna. *How to Make the World a Better Place for Women in Five Minutes a Day.* New York: Hyperion, 1992.

Maslach, Christina. *Burnout: The Cost of Caring.* New York: Prentice Hall Press, 1982.

Murdock, Maureen. *The Heroine's Journey.* Boston, MA: Shambhala, 1990.

Parry, Danaan. *Warriors of the Heart.* Cooperstown, NY: Sunstone Publications, 1989.

Small, Jacquelyn. *Becoming Naturally Therapeutic: A Return to the True Essence of Helping.* New York: Bantam Books, 1989.

Weiss, Elaine. *Family and Friends' Guide to Domestic Violence: How to Listen, Talk, and Take Action When Someone You Care about Is Being Abused.* Volcano, CA: Volcano Press, 2003.

Helpers' Resource Agencies

National Center for Victims of Crime
2000 M St. NW, Suite 480
Washington DC 20036
(202) 467-8700

(800) FYI-CALL (394-2255) (victim assistance)
(800) 211-7996, TTY (victim assistance)
Website: www.ncvc.org

National Organization for Victim Assistance
501 King St., Suite 424
Alexandria VA 22314
(703) 535-6682
Website: www.trynova.org

Workplace-Related Resources

Workplace-Related Reading Material

Bensimon, Helen Frank. "Violence in the Workplace." *Training and Development* 48 (January 1994), 27–32.

Family Violence Prevention Fund. *Domestic Violence: A Workplace Issue: A Training Resource Kit for Employers and Domestic Violence Service Providers.* San Francisco, CA: Family Violence Prevention Fund, 2000. Available from http://www.fvpf.org.

Family Violence Prevention Fund. *The Workplace Responds to Domestic Violence: A Resource Guide for Employers, Unions and Advocates.* San Francisco, CA: Family Violence Prevention Fund, 2000. Available from http://www.fvpf.org.

Kelley, Sandra J. "Making Sense of Violence in the Workplace." *Risk Management* 42, no. 10 (October 1995): 50–57.

Ketterman, Grace. *Verbal Abuse.* Ann Arbor, MI: Servant Publications, 1992.

Kinney, Joseph A., and Dennis L. Johnson. *Breaking Point: The Workplace Violence Epidemic and What to Do about It.* Chicago, IL: National Safe Workplace Institute, 1993.

Minor, Marianne. *Preventing Workplace Violence: Positive Management Strategies.* Menlo Park, CA: Crisp Publications, 1995.

Moskey, Stephen T. *Domestic Violence Policy Checklists for the Workplace: A Guide for Employers.* Cape Elizabeth, ME: Kettle Cove Press, 1996.

National Institute for Occupational Safety and Health Publications Dissemination. *Preventing Homicides in the Workplace.* Cincinnati, OH: DSDTT, 1993. DSDTT, 4676 Columbia Pkwy., Cincinnati OH 45226.

Scholder, Amy, ed. *Critical Condition: Women on the Edge of Violence.* San Francisco, CA: City Lights Books, 1993.

Shepard, Melanie. "The Effect of Battering on the Employment Status of Women." *Women and Social Work,* May 1988.

Texas Council on Family Violence. *Domestic Violence Is a Workplace Issue: A Manual for Employers.* Austin, TX: Texas Council on Family Violence, 1997. PO Box 161810, Austin TX 78716.

Workplace-Related Resource Agencies

The American Bar Association's Commission on Domestic Violence
740 15th St. NW, 9th Fl.
Washington DC 20005-1022
Website: www.abanet.org/domviol/workviolence.html

Corporate Alliance to End Partner Violence
2416 E. Washington St., Suite E
Bloomington IL 61704
(309) 664-0667
Website: www.caepv.org

Legal Momentum
395 Hudson St.
New York NY 10014
(212) 925-6635
Website: www.legalmomentum.org

National Association of Working
Women, 9 to 5
152 W. Wisconsin Ave., Suite 408
Milwaukee WI 53203
(414) 274-0925
Website: www.9to5.org

National Workplace Resource Center
on Domestic Violence
Family Violence Prevention Fund
383 Rhode Island St., Suite 304
San Francisco CA 94103
(415) 252-8900
Website: www.endabuse.org

Occupational Safety and Health
Administration (OSHA), U.S. Department of Labor
Website: www.osha.gov/SLTC/work
placeviolence

Publications Dissemination, DSDTT
National Institute for Occupational
Safety and Health
4676 Columbia Pkwy.
Cincinnati OH 45226-1998
(800) 35-NIOSH (356-4674)
Website: www.cdc.gov/niosh/home
page.html

Safe@Work Coalition
Website: www.safeatworkcoalition.org

Texas Council on Family Violence
PO Box 161810
Austin TX 78716
(512) 794-1133
Website: www.tcfv.org

Women's Bureau, U.S. Department of
Labor
Frances Perkins Bldg.

200 Constitution Ave. NW
Washington DC 20210
(800) 827-5335
Website: www.dol.gov/wb

Workplace Programs

Employee Assistance Program
Polaroid Corporation
549 Technology Sq.
Cambridge MA 02139
(617) 386-2000

Liz Claiborne, Inc.
Women's Work
Website: www.loveisnotabuse.com

Health-Related Resources

Health-Related Reading Material

Berne, Katrina. *Chronic Fatigue Syndrome, Fibromyalgia and Other Invisible Illnesses,* 3rd ed. Alameda, CA: Hunter House, 2002.

The Boston Women's Health Book Collective. *The New Our Bodies, Ourselves: A Book by and for Women.* New York: Simon and Schuster, 1984.

Campbell, Jacquelyn, and Janice Humphreys. *Nursing Care of Victims of Family Violence.* Englewood Cliffs, NJ: Reston Publishing Company, 1984.

Chernin, Kim. *The Hungry Self: Women, Eating, and Identity.* New York: Times Books, 1985.

Dalton, Katharina, with Wendy Holton. *Once a Month: Understanding and Treating PMS,* 6th ed. Alameda, CA: Hunter House, 1999.

Family Violence Prevention and Health Practice (an e-journal from the Family Violence Prevention Fund).

Available from http://endabuse.org/
health/ejournal.

Orbach, Susie. *Fat Is a Feminist Issue.*
New York: Berkeley Publishers,
1982.

Salber, Patricia R., and Ellen Taliaferro.
*The Physician's Guide to Domestic
Violence: How to Ask the Right Ques-
tions and Recognize Abuse... Another
Way to Save a Life.* Volcano, CA:
Volcano Press, 1995.

Schechter, Susan, with Lisa Tieszen
Gary. *Health Care Services for Battered Women and Their Abused Children: A Manual About AWAKE.*
Boston, MA: Children's Hospital,
1992.

Stark, Evan, and Anne Flitcraft. *Women
at Risk: Domestic Violence and
Women's Health.* Thousand Oaks,
CA: Sage Publications, 1996.

White, Kathleen, et al. *Treating Child
Abuse and Family Violence in Hospitals: A Program for Training and Services.* Lexington, MA: Lexington
Books, 1989.

Health-Care Protocols and Training Material

*Domestic Violence: A Guide for Emer-
gency Medical Treatment.* Trenton:
State of New Jersey, Division on
Women, Department of Community Affairs, 1986.

*Domestic Violence: A Guide for Health
Care Professionals.* Trenton: State of
New Jersey, Department of Com-
munity Affairs, 1990.

*Domestic Violence: A Guide for Health
Care Providers.* Denver: Colorado
Department of Health and the
Colorado Domestic Violence Coali-
tion, 1991.

*Domestic Violence: Identification, Inter-
vention and Nursing Documentation.*
Austin, TX: Austin Center for Battered Women, 1996.

*Start the Healing Now: What You Can
Do about Family Violence.* Austin:
Texas Medical Association and the
Texas Council on Family Violence,
1992.

Health-Related Videos

Amigas Latinas en Acción Pro-Salud (51
minutes). ALAS, 240a Elm St.,
Somerville MA 02114, (617) 776-
4161.

The Battered Women. Versions available
for RN, MD, counselor, and emergency-room personnel. New Jersey
Department of Community Affairs,
Division on Women, Domestic Violence Prevention Program, 101 S.
Broad St., Trenton NJ 08625-0801,
(609) 292-8840.

Crimes Against the Future (23 minutes).
March of Dimes Foundation, 1275
Mamaroneck Ave., White Plains NY
10605, (914) 997-4495.

*Domestic Violence: Recognizing the Vio-
lence* (30 minutes). Colorado Domestic Violence Coalition, 7700 E.
Iliff Ave., Unit H, Denver CO
80237, (800) 368-0406.

In Need of Special Attention (18 minutes). Select Media, 74 Varick St.,
Third Fl., New York NY 10013-
1019, (212) 431-8923.

*Video for Physicians Only! Battered
Women in Your Practice* (17 min-
utes). Network for Continuing
Medical Education, One Harmon
Plaza, Secaucus NJ 07094, (800)
223-0272.

Health-Related Resource Agencies

American College of Obstetricians and
Gynecologists
ACOG Resource Center
409 12th St. SW
Washington DC 20090
(202) 638-5577
Website: www.acog.org

American College of Physicians
Department of Public Policy
Independence Mall West
6th St. at Race
Philadelphia PA 19106
(800) 523-1546
Website: www.acponline.org

American Medical Association
Department of Mental Health
515 N. State St.
Chicago IL 60610
(800) 621-8335
Website: www.ama-assn.org

American Medical Women's Association
801 N. Fairfax St., #400
Alexandria VA 22314
(703) 838-0500
Website: www.amwa-doc.org

Black Women's Health Imperative
600 Pennsylvania Ave. SE, Suite 310
Washington DC 20003
(202) 548-4000
Website: www.blackwomenshealth.org

Black Women Physicians Project
3300 Henry St.
Philadelphia PA 19129
(215) 842-7124

Boston Women's Health Book Collective
34 Plympton St.
Boston MA 02118
(617) 451-3666
Website: www.ourbodiesourselves.org

Caribbean Women's Health Association
2725 Church Ave.
Brooklyn NY 11226
(718) 826-2942
Website: www.aidsnyc.org/cwha

Center for Women Policy Studies
National Resource Center on Women
and AIDS
1211 Connecticut Ave. NW, Suite 312
Washington DC 20036
(202) 872-1770
Website: www.centerwomenpolicy.org

Children's Safety Network
Education Development Center
55 Chapel St.
Newton MA 02458
(617) 969-7100
Website: www.childrenssafety
network.org

Feminist Women's Health Centers
14220 Interurban Ave. S., #140
Seattle WA 98168
(541) 344-0966
Website: www.fwhc.org

Indian Health Service
Federal Women's Program
The Reyes Building
801 Thompson Ave., Suite 400
Rockville MD 20852
(301) 443-0969
Website: www.ihs.gov

International Women's Health Coalition
333 7th Ave., 6th Fl.
New York NY 10010
(212) 979-8500
Website: www.iwhc.org

National Asian Women's Health Organization
One Embarcadero Ctr., Suite 500
San Francisco CA 94111
(415) 773-2838
Website: www.nawho.org

National Council of La Raza
Institute for Hispanic Health
1111 19th St. NW, Suite 1000
Washington DC 20036
(202) 785-1670
Website: www.nclr.org/content/pro
grams/detail/1452

National Health Resource Center on
Domestic Violence
Family Violence Prevention Fund
383 Rhode Island St., #304
San Francisco CA 94103
(888) Rx-ABUSE (792-8773)
Website: www.endabuse.org

National Institute of Mental Health
Violence and Traumatic Stress Research
Office
5600 Fishers Ln., Rm. 10-C-24
Rockville MD 20857
(301) 443-3728
Website: www.nimh.nih.gov/
about/index.cfm

National Latina Health Organization
PO Box 7567
Oakland CA 94601
(510) 534-1362
Website: www.latinahealth.org

National Minority AIDS Council
1931 13th St. NW
Washington DC 20009
(202) 483-6622
Website: www.nmac.org

National Resource Center for Women
and AIDS
Center for Women Policy Studies
1211 Connecticut Ave. NW, Suite 312
Washington DC 20036
(202) 872-1770
Website: www.centerwomenpolicy.org/
programs/aids.htm

National Women's Health Information
Center

U.S. Department of Health and
Human Services
Office on Women's Health
(800) 994-WOMAN (9662)
Website: www.4woman.org

National Women's Health Network
514 10th St. NW, Suite 400
Washington DC 20004
(202) 347-1140
Website: www.womenshealth
network.org

National Women's Health Resource
Center
157 Broad St., Suite 315
Red Bank NJ 07701
(877) 986-9472
Website: www.healthywomen.org

Native American Women's Health
Education Resource Center
PO Box 572
Lake Andes SD 57356
(605) 487-7072
Website: www.nativeshop.org/
nawherc.html

Nursing Network on Violence Against
Women, International
PMB 165
1801 H St. B5
Modesto CA 95354-1215
(888) 909-9993
Website: www.nnvawi.org

Physicians for a Violence-Free Society
American Association for the Surgery of
Trauma
Website: www.aast.org/pvs.html

Project Aware (Association for Women's
AIDS Research and Education)
San Francisco General Hospital
Building 90, Ward 95
955 Potrero Ave.
San Francisco CA 94109
(415) 476-4091

Share—Pregnancy and Infant Loss
Support
St. Joseph Health Center
300 First Capitol Dr.
St. Charles MO 63001
(800) 821-6819
Website: www.nationalshareoffice.com

Women's Health Initiative
Department of Health and Human
Services
PO Box 30105
Bethesda MD 20824
(301) 592-8573
Website: www.nhlbi.nih.gov/whi

Health-Advocacy Programs

AWAKE (Advocacy for Women and
Kids in Emergencies)
300 Longwood Ave.
Boston MA 02115
(617) 355-7979
Website: www.child-protection.org/
CPT/Providers/AWAKE.pdf

WomanKind
Fairfield Southdale Hospital
6401 France Ave. S.
Edina MN 55435
(612) 924-5775

Resources on Religious Issues

Reading Material on Religious Issues

The Advisory Committee on Social
Witness Policy of the General Assembly Council. *Turn Mourning
into Dancing: A Policy Statement on
Healing Domestic Violence and Study
Guide.* Louisville, KY: The Office of
the General Assembly, Presbyterian
Church, 2001. 100 Witherspoon
Street, Louisville KY 40202-1396,
http://www.pcusa.org/oga/publica
tions/dancing.pdf.

Alsdurf, James, and Phyllis Alsdurf. *Bat-
tered into Submission: The Tragedy of
Wife Abuse in the Christian Home.*
Downers Grove, IL: InverVarsity
Press, 1989.

Brown, Joanne Carlson, and Carole R.
Bohn. *Christianity, Patriarchy, and
Abuse: A Feminist Critique.* New
York: The Pilgrim Press, 1989.

Bussert, Joy M.K. *Battered Women:
From a Theology of Suffering to an
Ethic of Empowerment.* New York:
Division for Missions in North
America, Lutheran Church in
America, 1986.

Clarke, Rita-Lou. *Pastoral Care of Battered Women.* Philadelphia, PA: The
Westminster Press, 1986.

Fortune, Marie M. *Keeping the Faith:
Questions and Answers for the Abused
Woman.* San Francisco, CA: Harper,
1987.

Fortune, Marie M. *Violence in the Fam-
ily: A Workshop Curriculum for
Clergy and Other Helpers.* Cleveland,
OH: The Pilgrim Press, 1991.

Horton, Anne L., and Judith
A.Williams, eds. *Abuse and Religion:
When Praying Isn't Enough.* Lexing-
ton, MA: Lexington Books, 1988.

Jewish Women International. *Resource
Guide for Rabbis on Domestic Violence.* Washington, DC: Jewish
Women International, 1996. 2000
M Street NW, Suite 720, Washington DC 20036. Available from
http://www.jewishwomen.org.

Ketterman, Grace H. *Verbal Abuse.* Ann
Arbor, MI: Servant Publications,
1992.

Lateef, Shahida. *Muslim Women in India: Political and Private Realities.*
London: Zed Books, 1990.

Mathews, Alice. *A Woman God Can Use.* Grand Rapids, MI: Discovery House Publishers, 1990.

Spitzer, Julie. *When Love Is Not Enough: Spousal Abuse in Rabbinic and Contemporary Judaism.* New York: National Federation of Temple Sisterhoods, 1985.

Twerski, Abraham. *The Shame Borne in Silence: Spouse Abuse in the Jewish Community.* Pittsburgh, PA: Mirkov Publications, 1996.

Volcano Press. *Family Violence and Religion: An Interfaith Resource Guide.* Volcano, CA: Volcano Press, 1995.

Religious Resource Agencies

Christians for Biblical Equality
122 West Franklin Ave., Suite 218
Minneapolis MN 55404-2451
(612) 872-6898
Website: www.cbeinternational.org/new/index.shtml

Christian Lesbians.com
Website: www.christianlesbians.com

Church Women United
475 Riverside Dr., Suite 1626
New York NY 10115
(800) 298-5551
Website: www.churchwomen.org

Evangelical and Ecumenical Women's Caucus
PO Box 67
Davis IL 61019
Website: www.eewc.com

FaithTrust Institute
2400 N. 45th St., #10
Seattle WA 98103
(206) 634-1903
Website: www.faithtrustinstitute.org

The Feminist Sexual Ethics Project
Brandeis University Department of

Near Eastern and Judaic Studies
Mailstop 054
PO Box 9110
Waltham MA 02454
(781) 736-3228
Website: www.brandeis.edu/projects/fse

Jewish Women International
2000 M St. NW, Suite 720
Washington DC 200036
(800) 343-2823
(202) 857-1300
Website: www.jewishwomen.org

Kamilat
PO Box 391660
Mountain View CA 94039
7007 Georgetown Pkwy.
Fenton MI 48430
(877) KAMILAT (526-4528)
(810) 714-3664
Website: www.kamilat.org

The National Jewish Domestic Violence Hotline
(888) 883-2323

Priests for Equality
PO Box 5206
Hyattville MD 20782
(301) 699-0042
Website: www.quixote.org/pfe

Religious Coalition for Reproductive Choice
1025 Vermont Ave. NW, Suite 1130
Washington DC 20005
(202) 628-7700
Website: www.rcrc.org

Resource Center for Women and Ministry in the South
1202 Watts St.
Durham NC 27701
(919) 683-1236
Website: www.episcopalchurch.org/41685_3091_ENG_HTM.htm

Saheli
PO Box 3665
Austin TX 78764
(512) 703-8745
Website: www.saheli-austin.org

Task Force on Equality of Women in
Judaism
838 5th Ave.
New York NY 10021
(212) 249-0100

Women's Alliance for Theology, Ethics,
and Ritual (WATER)
8035 13th St.
Silver Spring MD 20910
(301) 589-2509
Website: www.his.com/~mhunt

Women in Mission and Ministry
Episcopal Church Center
815 2nd Ave.
New York NY 10017
(800) 334-7626

Military-Related Resources

Military-Related Reading Materials

Beals, Judith. *The Military Response to
Victims of Domestic Violence: Tools
for Civilian Advocates.* Washington
DC: The Battered Women's Justice
Project, 2003. Available from
http://www.bwjp.org.

*Defense Task Force on Domestic Violence
Compilation of Reports 2001–2003.*
Available from http://www.dtic.mil/
domesticviolence/reports/start.pdf.

Hansen, Christine. "A Considerable
Service: An Advocate's Introduction
to Domestic Violence and the Military," *Domestic Violence Report.*
Kingston, NJ: Civic Research Institute, 2001. Available from
http://www.civicresearchinstitute
.com/dvr_military.pdf.

The Miles Foundation. *The Guide to
Surviving Domestic Violence Associated with the U.S. Armed Forces.* PO
Box 423, Newtown CT 06470-
0423.

The Miles Foundation. *The Guide to
Surviving Sexual Assault Associated
with the U.S. Armed Forces.* PO Box
423, Newtown CT 06470-0423.

National Advisory Council on Violence
Against Women and the Violence
Against Women Office. *Toolkit to
End Violence Against Women.* Avail-
able from http://toolkit.ncjrs
.org/default.htm.

Military-Related Resource Agencies

Battered Women's Justice Project
2104 4th Ave. S., Suite B
Minneapolis MN 55404
(800) 903-0111, ext. 1 (Domestic
Violence/Criminal Justice and Military
Issues)
Website: www.bwjp.org

Department of Defense Domestic
Violence Task Force
Website: www.dtic.mil/domestic
violence

Department of Defense Family Advocacy Program
1745 Jefferson Davis Hwy.
Crystal Sq. 4, Suite 302
Arlington VA 22202
(703) 602-4990

Family Violence Prevention Fund
383 Rhode Island St., Suite 304
San Francisco CA 94103-5133
(415) 252-8900
Website: www.endabuse.org

The Miles Foundation
PO Box 423
Newtown CT 06470-0423
(203) 270-7861

National Center on Domestic and
Sexual Violence
7800 Shoal Creek Blvd., Suite 120 N
Austin TX 78757
(512) 407-9020
Website: www.ncdsv.org

National Domestic Violence Hotline
PO Box 161810
Austin TX 78716
(800) 799-SAFE (7233)
(800) 787-3224, TTY
Website: www.ndvh.org

RAINN: Rape, Abuse and Incest
National Network
635-B Pennsylvania Ave. SE
Washington DC 20003
(800) 656-HOPE (4673)
Website: www.rainn.org

Resources for Intervention and Prevention

Reading Material on Intervention and Prevention

Allen, N.E., and L.A. Hagen. "A Practical Guide to Evaluating Domestic Violence Coordinating Councils." Harrisburg, PA: National Resource Center on Domestic Violence, 2003. Available from http://www.vawnet.org.

Arnold, Rick, Bev Burke, Carl James, D'Arcy Martin, and Barb Thomas. *Educating for a Change.* Toronto, Canada: Between the Lines, 1991.

Chesler, Phyllis. *Women and Madness.* Garden City, NY: Doubleday, 1972.

Colodzin, Benjamin. *How to Survive Trauma.* Barrytown, NY: PULSE, 1993.

Davies, Jill. *Safety Planning with Battered Women: Complex Lives/Difficult Choices.* Thousand Oaks, CA: Sage Publications, 1998.

Doane, Sharon. *New Beginnings: A Creative Writing Guide for Women Who Have Left Abusive Partners.* Seattle, WA: Seal Press, 1996.

Family Violence Prevention Fund. "Preventing Family Violence: Lessons from the Community Engagement Initiative." San Francisco, CA: Family Violence Prevention Fund, 2004. Available from http://www.endabuse.org.

Family Violence Prevention Fund. *A Study of Family and Domestic Violence: Homicide Cases in San Francisco.* San Francisco, CA: San Francisco Commission on the Status of Women, 1993.

Freire, Paulo. *Pedagogy of the Oppressed.* New York: Continuum, 1970.

Fullwood, P. Catlin. "Preventing Family Violence: Community Engagement Makes the Difference." San Francisco, CA: Family Violence Prevention Fund, 2002. Available from http://www.endabuse.org.

Herman, Judith Lewis. *Trauma and Recovery.* New York: Basic Books, 1992.

Jordan, Judith V., Alexandra G. Kaplan, Jean Baker Miller, Irene P. Stiver, and Janet L. Surrey. *Women's Growth in Connection: Writings from the Stone Center.* New York: The Guilford Press, 1991.

Lerner-Robbins, Helene. *Our Power as Women: Wisdom and Strategies of Highly Successful Women.* Berkeley, CA: Conari Press, 1996.

Miller, Jean Baker. *Toward a New Psychology of Women.* Boston, MA: Beacon Press, 1976.

NiCarthy, Ginny. *Getting Free: You Can End Abuse and Take Back Your Life.* Seattle, WA: Seal Press, 1986.

NiCarthy, Ginny, Karen Merriam, and Sandra Coffman. *Talking It Out: A Guide to Groups for Abused Women.* Seattle, WA: Seal Press, 1984.

Pence, Ellen. *In Our Best Interest: A Process for Personal and Social Change.* Duluth: Minnesota Program Development, 1987.

Piercy, D. "Skills for Successful Collaborations: A Skill Building Curriculum in Negotiations, Collaborative Mindset, Strategic Thinking, Meeting Facilitation." Harrisburg, PA: National Resource Center on Domestic Violence, 2000. Available from http://www.vawnet.org.

Schaef, Anne Wilson. *Women's Reality: An Emerging Female System in a White Male Society.* New York: Harper, 1981.

Schmidt, K. Louise. *Transforming Abuse: Nonviolent Resistance and Recovery.* Philadelphia, PA: New Society Publishers, 1995.

Stone, Maria Fradella. *Domestic Violence Fatality Reviews: One Step Closer to a Solution.* Berkeley: Boalt Hall School of Law, University of California at Berkeley, 1995.

Stout, Karen D., and Beverly McPhail. *Confronting Sexism and Violence Against Women: A Challenge for Social Work.* New York: Longman, 1998.

Tavris, Carol. *The Mismeasure of Woman.* New York: Simon and Schuster, 1992.

National Advisory Council on Violence Against Women, "Toolkit to End Violence Against Women", Washington DC: National Advisory Council on Violence Against Women and the Violence Against Women Office. Available from http://www.ojp.usdoj.gov/vawo.

Whalen, Mollie. *Counseling to End Violence Against Women: A Subversive Model.* Thousand Oaks, CA: Sage Publications, 1996.

Resource Agencies for Intervention and Prevention

National Network to End Domestic Violence
660 Pennsylvania Ave. SE, Suite 303
Washington DC 20003
(202) 543-5566
Website: www.nnedv.org

FaithTrust Institute
2400 N. 45th St., #10
Seattle WA 98103
(206) 634-1903
Website: www.faithtrustinstitute.org

Family Violence Prevention Fund
383 Rhode Island St., Suite 304
San Francisco CA 94103
(415) 252-8900
Website: www.endabuse.org

Travis County Family Violence Task Force
Project Courage
PO Box 1748
Austin TX 78767
(512) 708-4423

Batterers' Resources

Batterers' Reading Material

Bancroft, Lundy. *Why Does He Do That? Inside the Minds of Angry and Controlling Men.* New York: G.P. Putnam and Sons, 2002.

"Coaching Boys Into Men." San Francisco, CA: Family Violence Prevention Fund, 2004. Available from http://endabuse.org.

Culligan, Joseph J. *When in Doubt Check Him Out.* Miami, FL: Hallmark Press, 1993.

Edleson, Jeffrey L., and Richard M. Tolman. *Intervention for Men Who Batter: An Ecological Approach.* Seattle, WA: Sage Publications, 1992.

Gil, Eliana. *Outgrowing the Pain: A Book for and about Adults Abused as Children.* New York: Dell, 1983.

Gondolf, Edward. *Men Against Women: What Every Woman Should Know about Violent Men.* Blue Ridge Summit, PA: TAB Books, Inc., 1989.

Gondolf, Edward. *Men Who Batter: An Integrated Approach for Stopping Wife Abuse.* Holmes Beach, FL: Learning Publications, 1985.

Gondolf, Edward W., and David M. Russell. *Man to Man: A Guide for Men in Abusive Relationships.* Bradenton, FL: Human Services Institute, 1987.

Johnson, Scott Allen. *Man to Man: When Your Partner Says No—Pressured Sex and Date Rape.* Orwell, VT: Safer Society Press, 1992.

Kivel, Paul. *Men's Work: How to Stop the Violence That Tears Our Lives Apart.* New York: Hazelden/Ballantine, 1992.

Paymar, Michael. *Violent No More: Helping Men End Domestic Abuse,* 2nd ed. Alameda, CA: Hunter House, 1993.

Paymar, Michael, and Ellen Pence. *Education Groups for Men Who Batter: The Duluth Model.* New York: Springer Publishing Company, 1993.

Russell, Mary Nomme, and Jobst Frohberg. *Confronting Abusive Beliefs: Group Treatment for Abusive Men.* Thousand Oaks, CA: Sage Publications, 1995.

Sonkin, Daniel Jay. *The Counselor's Guide to Learning to Live Without Violence.* Volcano, CA: Volcano Press, 1995.

Stordeur, Richard A., and Richard Stille. *Ending Men's Violence Against Their Partners: One Road to Peace.* Seattle, WA: Sage Publications, 1989.

Thorne-Finch, Ron. *Ending the Silence: The Origins and Treatment of Male Violence Against Women.* Toronto, Canada: University of Toronto Press, 1992.

"Toolkit for Working with Men and Boys to Stop Gender-Based Violence." San Francisco, CA: Family Violence Prevention Fund, no date. Available from http://www.end abuse.org/toolkit.

Batterers' Resource Agencies

EMERGE
2464 Massachusetts Ave., Suite 101
Cambridge MA 02140
(617) 547-9879
Website: www.emergedv.com

Men Against Sexual Assault
University of Texas at Austin
E-mail: egd3@mail.utexas.edu
Website: http://studentorgs.utexas
.edu/utmasa

Men Stopping Violence
533 W. Howard Ave., Suite C
Decatur GA 30030

(404) 270-9894
Website: www.menstoppingviolence.org

National Training Project
202 East Superior St.
Duluth MN 55802
(218) 722-2781
Website: www.duluth-model.org/
ntpabout.html

N.O. M.O.R.E. (National Organization of Men's Outreach for Rape Education)
c/o William and Mary School of Education
Room 320
PO Box 8795
Williamsburg VA 23187-8795
(757) 221-2191
Website: www.nomorerape.org

Texas Council on Family Violence
PO Box 161810
Austin TX 78716
(512) 794-1133
Website: www.tcfv.org

The White Ribbon Campaign
365 Bloor St. East, Suite 203
Toronto, Ontario, M4W 3L4, Canada
(800) 328-2228
(416) 920-6684
Website: www.whiteribbon.ca

Self-Help Resources

Self-Help Reading Materials

Davis, Martha, Elizabeth Robbins Eshelman, and Matthew McKay. *The Relaxation and Stress Reduction Workbook*. Oakland, CA: New Harbinger Publications, 1982.

Dowrick, Stephanie. *Intimacy and Solitude*. New York: W.W. Norton and Company, 1991.

Dowrick, Stephanie. *The Intimacy and Solitude Workbook: Self-Therapy for Lasting Change*. New York: W.W. Norton and Company, 1993.

Fanning, Patrick. *Visualization for Change*. Oakland, CA: New Harbinger Publications, 1988.

Folan, L. *Lilias, Yoga, and Your Life*. New York: MacMillan, 1981.

Francis, Cindy. *Life Lessons for Women*. Austin, TX: Newport House, 1992.

Gawain, Shakti. *Creative Visualization*. San Rafael, CA: New World Library, 1978.

Goldstein, Joseph. *Insight Meditation: The Practice of Freedom*. Boston, MA: Shambhala, 1994.

Johnson, Robert A. *Inner Work: Using Dreams and Active Imagination for Personal Growth*. San Francisco, CA: Harper and Row Publishers, 1986.

Karpinski, Gloria D. *Where Two Worlds Touch: Spiritual Rites of Passage*. New York: Ballantine Books, 1990.

Kauz, Herman. *Tai Chi Handbook: Exercise, Meditation, and Self-Defense*. New York: Doubleday, 1974.

Lark, Susan M. *Anxiety and Stress: A Self-Help Program*. Los Altos, CA: Westchester Publishing Company, 1993.

Moore, Thomas. *Care of the Soul: A Guide for Cultivating Depth and Sacredness in Everyday Life*. New York: HarperCollins Publishers, 1992.

Phelps, Stanlee, and Nancy Austin. *The Assertive Woman*. San Luis Obispo, CA: Impact Publishers, 1975.

Reed, Henry. *Dream Solutions: Using Your Dreams to Change Your Life*. San Rafael, CA: New World Library, 1991.

Steinem, Gloria. *Revolution from Within: A Book of Self-Esteem.* Boston, MA: Little, Brown, 1992.

Saunders, Charmaine. *Women and Stress.* New York: Crescent Books, 1990.

Wildwood, Christine. *Creative Aromatherapy.* San Francisco, CA: Thorsons, 1993.

Wildwood, Chrissie. *Erotic Aromatherapy.* New York: Sterling Publishing Company, 1994.

Resources Related to Women's History and Politics

Reading Material on Women's History and Politics

Agonito, Rosemary. *History of Ideas on Woman: A Source Book.* New York: Perigee Books, 1977.

Anderson, Bonnie, and Judith Zinsser. *A History of Their Own.* New York: Harper and Row, 1989.

Barstow, Anne Llewellyn. *Witchcraze: A New History of the European Witch Hunts.* San Francisco, CA: Pandora Books, 1994.

Davis, Angela. *Women, Race and Class.* New York: Vintage Books, 1981.

Ehrenreich, Barbara, and Deirdre English. *For Her Own Good: 150 Years of the Experts' Advice to Women.* New York: Doubleday Books, 1978.

Evans, Sara. *Personal Politics.* New York: Vintage Books, 1979.

Gordon, Linda. *Heroes of Their Own Lives: The Politics and History of Family Violence.* New York: Penguin Books, 1988.

Humm, Maggie, ed. *Modern Feminisms: Political, Literary, Cultural.* New

York: Columbia University Press, 1992.

Hymowitz, Carol, and Michaele Weissman. *A History of Women in America.* New York: Bantam Books, 1978.

Lerner, Gerda. *The Creation of Patriarchy.* New York: Oxford University Press, 1986.

Lightfoot-Klein, Hanny. *Prisoners of Ritual: An Odyssey into Female Genital Circumcision in Africa.* New York: Harrington Park Press, 1989.

Martin, Del. *Battered Wives.* Volcano, CA: Volcano Press, 1981.

Masson, Jeffrey Moussaieff. *A Dark Science: Women, Sexuality and Psychiatry in the Nineteenth Century.* New York: The Noonday Press, 1986.

McAllister, Pam. *This River of Courage: Generations of Women's Resistance and Action.* Philadelphia, PA: New Society Publishers, 1991.

Narasimhan, Sakuntala. *Sati: Widow Burning in India.* New York: Anchor Books, 1990.

Radford, Jill, and Diana E.H. Russell, eds. *Femicide: The Politics of Woman Killing.* New York: Twayne Publishers, 1992.

Schechter, Susan. *Women and Male Violence: The Visions and Struggles of the Battered Women's Movement.* Boston, MA: South End Press, 1982.

Showalter, Elaine. *The Female Malady: Women, Madness and English Culture, 1830–1980.* New York: Penguin Books, 1985.

Williams, Selma R., and Pamela Williams Adelman. *Riding the Nightmare: Women and Witchcraft from the*

Old World to Colonial Salem. New York: Harper Perennial, 1992.

Wollstonecraft, Mary. *A Vindication of the Rights of Woman.* New York: Everyman's Library, 1992. Originally published London: J. Johnson, 1792.

Resource Agencies Related to Women's History and Politics

American Civil Liberties Union
Women's Rights Project
125 Broad St., 18th Fl.
New York NY 10004
Website: www.aclu.org/WomensRights/
WomensRightsMain/cfm

Amnesty International USA
Stop Violence Against Women
5 Penn Plaza, 14th Fl.
New York NY 10001
(212) 807-8400
Website: http://women.amnestyusa.org

Bethune Museum and Archives
National Archives for Black Women's History
1318 Vermont Ave. NW
Washington DC 20005
(202) 673-2402
Website: www.nps.gov/mamc/bethune/
archives/main.htm

Elizabeth Cady Stanton Foundation
PO Box 603
Seneca Falls NY 13148
(315) 568-2703

Lesbian Herstory Archives
PO Box 1258
New York NY 10116
(718) 768-DYKE (3953)
Website: www.lesbianherstory
archives.org

National Organization for Women
1100 H St. NW, 3rd Fl.
Washington DC 20005

(202) 628-8NOW (8669)
Website: www.now.org

National Women's History Project
3343 Industrial Dr., Suite 4
Santa Rosa CA 95403
(707) 636-2888
Website: www.nwhp.org

National Women's Studies Association
7100 Baltimore Ave., #502
University of Maryland
College Park MD 20740
(301) 403-0524
Website: www.nwsa.org

Redstockings of the Women's Liberation Movement
PO Box 744
Stuyvesant Sta.
New York NY 10009
Website: www.afn.org/~redstock

United Federation of Teachers
Women's Rights Committee
52 Broadway
New York NY 10004
(212) 598-7738

Upper Midwest Women's History Center
749 Simpson St.
St. Paul MN 55104
(612) 644-1727

Women's Action Alliance, Inc.
370 Lexington Ave., Suite 603
New York NY 10017
(212) 532-8330

Women's Rights National Historical Park
136 Fall St.
Seneca Falls NY 13148
Website: www.nps.gov/wori/wrnhp.htm

Index

VIOLENT NO MORE: Helping Men End Domestic Abuse ... *2nd Edition*

by Michael Paymar, MPA, LSW

Based on the model domestic abuse intervention program in Duluth, Minnesota, *Violent No More* addresses abusive men directly, taking them step-by-step through the process of recognizing their abusive behaviors, taking a time-out when necessary, and learning how to express anger without violence. The changes are illustrated with the often-shocking stories of several previously abusive men — and of women who were abused.

304 PAGES ... 2 ILLUS. ... PAPERBACK $17.95

FREE YOURSELF FROM AN ABUSIVE RELATIONSHIP: Seven Steps to Taking Back Your Life

by Andrea Lissette, M.A., CDVC, and Richard Kraus, Ph.D.

A lifesaving guide for women who are victims of violence and abuse. *Step One* describes different kinds of abuse. *Step Two* is about abusers and who they abuse, with sections on children and senior citizens. *Step Three* deals with crises, stalking, rape, and assault. It includes an in-depth look at legal help and court proceedings. *Step Four* shows women how to live as survivors, with practical advice on money matters and work issues. *Step Five* discusses the decision to stay or leave, and *Steps Six* and *Seven* move from healing and rebuilding to becoming and remaining abuse-free.

304 PAGES ... 2 ILLUS. ... PAPERBACK $16.95

PEACE IN EVERYDAY RELATION- SHIPS: Resolving Conflicts in Your Personal and Work Life

by Sheila Alson and Gayle Burnett, Ph.D.

As the world becomes — or feels — more and more unstable, we must seek harmony close to home. We need the best possible relationships with spouses, families, friends, coworkers, and bosses. In this practical guide, two successful conflict-resolution specialists outline how we can negotiate both the big conflicts and the smaller disagreements in our daily lives — with neither side feeling like a loser. A special chapter addresses dealing with difficult people.

240 PAGES ... 1 ILLUS. ... PAPERBACK $14.95

DITCH THAT JERK: Dealing with Men Who Conrol and Hurt Women

by Pamela Jayne, M.A.

Ditch That Jerk is a women's guide to recognizing different kinds of abusive men — the potentially good, the definitely bad, and the utterly hopeless — and evaluating whether or not they will change. Based on the author's direct clinical experience with both victims and abusers, it was written specifically for women who underestimate the dangers of an abusive relationship or overestimate their ability to change the man controlling or hurting them.

Forthright and empowering, this book even includes "jerk tests" to help women decide if they should leave an abuser.

240 PAGES ... PAPERBACK $14.95

To order or for our FREE catalog call (800) 266-5592

HOW TO SPOT A DANGEROUS MAN BEFORE YOU GET INVOLVED

Sandra L. Brown, M.A.

This savvy, straightforward book offers help for women wanting to avoid bad choices and unsatisfactory relationships with men. The author, a therapist, describes eight types of dangerous men, their specific habits and characteristics. She also explains womens' innate "red-flag" systems — how they signal impending danger and why so many women learn to ignore them.

This practical guide teaches women tools that can help them choose partners wisely, avoid pain — and danger — and have long, happy relationships with men.

264 PAGES ... PAPERBACK $14.95

I CAN MAKE MY WORLD A SAFER PLACE: A Kid's Book about Stopping Violence

by Paul Kivel • Illustrations and games by Nancy Gorrell

This book shows children ages 6–11 what they can do to find alternatives to violence in their lives. Kivel explains public danger (gangs, fights, drug-related violence) and private danger (sexual assault and domestic violence) and gives suggestions for staying safe. Activities and games are used to encourage young readers to think about and promote peace. The drawings by Nancy Gorrell are playful and engaging, making difficult ideas easier to understand.

96 PAGES ... PAPERBACK $11.95

MAKING THE PEACE: A 15-Session Violence Prevention Curriculum for Young People

by Paul Kivel and Allan Creighton, with the Oakland Men's Project

This is a violence prevention curriculum for youth-group leaders and educators. The ready-to-use exercises, roleplays, and discussion guidelines show students how to explore the roots of violence in the community and their lives; deal with dating violence, fights, suicide, guns, and sexual harassment; and develop practical techniques for stopping violence.

192 PAGES ... 35 HANDOUTS ... PAPERBACK $24.95

MAKING ALLIES, MAKING FRIENDS: A Curriculum for Making the Peace in Middle School

by Hugh Vasquez, M. Nell Myhand, Allan Creighton, and Todos

This curriculum for grades 6–9 integrates with the Making the Peace program but also stands on its own. More than 30 innovative classroom sessions address diversity and violence issues that middle-schoolers face. Themes include: What respect is, Who am I / Who are my people?, Safety, and more. A valuable resource for middle-school personnel and teachers of violence prevention, youth development, conflict resolution, social studies, art, and theater.

224 PAGES ... 37 HANDOUTS ... PAPERBACK $29.95

To order or for our FREE catalog call (800) 266-5592

DAYS OF RESPECT: Organizing a School-Wide Violence Prevention Program *by Ralph Cantor, with Paul Kivel, Allan Creighton, and Oakland Men's Project*

This is a step-by-step guide for staging a collaborative school event that brings young people, teachers, parents, and the community together to create respect and tolerance in their school. The program emphasizes building non-violent relationships and includes planning outlines and checklists, timetables, permission slips, training exercises on gender and race, and evaluations.

64 PAGES ... 21 HANDOUTS ... PAPERBACK $17.95

HELPING TEENS STOP VIOLENCE: A Practical Guide for Counselors, Educators, and Parents

by Allan Creighton with Paul Kivel

Today's teenagers may be subjected to violence at home, at school, and in society. For several years, the Oakland Men's Project (OMP) and Battered Women's Alternatives (BWA) conducted seminars and workshops with teens and adults around the country, weaving issues of gender, race, age, and sexual orientation into frank discussions about male violence and its roots. This book by founders of OMP and BWA provides guidelines on how to help teenagers help themselves out of the cycle of abuse and find ways to deal with the violence in the world around them.

168 PAGES ... 16 PHOTOS ... PAPERBACK $16.95

KEEPING KIDS SAFE: A Child Sexual Abuse Prevention Manual ... *2nd Edition*

by Pnina Tobin, MPA, and Sue Levinson Kessner, M.S.

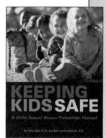

It is crucial to teach children how to recognize when they are in danger of being abused by strangers or people they know and how to obtain help. *Keeping Kids Safe* contains curricula for ages 3–7 and 8–11 with word-for-word scripts and workshops. Children are taught to distinguish between wanted and unwanted touch, and to say "No!" and get help. A Facilitator's Guide informs educators about myths and facts about child sexual abuse, and reporting procedures and follow-up methods.

160 PAGES ... 31 PHOTOGRAPHS ... PAPERBACK $24.95 ... SPIRALBOUND $29.95

TRAUMA IN THE LIVES OF CHILDREN: Crisis and Stress Management Techniques for Counselors, Teachers, and Other Professionals ... *2nd Edition*

by Kendall Johnson, Ph.D.

Written by one of the foremost trauma experts in the country, this book uses an interdisciplinary solution-based approach to show how schools, therapists, and families can work together to help children traumatized by natural disasters, parental separation, family violence, suicide, the death of a loved one, and the many other traumas a child may face.

352 PAGES ... 2 ILLUS., 14 TABLES ... PAPERBACK $19.95

ORDER FORM

NAME

ADDRESS

CITY/STATE   ZIP/POSTCODE

PHONE   COUNTRY (outside of U.S.)

TITLE	QTY	PRICE	TOTAL
When Violence Begins at Home (2nd ed.)		@ $24.95	
Violent No More (2nd ed.)		@ $17.95	

Prices subject to change without notice

Please list other titles below:

		@ $	
		@ $	
		@ $	
		@ $	
		@ $	

Check here to receive our book catalog ☐   *FREE*

SHIPPING COSTS
*By Priority Mail, first book $4.50, each additional book $1.00
By UPS and to Canada, first book $5.50, each additional book $1.50
For rush orders and other countries call us at (510) 865-5282*

TOTAL _____
Less discount @ _____ %   (_____)
TOTAL COST OF BOOKS _____
Calif. residents add 7½ sales tax _____
add Shipping & handling _____
TOTAL ENCLOSED _____
Payment accepted in U.S. funds only

☐ Check   ☐ Money Order   ☐ Visa   ☐ MasterCard   ☐ Discover

Card # _____ Exp. date _____

Signature _____

Complete and mail to:

Hunter House Inc., Publishers

PO Box 2914, Alameda CA 94501-0914
Phone (510) 865-5282 Fax (510) 865-4295
You can also order by calling **(800) 266-5592**
of from **www.hunterhouse.com**

WVB2 11/2005